Selected Letters of
Gustav Mahler

SELECTED LETTERS OF
Gustav Mahler

The original edition selected by
Alma Mahler
enlarged and edited with
new Introduction, Illustrations and Notes
by
KNUD MARTNER

Translated from the original German by
Eithne Wilkins & Ernst Kaiser
and Bill Hopkins

FARRAR · STRAUS · GIROUX

NEW YORK

CONTENTS

ILLUSTRATIONS

1*

INTRODUCTION TO THE ENGLISH EDITION

by Knud Martner

'In a man's letters, you know, Madam, his soul lies naked –
his letters are only the mirror of his heart!'

DR. SAMUEL JOHNSON

The idea of publishing Gustav Mahler's letters in a collected volume arose
soon after the composer's death, finally taking shape around 1920. Several
letters had already been published in Mahler's lifetime—almost certainly
without his approval—and in the decade following his death in May 1911
numerous of his private letters, as well as documents of a more official character,
appeared sporadically in various Austrian and German newspapers and magazines. Mahler would undoubtedly not have been pleased by this, and his pre-
sumed opposition may have been one of the reasons why Alma Maria Mahler
finally intervened in the autumn of 1920 and published the following notice,
though later events leave one with the impression that she may have acted from
less noble motives:

I learn from various quarters that recipients of Gustav Mahler's letters
plan to publish them in newspapers and magazines.

As I alone have the right to dispose of the literary inheritance of Gustav
Mahler as far as publication is concerned I draw attention to the fact that I,
as a matter of principle, will bring an action against any publication of Gustav
Mahler's letters which has not been given my consent.[1]

When Paul Stefan, the early and idealistic Mahler biographer, at about the
same time brought out a new and revised edition of his excellent biography of
Mahler, first published in 1910, he added three new books to his Bibliography,
under the heading 'In preparation'. The first, by Paul Bekker, another of
Mahler's earliest advocates, was entitled 'Gustav Mahlers Werke' and appeared

[1] *Musikblätter des Anbruch*, Vienna, September 1920.

a year later in Berlin as *Gustav Mahlers Sinfonien*. The second, to be published
by Ullstein & Co. in Vienna, and called simply 'Gustav Mahler' (probably a
biography) was to be a collaboration between two of Mahler's closest friends:
Friedrich Löhr and Bruno Walter. If the latter sounded exciting and promising
the third book sounded no less so. Its title was 'Gustav Mahlers Briefe, Band I'
(G.M.'s Letters, Vol. I), and it was to be published by E. P. Tal in Vienna.
No editor was named but Stefan implied in the foreword to his biography that
Alma Mahler was preparing such a collection of her late husband's letters.

Unfortunately, the advertised book by Löhr and Walter was abandoned
without explanation, having probably never got beyond the early stages. It is
not difficult to find reasons for the failure of this project. Bruno Walter left
Vienna in 1912 to take up an appointment as *Generalmusikdirektor* in Munich,
and from the beginning of the 1920s he not only conducted over most of Europe
but also began to work in the U.S.A. Quite as serious hindrances to the project's
accomplishment were Friedrich Löhr's failing health (he died in 1924), and the
two men's divergent opinions of Mahler and their different working methods
and temperaments. But in view of their intended co-operation it seems strange
that Walter mentions Friedrich Löhr neither in his 'Portrait'[1] of Mahler
(Vienna, 1936) nor in his autobiography (New York, 1947).

Although the promised volume of letters did not materialize immediately, its
forthcoming publication was further confirmed three years later, in 1923, by an
announcement printed in the back of Natalie Bauer-Lechner's posthumously
published *Erinnerungen an Gustav Mahler* ('Reminiscences of G.M.'). Besides
reminding us that it would only be the first volume of a work intended to include
one if not several more volumes, it also provided a subtitle 'Freundesbriefe'
('Letters to His Friends'). The publisher had remained the same, but the
editor's name was still not revealed. Indeed, although one might, of course, have
guessed that Alma Mahler was involved—as hinted at by Paul Stefan—it was
not until 1960 that she herself disclosed her role by a casual remark in her
fragmentary autobiography *Mein Leben* (Frankfurt/M.).[2] Writing of the
founding of the publishing firm Paul Zsolnay Alma Mahler remarked: 'Later
my *Mahler's Letters* was published; although this volume, too, had been
promised to another publisher [i.e. E. P. Tal], we [she and Franz Werfel] were
able to release it from the contract.'

Sure enough, a year later, on 1 October 1924, the Paul Zsolnay Verlag[3] in

---

[1] Thus subtitled in the second impression, Frankfurt/M., 1957.
[2] Though published a year earlier, in 1959, the English version (*And The Bridge is Love*)
is an abridged translation and does not include the passage cited.
[3] Paul Zsolnay, who six years later became Alma Mahler's son-in-law, simultaneously published the facsimiles of the sketches of Mahler's incomplete Tenth Symphony together with
Richard Specht's introduction to it.

Berlin was able to publish the result of Alma Mahler's endeavours, an extensive collection of letters from Gustav Mahler to his friends and colleagues, the final title of which had become *Gustav Mahler: Briefe 1879–1911*. It is this volume which forms the basis of the present collection of Mahler's correspondence.

Only eleven thousand copies of the original edition, including a new impression in 1925, were printed, and these were not long available, partly because under the Nazis, who came to power eight years later, the book automatically became forbidden reading and was among those volumes officially removed from public libraries, etc., and destroyed. After the Second World War the book became a collector's item, increasingly so as interest in Mahler's music developed from the late 1950s onwards. I only traced my copy of the book some ten years ago in an obscure second-hand bookshop in London, having searched for it all over the Continent.

The announcement in Bauer-Lechner's reminiscences had promised a collection of Mahler's 'Letters to His Friends, Vol. I', and this to all intents and purposes was what was published in 1924. It was not until sixteen years later, in 1940, that it was learnt what further volumes Alma Mahler had had in mind when she published her invaluable and now famous memoirs of her nine years of marriage to Gustav Mahler entitled *Gustav Mahler. Erinnerungen und Briefe* ('G.M. Memories and Letters'), a volume including, in particular, about 190 of Mahler's personal and sometimes highly intimate letters to his dearly beloved wife.

Whilst the latter has been available in several translations[1] including an abridged English edition (London, 1946)[2] this is the first time since 1925 that the former collection has appeared complete in another European language, the Czech and Russian editions being selections and including letters from Alma Mahler's *Memories and Letters* as well as abridgements of other important texts on Mahler.

The original German edition consisted of 420 numbered letters, to which twenty-three new letters have been added here, namely six to Anton Krisper (nos. 5–9, 15), thirteen to Albert and Nanna Spiegler (nos. 4, 10, 30, 65, 159, 246–7, 255, 260–1, 272, 277, 291), one each to Gustav Lewy (no. 14), Miss Gisella Tolney-Witt (no. 112) and C. F. Peter Verlag (no. 417), and one to an unknown correspondent (no. 227). Only those to Anton Krisper and Tolney-Witt have previously been published.[3] Strictly speaking there are 458 letters,

---

[1] American, 1946; Swedish, 1948; Italian, 1961; Czech, 1962; and Russian, 1964 (all abridged!).
[2] The third English edition, revised and enlarged by Donald Mitchell, and with an additional appendix of notes and chronology by the present writer, appeared in London, 1973.
[3] The Krisper letters by Hans Holländer in *Die Musik*, 1928, and the letter to Tolney-Witt in the *Neue Zürcher Zeitung* by Paul Nettl, 1958.

as the original letter no. 275 (now 308a/b) actually consists of two letters, and as Friedrich Löhr in his invaluable Notes incorporated fifteen letters and messages of varying length from Mahler to Löhr and members of his family.

Besides altering the arrangement of the letters I have also, in order to make the book more practical and useful as a work of reference, supplied it with various indexes, a biographical list, a key to the new and old numbering, new illustrations and additional notes. Finally, I have expanded the volume with a selection of thirteen letters *to* Gustav Mahler from his parents and sisters.

From an editorial point of view I was faced with two major problems when I began editing this volume. The first concerned the arrangement of the letters, the original order not seeming very satisfactory, the second, their dating. These matters are, of course, to some extent interrelated, both stemming—more or less—from the original German edition, towards which I felt I had certain moral obligations.

As can be seen from Alma Mahler's foreword to the original edition (p. 29) she divided the letters into four sections, arranging the letters within each section chronologically, the order of the recipients being somewhat casual. Alma Mahler justified this method by saying that 'not only the writer, but also his relationship to the letter's recipient is important', and that she felt the relationship would best be reflected in this way. I found and still find this point of view both sympathetic and interesting, and I do at least partially agree with it, but after long consideration I finally decided that I had to abandon her method and arrange the letters in another way.

One has to bear in mind that the present volume of letters is only a modest, though important and representative, selection of Mahler's enormous correspondence, and that Alma Mahler was not consistent in carrying out her method, which would at the very least have required her to collect all the letters to an individual recipient in the same section. Nor do we have both sides of the correspondence to provide the best way of understanding the extent and depth of the various relationships and to answer the numerous questions that arise. As it is, we are dealing with a volume of letters written solely by Mahler, a volume which, as far as most of the addressees are concerned, is far from complete. What is more, there is good reason to believe that the letters are a subjective selection made by the recipients and by Alma Mahler. In other words, the relationship between Mahler and his correspondents is not only incompletely represented, but in some cases I am afraid it has even been—more or less unconsciously—distorted, for example, by the suppression of personal remarks which were seemingly without public interest.[1] Almost all the letters to Anna von Mildenburg, for instance, are obviously abridged, and

---

[1] Wherever it has been possible I have restored the text.

even if we can guess the true nature of her relationship with Mahler from the published letters, it is still no more than intuition.

Soon after Mahler's death, Anna von Mildenburg published many of his letters to her in Austrian newspapers, not *in extenso*, but with the same omissions as here. She probably did so out of concern for her career and private life (two years earlier, in 1909, she had married the poet Hermann Bahr). By 1924 she would hardly have needed to worry about these matters; nevertheless we cannot say for sure whether it was she or Alma Mahler who wanted to conceal the former's early, passionate relationship with Mahler during his last years in Hamburg. Naturally, Alma Mahler was never pleased about this affair, or for that matter any of Mahler's earlier affairs, and did everything possible to conceal it, as is evident from her book on Mahler. I find it hard to believe it was out of consideration for Mildenburg's feelings that Alma Mahler in her book referred to her only as 'M'.[1] In an unpublished letter to the critic Ludwig Karpath (dated Munich, 1 December 1930) Anna von Mildenburg quoted several of Mahler's intimate and passionate letters to her in order to let Karpath know 'how things really were'.[2] This, however, is an extreme indication of the book's deficiencies and is certainly the exception rather than the rule.

That the correspondence is only one-sided would matter much less if more details of the individual addressees had been given. But the information we glean about the recipients in the original edition is mostly limited to names and titles, and is of hardly any use to a modern reader, for whom these meagre notes say nothing of the correspondent's relationship with Mahler.

Finally, as I mentioned above, Alma Mahler's method is not consistent, and however one reads the letters in her arrangement one cannot avoid flipping back and forth through the pages, and jumping backwards and forwards in time, thus disrupting any natural sequence there might be. This, at least, has been my experience; and matters are not improved by the lack of indexes.

The letters in this selection span most of Mahler's life—from his seventeenth year to his death—and it is therefore possible to read them as a kind of autobiography, although one with many gaps. I eventually decided, because of this, that the most sensible arrangement of the letters would be a strictly chronological one, as is usual in the publication of letters. But this decision confronted me with the further difficulty, already mentioned, of dating the letters. This

---

[1] It has always been rumoured in Vienna that Alma Mahler was responsible for the public not being allowed access to the many letters from Mahler to A. v. Mildenburg in the Austrian National Library (Theatersammlung) in Vienna. The reality is more prosaic: it is simply a matter of copyright.

[2] Letter in my possession. About that time Karpath was writing his memoirs (*Begegnung mit dem Genius*), published 1934, which contain about 190 pages on Mahler. Karpath did not make use of Mildenburg's disclosures as she requested in her letter, nor did he return it, as she asked.

problem was not new to me or to anyone who had ever occupied himself with Mahler's letters, for most of them are undated. Alma Mahler faced it when she edited the German edition we learn from her autobiography (*Mein Leben*): 'It was difficult to put the letters in order, because Gustav Mahler never wrote a date and I could only verify a date from the sense of the letter. No one else could have done that!'

Mahler was himself aware of his 'imperfection' in this respect and once 'excused' himself: 'As a matter of fact, the reason why I rarely date my letters is that I generally don't know what the date is!' (letter 191 to Max Marschalk).[1] Though this must be a joke, the fact remains that of the 443 numbered letters included in this volume Mahler personally dated only 108 according to the original German edition! Of the remaining 335, some have been dated more or less exactly by their recipients or by the editor from the postmarks or following their sense, and the rest are either left without any information regarding the year, month, season or place in which they were written, or at best with only one or two of these details. It may be added that a more careful study of Mahler's 'habit-of-dating-letters' reveals that he was as a rule more careful about dates when writing official letters.[2]

About fifty-five letters are said to have been dated from their postmarks but the number is undoubtedly higher.[3] It is usually taken for granted that this method of dating letters is infallible, and I was inclined at first to consider dates given thus as being beyond dispute. But after discovering several dubious cases I became convinced that a certain caution was necessary (cf. the letters to Berliner from London, 1892). Provided that the postmarks are clear and legible the method in itself is excellent, but the possibility of a blurred postmark being misinterpreted is obvious, especially if one is an amateur in that particular field—and without offending anyone I think we can presume that this is exactly what both the recipients of Mahler's letters and Frau Alma Mahler were. A skilled philatelist is able to establish the date of a letter within narrow limits, and sometimes exactly, not only from the date on the postmark but from the stamp (colours, motif and value) and from the postmark itself (its form and the way it has been printed, etc.). The combined skills of a philatelist and an editor

---

[1] I always considered it suspect that Marschalk ever asked the question which produced this reply, because at the time he did so, Marschalk had received sixteen letters of which only two according to the German edition were *not* dated by the sender. Of a total of twenty-five letters to Marschalk in the German edition, all but five were apparently dated by Mahler. When I was lucky enough to discover the original letters my suspicion proved to be well-founded: only seven of the letters carry the date in Mahler's hand.
[2] In an unpublished letter of 1 October 1892 to his sister Justine (in the Rosé Collection, Canada), Mahler writes: '*Do always date your letters! It can often be of importance!*'.
[3] About thirty letters which are given exact dates but also prefixed 'Undated', should be included in this group, though some of these dates may have been noted on the letters when they were received.

with a thorough knowledge of Mahler would certainly have been the ideal solution for a task such as this.

In dry figures the dating of the letters before and after my revision looks roughly as follows. For the sake of clarity I have distinguished only five alternatives:

Letters with:	*Before*	*After*
(a) exact dates (day, month and year)	210	231
(b) month and year only	103	151
(c) season and year only	49	36
(d) year and/or place of origin only	56	11
(e) dubious dates or none at all	25	14

The figures in the right-hand column may seem unimpressive, though they indicate some improvement; but they do not in fact give an accurate or final picture. Since it turned out, as I have mentioned, that several of the 'exact' dates given in the original German edition were in fact wrong, some of the letters I have been able to re-date correctly appear in both columns in (a). The actual number of letters where a new exact dating has been possible is thus not 21 but 34.

Unfortunately, many of the letters themselves have either vanished or are no longer accessible.[1] According to Alma Mahler's autobiography Mahler's letters —both those addressed to her and those she borrowed for the publication of the German selection but in many cases never returned, as well as other important papers concerning Mahler—were left in the loft of her house in Vienna when she fled from Austria in 1938. The upper part of the house was hit by a bomb at the end of the war and everything was burnt. It has therefore been impossible to make comparisons between the originals and the text as printed in the German edition of the letters, let alone to verify the dates given there and to see whether they were Mahler's or otherwise attributed. Alterations of the dates have thus had to be based on secondary sources except for the few letters to which I have had access.

In view of my reservations about the dates attributed to the letters, I had no other starting point than the assumption that all dates were unreliable, and had, hence, to re-examine every letter carefully in order to ratify given dates and to establish new ones where necessary and possible. This has, of course, involved taking every aspect of Mahler's life and surroundings into consideration, and

[1] Mahler's letters are spread all over the world in private and public archives. The greater part of the letters to Löhr are in private and inaccessible collections in France and Switzerland. All the letters to Mengelberg are located in Amsterdam, and most of those to Max Marschalk and Friedrich Gernsheim are in Berlin. The letters to Albert and Nanna Spiegler are in New York as are those to Bruno Walter.

using every available source of information about his works—manuscripts, dates of composition and publication, performances during his lifetime, etc.— as well as about the lives and works of those of his contemporaries who have any relevance to him; and finally having card-indexed all the letters with the necessary information on each, arranging this complicated jigsaw puzzle into a clear picture.

From a careful reading of the existing literature on Mahler it became obvious that the many discrepancies and repeated mistakes required the construction of a new chronology of Mahler's life, his activities as a conductor and his works. This is not the place to discuss in detail my various courses of action, but I should like to mention briefly two things which have been of special importance.

It is well known that Mahler worked almost uninterruptedly in various opera-houses in Austria and Germany from his twenty-first year until he left the Vienna Court Opera twenty-six years later. During the following two years he conducted only about forty performances at the Metropolitan Opera in New York, and for a season and a half after that was in charge of the New York Philharmonic Orchestra. All these engagements should have made it comparatively easy to follow his external activities—at least during the concert season—by reconstructing the day-to-day repertoires of the opera-houses where he worked, either from playbills in the theatre archives, or from contemporary newspapers and magazines. But during the Second World War many archives and libraries throughout Austria and Germany were destroyed, and what should have been a straightforward if tiresome task became instead a question of patchwork.

The other matter which has been of significance in my work as editor concerns the performance of Mahler's compositions during his lifetime, both his own and those given by other artists. In the literature on Mahler only Paul Stefan has tried to trace the diffusion of Mahler's works down to the year 1911. Stefan's list—recorded in his biography of Mahler in 1910 with later revisions— is far from complete, as he was of course aware, and contains many errors. Nevertheless, it forms an excellent basis for anyone who wishes to find out to what extent Mahler the composer was 'accepted' in his own time.

Mahler's much-quoted—and I am afraid, misquoted—remark that 'my time will yet come' (John vii, 6–8) has often been interpreted as if his works were little performed, but it should be noted that it was said in the context of the unparalleled success in those days of Richard Strauss; furthermore it is only to be expected that a composer will never be entirely satisfied with the number of performances his works receives. Not even Strauss himself was ever satisfied. Yet, given Mahler's relatively small output, he could hardly complain of disregard. Stefan recorded about 230 performances of Mahler's songs and symphonies, while I have been able to more than double this figure, and what is more important, to establish the dates of performance. The majority of these took place during the first decade of this century, as Alma Mahler correctly points out in her preface (see p. 27), and that is, of course, in direct proportion to the increase in the number of compositions published: by the turn of the century almost all Mahler's finished compositions had appeared, including the first three symphonies, and five volumes of various Lieder; the remaining compositions, i.e. the Symphonies nos. 4–8, the Rückert Songs and 'Das klagende Lied', came out during the first decade of this century, and in this later period an average of about fifty performances of his works took place each year.

After rearranging the letters in chronological order I decided, like Alma Mahler, to divide the letters into sections, but rather than four sections I found it more appropriate that they should form eight chapters corresponding to the main periods in the composer's external artistic life. Owing to its size I have broken the Vienna period into two parts, the dividing line being Mahler's marriage in 1902.

In the original edition the letters are annotated in two ways, with footnotes on the page, and with notes and commentaries collected in a separate appendix at the back of the book. Whereas the former were apparently provided by the editor,[1] the latter (except for one by Emil Freund) are by Friedrich Löhr, Mahler's friend from his early twenties.

These notes, and their division, have mostly been retained in this volume, but owing to the rearrangement of the letters a few of the original notes and comments have become obsolete or superfluous, and have consequently been omitted. On the other hand I have felt it necessary to provide the letters with a number of my own notes, inserted at the relevant points among the original ones. Each note is distinguished by the initials of its contributor:

(o.e.) = original editor; (F.L.) = Friedrich Löhr; (E.F.) = Emil Freund; (B.W.) = Bruno Walter; (K.M.) = Knud Martner.

All comments in square brackets are by the present editor.

The dates have also been provided by various contributors and are distinguished by three different notation forms:

(a) Dates, sender's addresses, hotels, etc., in roman type are those believed to have been on the letter as sent by Mahler.

(b) Dates which are prefixed 'Undated' are, of course, later additions provided

---

[1] It is obvious that the majority of the notes were written by the recipients but rewritten by Alma Mahler in the impersonal style in which they appear. This is confirmed by Karpath's personal notes which are in my possession.

either by the recipient or by the original editor. These are italicized. (Letter-heads are also italicized.)

(c) My own contributions are in square brackets, the previous dates being provided in the appendix of notes together with reasons for the change, if they are not evident from the footnotes on the page.

In the preceding pages there has been much talk of dates, and this will continue; it might be thought pedantic, but that does not make it either insignificant or superfluous. One might perhaps consider it unimportant whether a letter was written on one day or another, but, taken as a whole, such details placed in their right surroundings and order may help to form a picture of the writer and his development, not only as an artist but also as a man. Nor should it be forgotten that a false date, or a letter placed in the wrong order, may very well lead to wrong conclusions. Quite another thing, which I hardly need conceal, is that the task of dating Mahler's letters has been as fascinating as a good detective novel, if not so easy to approach.

It is obvious from the figures given above that the problem of dating the letters has not been completely solved. I realize, of course, that several letters never can be definitely dated, but there is a good chance of our being able to place many of the remaining letters, and I shall gladly receive any suggestions of improvements from readers, and if possible incorporate them in a new impression.

I have already mentioned that this edition of Mahler's letters represents only a modest selection of his vast correspondence, which runs to about 3,000 known letters. A complete edition (in German) is however in preparation under the editorship of M. Henry-Louis de La Grange and myself, and I appeal to anyone who has any material which might improve this enterprise to contact me.

Copenhagen, June 1977   *Knud Martner*

ACKNOWLEDGMENT

During the revision and editing of Mahler's letters I have encountered many problems which I would have been unable to solve if I had not been in the happy situation of knowing good friends who would indefatigably answer my flow of queries as well as otherwise render me advice and suggestions.

My friends are, of course, in no way responsible for my use of their knowledge and expertise, and I alone am to be blamed for errors and mistakes.

First and foremost my sincere thanks go to Mr. James W. Hart (Copenhagen), whose bilingual expertise has been invaluable to me and whose patience has been unbelievable. In the same breath and with the same gratitude I should like to thank Mrs. Susan Godfree (London), who has read and prepared my manuscript for the printer, and given me much advice and aid.

I am happy to express my thanks to the great Mahler biographer, M. Henry-Louis de La Grange (Paris), whose seemingly inexhaustible knowledge of even the smallest detail in Mahler's life has been of the greatest importance to me.

I am proud to count among my closest friends Mrs. Eleonore and Mr. Bruno Vondenhoff (Frankfurt/M.), both of whom out of love for Mahler's music have selflessly and expertly helped me with numerous difficult questions.

For much good advice and many suggestions I am especially indebted to Mr. Robert Becqué (Hoek v. Holland), Mr. H. J. Nieman (Wassenaar), Dr. Edward R. Reilly (Vassar College, Poughkeepsie), Mr. Paul Banks (Oxford) and Mr. David Matthews (London).

I should like to thank the following institutions and libraries for giving me access to their collections of Mahler letters: The Willem Mengelberg Stichting in Amsterdam (Miss Bysterus Heemskerk), Deutscher Staatsbibliothek in Berlin (D.D.R.), the Pierpont Morgan Library in New York and The Rare Room of the University of Pennsylvania (Philadelphia).

Last but not least I should like to thank Miss Judith Osborne of Faber and Faber Ltd. and Dr. Donald Mitchell of Faber Music Ltd. (London) for the patience and understanding both have displayed during the long preparation of this volume.

Finally my thanks go to my friend Per Munkgaard Thorsen (Copenhagen) who helped me with the illustrations.

K.M.

BIBLIOGRAPHY

Since Ludwig Schiedermair published the first book on Mahler (only thirty-eight pages) at the turn of the century, about a hundred biographies, studies, pamphlets etc. have appeared all over the world, but to list them all here would be irrelevant. The following list represents the titles which the editor has found most valuable.

Adler, Guido: *Gustav Mahler*, Vienna, 1916.
Bauer-Lechner, Natalie: *Erinnerungen an Gustav Mahler*, Vienna, 1923.
Bekker, Paul: *Gustav Mahlers Sinfonien*, Berlin, 1921.
Blaukopf, Kurt: *Mahler. Eine Dokumentarbiographie*, Vienna, 1976.
Gedeon, Tibor and Mathé, Miklos: *Gustav Mahler*, Budapest, 1965.
de La Grange, Henry-Louis: *Mahler*, Vol. I, New York, 1973.
Karpath, Ludwig: *Begegnung mit dem Genius*, Vienna, 1934.
Mahler, Alma: *Ein Leben mit Gustav Mahler* (manuscript).
        Gustav Mahler: Erinnerungen und Briefe, Amsterdam, 1940.
        Gustav Mahler: Memories and Letters (ed. by Donald Mitchell, and with new Chronology by K. Martner, London, 1973, and Seattle, 1975).
        Mein Leben, Frankfurt, 1960.
Mahler, Gustav: *Dopisy* (*Letters*), Prague, 1962.
Martner, Knud: *Gustav Mahler Werkverzeichnis*, Hamburg, *c.* 1980. (In prep)
        Gustav Mahler in Hamburg (manuscript).
Mitchell, Donald: *Gustav Mahler: The Early Years*, London, 1958.
        Gustav Mahler: The Wunderhorn Years, London, 1975.
Reilly, Edward: *Gustav Mahler und Guido Adler*, Vienna, 1978.
Stefan, Paul: *Gustav Mahler*, Vienna, 1910, second ed. 1920.
Vondenhoff, Bruno & Eleonore: *Gustav Mahler Dokumentation*, Tutzing, 1978.
Walter, Bruno: *Briefe 1894–1962*, Frankfurt, 1969.
        Thema und Variationen, Frankfurt, 1947.

GENERAL REFERENCE BOOKS

Deutscher Bühnen-Almanach, ed. Th. Entsch, Berlin, 1880–6.
Max Hesses Deutscher Musiker Kalender, Leipzig, 1886–1912.
Neuer Theater-Almanach, Berlin, 1890–1912.
Musikbuch aus Oesterreich, Vienna, 1904–11.

FOREWORD TO THE FIRST EDITION
by Alma Maria Mahler

I have done my best not only to edit this collection of letters faithfully, but also to arrange the correspondence in such a way as to give a picture of Gustav Mahler's life and development. There have been biographies and commentaries. Here now is the documentation.

So much has been written about Mahler that it seems unnecessary to provide an outline of his career. I would rather confine myself to recording some personal views and experiences that complement what is already known, thus, I hope, contributing to understanding of the letters and their writer.

This collection begins with a long, romantically enthusiastic letter written, at the age of eighteen, to a friend of his youth: the outpourings of a profoundly sensitive boy in love with Nature.[1] The tone, which undoubtedly has echoes of beloved voices, above all that of Jean Paul, is characteristic of Mahler's early years, all those years when he was working as Kapellmeister in small opera-houses. But what precedes these first letters, these first confessions? The childhood of genius is obscure, lit only by the lightning-flash of this or that anecdote. So what we know of Mahler as a child consists of a few characteristic details: for instance, that he would loiter outside the barracks to hear the bugle-calls, or how once, when he was four years old, during a visit to his grandparents, after a long search he was found in the attic, dreamily playing an old piano, now improvising, now effortlessly reproducing well-known tunes. It is also recounted that when the boy was once asked what he wanted to be when he grew up he answered: 'A martyr!'

None of these stories tells as much as one that, to me, seems to symbolize Gustav Mahler's spiritual destiny.

His father had taken the child Gustav for a walk in the woods. All at once he recalled something he had forgotten. He told the child to sit down on a log and wait until he came back. Then he went home. There, as usual, there was all the

[1] Now letter 2 to Josef Steiner (K.M.).

distraction, noise and tumult of family life. Only hours later was the little boy missed. It was already twilight when the agitated father hurried back into the woods. There, just where he had left him, he found the child sitting quietly on the log, his eyes wide with dreamy contemplation, untouched by fear or doubt, even though he had been there for many hours before evening fell.

There is something of the movingly heroic and, at the same time, of fairy-tale appealingness in this image of the solitary child patiently waiting in the dark woods. This is the child that Gustav Mahler always remained at heart. The cloud of dreamy thoughtfulness that wrapped him in solitude never quite left him, whether he was the young conductor in Olmütz [see letter 17], the all-powerful operatic director in Vienna or the celebrated master in New York.

The life to which he dedicated himself, the other side of his being, his ambition, made it necessary for him to fight continually against the danger inherent in this mystical abandonment. It was a tragic struggle. Outwardly that is evident in the fact that Mahler gave ten months of every year to operatic affairs, and only two months to his own creative work, an arrangement that caused him intense suffering. If people sometimes found him hasty, nerve-ridden, tyrannical and impatient, that was surely no more than the startled reaction of one constantly being waked out of his inner dream.

Yet there is a beautiful logic in his final return to that visionary childhood scene in the woods. Is not his farewell, *Das Lied von der Erde*, the ripe fruit of that far-off melancholy contemplation, the seed of it perhaps already germinating in the waiting child? It is between these frontiers that his life runs its course and that his letters trace it out.

A certain taste for endowing artists' lives with sentimentality has sought to mark Gustav Mahler down as a greatly unhappy man. That is false. He was good-humoured, active and energetic. Even the artist's gravest ill, doubt of his own genius, attacked him but very seldom, and soon would lose its hold on him. He believed in himself. Indeed, he had to believe in himself, his short life being such an incomparable crescendo.

After years of apprenticeship, of moving from one theatre to another, at the age of twenty-eight he became director of the Royal Opera-House in Budapest, then at the age of thirty-seven director of the Court Opera in Vienna, which meant that he was a king in the world of music—and that in an authoritarian age when the way ahead was sternly barred to youthful talent.

Gradually the financial anxieties and the burden of debt that embarrassed his early years diminished. His life became increasingly one of material ease. In his last years he could afford to live in princely style. His appreciation of beauty in outer things developed. Those disciples of his who try to make him an ascetic do not know that the capacity for sensuous enjoyment was an intrinsic part of what made him a complete human being.

In the end, too, success came to the creative musician. In his thirties his music was performed, causing astonishment and indignation, giving rise to heated controversy. But—*he had arrived*!

From the age of forty onward he gradually became famous as a composer. His symphonies were performed at the German music festivals. Willem Mengelberg was daring enough to conduct the Fourth Symphony twice on one evening.[1]

The first performance of the Eighth Symphony, in Munich [12 and 13 Sept. 1910], turned out to be the long-awaited, incomparable triumph, one such as no other composer of this age has experienced. For weeks beforehand all the newspapers were full of excited articles about the 'Symphony of the Thousand'. Each rehearsal was a celebration. Friends, eminent people, came from far and near. Mahler could now feel himself sought after, understood, cherished, loved! And when, on the evening itself, he came out to conduct, the whole audience rose to its feet and stood in solemn silence to mark its respect.

Soon afterwards we [again] left for America. What we experienced there was so wonderful that it scarcely seemed real. If in his journeyman years Gustav Mahler had been a sensitive romantic, in ever-impatient quest, and if in Vienna he was a ruthless commander, in America he became a serene monarch. He came under the spell of what he there encountered, the might of Nature, the generous enthusiasm of the people. He experienced things that must sound paradoxical to European ears: for instance, two ladies, returning home after a performance of *Fidelio* under his direction, resolved that 'Mr. Mahler' must have an orchestra of his own—and within twenty-four hours he had *his* orchestra.[2] And something else again that was profoundly exciting and momentous for him: his ensemble in New York consisted of the world's most glorious voices, and his joy in making music became infinite. In Vienna he had to work sparingly. Over there every rôle, down to the last, was filled by the great: Caruso, Bonci, Scotti, Chaliapin, Burrian, Sembrich, Fremstad, Farrar, Eames and many others, all joyfully owing unqualified fealty to his direction.

No, there was no respect in which life did not shower upon Gustav Mahler all that he deserved.

Just as life raised him to the heights, so too it did not spare him pain and grief. He was afflicted often and harshly. The first great sorrow of his life was the death of a brother, still a child, one whom he always mournfully said had

[1] Amsterdam, 23 October 1904. A.M. is not correct as it was Mahler who conducted both performances. See programme on p. 282 and note 316 (K.M.)
[2] Now it is A.M. who is romanticizing what actually happened. See note to letter 367, p. 441.

been more gifted than himself.[1] Later there was the death of his beloved mother. And four years before his own death we lost our elder child. His love for that child was immeasurable: she was all *his*! Every morning he would bring her into his study, where they would both have intense and impassioned discussions about things that remained unknown to me, for I scrupulously avoided disturbing their solitude.

And that child died.[2]

A short while later, merely in order to allay my forebodings, Gustav Mahler let himself be medically examined. So we learnt for the first time of the long-standing heart disease that was a threat to his life. Now he was overtaken by thoughts of death.

He said so often: 'All my works are an *anticipando* of the life to come.'

And, indeed, he had written the Sixth Symphony, the last movement of which has those three terrible blows, symbolic of catastrophes destroying the symphonic hero's life.[3]

It was the final rehearsal of this work, at Essen [27 May 1906], that had so frightfully disturbed his spirit. He had walked up and down in the Green Room, unable to suppress sobs and tears. Those few of us who were in the room with him scarcely dared to breathe or to look at him.

From year to year Gustav Mahler's life rose in an ever steeper curve, his experience growing riper, his work richer, his fame more splendid.

The letters written in his youth are full of real feeling, revelling in words, always full of strong poetry. Later the intensity of expression diminishes. A new tone appears: something concise, concentrated, restrained. It is not only the pressure of business that imposes a certain taciturn quality on the writer. It is something more. It is the taciturnity peculiar to the writer of music.

But it is especially in the more compact style of the mature letters that the reader will sense all the phases, achievements and moods of this great man. Mahler—I am impelled to believe—discovered for us a quite new value in music: that of ethical and mystical humanity. He enriched the symbolic world of music, which had until then comprehended love, war, religion, nature and mankind, by including Man as the solitary being circling, unredeemed on earth, throughout the universe—Man as the forlorn child for ever waiting in meditative quietude, amidst greenwood twilight, for the coming of the father. He set to music Dostoevsky's question to life: 'How should I be happy so long as anywhere some other creature suffers?' . . . *The Brothers Karamazov* is the source of these words that he loved above all else.

---

[1] A.M. alludes to Ernst Mahler who died in 1874 aged thirteen (K.M.).
[2] Maria Anna, nicknamed 'Putzi', who died on 12 July 1907 (K.M.).
[3] Mahler finally dropped the last 'blow' (K.M.).

I have here divided Gustav Mahler's correspondence into four sections. Each of these sections covers an historical period complete in itself. Within these sections the letters are arranged chronologically, but in such a way that no series of letters to any one correspondent is interrupted. For what is important is not solely the writer, but also his relationship to the letters' recipient. In this way there emerges a clear picture of all the bonds between them.

The letters collected in this volume are predominantly letters to Gustav Mahler's friends.

To all who have unselfishly helped me in this task I herewith express my heartfelt gratitude.

Alma Maria Mahler

NOTE ON THE EDITING OF THE LETTERS (FIRST EDITION)

by Alma Mahler

In this edition the spelling has been adapted to accord with modern usage, although Mahler for some time continued to use the older German spelling that prevailed in his youth. His method of writing is not reproduced typographically in so far as his habit of mixing the Gothic and the Latin hand is not represented: he customarily wrote place names and proper names, foreign words, dates and addresses, as well as anything he wished to emphasize, in Latin script, for the rest using Gothic letters. What is printed s p a c e d[1] is in his manuscript underlined; what is printed in Roman represents words omitted, as not infrequently happened, in the haste of writing. Italicized addresses and dates at the head of letters are given by him; those in Roman are supplied by the editor.

The overwhelming majority of the letters were not dated by Mahler himself. As he once remarked, the fact was that he usually did not know the date. Since at least a generation has passed since these letters were written, it will be understandable if exact dating has not always been achieved. The same applies to the identification of persons, musical works and performances, and to elucidation of much referred to in the letters. Every effort will be made to complete or correct documentation as opportunity arises.

The letters to F. Löhr have an apparatus, besides that of the footnotes, referring to a more detailed, separate appendix, which, because of its special nature, has been printed separately at the end of this volume.

[1] This applies to the German edition: for this edition read 'in italics' (K.M.).

NOTE ON THE EDITING OF THE LETTERS (FIRST EDITION)

by Alma Mahler

LIST OF LETTERS

2

2*

Supplement of Letters to Mahler

COMPARATIVE LISTS OF OLD AND NEW NUMBERING

I *The New Numbering*

The left-hand column refers to the original German edition, and the right-hand column to the corresponding number in the present edition.

1–2	27–35	53–51	79–91	105–93	131–157
2–1	28–36	54–52	80–95	106–94	132–198
3–31	29–37	55–53	81–97	107–193	133–224
4–3	30–38	56–61	82–99	108–96	134–118
5–11	31–39	57–66	83–108	109–98	135–101
6–12	32–40	58–67	84–113	110–102	136–110
7–13	33–43	59–70	85–114	111–103	137–123
8–58	34–45	60–71	86–116	112–105	138–100
9–62	35–46	61–73	87–121	113–104	139–128
10–16	36–47	62–74	88–125	114–106	140–129
11–17	37–48	63–75	89–119	115–107	141–152
12–18	38–49	64–76	90–131	116–109	142–145
13–19	39–50	65–77	91–133	117–115	143–146
14–20	40–54	66–78	92–134	118–117	144–147
15–21	41–55	67–79	93–137	119–120	145–148
16–22	42–56	68–80	94–111	120–122	146–165
17–23	43–57	69–81	95–179	121–124	147–166
18–24	44–59	70–82	96–200	122–126	148–167
19–25	45–60	71–83	97–213	123–138	149–169
20–26	46–63	72–85	98–214	124–127	150–171
21–27	47–64	73–86	99–220	125–132	151–172
22–28	48–72	74–84	100–222	126–135	152–173
23–29	49–68	75–87	101–235	127–136	153–174
24–32	50–41	76–88	102–237	128–140	154–175
25–33	51–42	77–89	103–69	129–142	155–201
26–34	52–44	78–90	104–92	130–139	156–206

157–208	197–185	237–405	276–321	316–317	356–387
158–209	198–154	238–309	277–324	317–318	357–396
159–210	199–168	239–236	278–354	318–327	358–419
160–212	200–170	240–238	279–279	319–328	359–420
161–230	201–187	241–290	280–294	320–353	360–423
162–232	202–180	242–239	281–311	321–266	361–434
163–233	203–181	243–243	282–314	322–278	362–438
164–130	204–202	244–248	283–342	323–329	363–366
165–141	205–186	245–249	284–281	324–344	364–367
166–143	206–203	246–257	285–282	325–346	365–381
167–144	207–223	247–258	286–292	326–331	366–395
168–151	208–199	248–259	287–283	327–335	367–442
169–153	209–205	249–265	288–289	328–336	368–413
170–176	210–226	250–270	289–300	329–339	369–422
171–195	211–211	251–268	290–284	330–340	370–429
172–149	212–234	252–271	291–306	331–355	371–428
173–150	213–192	253–275	292–307	332–356	372–388
174–182	214–161	254–274	293–297	333–349	373–362
175–183	215–377	255–276	294–301	334–397	374–364
176–155	216–215	256–280	295–286	335–436	375–406
177–156	217–216	257–299	296–287	336–351	376–383
178–158	218–218	258–313	297–288	337–350	377–372
179–160	219–225	259–357	298–295	338–371	378–375
180–177	220–219	260–252	299–323	339–352	379–378
181–162	221–228	261–253	300–332	340–392	380–384
182–163	222–231	262–262	301–293	341–348	381–382
183–164	223–241	263–263	302–303	342–359	382–399
184–178	224–245	264–264	303–310	343–360	383–407
185–188	225–240	265–250	304–316	344–376	384–416
186–189	226–242	266–254	305–325	345–380	385–415
187–190	227–251	267–267	306–338	346–441	386–345
188–191	228–256	268–312	307–341	347–404	387–361
189–194	229–330	269–333	308–343	348–411	388–389
190–196	230–319	270–334	309–326	349–412	389–370
191–197	231–320	271–337	310–347	350–432	390–368
192–204	232–217	272–390	311–302	351–424	391–358
193–184	233–229	273–273	312–315	352–433	392–363
194–207	234–269	274–285	313–296	353–373	393–365
195–221	235–298	275 { 308a	314–304	354–440	394–379
196–244	236–322	275 { 308b	315–305	355–386	395–385

396–369	401–414	405–398	409–431	413–394	417–427
397–401	402–374	406–410	410–439	414–400	418–430
398–409	403–391	407–418	411–402	415–421	419–437
399–425	404–393	408–426	412–403	416–408	420–443
400–435					

II *The Old Numbering*

The left-hand column refers to the present edition, and the right-hand column to the corresponding number in the original German edition.

1–2	31–3	61–56	91–79	121–87	151–168
2–1	32–24	62–9	92–104	122–120	152–141
3–4	33–25	63–46	93–105	123–137	153–169
4	34–26	64–47	94–106	124–121	154–198
5	35–27	65	95–80	125–88	155–176
6	36–28	66–57	96–108	126–122	156–177
7	37–29	67–58	97–81	127–124	157–131
8	38–30	68–49	98–109	128–139	158–178
9	39–31	69–103	99–82	129–140	159
10	40–32	70–59	100–138	130–164	160–179
11–5	41–50	71–60	101–135	131–90	161–214
12–6	42–51	72–48	102–110	132–125	162–181
13–7	43–33	73–61	103–111	133–91	163–182
14	44–52	74–62	104–113	134–92	164–183
15	45–34	75–63	105–112	135–126	165–146
16–10	46–35	76–64	106–114	136–127	166–147
17–11	47–36	77–65	107–115	137–93	167–148
18–12	48–37	78–66	108–83	138–123	168–199
19–13	49–38	79–67	109–116	139–130	169–149
20–14	50–39	80–68	110–136	140–128	170–200
21–15	51–53	81–69	111–94	141–165	171–150
22–16	52–54	82–70	112	142–129	172–151
23–17	53–55	83–71	113–84	143–166	173–152
24–18	54–40	84–74	114–85	144–167	174–153
25–19	55–41	85–72	115–117	145–142	175–154
26–20	56–42	86–73	116–86	146–143	176–170
27–21	57–43	87–75	117–118	147–144	177–180
28–22	58–8	88–76	118–134	148–145	178–184
29–23	59–44	89–77	119–89	149–172	179–95
30	60–45	90–78	120–119	150–173	180–202

181–203	221–195	261	301–294	340–330	380–345
182–174	222–100	262–262	302–311	341–307	381–365
183–175	223–207	263–263	303–302	342–283	382–381
184–193	224–133	264–264	304–314	343–308	383–376
185–197	225–219	265–249	305–315	344–324	384–380
186–205	226–210	266–321	306–291	345–386	385–395
187–201	227	267–267	307–292	346–325	386–355
188–185	228–221	268–251	308a)	347–310	387–356
189–186	229–233	269–234	308b) }–275	348–341	388–372
190–187	230–161	270–250	309–238	349–333	389–388
191–188	231–222	271–252	310–303	350–337	390–272
192–213	232–162	272	311–281	351–336	391–403
193–107	233–163	273–273	312–268	352–339	392–340
194–189	234–212	274–254	313–258	353–320	393–404
195–171	235–101	275–253	314–282	354–278	394–413
196–190	236–239	276–255	315–312	355–331	395–366
197–191	237–102	277	316–304	356–332	396–357
198–132	238–240	278–322	317–316	357–259	397–334
199–208	239–242	279–279	318–317	358–391	398–405
200–96	240–225	280–256	319–230	359–342	399–382
201–155	241–223	281–284	320–231	360–343	400–414
202–204	242–226	282–285	321–276	361–387	401–397
203–206	243–243	283–287	322–236	362–373	402–411
204–192	244–196	284–290	323–299	363–392	403–412
205–209	245–224	285–274	324–277	364–374	404–347
206–156	246	286–295	325–305	365–393	405–237
207–194	247	287–296	326–309	366–363	406–375
208–157	248–244	288–297	327–318	367–364	407–383
209–158	249–245	289–288	328–319	368–390	408–416
210–159	250–265	290–241	329–323	369–396	409–398
211–211	251–227	291	330–229	370–389	410–406
212–160	252–260	292–286	331–326	371–338	411–348
213–97	253–261	293–301	332–300	372–377	412–349
214–98	254–266	294–280	333–269	373–353	413–368
215–216	255	295–298	334–270	374–402	414–401
216–217	256–228	296–313	335–327	375–378	415–385
217–232	257–246	297–293	336–328	376–344	416–384
218–218	258–247	298–235	337–271	377–215	417
219–220	259–248	299–257	338–306	378–379	418–407
220–99	260	300–289	339–329	379–394	419–358

420–359	424–351	428–371	432–350	436–335	440–354
421–415	425–399	429–370	433–352	437–419	441–346
422–369	426–408	430–418	434–361	438–362	442–367
423–360	427–417	431–409	435–400	439–410	443–420

KEY

(o.e.) = original editor (i.e. of the German edition)

(F.L.) = Friedrich Löhr

(E.F.) = Emil Freund

(B.W.) = Bruno Walter

(K.M.) = Knud Martner

[ ] = Knud Martner's editorial additions

⟨ ⟩ = cuts made by Alma Mahler in original German edition and now restored by Knud Martner

{ } = words omitted by Mahler in the haste of writing and supplied in the original edition by Alma Mahler

† = further notes are to be found at the back of the book, under the letter number

Italic type used for address and/or date = omitted by Mahler and supplied by Alma Mahler or the recipient

Roman type used for address and/or date = supplied by Mahler in the original

Italic type used in text of letter = words emphasized by Mahler and underlined in the original

Bold type used in text of letter = words written in English by Mahler in the original

I
VIENNA, BAD HALL, LAIBACH AND OLMÜTZ
1877–1883

1877

Undated. Iglau [July 1877]

My dear and revered Master,

   You cannot imagine the joy that your esteemed letter has given me; I really do not know what to say in gratitude for so much kindness. But even if I were to write page after page in the attempt to express my thanks, it would not amount to anything but: 'how very like you'. Let me assure you, this is not just empty talk, but something I really and truly mean.—Your 'wohltemperiertheit'2 will forgive me if I modulate out of this gentle adagio of my feelings, through the dissonances of my anger, into a tempestuous finale that is really to be understood as 'ungemein rubato'.3 For the fact is I came in several bars late at the matriculation concert here in Iglau, or rather I arrived a few days late, so I could not sit for the matriculation exam with the others and was forced to postpone it for two months. But I hope that I shall nevertheless complete to your entire satisfaction the holiday task that you set me.

   With sincere assurance of my profound respect and gratitude, I remain

Your devoted pupil
Gustav Mahler

PS. Please have the kindness, if opportunity occurs, to convey my respects to Herr Direktor Hellmesberger4 and Herr Prof. Krenn.5 My parents ask to be remembered to you.

---

1 Further notes to be found at the back, under the letter number, are indicated by a 'dagger'.
2 'Wohltemperiertheit' is a pun on Bach's *Das Wohltemperierte Klavier* (The Well-tempered Klavier) and the German 'Wohlgeehrte' ('esteemed master'). Mahler doubtless played Bach's work during his lessons with Epstein who taught him at the Conservatory (K.M.).
3 'Exceedingly rubato'. This unusual expression-mark is used by Mahler in his unfinished Piano Quartet (1876) at the end of the only existing movement (K.M.).
4 Joseph Hellmesberger (1828–93), director of the Conservatory in Vienna (K.M.).
5 Franz Krenn (1816–97), Mahler's teacher in composition (K.M.).

1879

2a *To Joseph Steiner*†

Puszta-Batta, 17 June 1879

Dear Steiner,

Don't be cross with me for taking so long to reply; but everything around me is so bleak, and behind me the twigs of a dry and brittle existence snap. A great deal has been going on since I last wrote. But I can't tell you about it. Only this: I have become a different person; whether a better one, I don't know, anyway not a happier one. The greatest intensity of the most joyful vitality and the most consuming yearning for death dominate my heart in turn, very often alternate hour by hour—one thing I know: I can't go on like this much longer! When the abominable tyranny of our modern hypocrisy and mendacity has driven me to the point of dishonouring myself, when the inextricable web of conditions in art and life has filled my heart with disgust for all that is sacred to me—art, love, religion—what way out is there but self-annihilation? Wildly I wrench at the bonds that chain me to the loathsome, insipid swamp of this life, and with all the strength of despair I cling to sorrow, my only consolation.— Then all at once the sun smiles upon me—and gone is the ice that encased my heart, again I see the blue sky and the flowers swaying in the wind, and my mocking laughter dissolves in tears of love. Then I *needs must* love this world with all its deceit and frivolity and its eternal laughter. Oh, would that some god might tear the veil from my eyes, that my clear gaze might penetrate to the marrow of the earth! Oh, that I might behold this earth in its nakedness, lying there without adornment or embellishment before its Creator; then I would step forth and face its genius. 'Now I know you, deceiver, for what you are! With all your feigning you have not tricked me, with all your glitter you have not dazzled me! Lo and behold! A man surrounded by all the glamorous gambols of your falsity, struck by the most terrible blows of your scorn, and yet unbowed, yet strong.' May fear strike you, wherever you hide! Out of the valley of mankind the cry goes up, soars to your cold and lonely heights! Do you comprehend the unspeakable misery here below that for aeons has been piling up mountain-high? And on those mountain peaks you sit enthroned, laughing! How in the days to come will you justify yourself before the avenger, you who cannot atone for the suffering of even one single frightened soul!!!

2b.   18 June

Yesterday I was too exhausted and upset to go on writing. Now yesterday's
state of wild agitation has yielded to a gentler mood; I feel like someone who has
been angry for a long time and whose eyes at last fill with assuaging tears. Dear
Steiner! So you want to know what I have been doing all this time? A very few
words suffice.—I have eaten and drunk, I have been awake and I have slept, I
have wept and laughed, I have stood {on} mountains, where the breath of God
bloweth where it listeth, I have been on the heath, and the tinkling of cow-bells
has lulled me into dreams. Yet I have not escaped my destiny; doubt pursues
me wherever I go; there is nothing that affords me complete enjoyment, and
even my most serene smile is accompanied by tears. Now here I am in the
Hungarian Puszta, living with a family who have hired me for the summer; I
am required to give the boys piano lessons, and occasionally to send the family
into musical raptures, so here I am, caught like a midge in the spider's web, just
twitching. Yet 'the Moor has done his work: the Moor can go'.[1] But in the
evening when I go out on to the heath and climb a lime tree that stands there all
lonely, and when from the topmost branches of this friend of mine I see far out
into the world: before my eyes the Danube winds her ancient way, her waves
flickering with the glow of the setting sun; from the village behind me the chime
of the eventide bells is wafted to me on a kindly breeze, and the branches sway
in the wind, rocking me into a slumber like the daughters of the elfin king, and
the leaves and blossoms of my favourite tree tenderly caress my cheeks.—
Stillness everywhere! Most holy stillness! Only from afar comes the melancholy
croaking of the frog that sits all mournfully among the reeds.—

Then the pallid shapes that people my life pass by me like shadows of long-
lost happiness, and in my ears again resounds the chant of yearning.—And once
again we roam familiar pastures together, and yonder stands the hurdy-gurdy
man, holding out his hat in his skinny hand. And in the tuneless melody I
recognized Ernst of Swabia's salutation, and he himself steps forth, opening his
arms to me, and when I look closer, it is my poor brother;[2] veils come floating
down, the images, the notes, grow dim:

Out of the grey sea two kindly names emerge: Morawan, Ronow![3] And I see
gardens, and many people there, and a tree, with a name carved in its bark:
Pauline. And a blue-eyed girl bends sideways—laughing, she breaks a bunch of
grapes from the vine for me—memory causes my cheeks to flush for the second

---

[1] A well-known quotation from Schiller's play *Die Verschwörung des Fiesko zu Genua* (1783)
(K.M.).
[2] Allusions to *Ernst von Schwaben*, an opera that Mahler had sketched to a libretto by Josef
Steiner, and to Mahler's younger brother Ernst (1861–74) (o.e.).
[3] Dairy farms near Caslau [twenty-five miles north of Iglau], in Bohemia, which Mahler
visited during the summer holidays of 1875 and 1876 (o.e.).

time—I see the two eyes that once made a thief of me—then once again it all recedes.—Nothingness!—Now, over there, that fateful umbrella rises, and I hear the prophetic voices foretelling, from its ribs and entrails, like a Roman augur, the misfortune that is to befall me. Suddenly a table rises out of the ground, and behind it stands a spiritual figure veiled in blue clouds: it is Melion[1] hymning the 'Great Spirit', at the same time censing him with genuine Three Kings tobacco! And beside him the two of us sit like altar-boys about to serve at Mass for the first time.

And behind us a grinning goblin hovers, decked out in piquet cards, and he has Buxbaum's[2] face and calls out to us in a terrible voice, to the melody of Bertini's[3] Études: 'Bow down! for this glory too shall turn to dust!' A cascade of smoke from Melion covers the whole scene, the clouds become ever denser, and then suddenly, as in Raphael's painting of the Madonna, a little angel's head peers out from among these clouds, and below him Ahasuerus stands in all his sufferings, longing to ascend to him, to enter the presence of all that means bliss and redemption, but the angel floats away on high, laughing, and vanishes, and Ahasuerus gazes after him in immeasurable grief, then takes up his staff and resumes his wanderings, tearless, eternal, immortal.

O earth, my beloved earth, when, ah, when will you give refuge to him who is foresaken, receiving him back into your womb? Behold! Mankind has cast him out, and he flees from its cold and heartless bosom, he flees to you, to you alone! O, take him in, eternal, all-embracing mother, give a resting place to him who is without friend and without rest!

2c.   19 June
Dear Steiner,

Now for the third day I return to you, and today I do so in order to take leave of you in merry mood. It is the story of my life that is recorded in these pages. What a strange destiny, sweeping me along on the waves of my yearning, now hurling me this way and that in the gale, now wafting me along merrily in smiling sunshine. What I fear is that in such a gale I shall some day be shattered against a reef—such as my keel has often grazed!

It is six o'clock in the morning! I have been out on the heath, sitting with Fárkas the shepherd, listening to the sound of his shawm. Ah, how mournful it sounded, and yet how full of rapturous delight—that folk-tune he played! The flowers growing at his feet trembled in the dreamy glow of his dark eyes,

[1] Franz Melion was Mahler's tutor at the grammar school that he went to from 1875 to 1877 (o.e.).
[2] Unidentified (K.M.).
[3] Henri Bertini (1798–1876), the well-known composer of études (K.M.).

and his brown hair fluttered around his sun-tanned cheeks. Ah, Steiner! You are still asleep in your bed, and I have already seen the dew on the grasses.—I am now so serenely gay and the tranquil happiness all around me is tiptoeing into my heart too, as the sun of early spring lights up the wintry fields. Is spring awakening now in my own breast?! And while this mood prevails, let me take leave of you, my faithful friend!

Write to me soon, very soon, for I am so utterly alone here, with no soul to speak to, no books to read.

With all my good wishes,

Yours sincerely,

Gustav Mahler

My present address is: Herr Moritz Baumgarten, Tétény, Hungary.

3.   *To Emil Freund* (Vienna)†

Batta, June 1879

Dear Emil,

I have waited until today hoping that Herr Baumgarten would pay me my monthly salary. But since he still shows no signs of doing so, I have no choice but to go, as soon as I have finished this letter, and ask him for a loan, so that I can enclose 11 fl.

When your letter came, I was suffering from the most terrible yearning—I simply can't stand it any longer.

I am very pleased to be able to tell you that the family is going to the seaside, to Norderney, on 12 August, which means that I shall then be as free as a finch, I hope I shall then be able to look you up in Seelau or, better still, that you will come and fetch me. Meanwhile, keep your nose to the grindstone so that you can take some time off while I am staying with you. It would be rather a bore to have your parents' prophetic wisdom (I mean with reference to being ploughed in your State exam) looming behind us all the time.

Yours,

Mahler

4.   *To Albert Spiegler*†

Batta, 16 July 1879

Dear Albert,

Many thanks for your writing to me. It is really a high holiday for me whenever a letter strays into this hermitage of mine here. I received your reminder just as everything had been settled. I will say nothing of my sufferings. How could I describe them to you, who have not yet borne the woes of loneliness, nor the torments that heartless people cause one, nor the disgust evoked by this shallow scrambling as in an ant-hill!

On 10 August (I expect to write to you before that) I am coming to Vienna, thence continuing my journey to Iglau. I hope I am *sure* of seeing you there. You cannot imagine, dear Albert, how I yearn to see human beings again, and how I long once again to hear the sound of the organ and the peal of the bells. A breeze as of heavenly wings blows through me when I see the peasants in their finery at church. They kneel in prayer before the altar, and their songs of praise mingle with the sound of drums and trumpets.—Ah, it is long since there was any altar left for me: only, mute and high, God's temple arches over me, the wide sky.—I cannot rise to it, and would so gladly pray. Instead of chorales and hymns it is thunder that roars, and instead of candles it is lightning that flickers—

Storm on, storm on, I understand your language not, ye elements, and when ye jubilate to God, to my human ear it sounds like wrath!

Write soon. Everyone else is silent.

Ever,
Gustav Mahler

5. *To Anton Krisper* (Laibach)†

Undated. Postmark: Vienna, 22 September 1879
Café Imperial

My dear Anton,

I have just arrived in Vienna and have been visiting the places where together we so often shared our joys and sorrows. I am the unhappiest of fortune's favourites ever to have writhed amidst roses. A new name[1] is now inscribed in my heart alongside yours—true, only whisperingly and blushingly, but no less powerfully. When are you coming to Vienna? Write straight away. I am now moving into familiar lodgings. Ah, that I might be nearer to the good old times! I dare say I am a real fool. So be it! Children are better than old men.

I am too restless to be able to write more. My parents greet you cordially, as does also your loyal

Gustav Mahler

Wien, III. Rennweg 3. Parterre, Door 10 B.

---

[1] Josephine Poisl, daughter of the postmaster in Iglau. See Notes (K.M.).

6. *To Anton Krispert*†

My dear Anton,

To make certain that this letter reaches you I am sending it to your old address. Also, do not be surprised if it turns out to be a somewhat short one—I still suspect that I am only writing for the benefit of the four winds.

Why can it be that you still fail to give any signs of life, so that I don't even have a remote idea where you are to be found?

My curriculum vitae for these two months can be given in a few words: I have

– – – – –

I resume after a break of half an hour, because that old crow of a chambermaid forgot to fill the lamp, so I had to run around to all the paraffin dealers in Cottageverein until one of them took pity on me and opened up his shop—it is now in fact half past ten.

So—to return to my curriculum. Dear friend, I have been quite dreadfully entangled in the delightful fetters of the darling of the gods: the hero now 'sighs, wrings his hands, groans and weeps' etc., etc. For the most part I have really spent the time poking around in sweet sufferings in the most various ways, arising in the mornings with 'Ah' and going to sleep with 'O'; dreaming, I have lived, and waking, I have dreamt, and in this way the two months have gone by and now the little Christ-child is here—and should be bringing me something *really* lovely. In a week I shall be in Iglau and shall awake from my rosy dreams into a still rosier daylight.

A fresh shadow is now hovering in the background of my dream-pictures too, only I must first await its bearer. When he shows himself I will tell you more about him—I can only suppose that it is an ancient Nordic king who will startle me out of my peace with his heroes and carousels. I have also been tippling a little at the fount of Hippocrene—out of the abundance of the heart the mouth speaks.—

And now enough of detestable smiling—I have force myself to adopt a cheerful pastoral style so as not to lapse into the old, trite lamentations. I do not want to sigh, yet nor do I want to smile. In my φρῆν [brain] are quartered some squadrons of imprecations and curses; I want them to march forth now. 'The Devil take this whole shoddy existence!' My eyes are like dried lemons—there is no longer even a single drop in them. I must experience all the afflictions of this world, and am not to be spared a single one.

This will seem enigmatic to you—I fear that soon I shall be in a position to provide you with a dreadful explanation. Until then a hearty farewell, and do write soon. I will now go to sleep, since I need the rest.

Good night, dear Anton, good night!

Your loyal

Gustav Mahler

Wien, Cottageverein, Karl Ludwigstrasse No.24

If you can, lend me five Spiesse,[1] but *only* if this is *absolutely* convenient.

Vienna, 14 December. I have now been carrying this letter around in my pocket for two weeks already. *Reply immediately!* On Friday I shall be going home.

1880

7. *To Anton Krispert*†

Undated. Postmark: Vienna, 18 February 1880

My dear Anton,

I am now sitting down late at night in my new quarters. Numerous books lie before me and the chibouk[2] is steaming. However I do not relish smoking and I am too preoccupied to be able to read anything either.

My thoughts constantly turn to you. And then I think it is better to leave the books in peace and I want at once to be entirely in your company. If I had written to you half an hour ago, the old tears and sighs would once more have poured on to the paper. But now I am much calmer. A book is a veritable Leyden jar for pain, absorbing and gathering into itself the whole current of feelings—from time to time, of course, the battery discharges should one come too near to it, and returns everything to the originator again in bright sparks. This is truly the first time for a long while that I have found such calm words. However I have also saved them for you so that you can see how tractable I am and how willingly I fulfil your wishes.

In the next room lives a young lady who stays at her spinet the whole day long. Of course she does not know that on account of it I am going like Ahasuerus to have to take up my walking stick again. Heaven knows whether I will ever settle down anywhere. There is always some heedless fellow to drive me from one room to another. My present one is at: VI., Windmühlgasse No. 39, First floor, Door 18.

---

[1] Viennese slang for a coin, presumably Gulden. See also letter 334, p. 292 (K.M.).

[2] A long straight-stemmed Turkish pipe (K.M.).

Write and tell me what has been happening to you. When will you be coming to Vienna? Wasn't it arranged that you would spend the second term here? But come anyway, as you are under no obligation to stick around in that seaside town. You won't be missing anything there, and you will lose nothing by coming here. Write soon!

With all good wishes,
Yours,
Gustav

8. *To Anton Krisper†*

Undated. Postmark: Vienna, 3 March 1880

Dearest Friend,

Why this silence? Have you not received my letter? My life continues on its familiar daily round. Spring arrived overnight and with it the old yearning and melancholy. I have just written some lines of poetry which I pass on to you because they will best reveal my inner thoughts to you.

Vergessene Liebe[1]

Wie öd' mein Herz! Wie leer das All'!
Wie gross mein Sehnen!
O, wie die Fernen Tal zu Tal
sich endlos dehnen!
Mein süsses Lieb! Zum letzten Mal!?
Ach, muss ja ewig diese Qual
in meinem Herzen brennen!

Wie strahlt' es einst so treu und klar
in ihren Blicken!
Das Wandern liess ich ganz und gar
trotz Winters Tücken!
Und als der Lenz vergangen war,
Da tat mein Lieb ihr blondes Haar
wohl mit der Myrthe schmücken!

Mein Wanderstab! Noch einmal heut
komm aus der Ecken!
Schliefst du auch lang! Nun sei bereit!
Ich will dich wecken!

[1] See Notes for translation.

Ich trug es lang mein Liebesleid
Und ist die Erde doch so weit—
    So komm, mein treuer Stecken!

Wie lieblich lächelt Berg und Tal
    in Blütenwogen!
Kam ja mit seinem süssen Schall
    der Lenz gezogen!
Und Blumen blühn ja überall
Und Kreuzlein steh'n ja überall—
    die haben nicht gelogen!

Most important of all, I must tell you about a plan for a summer trip I want to make with Heinrich and Rudolf Krzyzanowski in July; we are most certainly counting on your coming with us.

On foot through the Bohemian Forest (the only virgin forest in Europe—a strange and individual race of people with wonderful women), then likewise through the Fichtelgebirge. Eger—Beireuth [*sic!*]—Nuremberg—then finally to Oberammergau for the Passion Plays—this will take us less than three weeks, and then we shall go straight home (with you spending a few days with me in Iglau if possible). Does this proposal not appeal to you? It would really be quite splendid, and besides, we did in fact discuss this last summer. I beg you to write back straight away to your ever loyal

Gustav Mahler

9. *To Anton Krisper*†

Undated. Postmark: Vienna, 14 March 1880

Dear Anton,

I am extremely concerned at still not having had any answer from you. Where can you be? And what can you be doing? Am I to be left in ignorance—I who am perhaps besides your parents the only person in the world who has your interests at heart? Or are you unwell?—Ah, dear Anton, that is what I am—already I feel a terrible yearning to see you and to be with you.

I am so solitary!

I do not know whether I shall be able to bear it for much longer. I feel as if I am about to collapse at any minute!

I have just been fighting a major battle—and I still have not got to the end of it. I cannot explain this to you—

For the first time this world has got hold of me just where it matters and the faded commonplaces, the threadbare old wives' tales, which I never heard with more than a pitying smile, have dragged me into their own ranks like water sprites, and now I am engulfed by the waves.

I beg you to write immediately if you do not want me to think that you are angry with me. I embrace you—

Your loyal friend,
Gustav

My address: G.M. Wien, Windmühlgasse, No. 39, First floor, Door 18.

10. *To Albert Spiegler* (Vienna)†

Undated. Postmark: Bad Hall, 21 June 1880

As an oddity, dear fellow, I am writing to you from this garden.[1] The house over which I have put the X is where I live. I must say, the district is much more beautiful than this woodcut supposes, with its tear-blurred eyes, through which it sees everything desolate and pale. My own condition is in keeping with the circumstances. I neither let courage hold arbitrary sway—as you suppose—nor do I try to combat this distress with a joke; yet I still stand upright, and hope to do so for all time. For it would be too pitiful if bluebottles could bring one to the point of moaning. If I complain, there is another reason—which you do not know—one that has arisen not only *now*—and which, above all, is not so trivial that you should merely shrug your shoulders over it.

Where is Lipiner?[2] It is thoroughly inconsiderate of him to wander about the world with *Rübezahl* in his bag and never to give a sign of life to me, wailing for it. I do not know at *all* if it is still in existence—for it is the only copy I possess— and should dearly like to do more work on it. Though I am so cross I have almost lost all urge to do so. Please do give me his address, and yourself do something towards getting my manuscript back to me.

When I think that with all my other trials I must also put up with this, of my own creating, I overflow with bitterness. I beg you, do *not* forget to do something about this matter *at once*. I would write to Lipiner myself, but I do not know where he lives.

---

[1] The letter-heading is an engraving of rolling fields surrounding the village of Pfarrkirchen, as can be seen in Plate 1 which reproduces the first page of the holograph and clearly shows the cross which Mahler placed over his house. There are two further crosses over the second word in the fourth line from the bottom; these are explained by a note which Mahler wrote at the very top of the page: 'I've marked two little crosses below—over the word "blue-bottles"—to show where you would find the theatre and [Bad] Hall if the picture were extended.' (K.M.).
[2] The poet Siegfried Lipiner, see p. 452 (K.M.).

[Rudolf] Krzyz[anowski], to whom I wrote, also seems to have forgotten that I am still in this world.

When leaving Vienna I forgot to pick up the *index*. I had left it with the Faculty porter so that the professor's certificate of attendance could be supplied (at the beginning of the summer term), and then forgot to pick it up. Whenever you happen to be at the university, please ask about it. Won't you visit me some time in Hall? You would live cheaply and well here.

As for the Jean Paul,[1] the aforementioned copy would certainly suffice me. But how does one lay hands on the price of it? *Once again* I appeal to you to send me Lipiner's address and see that he sends back *Rübezahl*.

With best wishes,
Gustav Mahler

Hoping you will answer soon.

---

11. *To Emil Freund* (Vienna)†

Vienna, 1 November 1880

Dear Emil,

I have been through so many emotional crises recently that I find it almost impossible to speak to anybody who knew me in happier days.

In return for your upsetting news,[2] I am afraid I have equally upsetting news for you. My friend Hans Rott has become *insane*![3]—And I fear that a similar fate may befall Krisper.

—This news reached me at the same time as your letter—and at a time when I myself was in dire need of comfort. Misery is at home everywhere, and clothes itself in the strangest guises, as though to mock poor human beings.

If you know one happy person on this earth, tell me his name quickly, before I lose the last of what courage remains in me.—Anyone who has watched a truly noble and profound nature struggling against the most shallow meanness, and perishing, can scarcely suppress a shudder when he considers the chances of saving his own poor skin. Today is All Saints.—

If you were here by this time last year, then you will know in what mood I greet this day.

Tomorrow will be the first All Souls' Day I have ever known! Now for {me} too there is a grave on which to lay a wreath. For a month now I have been an out-and-out vegetarian. The moral effect of this way of life, with its voluntary

---

[1] The German novelist Jean Paul (Friedrich Richter) (1763–1825) (K.M.).
[2] See Note by E. Freund (p. 388.)
[3] Hans Rott (1858–84), contemporary of Mahler's at the Vienna Conservatory (o.e. + K.M.).

castigation of the body, causing one's material needs to dwindle away, is enormous. You can judge for yourself how utterly I {am} convinced of it, when I tell you that I expect of it no less than the *regeneration* of humanity.

All I can tell you is: let yourself be converted to a natural way of living, but one in which you eat suitable food (compost-grown, stone-ground, wholemeal bread) and soon you will see the fruits of your endeavours.

My fairy play[1] is finished, at long last—truly a child of sorrow, more than a whole year's labour.—But it has turned out to be worth it. The next thing is to use all means at my disposal to get it performed.

Do write again to your faithful

Gustav Mahler

Incidentally, there is no need for you to carry the *laconical* to such extremes.

1881

12. *To Emil Freund*†

Undated. 18 August 1881

Dear Emil,

This time I am attacking you from the rear—i.e. I am coming from Wlaschim. So please do expect me in Čzechtitz, Gasthaus zur Post, tomorrow, Friday, at *9.00 a.m.* No more for the moment. See you soon!

Gustav Mahler

13. *To Emil Freund*†

Iglau, September [1881]

Dear Emil,

It is only now, just before leaving Iglau, that I find time to send you a few lines.

I leave tomorrow.

I can sincerely assure you and your family that those days spent in Seelau after so long an absence were most delightful, just as in old times. Please convey my warmest thanks to your parents for their kind hospitality.—

Now let me tell you about an encounter I had.

---

[1] 'Das klagende Lied' ('The Song of Lament') (o.e.).

Recently, while walking across the square, I suddenly heard a voice from on high calling out: 'Herr Mahler, Herr Mahler!'

Looking up, at a window on the third floor I saw Frl. Morawetz (the youngest one, who was at your house), who in her simplicity, and perhaps too in her pleasure at seeing me, could not refrain from hailing me.—

I have been doing my best for her in Iglau, taking her around here, there and everywhere, and she is so grateful she cannot stop thanking me. Even as I write these lines to you, she is in the next room with my sister. Since I have kept her waiting for some time, I hasten to bid you a hearty *farewell*.

Yours,
Gustav

Please convey my kindest regards to your family and also to Frl. Wiener. *My address* is: G.M., Kapellmeister at the Landestheater, Laibach.

1882

14. *To Gustav Lewy* (Vienna)†

Trieste, 4 April 1882[1]

Dear Sir,

I shall be coming to Vienna next week and would ask you, at your leisure, to call me to mind. I would have been on my way there now, but I do not wish to miss the opportunity of seeing Italy, now that I am so near.

Yours faithfully,
Gustav Mahler

1883

15. *To Anton Krisper*†

Undated. [Vienna, before 10 January 1883]

Dear Anton,

Please accept my somewhat belated wishes for the New Year. May this also be the first communication after a long silence. Your last letter reached me when

---

[1] Letter-card. Postmark: Trieste, 5 [April 1882]. Arrival postmark: Wieden in Vienna, 6 [April] 1882 (K.M.).

I was in Iglau, and you will find it not without interest to learn that in that same place I was conducting a performance[1] in which the prima donna was a Fräulein Hassmann, who moreover is the shallowest creature of all the women I have encountered for a very long time. However, I did not stay there for long, but instead embarked on a jolly existence in Vienna—in other words, I have moved into new quarters every fortnight. I have now been in Vienna three months and, aside from various hotels, I am already at my fifth address. You can easily imagine that my work has not been going particularly well; now that I ought to be in the best frame of mind I am being disturbed again by the screaming of a small child—thus I escape one vexation only to come up against another. Nonetheless I hope to have the first act of *Rübezahl* ready soon. Furthermore, since you saw it the libretto has taken a completely new form. In fact much of it has not come off badly.

When are you thinking of coming to Vienna again? And what are you doing now? Have you been working, and do you feel well? I beg you to subdue your metaphysical ardour for once and let me have simple and truthful answers to these prosaic questions.

I myself would be in an excellent humour if only that wretched child would refrain from interrupting my finest work.

Accept my best greetings and write to me soon! My address is:

Gustav Mahler

I. Wipplingerstrasse 12, Second Staircase, Fourth Floor right.

16. *To Friedrich Löhr*†

Undated. Postmark: Olmütz, 20 January 1883
Postcard

Dear Fritz,

Simply cannot find time to write to you properly. Sending the stuff soon. My address is: G.M., Kapellmeister, Olmütz, Michaelergasse 1, first floor. Am extremely depressed.

Very best wishes to you and your family,

Yours,
Gustav

---

[1] Of Suppé's *Boccaccio*, on 19 September 1882 (K.M.).

17. *To Friedrich Löhr*†

Olmütz, 12 February 1883

My dear Fritz,

It has been a real struggle to pull myself together to the point of writing to you. I am paralysed, like one who has been cast forth from heaven. Since the moment I crossed the threshold of the theatre in Olmütz, I have felt like a man about to face the Day of Judgement.

Take a thoroughbred horse and yoke it to a cart with oxen—all it can do is to pull and sweat along with them. I hardly dare to bring myself to your attention —I feel so besmirched.

I know that you and your family won't bear me a grudge for not having thanked you for all your great kindness. Not a day passes without my thinking nostalgically of {the} hours, so dear to me, that I spent with you all. How well I was looked after! And how bitter the contrast between then and now! I am more or less always alone—i.e. if I am not rehearsing—So far—thank God—what I have been conducting is almost exclusively Meyerbeer and Verdi. By dogged scheming I have succeeded in getting Wagner and Mozart out of the repertory; —for I could not endure rattling off, say, *Lohengrin* or *Don Giovanni*—in this place here.—Tomorrow we are doing *Joseph in Aegypten*.[1] An extremely charming work, with something of Mozart's grace.—I really did get great enjoyment out of rehearsing it. And I must say—despite their incredible lack of sensibility, these people I have to work with here do now and then pull themselves together a bit for my sake, and this time they have tried somewhat harder —though I'm afraid it's only a way of showing they're sorry for this 'idealist'— a very contemptuous epithet, this—for the idea that an artist can become utterly absorbed in a work of art is quite beyond them. At times, when I'm all on fire with enthusiasm, when I'm trying to sweep them along with me, give them some impetus, I see these people's faces, see how surprised they are, how knowingly {they} smile at each other—and then my boiling blood cools down and all I want is to run away and never go back. Only the feeling that I am suffering for my masters' sake, and that some day perhaps I shall kindle a spark in these poor wretches' souls, fortifies me, and in some of my better hours I vow to endure with love and understanding—even in the face of their scorn.— You will smile at the dramatic tone in which I speak of these trivialities.—But isn't this actually the prototype of our attitude to the world? Only here it happens to be concentrated on one single point.—

As for the rest of my life, it is not much better.—In the restaurant I starve because only meat dishes are served here. In the flat where I live there are only

[1] Opera by Étienne Méhul (K.M.).

two pianos and they are played for only a few hours every day. Unfortunately those are precisely the hours when I am at home. I have nothing at all to read! Couldn't you provide me with something again?

Very best wishes to your family, and do look after yourself!

Yours,

Gustav

I shall write to Heinrich[1] as soon as possible—please convey my regards to him and also to his fiancée and her sisters. Also my regards and thanks to Reiff.

---

[1] Heinrich Krzyzanowski (K.M.).

II

KASSEL
1883–1885

1883 continued

18. *To Friedrich Löhr†*

Undated. Kassel, end of June 1883

What am I to say to you, my dear Fritz?[1] What can I say to you, when words fail me and yet I can't remain silent! I know you will not be bowed down under the heavy cross that God has laid on your shoulders, but will bear it manfully. How gladly I should relieve you all of even a small part of that burden! I shall see you soon. Until then do remain the old, strong Fritz I know and don't forget

Your
Gustav

19. *To Friedrich Löhr†*

Iglau, Sunday?, [22?] July 1883

My dear Fritz,

Just now, on my return from Bayreuth, your present arrived, at a moment when it is like a ray of light from heaven, falling into the darkest darkness that surrounds me.

I have no words to say what these lines of yours and, with them, you yourself mean to me.—So it is that your staunch love sees right through the desolate shell of my present existence and gazes deep into my heart, and you believe in me, when I no longer know how to believe in myself.—It would be hard to describe what is going on in me. When I walked out of the Festspielhaus, incapable of uttering a word, I knew I had come to understand all that is greatest and most painful and that I would bear it within me, inviolate, for the rest of my life. So I returned home, only to find those whom I love so poorly, so—(. . .)[2] my beloved parents with those three iron rings around their chests

---

[1] Friedrich Löhr's elder brother had died a few days before this letter was posted (o.e.).
[2] Here several lines have been omitted without explanation; they cannot have related solely to Mahler (o.e.).

3*

and their poor tormented hearts[1]—and I myself am so hard and cruel to them—yet I can't help it, and I go on tormenting them to the utmost.—And I am supposed to leave in three weeks, in order to start work in my new 'profession'!—

I met Heinrich in Eger and we did a bit of walking in the Fichtelgebirge, and also went to Wunsiedel.[2] While I write these lines to you the newly wedded couple[3] is already in Thuringia, getting on with their tour and enjoying life. How I long to see you again. It was actually my firm resolve to look you up in Vienna, but, alas, it has turned out to be impossible. As soon as I arrive in Kassel, I'll send you my new address, and at the first opportunity I shall also send picture postcards of the place. I shall be in Iglau until 10 August. Please convey my very best wishes to your family. I'll write more soon.

Yours ever,
Gustav

20. *To Friedrich Löhr†*

Kassel, 19 September 1883
c/o [Adolf] Frank, Mittlere Karlstrasse 17, Second Floor

My dear Fritz,

Just a few lines! As so often happens when great distances come between two people, I—who have been accustomed to talk to you about everything so long as we were face to face—find it hard to get used to this unsatisfactory means of communication.

Once again everything has taken its usual course.—Of my own free will I have let myself be shackled, chain upon chain, and so have returned to that same disgraceful old condition of bondage.—

I mean to fight my way bravely through it, even though to me too the 'crooked ones in the dark' whisper 'go round!'[4]

I should dearly like an explanation of some allusions in your last letter.—Although I have an inkling of what you mean, I should be glad to hear it from yourself.—Tonight I am conducting *Robert der Teufel*—the Herr Hofkapellmeister[5] has an option on all the classics; he is the cheerfullest 4/4-beat man ever to come my way. I, of course, am the 'most stiff-necked young man in the

---

[1] Both Mahler's parents were suffering from grave illnesses, from which they died six years later, in 1889 (o.e. + K.M.).

[2] Home of the poet Jean Paul (K.M.).

[3] Heinrich Krzyzanowski had recently married (o.e.).

[4] A quotation from Ibsen's *Peer Gynt*. See also Notes (o.e.).

[5] Wilhelm Treiber (1838–99), court conductor at the Kassel Theatre from 1881 (K.M.).

world', who absolutely refuses to be initiated into the mysteries of art by him. Rudolf Krzyzanowski is now conductor in Laibach, where I had my first job.[1]— Of Heinrich I know nothing at all! Not even his address! Could you not get it for me?

Very cordial greetings to your family.

I hope I shall soon be able to write to you at greater length.

Gustav

20 September

I simply can't remember the name of the street where you and your family live. Shall have to wait until I can get it from my parents.

Do write soon!

21. *To Friedrich Löhr*†

Kassel, 10 October 1883
Mittlere Karlstrasse 17, Second Floor

Thanks, dear Fritz! Many thanks for your good letter.—I feel just the way you do! I do not want to make so much ado about the anxious hours I some-times experience;—one of which has just taken its leave of me.

If you can occasionally send me something to read, you will satisfy an urgent need of mine. Mountain spirits[2] are not visiting me at present for they know they would be sent away again.

But to make up for that there are poltergeists—upstairs *and* downstairs—the old plague!

I wrote to Heinrich, but I don't know if he got the letter, for the address he had scribbled on a mere postcard was rather difficult to decipher. Next time you write to me, please don't forget to let me have detailed news of your family, of every single one—there's a good fellow. I am so glad of every little scrap of news. Please convey my warmest greetings to them—to every single one of them.

I did receive Basler's letter,[3] but I am afraid I cannot fulfil his wish at the moment; later on, perhaps.

How often I think with deep nostalgia of that first walk of ours out to Heiligenstadt, and of the later ones too—right down to the one that took us to the look-out tower in the beautiful Wienerwald near Perchtoldsdorf—and how

---

[1] Mahler passes over the short summer engagement in Bad Hall in 1880 (o.e.).

[2] Mahler is referring to work on his opera in progress, *Rübezahl* (o.e.).

[3] Ludwig Basler, Land official and amateur singer (o.e.).

I sweated that time, and had to borrow a shirt of yours.—That was our last walk! When will there be another?

That's all I can manage to put on paper today—except for most affectionate greetings from

Yours,
Gustav

22. *To Fr. Löhr's Mother*

Undated. Kassel, end of December 1883

To all of you most heartfelt good wishes for the New Year from the forlorn hope of Kassel.

1884

23. *To Friedrich Löhr†*

Undated. Kassel, April 1884

My dear Fritz,

It will amuse you to hear that this is the fourth or fifth of the letters I have been writing to you and that the rest of them are still patiently lying in my desk. And even today—as is bound to happen when one has been silent for a long time—I don't know where to begin. Well, let me start off by telling you how constantly and affectionately I have thought of you and that my dearest hope is to see you soon and spend a few days with you in the spirit of our old, unchanging friendship.—But how could I express in so many words all that flashes through my heart and mind, when now I turn to you just as in old times. Many, many thanks for your springtide greetings, your faithfulness!

Heinrich [Krzyzanowski] told me, my dear Fritz, of the sorrows that befell you on Christmas Day. So I may as well tell you that I was afflicted in the same way on the same day, and that with that day there began a period of unceasing and intolerable struggle to which there is as yet no end in sight, a struggle I have to endure day in, day out, indeed hour by hour.

The summer holidays begin here on 24 June; I hope I shall manage to be in Vienna at the beginning of July. Please do let me know soon what your life is like and how your family is getting on. And please convey my sincere thanks to your mother for her very kind New Year's greetings.

My warmest regards to her and to your father, and likewise to your sisters!

Yours ever,
Gustav

24. *To Friedrich Löhr*†

Kassel, 22 June 1884

My dear Fritz,

Briefly, the news is that I shall go to Iglau without touching Starnberg or Kissingen, shall be in Vienna at the beginning of July and shall then come to you in Perchtoldsdorf. As you will see from the date, you were absolutely right —and it was a real joy to get your affectionate note. In the last few days I have had to write some music helter-skelter for *Der Trompeter von Säkkingen* which is going to be performed in the theatre tomorrow with *tableaux vivants*. I polished off this opus inside two days, and I must confess I am very pleased with it. As you can imagine, it has little in common with Scheffel's affectation, indeed leaves that author a long way behind. Your letter arrived just as I was entering the last note in the score; as you can imagine, it was more like a heavenly than an earthly voice.

Now let us postpone everything until our speedy reunion. Very best wishes to all your family.

Yours ever,
Gustav

25. *To Friedrich Löhr*

Undated. Iglau, 29 June 1884

Dear Fritz,

Tomorrow morning, if all goes well, I shall be off to Vienna, and I expect to be with you in Perchtoldsdorf the day after tomorrow, that is, on Tuesday afternoon, and to spend a few days with you and your family. I am tremendously looking forward to seeing you all. In any case I'll write from Vienna giving you the exact time of my arrival in P. Best wishes to your family

from
Gustav

26.   *To Friedrich Löhr*†

Iglau, 20 July 1884

My dear Fritz,

Before all else, my profoundest thanks to all of you for the love and attention
with which you made me at home in your house; I really did feel at home among
you during those days, the first after having been abroad for so long.—You find
me buried among the books which came the day after my own return. I have got
much pleasure out of *Ponce*,[1] even though it is only too obvious that a performance of this play could not make an impression on any audience in the world. It
is so entirely a play to read; the most beautiful and delicate parts of it are bound
to be missed by anybody merely listening to the spoken words. I have also
managed to get on quite well with Boisserée,[2] and once again a large and rich
area of that period has opened up to me. What strikes me as very odd indeed is
the few glimpses of Goethe one gets from the book. If I understand aright, what
it amounts to is that 'the old man', as he often calls Goethe, was up to that time
entirely averse to art of the at once German and Christian tradition, and
Boisserée indeed repeatedly expresses his pleasure in having converted Goethe.
At that time Goethe was beginning to write his *Dichtung und Wahrheit* [*Poetry
and Truth*]—and a number of things in it strike me as having been very noticeably
reconstructed—e.g. the passage about his stay in Strassbourg, which is full of
references to the Gothic. On the other hand, his enthusiasm for it seems to be
more of an aesthetic nature, and perhaps that is the element that bothers you.
What I should enjoy (and what I've also, alas, plenty of time for) is to devour a
large chunk of Goethe literature, in order to construct the good white light from
all the various rays; I cannot let that dissonance have, as it were, the last word
about the master for whom I have such a profound veneration.—That woman
Dorothea Schlegel, who appears so often, doesn't particularly appeal to me; I
should be tempted to call her the female ⟨Klein⟩ if it were not that I feel too much
reverence for her sex to connect it with that name; the same goes for her husband Friedrich, who also remains something of a dark horse; oddly enough it
is whenever they adopt a cordial note that I don't trust them. Among all those
who have appeared hitherto it is friend Bertram whom I like best.—This
writing-paper I am using at the moment could make a lamb go berserk; please
understand that I can't go on writing until my little brother Otto goes to the
paper shop to get me a better sort.

---

[1] *Ponce de Léon*, comedy in five acts by Clemens Brentano (o.e.).
[2] Sulpiz Boisserée (1783–1854), of Cologne, amateur of the arts and collector, friend of
Goethe (o.e.).

When are you coming? Let me know soon! Best wishes to your whole family:
Mamma, Papa, Louise, Ernestine, Gretel.

Yours,
Gustav

27. *To Friedrich Löhr*†

Undated. Iglau, summer 1884

My dear Fritz,

With what joy {I} received the definitive news of your imminent arrival! I
couldn't help laughing, you crazy fellow, about your qualms, which I couldn't
understand even after re-reading your first letter. How could there still be any
misunderstandings between us? We have always been candid and open with
each other and surely we can put our trust in such utterly carefree friendship,
unclouded by doubts.

We are all looking forward to having you here among us. If I understand you
rightly, you are taking the midday train (1.45 p.m.) from Vienna on Monday,
arriving in Iglau at 7.00 p.m., at which hour I shall be at the station to meet you.
Incidentally, you will find sister Poldi[1] here, and perhaps her husband as well.
I am sorry to say you must be prepared for yet another surprise; outside the
window of the room we are going to share (it is the only one that is completely
separate from the rest of the house, which is why I should like to keep it, for
both our sakes) our worthy neighbour has erected a pig-sty, the charming
inhabitants of which will sing us a lullaby almost every night and always
serenade us at dawn. There is, into the bargain, a flock of high-spirited hens
who lay their eggs every morning and proclaim that event to all and sundry
with odious cackling.

Longing to see you!

Warmest greetings to all from the family and myself.

Yours,
Gustav

I shall meet you at Iglau station on Monday evening.

---

[1] Leopoldine Mahler (1863–89), married Ludwig Quittner by whom she had two children,
Anna, b. 4 Nov. 1884 and Heinrich b. 9 March 1887 (K.M.).

28. *To Friedrich Löhr*†

Undated. Kassel, [end of August] 1884

My dear Fritz,

I arrived here yesterday and already have my first rehearsal behind me. I had scarcely set foot in the streets of Kassel when the same terrible old spell befell me, and I don't know how to regain my balance. I have seen her[1] again, and she is as enigmatic as ever! All I can say is: God help me! You will have noticed, in the last days of the time we spent together, how now and then some sombre forces took hold of me—it was my dread of the inevitable. I am going to see her this afternoon, 'I am going to call on her', after which my situation {will} at once take on definite shape.

I stopped in Dresden for two days and saw a delightful performance of *Così fan tutte*[2] on the first day, and the next day—*Tristan*! Unfortunately Kapellmeister Schuch (who conducted the performance) asked me to go and see him in the intervals, and you can imagine how very disturbing that was. However, he was very amiable, introduced me to the singers, and asked me to write to him. He proposes coming to Kassel at some convenient time to watch me conduct. It is not inconceivable that I may still get a job in Dresden after all. As for the performance, I can report that it was a case of 'good team-work', and Frl. Malten's rendering of Isolde positively enraptured me.—Unfortunately that is all. However well and, to me, amazingly Schuch wields his baton, his approach was not at all to my liking. I also saw Überhorst[3] (it was he, incidentally, who introduced me to Schuch) and was very grateful for the sympathetic interest he took in me.

I am still staying at the hotel. My address, by the way, is simply: Royal Theatre, Kassel.

I cannot close without saying how much we all missed you and how all my family have taken to you. Give everyone my very best wishes, and write soon.

Ever yours,

Gustav

---

[1] Johanna Richter, a soprano at the Kassel Theatre (o.e.). See also Notes.
[2] Given on 23 August. *Tristan* was performed on 24 August and repeated the following day (K.M.).
[3] Karl Überhorst (1823–99), stage manager of the Dresden Court Opera (K.M.).

1885

29. *To Friedrich Löhr*†

Kassel, 1 January 1885

My dear Fritz,

On this morning of New Year's Day let my first thoughts be devoted to you. It was a strange way indeed that I spent the first minutes of this year. Yesterday evening I was alone with her,[1] both of us awaiting the new year's arrival almost without exchanging a word. Her thoughts were not bent on the present, and when the bell chimed and tears gushed from her eyes, it overwhelmed me that I, I might not dry them. She went into the adjacent room and stood for a while in silence at the window, and when she returned, still weeping, the nameless grief had risen up between us like an everlasting partition-wall, and there was nothing I could do but press her hand and go. As I came out of the door, the bells were ringing and the solemn chorale resounded from the tower.

Ah, dear Fritz—it was all as though the great director of the universe had meant to stage manage it perfectly. I wept all through the night in my dreams.

My signposts: I have written a cycle of songs,[2] six of them so far, all dedicated to her. She does not know them. What can they tell her but what she knows. I shall send with this the concluding song, although the inadequate words cannot render even a small part.—The idea of the songs as a whole is that a wayfaring man, who has been stricken by fate, now sets forth into the world, travelling wherever his road may lead him.

My 'Trumpeter music' has been performed in Mannheim[3] and is shortly to

Theater und Kunst.

* (Großh. Hoftheater.) In Karlsruhe: Freitag den 5. Juni. 14. Vorstellung außer Abonnem. Zum Vortheil des Hoftheater=Pensionsfonds: **Der Trompeter von Säckingen,** Dichtung von V. v. Scheffel, für die Darstellung mit lebenden Bildern eingerichtet von Ewald. Musik von Mahler. — **Der Barbier von Sevilla,** komische Oper in 3 Aufzügen. Musik von Rossini. Anfang ½7 Uhr.

Fig 1. Announcement of the Karlsruhe performance (5 June 1885) of *Der Trompeter von Säckingen*

[1] Johanna Richter (K.M.).
[2] 'Lieder eines fahrenden Gesellen', probably only the poems, four of which Mahler later set to music and had published in 1897 (K.M.).
[3] This performance did not materialize (K.M.).

be performed in Wiesbaden[1] and Karlsruhe. All of course without any instigation whatsoever on my part. For you know how little this work in particular concerns me.

I spent Christmas Eve alone, although she had invited me to her place.

Dear Fritz! All that you know about her is mere misunderstanding. I have begged her forgiveness for everything, casting my pride and egoism from me. She is everything that is lovable in this world. I would shed every drop of my blood for her. But I do know that I must go away. And I have done everything to that end, but still I see no way out. Farewell! I must go now, to pay my New Year calls. Write to me soon, dear Fritz. And give me news of your family too!

Gustav

30. *To Albert Spiegler*†

Undated. Postmark: Kassel, 23 January 1885

Dear Albert,

I was very glad to get another sign of life from you. But it was certainly a very scanty one. I have no news of you all and do not know, as things now stand, how long it may be before I see any of you again. The fact is I have been appointed (most probably from the beginning of next summer) (first) conductor at the Leipzig Stadttheater—together with Nikisch, with whom I rank exactly equal. The contract is for six years, and it will be hard for me to get away during this time—at the utmost, for three or four weeks at the height of summer, when all of you vanish anyway. As you see, fortune favours me, so to speak. But, believe me, without making me one iota happier. I live like a Hottentot. There is no one to speak a rational word to. The people of Kassel are such blockheads that I would rather talk to a Viennese cabby. Have done some work[2]—even if only 'for the bottom drawer'. I now have the power and opportunity to perform my own compositions, if I wish; but in view of the oafishness prevailing here the thought of performances is so boring that I do not lift a finger.[3]

Send me *Sax*'s[4] address. I have been wanting to write to him for ages—but where to? My warm thanks to all for the New Year greetings—Adler,[5] Pernerstorfer and Bondi.[6] *Perhaps via Friedjung[7] it would be possible to get an announce-*

[1] This performance did not materialize (K.M.).
[2] Almost certainly a reference to 'Lieder eines fahrenden Gesellen' (K.M.).
[3] At this point we only know with certainty that Mahler had completed *Das klagende Lied* and the three songs to Josephine Poisl (K.M.).
[4] Hans Emmanuel Sax (1858–96), see Notes, letter 49 (K.M.).
[5] Victor Adler (1852–1918); he later became leader of the Austrian Socialist Party (K.M.).
[6] Engelbert Pernerstorfer, editor of the Viennese monthly *Deutsche Worte* (1881–4); see Notes, letter 35. Seraphim Bondi, a Viennese lawyer; see Notes, letter 36 (K.M.).
[7] Heinrich Friedjung (1851–1920), historian and journalist (K.M.).

ment of my new appointment into the Viennese newspapers. If possible with a little 'obituary' as well. It could be very helpful for my future—although I no longer have many more rungs to climb. But my ultimate goal is and must remain Vienna—there is nowhere else where I can feel at home. Do write to me soon, dear Albert—and above all give me detailed *news* of *yourself* and our *friends*! Best wishes from me to *all*! To your family I send my warmest best wishes for recovery from the grave blow. I can imagine how hard life now is for you all. Write soon!

Yours ever,

Mahler

31. *To Julius Epstein* (Vienna)†

Kassel, 26 March 1885
Wolfsschlucht 13

Dear Herr Professor,

You are so kind to keep a small place in your memory for me still. This encourages me to give you some news, which also includes a request.

As you will see from the enclosed newspaper cutting, a big music festival is to take place here under my direction in June, and the Ninth Symphony is among the works to be performed.[1]

Since this is certainly an unusual expression of confidence in a young man on the part of what one might almost call an entire country—it comes from the big musical societies of Hesse and to some extent of Hanover—it is perhaps pardonable if I wish people in Vienna to hear of it too.—Would you show me this great kindness? I am still as 'arrogant' as I used to be, am I not?

By the way, before the end of the year I shall be taking up an appointment as conductor at the Stadttheater in Leipzig.

Please do remember me to Herr Hofkapellmeister Hellmesberger and to Professor Krenn and—please forgive me for taking such liberties.

I remain, as ever, your devoted pupil,

Gustav Mahler

---

[1] Beethoven's Ninth was not, however, performed at the music festival in Kassel which took place between 29 June and 1 July 1885 (K.M.).

32. *To Friedrich Löhr*

Kassel, 1 April 1885

Dearest Fritz,

There is nothing I can say.[1] I had such forebodings during these last days. Nameless anxiety and sorrow befell me.—I kept on wanting to write to you, and always something held me back.

The sacredness of your feelings compels me to silence about my own.

Briefly let me just tell you that we shall spend the next year together. Today I have sent in my resignation, and presumably it will be accepted.

My only plan for the next year is to be together with you. I am so torn apart. My heart bleeds from many wounds.

Tell your dear family from me how intensely I am with you all and mourn with you all. Write soon! And think of me.

Gustav

33. *To Friedrich Löhr*†

Undated. Kassel, April 1885
Sunday afternoon

My dear Fritz,

My windows are open and the sunny, fragrant spring is gazing in upon me, everywhere endless peace and repose. In this fair hour that is granted me I will be together with you.—My thanks for everything, letter, flowers and verses. What I felt above all was 'I wear a little golden ring—' (very recent, I suppose)— then 'Winter had come' and 'Last night was that leave-taking' and 'A blind man speaks of colours'!

—You think too well of me when you call my decision 'great'. Inevitable necessity has wrung from me what lucid insight could not bring about.

Much has happened since I wrote to you in Starnberg; the most grievous thing was still to come. When we are together again you shall learn all. For the present it suffices to say that I was near to the loveliest fulfilment and then at a stroke lost all—through no living being's fault.—For a long time I did not know where to turn—there was one sole sombre wish in me: to sleep—and not to dream!

With the coming of spring all has grown mild in me again. From my window I have a view across the city to the mountains and woods, and the kindly *Fulda* wends its amiable way between; whenever the sun casts its coloured lights

---

[1] Löhr's mother had died on 28 March (o.e.).

within, as now, well, you know how everything in one relaxes. That is the mood I am in today, sitting at my desk by the window, from time to time casting a peaceful glance out upon this scene of carefree calm. The people round about me, who torment me unspeakably with the racket of their affairs, are all out today. No sound of daily doings penetrates to me here, only from time to time the bell announcing that human beings belong together. And lo, all at once you are so close to me and I scarcely feel that we are in fact separated by such immense distances. I see us on those glimmering paths there among meadows and hills and am with you and have you to myself.—You will believe me when I say I cannot now report to you on the external circumstances of my life.—You want to know if I enjoyed the 'music festival'.[1]—As for that, it is as with any fulfilment one expects from outside. Do you suppose anything good can come of it when a few choral societies get together in order to produce art?—It is the fashion now to be musical—patriotic—festive.—My appointment caused terrible strife among the various parties, and in fact the whole thing was nearly wrecked as a result.—They can't forgive me my youth; that goes especially for our profession.—Our orchestra is on strike because the Herr Hofkapellmeister[2] feels he has been made to look a fool, and the Herr Intendant[3] has even had the brazenness to appeal to the nobility of my feelings in the hope of {persuading} me to withdraw. Of course I let him have a piece of my mind, and now I am a dead man so far as the theatre here is concerned.

—But in three and a half months all that will be behind me, the music festival, the theatre, and my official duties, and I hope to be with you. You know, I think, that all during July I shall be in Leipzig, on probation. When that is over, I shall go to Vienna and look for pupils and see to it that, until I start my job in Leipzig (July 1886), my time belongs only to myself and to those who care for me.—I think of spending August and September in Iglau, and I am sure you will come and stay with us there for some time. Then we shall go to Vienna together. That's how I have worked it all out. Why don't you write anything about your sisters? And how is your Papa? I am so very fond of you all. How I look forward to once more sitting at your table, where I feel so much at home, so sheltered.—When I get to Vienna, Bertl too shall have her proper lessons.[4] Does Louise still have her painting lessons with Hofmann? How are Ernestine and little Gretel!—Write soon and tell me how you are all getting on.

Gustav

---

[1] The great music festival in Kassel on 29 and 30 June and 1 July, at which Mahler conducted Mendelssohn's *St. Paul* (o.e.).
[2] Wilhelm Treiber (K.M.).
[3] Adolf Freiherr von und zu Gilsa (K.M.).
[4] Before going to Kassel Mahler had begun giving my sister Bertha piano lessons (F.L.).

34. *To Friedrich Löhr*

Kassel, 12 May 1885

My dear Fritz,

I am worried by your silence! Do send me a word to say how you and your family are getting on.—I haven't had any news at all from Heinrich either.—

As for my own affairs, I can only say that they are becoming still more and more confused.—My dismissal here comes into force on 1 July. After that I shall go to Leipzig for a month.[1] What is to happen after that is just as obscure to me as what we shall be doing in fifty years from now.—Here battle rages— 'Up Mahler!'—'Up Treiber!'—the parties go on skirmishing, and—it is I who take the beating.—The Herr Intendant has also finished with me, that is, since I told him candidly that I don't share his views on artistic matters, he regards me as a fellow lacking in all proper sense of subordination and has put me on his black list. At the same time a lot of work is being put into preparing for the music festival. I have to do a great deal of travelling around in secret, visiting all the associations and rehearsing with them, and since I am pretty often short of funds that doesn't altogether go smoothly either.

My sphinx stares at me ceaselessly with threateningly enigmatic gaze—for the rest I am treated as practically a lunatic—partly with benevolent pity, partly with spiteful curiosity.—Well, there you have my latest bulletin, and you can fill in the rest, imagining what it's like, just the way you always did.—

Here with us May has not lived up to its promise; I am frozen stiff in body and soul.

The news I receive from my family is rather distressing; nothing is as it ought to be, and I, to whom they all look as their sheet-anchor, am myself foundering. But I lose neither heart nor resolution, and I know I am doing the right thing.—I could not stay here any longer except at the cost of all that I am, and the thought that I have forced my way out of it is all that supports me in my present tribulations.

Do write me a few lines whenever you can manage it, let me know how you all are and what your plans are for the summer.

My best wishes to all of you,

Yours,
Gustav

---

[1] The trial in Leipzig was finally cancelled (K.M.).

35. *To Friedrich Löhr*†

Kassel, 28 May 1885

Dearest Fritz,

How well you know my malady! You can certainly boast of offering the right remedy, for who always thinks of others as lovingly and unselfishly as you! You are the only person in the world to whom I am utterly devoted and who never-theless doesn't ever cause me pain. All my thinking here amounts to the one thought: away from here and to you, and your sister and your family.—My situation here and the threads of my life are becoming more and more entangled there is nothing for it now but Alexander's sword.—If I wrote to you recently that my relationship to 'her' had entered into a new and final stage, that was nothing but the ruse of a cunning theatre manager who announces a 'last per-formance' only to offer, the following day, a very last one. What was final has now given way to the definitely final. But since there are now only three weeks between me and our parting for ever, it doesn't seem very probable that there will be any 'widespread demand' leading up to yet another very—very last.—But I cannot vouch for anything.—

What are my prospects with regard to Vienna? Shall I be able to find a few pupils there? The thought of it causes me considerable anxiety, since here, as you can imagine, I have not managed to save anything. I shall indeed, find it very difficult to escape landing in the 'debtors' prison'.—What it will mean to me to be without a 'position' and 'duties' once again for an indefinite period and to live with you—it's beyond words. How I long to spend a few days with you and your family in Perchtoldsdorf—but I scarcely think it will be possible this time, since I shall almost certainly not get to Vienna before October. But to make up for that I hope you will be with us in Iglau in September. You will come, won't you?—I am not coming to Starnberg, because for 'various' reasons it is impossible. I cannot imagine where our friend Heinrich [Krzyzanowski] picked up that information. Your letters from Clothilde[1] and the other docu-ments I am keeping safely and shall deliver same to you as soon as we meet.

Please send me the issue of *Deutsche Worte* in which your essay appears.[2]

Affectionate greetings to you all! Write one more letter to me in Kassel!

Yours ever,
Gustav

---

[1] Clothilde Tschuppik, H. Krzyzanowski's sister-in-law (F.L.).
[2] 'Über einige Einflüsse der Antike auf unsere Kultur' (K.M.).

36.   *To Friedrich Löhr†*

Undated. Kassel, [end of] *June 1885*

Dearest Fritz,

Why don't you write? How are you all getting on?—Today I have a number
of things to tell you.—First of all I want you to know that I have been appointed
first conductor in Prague by Angelo Neumann, starting from August, and that I
shall be conducting *Lohengrin* there that very day for the first time. In the course
of the year I shall be rehearsing the *Nibelungen—Tristan—Meistersinger*! I have
to be there by 15 July to conduct the initial rehearsals, so I shall be able to spend
only a few days at home at the beginning of July.—I definitely count on seeing
you there; and once I am installed in Prague, you could come and stay with me
for some time.

—So you see I am getting on fast in 'the world'! Under Neumann's direction
the theatre will become really important—and it will offer me extremely important scope—I am afraid all this glory will last only one year, for the year after I
am tied up in Leipzig, and Direktor Staegemann has just written telling me I
had better give up all hope of his releasing me from my contract with him.—
Well, it's all to the good to have the Herren Direktoren fighting over me!

—The music festival is also making rapid headway. It will be launched in the
next few days with colossal pomp and ceremony.—I have become downright
popular, a sort of lion of the day.—Well, so that's off my chest.

Apart from the fact that I am in financial straits, things have generally
improved. All the jobs and prospects before me have helped me, sanguine type
that I am, to get over many a bitter experience. I shall almost certainly leave her
without so much as a word of farewell! For a whole month I haven't set eyes on
her except at rehearsals. How it has come to this is something I may tell you
about when we meet. Sometimes, when I start up out of my sleep, I simply
cannot believe it.

Do write me a few lines.

I am so busy now that I can hardly find time and leisure for this rather confused communication. Greetings to your family.—Also to Seemüller,[1] Bondi!
Reiff!

Very best wishes,

Yours,

Gustav

---

[1] Josef Seemüller, German scholar. See Notes (o.e.).

37. *To Friedrich Löhr*

Münden, 5 July 1885

Dear Fritz,

In great haste very best wishes for today.[1]—I still have so much to do that I cannot sit down even for an hour to think about you properly.

So far as I am concerned everything has turned out extremely well up to now. Honours and love have been simply showered upon me.[2]

A ring with a large diamond, a gold watch, a laurel wreath, an album, etc. etc.!—Incidentally the bailiffs have sequestered my old watch and most probably I shall have to dispose of many of these recent precious gifts in order to pay for my journey to Iglau, on which I start tomorrow.

My most affectionate greetings to your family.—Always be my faithful friend, dear Fritz!

Gustav

I arrive in Iglau on Thursday and in Prague on 13 July.

38. *To Friedrich Löhr†*

Iglau, 10 [July] 1885[3]

Dear Fritz,

Now I am at home again, and to be frank I am in a rather absent-minded, drowsy state of mind. Much to my distress, when searching for my luggage-receipt on my arrival in Prague, I found my letter to you.—I am sure you will not take it amiss, you will regard it as a forgivable blunder, if I tell you that quite apart from being terribly tired I have also been suffering from a rather formid-able attack of tonsillitis.

—You can imagine how I should love, how we should all love, to have you here with us; but perhaps it is better if we wait and you come to us when I am in Prague and settled in there. There of course you will consider yourself my guest (to the limit of the means at my disposal). We shall be able to see much more of each other.

So in the end, dear Fritz, it did all turn out rather nicely, of course only after all the accumulated electricity on both sides had been discharged, myself naturally being the first from whom the sparks flew.—I shall tell you all about it when you come to stay with me.

[1] F. Löhr's birthday (K.M.).
[2] A reference to the music festival in [Kassel]. Mahler had gone to Münden to say good-bye to the choral society he had conducted (F.L.).
[3] By mistake Mahler wrote June instead of July (F.L.).

Shall I send back your letters (from Clothilde etc.) now or wait until you come.—

I do beg you to let me have some news soon about 1. your family, 2. yourself particularly, with reference to past, present and future. I have told you all about myself! I am on the point of, as they say, making a name for myself. All the very best to you and warmest regards to your family,

Yours,
Gustav

III
PRAGUE AND LEIPZIG
1885–1888

1885 continued

39. *To Friedrich Löhr*†

Prague, 28 November 1885
Rittergasse 24

My dear Fritz,

How are you? Am I not entitled to ask you? The last news I had from you was about your having been in Starnberg, so I have all the time been hoping that one day you would feel you ought to write a few lines to me.—What I am doing is difficult to describe. What I should like best is to begin my letters with sighs, by now an old habit of mine! Something quite pleasant I can tell you is that I have now conducted *Die Meistersinger* three times and that I shall shortly be doing *Rheingold* and *Walküre*. It is probably inevitable that such tasks entirely absorb a musician—especially if he is like me, having to enter the lists to fight for what is holy.

Nevertheless the time now seems as empty and sombre as any I can remember, and what I long for and feel as a profound need is a heart-to-heart talk with you. But the words of love uttered here among these wretched rocks echo back with a sound so hollow that one starts at the sound of one's own voice. How often have I thought: if now, at this moment, Fritz came into the room, everything could suddenly be expressed in words again and one would immerse oneself in the curative springs of friendship! So much has happened since we saw each other last. And how much poorer we have both become since then! Perhaps if you remember the days when I came from Olmütz to rehearse the choirs at the Italian season[1] in Vienna—that might give you a fairly good picture of what I am like now—just with the difference that I was younger then and so full of hope and not yet saddened by the changes that earthly life must undergo —just as a man forgets the dust of his journey when he sees the cool of a well-spring ahead. Dear Fritz! Oh, if you knew of all that has come over me again! You must come here in order to – – – – –

[1] From 31 March to 4 May 1883 Mahler was engaged as a chorus coach at the Carl Theatre in Vienna which gave a season of Italian operas. Nine different operas were given 28 performances, four of which took place at the Court Opera (K.M.).

39a.

3 December 1885

in order to?—probably to give me a good thrashing! A thrashing's what I deserve! I keep on stumbling from one idiocy into another. In this short pause I have landed myself in something it will take a long time to get out of. Do come! I will tell you all! But I can't write about it.—

If only I knew how you all are! Your Papa, your sisters! As you know, I take up my appointment in Leipzig in August '86. Since I am doing 'so well' here, playing first fiddle, as it were, whereas in Leipzig I shall have a jealous and very capable rival in Nikisch, I have moved heaven and earth to get out of it. Alas, it has all been of no avail and I shall just have to go.

39b.

28 December '85

If all goes well I shall post this letter today.

Many thanks for your present! It was almost a silent reproach to me! *Rheingold* and *Walküre* have been successfully delivered, particularly the latter turning out really well. You must come and hear it! Do, do write, you old procrastinator! Do really write!

My warmest regards to *all* of you and best wishes for a happy 1886.

Ever your
Mahler

1886

40. *To Friedrich Löhr*

Undated. Prague, beginning of February 1886
Postcard

Dear Fritz,

I am overjoyed at the prospect of seeing you soon. Please let me know what time you will arrive. If I have no rehearsal I shall come to the station to meet you—if not, come straight to my flat: Langegasse 18—everything will be prepared for you. I share the flat with a colleague[1]—just so you are forewarned. I now wear a moustache only. Write immediately!

Yours,
Gustav

[1] The Swedish baritone Johannes Elmblad (K.M.).

41. *To Max Staegemann* (Leipzig)

Prague, 3 June 1886
Langegasse 18, I

Dear Herr Direktor,

The time approaches when I shall be assuming my new position under your direction, and I take this opportunity of getting in touch with you.

First of all I would respectfully ask to be allowed to inaugurate my appointment by conducting *Tannhäuser*.[1] This opera offers an opportunity both to introduce myself as an orchestral conductor and to prove my control of massed voices and of the structure of operatic ensembles. Since I am leaving here on excellent terms with Direktor Neumann, I shall have no difficulty in getting away, if you think it desirable, before expiry of my contract (1 August) and arriving in Leipzig as soon as may be necessary.

However, this would of course have to be arranged with all possible speed.

I would therefore ask you to inform me of your wishes at your earliest convenience.

I remain, dear sir, with deep respect,

Yours faithfully,
Gustav Mahler

42. *To Max Staegemann*

Prague, 7 June 1886

Dear Herr Direktor,

Thank you very much indeed for your kind answer and all your helpfulness. I shall be able—with Direktor Neumann's agreement of today—to arrive in Leipzig on approximately 24 or 25 July and make the best use of the time you have allowed me for preliminary rehearsals (*Meistersinger*, etc.). May I repeat my request to be allowed to begin with *Tannhäuser*, since in the present situation this should cause no difficulties?—Perhaps you will be so kind as to let me know about this at your convenience; and pray avail yourself of my services if there should be anything you would like me to do for you on the journey from Prague to Leipzig.

I remain, dear sir,

Your most obedient servant,
Gustav Mahler

[1] In the end Mahler made his first appearance in Leipzig with *Lohengrin* on 3 August 1886 (K.M.).

43. *To Friedrich Löhr* (Vienna)†

Undated. Prague, 30 June 1886

Dear Fritz,
    Just a brief message! I shall be here up to 15 July. Then I shall be going to
Iglau, where I shall be up to the 24th, and then go straight on to Leipzig!
    Tomorrow we are doing Gluck's *Iphigenie* in Wagner's adaptation. You can
imagine what sort of a day it will be. Then I shall probably do *Fidelio* before
leaving.
    Where shall I see you, have a chance to talk to you. Here in Prague or not till
Iglau? Please let me know soon.
    I did have a letter from Heinrich. Everything seems to be going all right with
them.
    Warmest greetings to your family,

Yours,
Gustav

44. *To Max Staegemann* (Leipzig)†

Undated. Prague, June or beginning of July 1886
Prague, Langegasse 18
not [Hotel] blauer Stern

Dear Herr Direktor,
    Fräulein Hudl's having been indisposed, so that she could not come to an
audition until yesterday, is the reason why I report to you about her so belatedly.
    The voice is definitely beautiful, with a warm timbre—middle range and
depth not at all bad, indeed I cannot help wondering whether the lady is not a
mezzo-soprano.—
    However, she is the veriest beginner! Although she was engaged for a whole
season at Olmütz, she sang only three parts there—the reasons are unknown to
me—namely Agathe, Gretchen and Leonore (*Trovatore*)!
    I got her to sing me various things from these and from other parts (Elsa,
Elisabeth), and it was apparent that she has not been in good hands hitherto, but
that she is definitely trainable.
    I do not know what you need the lady for, but for the time being I could not
recommend her for exclusively leading roles in Leipzig.
    I have looked through the *Gioconda*[1] opera, and definitely disliked it.

[1] *La Gioconda* (Milan, 1876) by A. Ponchielli (K.M.).

In any case *Dejanice*,[1] about which I wrote to you, is far superior. I do not know whether Leipzig audiences have a taste for *Aïda*, in which case they might also like *Dejanice*.

Incidentally, I have several times been to the Bohemian National Theatre here and have heard a number of works by *Smetana*, Glinka, Dvořák, etc., and I must confess that Smetana in particular strikes me as very remarkable.

Even if his operas will certainly never form part of the repertory in Germany, it would be worth while presenting such an entirely original and individual composer to audiences as cultivated as those in Leipzig.

It would indeed be quite interesting to produce something by Spontini[2] again! All in all, in such matters one must reckon with the prevailing conditions and the singers at one's disposal. It is often a singer's particular suitability for a part that makes for an opera's success.

With deepest respect, I remain,

Yours faithfully,
Gustav Mahler

45. *To Friedrich Löhr*

Prague, 5 July 1886

Dear Fritz,

My most heartfelt wishes to you this day.

I have just got in from a *Fidelio* rehearsal and am, as you can imagine, quite worn out.—*Iphigenie* is now over—as successful as one could reasonably expect.

I definitely count on seeing you in Iglau between 20 and 24 July! On the 25th I leave! I am so looking forward to seeing you.

I dare say we both have a lot to tell each other.

Very best wishes to your family,

Gustav

46. *To Friedrich Löhr*†

Undated. Leipzig [18] *August 1886*

My dear Fritz,

I put off writing to you until I had got over the worst difficulties of starting here.—But since there is no sign of any easing up I shan't wait any longer, even

---

[1] *Dejanice* (Milan, 1883) by the Italian composer Alfredo Catalani. Neither this opera nor *La Gioconda* were produced at the Leipzig Stadttheater (K.M.).
[2] Mahler got the chance to conduct a performance of Spontini's *Ferdinand Cortez* on 10 May 1888 (K.M.).

4

though the situation is not particularly propitious, because I feel an urgent need to talk to you again. I quickly established my position—which at times is also an opposition—as you can see from one of the two enclosures. This enclosure is doubly interesting in that it shows a dim obscurantist entering my very own camp in order to stab me in the back.—Anybody who reads the stuff is no doubt bound to think I am one of those elegant conductors of the Mendelssohn school.

What I must tell you first is that the performance really made a magnificent impression—it had all the boldness and brilliance one could wish for—*Tannhäuser* was sung by Schott,[1] who was wonderful. You would enjoy meeting that sturdy, earthy fellow. Lest you think I am always treated in such a manner I am also sending you a different kind of criticism about my *Rienzi*.—

Now I am again as lonely as ever. If only I could have you here with me just for a few days.

Is it really impossible to come for a short while?—You would stay with me and have your meals with me!—

Rudolf[2] wrote at the last moment saying that he couldn't come, because it had turned out to be impossible to break his journey, and so, as you may know, he went to Starnberg.

F.[3] often writes to me—there is an exceedingly melancholy and resigned note in her letters that hurts me very much.—She tells me that Elmblad[4] has come from Rome with his wife and that he now appears to be very happy.—He hasn't written to me yet—and oddly enough, he hasn't yet called on her, though he has been seeing quite a number of his other colleagues.

The photographs of your sisters were a great delight to me and now all of them and those of you and Uda[5] are standing on my desk, all gazing into my face, which is sad with longing and homesickness.

During the beginning of my time here I was constantly with Schott, about whom I have a great deal to tell you. Now, since he has left, I am always alone.

Tonight I am conducting *La Juive*[6]—I am utterly fascinated by this wonderful, magnificent work, and rank it among the greatest ever created. Do come—I must play it to you.

---

[1] Anton Schott (1846–1913) (K.M.).
[2] Rudolf Krzyzanowski (K.M.).
[3] The soprano Betty Frank (1864–191?) with whom Mahler had an affair in Prague. See Notes (K.M.).
[4] The Swedish bass singer Johannes Elmblad (1853–1910), engaged at the Prague Theatre 1883–87 and 1890–94. His first wife was the Australian pianist Maggie Menzies (died 1887). In 1888 he married the Swedish poet Sigrid Pettersson (1860–1926) (K.M.).
[5] F. Löhr's fiancée, Ludovica Czilchert, later his wife. Mahler at that time had not yet met her (o.e. + K.M.).
[6] An opera by the French composer J. Halévy which Mahler conducted on 18 August (K.M.).

Best wishes to your sisters and your father and Uda—and Lipiner and any-one else who is near and dear to you.

Do write soon!

Gustav

How are things with my father? Please do understand that if he is in a bad way, *he* must in no circumstances be told—not even by the doctor; but you must let *me* know.

47. *To Friedrich Löhr†*

Undated. Leipzig, August 1886
Gottschedstrasse 4. II

My dear Fritz,

I hope you got my last letter. If so, I must give you a good telling off! We mustn't have any more of that sort of thing, like the time when we once lost sight of each other for quite a while.—I at least promise that from now on I shall not leave any letter unanswered.

My situation here is still very far from clear. I am simply dying of longing and homesickness. I have met some really tip-top people, and almost every-where I have been welcomed in the most cordial way. The Direktor[1] has introduced me to his family, and I have already spent wonderful hours with them. If you could see those splendid organ-pipes with the loveliest voix celeste[2] at the top—you would realize why I was incapable of uttering a word of thanks, so that I seemed almost rude, at any rate cold.

Anyway, my 'business interests' compel me to put cotton wool in my ears to keep out these siren voices.—There are a few excellent people among our men. Above all our leader, a truly warm-hearted young Dutchman by the name of Petri,[3] who reads my baton's most cryptic indications and transforms them into music. And then Schelper[4] and many others.—

It will 'interest' you to hear that where Prague is concerned things look pretty bad at the moment. The brave duellist[5] has received many a wound on that great duelling-ground. Just a few days ago Neumann suggested I should come back to him. I should like to, but they would never let me go here—and I have made up my mind to see it through for a time.

[1] Max Staegemann (o.e.).
[2] No doubt a reference to Staegemann's children, Helena and Erna, who both studied singing and later took up professional careers. See also Notes (K.M.).
[3] The Dutch violinist Henri Petri (1856–1914), father of the pianist Egon Petri (K.M.).
[4] Otto Schelper (1840–1906), in those days a noted baritone singer (K.M.).
[5] Karl Muck (1859–1940), conductor and Mahler's successor in Prague (F.L. + K.M.).

Just think, poor F.[1] has for a long time gone on struggling with her feelings and now, only a few days ago, she asked me point-blank whether my feelings for her amounted to anything more than friendship. I answered with equal sincerity, and now, brave and sensible as she is, she seems to have come to terms with it.

Elmblad and his wife are living in Prague, in the grandest style. He hasn't yet answered my letter.

My warmest greetings to your dear sisters, to *Uda*, and your father! Write soon!

Ever yours,
Gustav

48. *To Friedrich Löhr*

Undated. Leipzig, 1 October 1886

Dearest Fritz,

Very many thanks for your letter, which means so much to me, and also for the enclosures, which I am returning to you herewith. I wrote to Elmblad, and his wife has sent me the enclosed letter. Read page 4 directly after page 1. The main reason for my letter of today is this: please let me have Rudolf's[2] exact address at once. It may be that I have something for him, which might have to be settled instantly.

I am in great anxiety about my mother, who is ill again!

Greetings to your family. Shall write again soon.

Yours,
Gustav

49. *To Friedrich Löhr*†

Undated. Leipzig, October 1886

Dearest Fritz,

In great haste! (at the theatre)

My father will be in Vienna in the next few days. Please see that, if there is no hope of his complete recovery, it is kept from him. This is necessary, considering his temperament! Of course I beg you to let me know the entire truth regardless!

I am afraid my plans for Rudolf have once again come to nothing; but I shall

---

[1] Betty Frank (K.M.).
[2] Rudolf Krzyzanowski (K.M.).

go on trying, wherever there seems to be a chance. Tell him not to lose hope. (I know how hard that is.)

Very best wishes to your family, Uda—Rudolf—Sax, Lipiner,

Yours,
Gustav

50. *To Friedrich Löhr†*

Undated. Leipzig, October? 1886

My dear Fritz,

First of all many, many thanks for all you have done for my father.—You can imagine how distressing it all is for me.—It is not given to me to have a relationship with my own people, and so I have to watch them going down without stirring a hand. At times I feel I am a solitary stranger everywhere! My whole life is one great homesickness.

You ask how I am getting on with Nikisch! Often I am quite happy about him, and I can look forward to a performance with him conducting as confidently as if I were going to conduct myself—even though the greatest heights and the greatest depths are a closed book to him.—But how seldom I myself have a chance to bring them out—mostly I have to be satisfied with preventing downright crudities, and must allow things to take their course left and right of me.

There is no personal contact between us. He is cold and reserved towards me —whether out of vanity or out of mistrust—I really don't know! In short, we pass each other by without a word!—Otherwise I receive plenty of recognition, often from people who are near and dear to me. I am at present rehearsing *Armida*.[1]—Just recently Reinicke invited me to meet Rubinstein (only me)![2] Unfortunately he had never heard of me, so I could only 'look and not do'. On such occasions it is always painful being simply an unknown quantity. What then happens is that I say nothing, not wanting to be a bore; after all, I know how much I myself am irritated by admiring nobodies and how ridiculous such people seem to me.

I have met a beautiful person here in Leipzig—and let me tell you at once— the sort that tempts one to do foolish things.[3]—Do I make myself clear, *amice?*

[1] Gluck's opera which was first performed at Leipzig on 6 December 1886, with Mahler conducting (K.M.).
[2] Karl Reinicke (1824–1910), German composer and conductor of the Gewandhaus Orchestra. Anton Rubinstein (1829–94), Russian pianist and composer. Mahler very much liked his opera *The Demon* which he later conducted in Hamburg and Vienna (K.M.).
[3] A reference, without doubt, to Mrs. Marion Mathilde v. Weber (1856–1931), wife of Karl v. Weber (1849–97) who asked Mahler to complete Weber's *Die drei Pintos* (K.M.).

—But this time I mean to be careful, or else I shall be in trouble again.

I have been reading a great deal, and I shall shortly send you a small reading-list.—How have things turned out for Rudolf? Naturally, he doesn't dream of letting me know.

Elmblad has written to me. The letter (. . .)[1]

I am afraid your misgivings seem to be justified. As F. tells me, the two of them are again well on the way to making each other thoroughly unhappy.—

I have also had some news from Heinrich. He is working hard. Affectionate greetings to all of you, and do write to me soon!

Yours,
Gustav

Too lonely! Too lonely!

51. *To Max Staegemann*

Leipzig, 6 November 1886

Dear Herr Direktor,

I ought now to profess myself astonished at your astonishment—yet I know that would not suit my face.

I beg you to treat me as frankly and straightforwardly as I confidently expect you to do in your dealings with me.

You yourself know that up to a certain date it was tacitly agreed between us that, whenever the *Nibelungen*[2] should be put on here, I should share the conducting of these works with my colleague. The evidence for this is available.

You know too that my abilities and my constitution would make it impossible for me to remain in a position in which I was excluded from tasks of this kind.

I beg you also to bear in mind that, if only for reasons of professional advancement, this exceptional opportunity of gaining public confidence must not be withheld from me.

I make so bold also to remind you that I have hitherto proved myself not unworthy of *your* confidence and favour—and I can assure you that I shall earnestly endeavour to keep it for ever.

I very much hope that in this letter I have not again failed to make my meaning

[1] Three short words here cannot be deciphered with certainty (o.e.) [but are probably 'lege ich bei'—'I enclose the letter' (K.M.).]

[2] Staegemann had only recently obtained the rights from Bayreuth to produce the *Nibelungen* (K.M.).

clear, and I sincerely beg you for an answer of the sort that the kindness you have hitherto shown me justifies my hoping for.

With deep respect, I remain,

Your obedient servant,
Gustav Mahler

---

52. *To Max Staegemann*

Leipzig, 26 November 1886

Dear Herr Direktor,

Permit me to inquire most respectfully whether the announcement in today's issue of the *Leipziger Tageblatt*[1] regarding the musical direction of the *Nibelungen* is in accordance with your own views.—I believe I may now consider myself entitled to ask for some clarification of this to me vital matter.

With deep respect, I remain,

Your most obedient servant,
Gustav Mahler

---

53. *To Max Staegemann*

Leipzig, 27 November 1886

Dear Herr Direktor,

After careful consideration of the prevailing circumstances I have come to the conclusion that it would be very unfair if I were to attribute any blame to you for this situation, which has now become so embarrassing to me.

On the contrary, it is quite clear to me that from your point of view you are entirely in the right and cannot act otherwise.

While drawing your attention to my letter of December last year, in which I foretold what has now happened, I wish to express to you personally my sincerest regret for all the steps that I shall henceforth see myself compelled to take.

I herewith ask to be released from my contract.—Now that I have put this into words, you will, I hope, believe that I mean it entirely seriously, and for my part I declare myself ready to make any sacrifice in order to obtain this favour, for which—I do recognize—you too will have to pay dearly.

It goes without saying that I leave it entirely to you to determine the date of my departure hence, according to your needs and convenience; only I beg you,

[1] That Nikisch was to conduct the *Nibelungen* (K.M.).

in the interests of both of us, not to give a negative answer to this request of mine.

Assuring you of my unalterable esteem, I remain,

> Your most obedient servant,
> Gustav Mahler

54. To Friedrich Löhr

Undated. Leipzig, 25 December 1886

My dear Fritz,

Do tell Rudolf instantly to collect all the testimonials he can get hold of and to send them to Herr Direktor Staegemann here, accompanied by a letter as follows:

'Dear Herr Direktor, I am so-and-so. For two years I was Kapellmeister at the theatres in Laibach and Wurzburg, and subsequently conductor of the choral society in Hanover. Before that I passed out of the Vienna Conservatory, receiving the first prize. I can do such-and-such, and I should be most grateful if in the event of your having a vacancy you would consider me for the job. I shall gladly accept a trial engagement whenever you think fit. Yours, etc. R. Krz.'

My own affair has become a little more complicated—in so far as yesterday I received: I. Contract signed by Pollini (who has tied himself down, whereas I have to make up my mind by 18 January '87); II. an offer from the Court Theatre in Karlsruhe (to become Mottl's successor); III. a splendid offer from Neumann in Prague.

Now four carrots are dangled before the donkey! What am I to do?

As a result of all I have experienced I have made up my mind not to do anything, just to wait and see what wheel I come under.

Last night I spent a sad Christmas Eve once again sitting at home all by myself, gazing out, seeing all the windows opposite aglow with Christmas trees and candles.—And then I thought of my poor joyless people at home, sadly sitting in the dark, waiting—and then again I saw before me yourself and your family, the old congenial circle, now lost to me—and then—then I no longer saw anything because a veil of moisture moved before my eyes, and the whole world, through which I am destined to wander without rest, was blotted out by a few tear-drops.

I do beg you, dear Fritz, to push Rudolf a bit. Has he been to the Hotel Imperial to see the agent? Allowing for the possibility that he did not get my letter, I am putting it down again: He should instantly go to see H[err] Ledner, the representative of Entsch the agent in Berlin. Ledner is at the moment at the Hotel Imperial in Vienna. I have already informed him, and he is willing to try to get Rudolf to Hamburg. L. doesn't know anything about Leipzig, because I am seeing to that myself.

Make sure that Rudolf keeps me informed instantly of whatever he does.

I am with you in spirit during these days!

Yours ever,
Gustav

What do you mean by 'absolutely impossible to delay much longer'? Do you realize, my dear fellow, that this worries me a great deal? I do beg you to wait a little longer if it is at all possible.[1]

Please one of these days let me have the collection of poems you would like to publish, perhaps I can do something about it.—The fact is I know a crazy publisher who is quite capable of such a thing!![2]

1887

55. *To Friedrich Löhr*

Undated. Leipzig, [early] *January 1887*
Gottschedstrasse 4, 2nd Floor

My dear Fritz,

Why have you not written for so long? Surely you must have had my last letter?

A new crisis is developing in my situation. To save you from long discussion I shall give you the dry facts, which are the result of the most hectic and complicated goings-on.

As you probably know, my colleague Nikisch has received a brilliant offer.

If he leaves, I shall take his place as first conductor with a completely free hand.—If he stays, I shall go to Hamburg, to be in charge of the opera-house there, having been offered really splendid terms. There my salary would be 6,000 marks per annum, I would get three months' holiday, have the exclusive right to the *Nibelungen, Meistersinger, Tristan, Fidelio, Don Giovanni,* and the right to give notice after the first year. You can imagine I naturally wish to go to Hamburg—but I am not free to choose, because if Nikisch decides to go to Budapest Direktor Staegemann will not release me from my contract. The

---

[1] The reference is to my marriage (F.L.).
[2] Löhr never did publish any of his poems (K.M.).

4*

matter will be decided by 15 January at the latest. I have made the stipulation (in both cases) that Rudolf (Krzyz.) shall be appointed at the same time.— Please inform him of this and send me his address immediately. He would of course have to accept a modest position to begin with—but I should see to it that he would gradually be given scope worthy of his abilities.—

As a result of all this I have simply lost all contact with 'myself'—though I have remained pretty much my old self and am just on the point of once again committing a number of 'follies'.[1]—Sometimes I am so anxious that I simply want to run away.—I simply do not dare to think of home.

Dear Fritz, do write to me and tell me how you are all getting on!

Elmblad's wife has gone off to Paris again! Neumann continues to sigh mightily for my coming! F. ditto![2] The Leipzig people show considerable respect for me; Nikisch and I have come a good deal closer to each other, and we get on like good colleagues.

Most affectionate greetings to you all, and please write soon to your present somewhat confused

Gustav

56. *To Friedrich Löhr*†

Undated. Leipzig, [January] *1887*

Dear Fritz,

I am really very much worried about your having so hastily decided to take this important step! What are the two of you going to do? Do write to me about it fully![3]

I have received very grievous news from home. My mother too is ill, and my poor, poor sister[4] is all alone there at this difficult time. The decision about my situation here has become somewhat more imminent, since Nikisch has now definitely decided to stay on and Staegemann has declared his readiness, in principle, not to put any obstacles in my way.

For the last few days I was in Berlin with Spiegler, and spent some time with Braun. Both of them are still their old selves, except that I found Spiegler infinitely more mature than he used to be. He is now so free and independent that I am really delighted with him. Unfortunately he is going away again soon, and I shall again be left—to my own melancholy company.

---

[1] His feelings for Marion Weber had intensified and were about to reach their climax, and he *was* in fact about to run away with her (K.M.).

[2] Betty Frank in Prague (K.M.).

[3] Reference to my marriage. The letter must therefore have been written before 17 February 1887, which was my wedding day (F.L.).

[4] Justine, who later married Arnold Rosé (F.L.).

Yesterday I moved into a new flat, which is really almost too magnificent for me.[1] I almost begrudge it to myself. If any of you come here to see me, you will of course stay with me.

At the moment it seems not improbable that I shall go to Karlsruhe, starting in the autumn.—

Please, please do write soon and tell me all about yourself! Best wishes to you all!

Yours,

Gustav

Best wishes to Louise and my gratitude for her having remembered me.
20 marks enclosed.

57. *To Friedrich Löhr*

Undated. Leipzig, [18] *February 1887*

My dear Fritz,

Just a few lines—Nikisch has suddenly fallen ill, and I must do all the work single-handed—

My most heartfelt, ever constant good wishes to you and your wife for ever!

You know how dearly I should like to be with you both even if only for a few moments.—Alas, it is my fate all through life to be obliged to leave my dear ones alone when perhaps they need me most.

My thoughts go out to you both all the time, and I keep on picturing your Jean Paul-ish hermitage—

My affairs are becoming steadily more incomprehensible.—I have conducted *Die Walküre*[2] here (as a result of my colleague's sudden illness), and this has put me in a very strong position.

At the same time I have received an offer from New York, an invitation to replace Anton Seidl[3]—perhaps I shall end up by accepting it!—

A thousand greetings to you both. Do write whatever can be written—perhaps Uda will help you a bit.

I must go—to rehearse with Lucca,[4] who is giving a guest performance here tomorrow.

Yours affectionately,

Gustav

[1] Gustav Adolfstrasse 12 (F.L.).
[2] On 9 February (K.M.).
[3] Anton Seidl (1850–98), noted Hungarian conductor who at that time was in charge of German Opera at the Metropolitan in New York (K.M.).
[4] Pauline de Lucca (1841–1908) appeared on 19 February in *Carmen*, and on 22 February in *Der widerspänstigen Zähmung* by Goetz (K.M.).

58. *To Emil Freund* (Vienna)

Leipzig, April 1887

Dear Emil,

You can imagine how shocked I was and how deeply I felt with you all when I received the sad news.[1] And yet I had to put off writing you even a few lines from day to day because of the enormous pressure of work.—If you can bring yourself to do so, please let me have more details of what happened and tell me, too, how you are faring in Seelau. I expect to be in Iglau in the middle of July, so I count on seeing you and on our having a good talk—but I simply haven't the time to write a letter. At any rate you know I am getting on all right, and also that I too have my allotted share of suffering—that is something we all must take in our stride.

Please convey my kindest regards to your family and do write to your old friend

Mahler

59. *To Friedrich Löhr†*

Undated. Leipzig, about the end of April 1887
Gustav Adolfstrasse 12

My dear Fritz,

I simply cannot understand why you don't write me even so much as a word —and precisely now when I so much need to have news of you.

I dare say you know that for about the last three months I simply haven't been able to call my soul my own—owing to my colleague's[2] illness I have to do two men's work. I conduct big operas almost daily, literally almost never getting away from the theatre. You can imagine how exhausting that is for someone who takes art seriously and what a strain it is carrying out such great tasks with an utter minimum of preparation. Now it is I who am busy 'getting up' *Siegfried*.[3]—I have gone up a good deal in the public's estimation, very often get 'curtain calls', and so on.

I am positively on terms of friendship with my chief, and treated as a member of the family. They are almost the only people here whom I visit. Nikisch will probably be back from Italy next month, and then my life ought to become a

---

[1] The death of Dr. Emil Freund's brother (o.e.).
[2] Arthur Nikisch (K.M.).
[3] The première was on 13 May 1887 (K.M.).

little more human. Of course all this also means an increased prospect of my staying on here, since I really no longer have any reason to go away.

The latest turn of events means that to all intents and purposes I am now on an equal footing with Nikisch and need have no qualms about fighting him for the upper hand, which I am certain to gain if only on grounds of physical superiority. I don't think Nikisch will stand the pace, and sooner or later he will take himself off.

I am terribly worried about Rudolf.[1] I keep on writing and talking to everyone, hitherto without any result. It is awfully difficult for a beginner to get a footing. But I am not giving up hope. In the end I shall pull it off for him.

My family continues to cause me deep concern, and this is another reason for my willingness to plunge into this work; for I must not and will not let my mind dwell on all these things that I cannot do anything about. I wonder when things will improve.—

How often now I think of you and your wife, wondering why I hear nothing from you. Perhaps my appeal will touch your wife's heart and make her press the pen into your hand.

Remember me very affectionately to your family and thank Louise for her greetings. How I should like to see you all again!! A thousand greetings to all—and do write at long last to

Your
Gustav

1888

60. *To Friedrich Löhr*†

Undated. Leipzig. Delivery postmark: 4 January 1888

Dear Fritz,

I must write you a few lines. It is all I can manage now in this trilogy of the passions and whirlwind of life!

Everything in me and around me is in a state of becoming! Nothing is! Let me have just a little longer to see it through! Then you shall know all!

Fondest greetings to you all from
Gustav

I am thinking of you!

---

[1] R. Krzyzanowski was still unemployed (K.M.).

61. *To Max Staegemann*

Leipzig, 5 January 1888

My very dear Herr Direktor,

Do not take my writing to you amiss when, after all, I should not have far to go to see you.

For some time I have been aware of some ill-humour on your part, which must doubtless to a large extent be attributed to the petty worries and vexations with which you ceaselessly have to contend; but I nevertheless cannot help seeking the reason for it also to some slight extent in myself.

I fear this ill-humour might grow and in the end seriously imperil our excellent relationship, which has been such a source of happiness to me, making my appointment such a pleasant one. I freely admit that you have reason enough to complain of me, since for a long time now I have ceased to carry out my duties in the way you had come to expect of me.

I know too that so far as you are concerned there is no need for me to make excuses, since the cause of my negligence will doubtless make you regard it in a milder light. You yourself, who have from the very beginning promoted the good cause so energetically and disinterestedly, are certainly also the first to make a sacrifice on behalf of its success and to dispense, for a time, partially, with the work of one whose energies you are entitled to claim in their entirety for your institution.

Just a little patience, a little longer!

Give your uneasiness no ground to grow on and remain a little well disposed to me.

Allow two more months to pass, and you shall see that I shall once again be 'as of old'.[1]

And now—no hard feelings!

I did want to say a great deal more—but I have just reflected that it is better to close at this point, postponing the second part of my letter until some more favourable time. Assuring you that your regard and friendship are among my most precious possessions, which I would fain keep, I remain, as ever,

from the bottom of my heart
your devoted
Gustav Mahler

PS. (There I am, talking as 'a man of feeling'. Well, even a conductor may sometimes have 'feelings'.)

---

[1] In March of this year Mahler completed his First Symphony (o.e.).

62. *To Emil Freund* (Vienna)†

Leipzig, 17 January 1888

Dear Emil,

Please *don't* come to the first night,[1] for it would mean not having the slightest chance to get together. During the first few days I shan't have even a *single* moment to spare. As you know, all the world and his wife are here and I shall have to be at the beck and call of the high and mighty.

It would be much better if you came the following week, when we shall be able to get together in peace and quiet and have a real talk.

So I am not getting you a ticket for the first night—anyway, they're probably sold out by now.

Kindest regards to all,

Yours,
Gustav Mahler

63. *To Friedrich Löhr*

Undated. Leipzig, January or February 1888

Dearest Fritz,

It weighs on me not being able to tell you anything! Forgive me this silence, dear, fellow—you shall know all in time. At least I can reveal that I have filled many a sheet of music-paper—and that everything in that quarter has turned out splendidly—dear God, perhaps in every quarter! Yes! It is all very beautiful and great![2]

Farewell Fritz—and *you* write to me!

Yours,
Gustav

My love to all the family!

64. *To Friedrich Löhr*†

Undated. Leipzig, [middle of] March 1888

My dear Fritz,

Well! My work is finished![3] Now I should like to have you by my piano and play it to you!

[1] The première on 20 January of Weber's opera *Die drei Pintos* (o.e.).
[2] Undoubtedly a reference to Mahler's First Symphony (K.M.).
[3] Mahler's First Symphony (o.e.).

Probably you are the only person who will find me unchanged in it; the others will doubtless wonder at a number of things! It has turned out so overwhelming it came gushing out of me like a mountain torrent! This summer you shall hear it! All of a sudden all the sluice-gates in me opened! Perhaps one of these days I shall tell you how it all happened!

I am returning your work herewith, with thanks.

I should dearly like to be able to say a few words to you about the little arrival in your family—it is so odd to think of you as a father![1]

I can't do it today! Spring is driving me out of the house! I must get out—and once again take deep breaths of fresh air. For the last six weeks I have seen nothing but my desk!

Fondest greetings—and write soon about how you and your wife are. Greetings to everyone!

Yours,
Gustav

65. *To Albert Spiegler* (Vienna)†

Undated. Postmark: Leipzig, 2 May 1888
Vienna delivery postmark: 4 May 1888

Dear Albert,
Greetings to you in your quiet haven from one who is tossed on the high seas by all the storms that be. Though the sails are in tatters, the helm is still in one piece! I shall survive, salvaging many a precious possession from many a shipwreck. Thanks for 'letters'!

Yours,
Gustav

66. *To Max Staegemann*

Leipzig, 16 May 1888

Dear Herr Direktor,
In the matter of the prevailing difference between myself and Herr *Goldberg*,[2] about which you are informed, I must again return to my request to be released from my contract.

While standing by and herewith explicitly repeating that request of mine,

---

[1] Maria (Maja) Löhr, born on 9 March 1888. She died in 1964 (K.M.).
[2] Albert Goldberg (1847–1905), stage director at the Leipzig Stadttheater (K.M.).

I should like to be allowed to state the grounds on which I consider myself justified in insisting on release from my contract. These grounds are as follows:

First of all, I consider it entirely incompatible with the authority vested in me as conductor, and essential to the performance of my duties, that I should with impunity be exposed before the opera-house's employees in the way that has resulted from Herr G.'s behaviour to me. I therefore find myself, after that incident, no longer able to carry out my duties with the authority that is just as necessary in my interests as in yours and that of the artistic institution to which I belong. My view is thus primarily that that episode has made the further performance of my contractual duties downright impossible and for this reason alone I am therefore entitled to require that my contract with you should be dissolved.

Secondly, I am also of the opinion that you have in fact already granted my request for release. As I have already informed you, after the incident in question Herr G. called out to me, in front of the employees there assembled, these very words: 'You have conducted here for the last time today etc.!' Even if it cannot be assumed that, at the moment when Herr G. uttered those words, he did so explicitly on your behalf, I considered it my duty, in writing my letter of the following day, to draw your particular attention to those words, in order to learn to what extent you endorsed this behaviour of Herr G.'s.

You will recall expressly stating, with reference to my letter, during the conversation that I had with you that same day: 'Anything Herr G. does is done by me—He is myself etc. . . .'

From this I believe I am entitled to conclude that you are also in agreement with the dismissal distinctly formulated by Herr G. in his words to me.

After the above statement of the situation I hope and trust that you will {acknowledge} the legitimacy of my point of view and, in any case, in the interests of all concerned, will not fail to grant the release from my contract for which I ask.

Assuring you of my highest esteem, I am,

> Your most obedient servant,
> Gustav Mahler

67. *To Max Staegemann*

Leipzig, 17 May 1888

Kapellmeister Gustav Mahler

respectfully requests to be relieved of his duties pending termination of his contract.[1]

[1] This time Mahler's resignation was accepted, and he left Leipzig shortly after (K.M.).

68. *To Friedrich Löhr*†

Undated. Iglau, [September] *1888*

Dear Old Man,

On Sunday evening I shall be arriving in Vienna, on very important business. —Do please send a line to me at the Hotel Höller, saying when I can see {you} in town, for our first meeting. We can arrange everything then. My brother Otto will probably be with me.

Ever yours,

M

IV

BUDAPEST
1888–1891

1888 continued

69. *To the Members of the Budapest Opera-House†*

Budapest, [10 October] *1888*

Ladies and gentlemen,

Today I have the honour of assuming the leading position in an establishment that is in every respect fitted to be a home for and an ornament to this country's art.—First of all I should like to thank our revered chief, the Secretary of State, Herr von Beniczky, for the confidence he has shown in me by conferring upon me an office at once so responsible and so eminent, and I hereby pledge myself to devote myself to my duties wholeheartedly and single-mindedly. I also wish to address a few words to you, ladies and gentlemen.

It is with pride and pleasure that I see gathered around me a throng of artists whom any general might be proud to lead to victory. It must fill each one of us with pride to belong to an establishment promoted so benevolently and munificently by that noble patron of the arts, His Majesty the King, an establishment towards which the highest representatives of the kingdom have always been open-handed, one that forms—and which should form—the focal point of Hungary's artistic endeavours and at the same time is the pride of the nation.— Yet what stringent demands we must make on ourselves in our awareness of our duty to maintain and enhance the significance of such an establishment.—

Ladies and gentlemen, let us vow to dedicate ourselves wholeheartedly and with utter devotion to the proud task that falls to us! *To perform our tasks with the utmost rigour,* with complete absorption in and devotion to the work as a whole—let that be the motto inscribed on our banner.

Do not expect either promises or acts from me in the immediate future. Nor shall I present you with a programme today.

Let us first get to know one another and collect ourselves for the difficult work that lies ahead of us.

If I promise one thing today, it is that I shall set an example in being keen on the work and always sincere in intention.

Let us set to work—each one to his task! Then our labours will be crowned with success.

I conclude now in the joyful hope that as true artists you all agree with what I have said and will support me in the difficult task ahead of us.

Gustav Mahler

70. *To Max Staegemann* (Leipzig)

Budapest, 20 December 1888

My very dear Herr Direktor,

The enclosed letters will clarify the situation for you. I beg you to treat them as in previous cases, as confidential.

Are you yet able to reach a decision? And what line shall I take in the matter?—I am in a dreadful 'Soubrette scrape'!

I take this opportunity of wishing you and yours a happy Christmas and New Year and hope you will sample the 'genuine Magyar' specialities that I am sending by the same post.

The sausage must be fried. Do please be careful in opening the various tins, since one small one contains paprika and might easily have a distressing effect on nose and eyes.

I expect to spend a very lonely Christmas Eve this year—the theatre will be closed—and I have as yet no acquaintances at all here.

I am now well into the *Nibelungen* rehearsals, but am in serious straits about a tenor and have the most ridiculous difficulties in all directions.—But I shall not give up![1]

Please remember me very kindly to your family—I take it that these greetings will also reach our friend Perron[2]—wishing you all some days of repose and jollity.

Your most obedient servant,
Gustav Mahler

Please do not leave the packages at the Post Office too long, or the fruit will go bad.

Just for fun I am sending you both Artner's[3] letters herewith, so that you can enjoy them to the full.

---

[1] The première of *Rheingold* was on 26 January and of *Walküre* on the 27th. Mahler did not succeed in putting on the last two parts of the *Nibelungen* (K.M.).

[2] Karl Perron (1858–1928), baritone at the Leipzig Theatre (K.M.).

[3] Josephine von Artner (1867–1932), Czech soprano, at that time appointed to the Leipzig Stadttheater. She later joined Mahler in Hamburg, and she sang in the first performance of his Second Symphony (K.M.).

1889

71. *To Friedrich Löhr†*

Undated. Budapest, April 1889

Dearest Fritz,

I am immensely looking forward to our meeting!

My hotel is called the Hotel Tiger and is in the Palatingasse (in Hungarian Nádor-utcza); but please do in any case let me know in good time when you will be arriving, because I should like to meet you at the station. Should I be prevented, just come straight to my hotel, where everything will be prepared for you.

As regards Otto, I am very disturbed to hear that he means to suspend work for so long.

He cannot play at home, of course. What I should really prefer is for him to spend several days in Iglau and then to go back to Vienna and resume the old routine.

Looking forward to seeing you soon,

Yours,
Mahler

Very best wishes to all your family.

72. *To Friedrich Löhr†*

Undated. Munich [July 1889]

Dear Fritz,

At last I have been sent home from hospital.[1]—I am still in pain and fairly run-down. I hope I shall pretty soon be on the mend. Today I am going to Bayreuth for five days, and from there to Marienbad for three weeks.—I hope to be in Vienna in the middle of August.

Yours affectionately,
Gustav

---

[1] After an operation (o.e.).

73. *To Friedrich Löhr*†

Dear Fritz,

Herewith 47 fl., of which 31 fl. 60 kr. are for the landlady—10 fl. for Berta and 5 pocket-money for Otto.

In a fortnight I shall be in Vienna.

Very best wishes,

Yours,
Gustav

74. *To Friedrich Löhr*†

Dear Fritz,

So I shall be coming to Vienna at the end of next week with Justi.

If I can conveniently stay with you, without disturbing you in any way, I shall come to you—but if not, I would ask you to take a quiet room for me for a few days in a pleasant hotel as close as possible to your flat.—I think the latter arrangement would in fact be altogether preferable.

Please do not tell anyone that I am coming.—I shall explain why when I see you.

So after all this time we shall once more spend a few days together.—

If I can, I shall arrange to be with you no later than Sunday (a day on which I am sure you can manage to be free).—

Very best wishes,

Yours,
Gustav

75. *To Uda Löhr*†

Dear Uda,

Many thanks for your sweet letter. Herewith 75 fl. for September and October.

I am in the midst of work—*Lohengrin* on Sunday![1]

---

[1] The first performance in Budapest was on 15 September 1889 (K.M.).

Very bad news from home—the catastrophe is awaited hourly.—In no circumstances can I leave here before Monday.

Would it be possible, if the worst should happen before I can get there, for you to go to Iglau for one or two days to support my sister?

For I do not know how they can manage alone!

In that event I would telegraph you—would you then let me know whether you can do it or not?—There has been no improvement in my condition so far.[1] I take morphia in order to get through rehearsals.

—Very best wishes to you all,

> Yours sincerely,
> Mahler

76. *To Friedrich Löhr*†

> *Undated. Budapest, October 1889*

Dear Fritz,

I have just received mail from Iglau.—Do please let me know by return, in detail, whatever you may know—especially about the new arrangements.

I hear that Justi is going to stay with you for a short time. What are we going to do with Emma?

Any expenses that may arise need of course be no object; all that matters to me now is that the brief transitional period up to the time when I can have my two sisters with me should be as tolerable as possible for them.

I can't get away at the moment.

> Ever,
> Gustav

77. *To Friedrich Löhr*

> *Undated.* [Budapest, October 1889]
> *Delivery postmark:* [Vienna] *1 November 1889*

Dear Fritz,

You will receive by the same mail a money order for 86 fl. 69 kr.—I beg you to give me, for my orientation, precise figures as to what now, when, after all, the situation is doubtless consolidated to some extent, how much I shall have to send regularly every month for the two children[2]—and I must admit I cannot

---

[1] A reference to the operation Mahler had had to undergo during the summer (o.e. + K.M.).

[2] Mahler's sisters, Justine and Emma (o.e.). [Translators' note: In this sentence Mahler lost the thread of his construction.]

quite suppress a slight groan.—Alois,[1] in Brünn, also has to be constantly supplied with money, and here expenses seem to be turning out considerably higher than I had originally hoped, and these owing to Justi's singularly sensitive and debilitated constitution.—Well—with God's help! Tomorrow I shall ask for an advance! The enclosed letter is for Emma. My condition improves daily. Very best wishes,

Gustav

I am just negotiating with Levi[2] in Munich for Rudolf,[3] whom I am most strongly recommending for a vacancy there as conductor at the Court Theatre. I have high hopes that it will come off.

—He doesn't know anything about it yet—I want the news to come to him as a surprise from there.

78. To Friedrich Löhr†

Undated. Budapest, beginning of November 1889

Dear Fritz,

I enclose 60 fl. Please do get Otto whatever he needs.—I thought Otto {had} a winter coat; I no longer have mine.—So if it is absolutely necessary, please get him that as well (remaining within the most modest limits) and let me know what it costs. Please write and tell me what Otto's health {is} like now—and {what} sort of efforts he is making.

Anyway, I hope to see you both here on 6 November!

Ever,
Gustav

Did he get my 20 fl.?

79. To Friedrich Löhr†

Undated. Budapest [in November 1889
Delivery postmark: [Vienna] 15 November 188(

Dear Fritz,

Just a line in haste![4] Here is the certificate. I suggest the two of you shoul(

[1] Mahler's brother, then aged 22, in business (o.e.).
[2] Herman Levi (1839–1900), German conductor (K.M.).
[3] Krzyzanowski who after engagements in Halle and Elberfeld was appointed Kapellmeister i*
Munich from August 1890 (K.M.).
[4] Written in pencil (F.L.).

not arrive here until Tuesday morning.—Otto can take some leave and stay longer, say over Sunday. If you want to arrange things differently, it is all the same to me. Only do be sure to let me know what time you arrive.

All for now!

Gustav

PS. But do come too![1]

80. *To Friedrich Löhr*

Undated. Budapest, Winter 1889

Dear Fritz,

Now I should really like to get some news of you all—your postcards, which I was looking forward to, remained, alas, in the singular.—Forgive me writing nothing today—I am in such haste—I daresay Justi will tell you all about everything. It does worry me still being without news.

Today I am sending you 100 fl., which leaves another 300 fl. that you have {to} get from me.—Please let me know when you want the rest; naturally it is at your disposal at any moment.

Do write soon.

Remember me to Uda and the family.

Gustav

81. *To Friedrich Löhr†*

Undated. Budapest, Christmas 1889

Dear Fritz,

I shall arrive with Justi at noon on Monday (the same train that you took). Justi will then remain with you, and I shall go on to Iglau, to settle things there.

Perhaps someone will meet us at the station.

Ever yours,
Mahler

† For the first performance of Mahler's First Symphony in Budapest [on 20 November 1889] (o.e.).

1890

82. *To Friedrich Löhr†*

Undated. Budapest, February 1890

Dear Fritz,
    There's always one of us ill in bed! For weeks I have been meaning either to come myself or to write—but, believe me, I simply haven't the time.
    —There is a great deal to talk over with you! What do you think—can't you get away for a few days and slip over here to see me? It would do you no harm to get out of harness for a bit.
    If not, then I shall somehow get over to you.
    I shall 'compose' Sax's poem—a heavy obligation, I can tell you!
    By all means do be strict with Emma. There is still far too much of the old devil in her.
    I am also sending a money order today for the 50 fl. you need. For the summer I have worked out a very nice plan, which I shall tell you about one of these days —preferably when we meet, so that we can discuss it.
    Everything is a mad rush here—I have no time to draw breath.

Ever yours,
Mahler

83. *To Friedrich Löhr*

Undated. Budapest, Spring 1890

Dear Fritz,
    Please find enclosed the sum for the Ministry of Finance. I am so madly busy —have to bottle up so much vexation that I am incapable of writing!—How is Otto turning out? Do come here.—At the moment I don't know when I shall be able to get away.
    Write soon to your care-worn

Gustav

84. *To Friedrich Löhr*†

Undated. Budapest, May 1890
[Express letter]

Dear Fritz,

On Wednesday and Thursday I shall be in Trieste, Hotel Delorme. Please send a few lines to let me know if Uda received my last letter and when she will be able to answer it.

From there I go to Venice; I shall send you my address when I get there.— I am travelling, together with Justi, for nothing, having been able to get myself a free pass on the Southern Railway.

In great haste,

Yours,
Gustav

Answer express, as I send this.

85. *To Friedrich Löhr*†

Undated. Budapest [May 1890]
Vienna delivery postmark: 9 May 1890

Dear Fritz,

I received your explanatory letter just a short time before leaving, when I had already posted my express letter.[1]

Here are 30 fl. for clothes for Emma.—Do get everything ready in the Hinterbrühl, so that we can go out there at the beginning of June. As soon as I have found out about my round-trip here, I shall let you know the various addresses where letters will reach me.

Affectionate greetings from

Gustav

86. *To Uda Löhr*†

Undated. Budapest, May 1890

Dear Uda,

May I ask a favour of you?—For reasons of economy I shall perhaps have to

---

[1] This letter is not extant and I do not recall what is meant (F.L.)—probably no. 84 in this collection (K.M.).

send Justi to Franzensbad[1] by herself. For this eventuality I have been recommended a doctor, whose address I enclose, whose wife is prepared to give my sister full board and look after her.

What I now want to ask you is this—could you go there within the next few days—see what sort of place it is and inquire whether and if so how it would work.

Please use my name, since I am just writing to him too.

Affectionate greetings, looking forward to seeing you all soon.

Yours sincerely,
Mahler

⟨Dr. Fellner, I, Grünangergasse 2.⟩

87. To Friedrich Löhr

Undated. Bologna, May 1890

Dear Fritz,

In a few days our address will be: Hotel Milano, Milan! We are going there by way of Florence and Genoa.

Send me some news of yourselves and let me know whether, coming on the Southern Railway train on 1 or 2 June, we can get out at Mödling, which would be very desirable, since it would save us all sorts of trouble.—

The weather and things in general have turned out very well.—

Best wishes from me and Justi to all

from your
Gustav

88. To Uda Löhr†

Florence, 18 May 1890

Dear Uda,

We are just sending off to you a box of clothes that are only a burden to us on the journey. Please unpack them and hang them up.

I am also writing to Budapest and having 700 fl. sent off to you, so that the rent can be paid on moving in.

We shall probably arrive in Mödling on 31 May and I hope we shall be able to move straight into our flat. I hope to find news about this from you in Milan.

Will the flat be ready? That would be very nice!

[1] A small spa in Bohemia, near Karlsbad (K.M.).

We've been having a glorious time and are now looking forward to enjoyable
days at Genoa, Milan, Lake Garda and Laibach. Justi is positively flourishing;
the journey is doing her a world of good.

Do send some news too of yourself and the children.

Very best wishes from me and Justi.

Gustav Mahler

Address: Hotel Milano, Milan.

9. *To Friedrich Löhr*

Undated. Milan, end of May 1890

[Arrival postmark: 23 May 1890]

Dear Fritz,

We shall arrive in the Hinterbrühl on Tuesday evening, hoping to find some
of you there.

I am today writing to Budapest and having an advance of 800 fl. sent direct
to you. We can reckon up when we meet. This damned money!—I am coming
to the end of it here too.

See you soon!

Gustav

I shall telegraph the exact time of my arrival.

10. *To Uda Löhr*†

Undated. Budapest, August 1890

Dear Uda,

I hope you have by now received the remittance! {Judging by} a remark of
Berta's on the last post{card} the worthy Hinterbrühl post office with {that}
worthy Herr Meier must have taken its time. (. . .)[1]

It is really too bad that Fritz had to leave![2]

What is Otto's health like? And how is Emma behaving? I am still having
quite a pleasant time here, since I still have my afternoons free.

So I am still taking delightful solitary walks.

I think it will be better if I send the Sept{ember} money by post.

Here I have omitted a sentence of no importance which it would be improper to elucidate
(F.L.).

I had had to make a second visit to Sax in Aussee (F.L.).

This time your Mama has fortunately had good luck with the weather. So I dare say you will be busy taking her for walks in the Kienthal.
Fond greetings from

         Gustav Mahler

91. *To Friedrich Löhr*†

         Undated. Budapest, September 1890

Dearest Fritz,
     I am afraid I can manage only a few hasty lines.
     I should be glad if you would now settle the freight bill for me. So then I shall still owe you 412 fl.—You can have the money back any time it suits you.— You can either have the whole sum on 1 October—or, if you prefer, in two or three instalments—write and tell me.
     I am horrified to hear you are now so harassed.—See that you don't take these worries to Italy with you. Another thing on my mind is the move to Vienna.—Won't it all be too much of a strain for Justi? Have you got the furniture yet? Who is the lady who has been taken on?—When do you start out? Don't bother about the receipts! The outlook for reduced fares is very dim—I have tried, but I have little hope.
     I shall write again at greater length before you leave.
     In great haste,

         Yours,
         Gustav

92. *To Bernhard Pollini* (Hamburg)†

         Budapest, 11 October 189c

Dear Sir,
     I am unfortunately unable to modify my requirements to meet your proposal: and deeply regret the possible failure of our negotiations: all the more since I had already taken preliminary steps in the justifiable hope of being able to realize my intentions.

         I remain, sir,
         With great respect,
         Your obedient servant,
         Gustav Mahler

93. *To Bernhard Pollini*†

Budapest, 14 October 1890

Dear Sir,

In reply to your esteemed letter of the 9th inst., I am now prepared to accept your proposal, on condition that you approve my salary without any deduction, i.e. that you bear the responsibility for taxation requirements, pension contributions and any other similar deductions.

In the hope of having established my readiness to make certain concessions I must, however, state most emphatically that I am not in a position to accept any further reduction of my demands, and am therefore looking forward to your final decision in the matter.

I remain, sir,
Your obedient servant,
Gustav Mahler

94. *To Bernhard Pollini*

Budapest, 7 November 1890

Dear Sir,

I received your esteemed letter of 2 November with the enclosed contract on my return to Budapest. After reading same I must return to a matter that you have probably disregarded as a result of the new course of our negotiations, but which I, as you will gather from the relevant letter, regard as an issue of much importance.

I should have accepted your offer of 12,000 marks annual salary if you had been prepared to be responsible for the customary deductions such as tax and pension contributions.

Having given ample evidence of my willingness to come to terms with you, I must now ask you to make this concession and allow me to enter a clause to this effect in the contract I have received.

There will then be no further obstacle to my joining the staff of your establishment.

I am, sir, with great respect

Your obedient servant,
Gustav Mahler

5

1891

95. *To Friedrich Löhr†*

Undated. Budapest, [January 1891]
Delivery postmark: Rome, 28 January 1891

Dearest Fritz,
  It is a great piece of luck that I have to write to you—for otherwise you would
have to wait heaven knows how long for a letter.—Heaven knows, I did write
one, then put off sealing it for so long that it got lost. It is really abominable of
me to leave {you} quite without word down there.—But what is the use of
dragging the reasons into the light of day. Let it pass! (. . .)[1]
  I am leading a life devoted entirely to external affairs. And in this respect I
have achieved much that is profitable, even experience a number of pleasant
things. What will interest you is that Brahms heard me conduct *Don Giovanni*[2]
here and forthwith became my fiercest partisan and benefactor. He has distinguished me in a way that is quite unheard of with him, indeed treats me on
terms of real friendship.—
  I had already heard of the disaster with Hausmann.—You will soon have the
joy of going for walks on the Aventine with Berta.—But it is far from impossible
that you will suddenly be descended on by {me} too!
  All sorts of things are going on—who knows what wind will suddenly waft
me away from Budapest.
  I close in haste, or else this letter will not get posted either.
  Greetings to Uda and the child.

Yours affectionately,
Gustav

96. *To Geza v. Zichy* (Budapest)†

Undated. Budapest, March 1891

Your Excellency,
  With reference to our conversation today I wish to express my willingness—
without prejudice to any rights covered by my contract—to terminate my

---

[1] A paragraph relating to the urgent reason for writing this letter has been omitted for
personal reasons (F.L.).
[2] On 16 December 1890 (K.M.).

present contract and enter into a new one with Your Excellency, on the basis of the new statutes.

This new contract would have to stipulate:

I. Duration of the contract: from date of signature to 1 October 1892.

II. The conditions remain essentially as before, with the exception of those special clauses that are at variance with the new statutes and which would have to be modified in accordance with them.

III. Should no new contract have been made with me by 15 May 1892, I am then to receive in settlement a payment of 25,000 florins—in other words, twenty-five thousand Austrian gulden—payable in cash and without any deduction by the accounts department of the Royal Opera-House.

IV. The stamp duty, which I have paid for 10 years in advance, and the sums I have contributed to the pension fund of the Royal Opera during my term of office, to be refunded to me on the same date by the accounts department of the Royal Theatre (. . .)[1]

---

[1] The rest of the letter is missing (o.e.).

V

HAMBURG
1891–1897

1891 continued

97. *To Friedrich Löhr†*

Undated. Hamburg, [September] *1891*

My dear Fritz,

Welcome home.—I wish I could see you at once, while you are still tanned by the southern sun! But alas, alas! We must wait at least nine months. (Don't you agree that's long enough to give one offspring? This joke is of course not intended for the family.)—I am homesick.

Many letters which I have begun writing to you—most of them dating from Budapest—are still in my folder.—I don't know how it's happened—but putting my thoughts into writing has become intolerable. So today I shall again confine myself to sending heartfelt greetings, from these foreign parts that, alas, will not release me as long as I live, to you at home, in the surroundings that you will have hailed with double joy after so long and unaccustomed a separation. One thing I want to know as soon as possible: what form your material life is to take on henceforth. (. . .)[1]

I have done a great deal of reading this year, and many of the books have made a lasting mark, indeed brought about a revolution—or rather, progressive development—in my view of the world and my attitude to life.—However, this is something I can only talk about when we meet.—

I hope to tell you a great deal about it in the summer.[2]

I hope, my dear Fritz, we are the same as we used to be—we cannot be different, can we, old man?—Has it never yet struck you that we have already seen the next generation growing up—the new ideas that we fought for having already become commonplaces—indeed, that we already have to fight the young in order to preserve what we have made our own?—Just think about it, and you

---

[1] A fairly long passage is here omitted for personal reasons (F.L.).
[2] Translators' note: Mahler actually writes 'in the summer this year'. [Like most musicians Mahler's 'year' corresponds with the concert season, i.e. from September to June (K.M.).]

Stadt-Theater.

Freitag, 27. März. 201. Ab.-Vorst. 28. Freitags-Vorst.
Mit Bewilligung des Hohen Senates.
Unter Mitwirkung des gesammten Opern-Personals.
Die Schöpfung.
Oratorium in 3 Abtheilungen von Joseph Haydn.
Gabriel: Fr. Brandt; Uriel: Hr. Cronberger;
Rafael: Hr. Lißmann; Adam: Hr. Ritter; Eva:
Fr. Lißmann.
Hierauf: **Solo-Gesangsvorträge**
von Fr. Heink, Fr. Brandt und Herrn Landau.
Preise der Plätze: 1. Rang, Parquet und
Parquetloge M. 4. 2. Rang Mittelloge u. 1. Parterre
M. 2.50. 2. Rang Seitenloge und Sitzparterre M. 2.
3. Rang Mitte M. 1.50. 3. Rang Seite M. 1.20.
Gallerie-Sitzplatz 75 ₰.
Anfang 7 Uhr. Ende nach 9½ Uhr.
Sonnabend, den 28. März: Keine Vorstellung.
Sonntag, den 29. März. 6. Extra-Vorstellung.
Bei gänzlich aufgehobenem Abonnement.
**Erstes Wiederauftreten des
Herrn Max Alvary nach seinem Urlaube.
Unter Leitung des Capellmeisters Herrn
Gustav Mahler von d. Kg. Oper in Budapest.
Tannhäuser,** gr. rom. Oper von R. Wagner.
Tannhäuser: Hr. Alvary; Elisabeth: Fr. Klafsky;
Landgraf: Hr. Wiegand; Venus: Fr. Brandt; Wolf-
ram: Hr. Lißmann; Hirt: Fr. Heink. Große Preise.
Montag, 30. März. 202. Ab.-Vorst. 30. Montags-Vorst.
**Unter Leitung des Capellmeisters Herrn
Gustav Mahler von d. Kg. Oper in Budapest.**
Zum 12. Male: **Cavalleria rusticana,**
(Sicilianische Liebesrache).
Oper in 1 Akt von Pietro Mascagni.
Santuzza: Fr. Brandt; Turiddu: Hr. Cronberger;
Lucia: Fr. Heink; Alfio: Hr. Greve; Lola: Frl. Gelber.
Hierauf: **Auftreten d. Herrn Heinrich Bötel.**
Der Postillon von Lonjumeau.
Kom. Oper von A. Adam.
Große Preise. Anfang 7 Uhr.
Dienstag, 31. März. 203. Ab.-Vorst. 30. Dienst.-Vorst.
**Auftreten des Herrn Max Alvary.
Unter Leitung des Capellmeisters Herrn
Gustav Mahler von d. Kgl. Oper in Budapest.
Siegfried,** in 3 Akten von R. Wagner.
Siegfried: Hr. Alvary; Brünnhilde: Fr. Klafsky;
Mime: Hr. Landau; Wanderer: Hr. Greve; Alberich:
Hr. Ritter; Fafner: Hr. Wiegand; Erda: Fr. Heink;
Stimme des Waldvogels: Fr. Brandt. Große Preise.

Fig 2. Mahler's first appearances in Hamburg, March 1891

will look around you in this fair world with as much head-shaking as I do when I sometimes stick my head out into it.

Now do write soon!

Affectionately your old

Gustav

I saw Heinrich and Rudolf this summer.

98. *To Heinrich Krzyzanowski* (Innsbruck)†

Undated. Hamburg [November] *1891*

Dear Heinrich,

You cannot imagine how glad I was to receive a sign of life from you!—Recently, in particular, I have had all sorts of worries about you.—I have had no news of you at all—I do not even know where to direct my thoughts and anxieties.—{I} hasten to assure you of one thing—that is, that my *feelings* towards you have not changed and that you can rely on me *in any situation.*—I also realize how hard it is, especially for you, to say to someone else: Help me! At the risk of offending you, you old snail completely withdrawn into your shell, I am now telling you to *let me know* and *count on* me *if* you do really need my help.

—I am afraid I cannot give a straight yes or no to your offer of an opera.[1] Send me your ideas and plans.—If I am stimulated, I shall joyfully set to work! —You do know I never set out 'to do something'—sometimes on my zigzag way through life, the threads of which we find incessantly becoming entangled, a sudden impulse throws me on to some course or other. That is when I 'do something'. Now that I have so many fairy-tales, songs and symphonies 'in my drawer', it is quite possible that I might suddenly find myself writing an opera—which then, of course, has every chance of being produced.

From your 'hint' I gather that I should have to give you an 'advance'.—My circumstances are very complicated. It would take too long to explain it all to you. I could not really make you an advance payment. Nor would that be appropriate between us.—It will be a heartfelt pleasure to share with you the little I have for my own needs—regardless of whether you write a libretto for me or not.—Do write, old fellow, and tell me how you are faring—*as soon as possible!*

—What takes you to *Innsbruck?* Would you not like to come up to Hamburg for a while? I can offer you a good bed, a proper desk and the indispensable bread-and-butter.

[1] See letter 99 (K.M.).

5*

Perhaps you can find some little cranny here through which you can slip into a suitable post.—But if you want to stay in Innsbruck and I can help you in some other way—money or books, etc.—let me know at once.

At any rate, do write now and tell me how you are getting on, what your plans are and what you need.

Ever yours, in haste,
Gustav Mahler

99. *To Friedrich Löhr*†

Undated. Hamburg, [28 November] *1891*

My dear Fritz,

Now, after writing so many letters to you in my head it is really time to send a written one.—

Now the second Christmas Eve is approaching that we shall spend far from each other—I no doubt alone again this time, as in that first year in Leipzig!— How much has happened since then, and how everything has changed! Only— strangely—I think—I have not changed at all.—Only there is now too much winter in me—if only spring would come again.

One thing I must tell you is that I have had a meagre sign of life from Heinrich in Innsbruck.[1]—He writes nothing at all about himself—but he offers to write a libretto for me—in barren words that merely {outline} the business aspect of such a collaboration.—I can see he's having a solitary struggle down there and fighting the very same penury that we all know so well.

Rudolf, as I learn from a laconic announcement of his, is engaged in Prague from the beginning of next year.[2] I cannot make out with any certainty whether in a leading position (as one of my successors) or not; but I hope so.

I wish from the bottom of my heart that the time were near when at long last Otto would have his examination and his year of military service behind him, so that this infinitely complicated process of providing money would become simpler for me;—it is beginning to wear me down and I long for the day when I am no longer obliged to earn so much money. Besides, it is very doubtful how much longer I shall be in a position to do so.

I should love to come to you for Christmas—I dare say I should have the time—but it would be too expensive.—In the Christmas month no big operas are done here—so I really can spend my time going for walks.—That would be

[1] See letter 98 (K.M.).
[2] R. Krzyzanowski was Karl Muck's successor as first Kapellmeister in Prague from 1892 to 1895 (o.e.).

by no means disagreeable if only one had the right companion. In that respect, as you will already have gathered, I'm pretty badly off here this year.

Yesterday I gave a big orchestral concert in Lübeck.[1] I enclose the programme, which, by the way, I should like you to pass on to Justi, since I cannot find the other one I had put aside for her.

Bülow[2] lives here, and I go to all his concerts; it is droll how he takes every opportunity of sensationally 'distinguishing' me *coram publico* in his abstruse fashion. At every fine passage he casts me coquettish glances (I sit in the front row).—He hands the scores of unknown works down to me from the dais so that I can read them during the performance.—The moment he catches sight of me he ostentatiously makes me a deep bow! Sometimes he addresses me from the dais, and so on.—Nevertheless my attempt to get him to conduct one of my works was a failure.—When I played my 'Todtenfeier'[3] to him, he became quite hysterical with horror, declaring that compared with my piece *Tristan* was a Haydn symphony, and went on like a madman.—

So you see I am myself beginning to believe: Either my stuff is abstruse nonsense—or——well! You can work it out and decide for yourself! I am getting tired of it!

Very best wishes and to Uda,

Yours,
Gustav

100.   *To Emil Freund* (Vienna)†

Undated. Hamburg [late Autumn 1891]

Dear Emil,

Thank you very much for your letter and the trouble you have gone to for me. I wrote to Spitz about the army tax[4]—unfortunately without thinking of you— and he informed me in a very off-hand manner that he would try an appeal, though he could not count on its being successful.—

My claim against Otto's capital on Justi's behalf does not seem to be making any progress either, and yet the matter is *more important* to me than you can imagine. Believe me, dear Emil, I shall sleep *far better* when this affair has been settled once and for all—do everything in your power.

---

[1] 27 November 1891. See also Notes (K.M.).
[2] Hans von Bülow (1830–94), German pianist and conductor, in charge of the Philharmonic Concerts which took place in the 'Convent Garten' in Hamburg (K.M.).
[3] At that time this was still Mahler's name for the first movement of his Second Symphony (o.e.).
[4] Mahler had to compensate for not doing military service (K.M.).

This Herr Dr. *Spitz* does not see to *anything whatsoever*.

What about that *mistake in the accounts* and the interest I was still supposed to get?—

I am simply furious about the way my lawyer persistently ignores my express wishes.—Please, Emil, press him for all you are worth and let me know what happens.

What you have gathered from my letters about my 'mood' is right enough.— I have been through so much in the last few weeks—without any evident material cause—the past has caught up with me—all I have lost—the loneliness of the present—all sorts of things—you know these moods of mine from earlier years—when I would be overcome by sadness even while among my friends— when I was still all youth, vigour and stamina—so you can well imagine how I spend these long, *lonely* afternoons and evenings here.—*No one* with whom I have anything in common—whether a share in the past or shared hopes for the future.—

Besides, in the last few weeks I have been reading something so remarkable and strange that it may very well have an *epoch-making* influence on my life.[1]— Perhaps we shall talk about it one of these days.—

Oh, anything, anything, but this eternal, eternal loneliness! It was there when I was up in Norway, roaming about for weeks on end without speaking a word to a living soul—and that after already having had my fill of keeping silence—and now back in this atmosphere in which I cannot get so much as a single breath of fresh air.

Don't show this letter to Justi! I do not need to tell you I should *gladly* make any sacrifice—but I assure you I cannot bear this much longer.—

—I have to economize here more than I have ever had to since Vienna.— Otto *must* take his examination this year!

He seems to be still pretty green.—

I was very pleased by what you wrote about Justi. Please write more often and tell me about *everything*!

Yours ever,
Gustav

---

[1] Friedrich Nietzsche (o.e.).

1892

101. *To Emil Freund†*

Undated. Hamburg, [Spring] *1892*
Bundesstrasse 10, III

Dear Emil,

I should have sent you the enclosed ages ago; you will see for yourself what you (or, as the case may be, I) have to do about it.—I should very much like to hear your views (actually I should have expected to hear them long before this) on the *Otto* developments and indeed in general. What ever was the matter with you that kept {you} confined to your room so long?! I hope you are quite all right now.

You can imagine the worries I have with this perpetual movement of the 'molecules' making up my family. Please do drop me a line soon.

Very best wishes, with regards to your Mama.

Yours ever,
Mahler

102. *To Arnold Berliner* (Hamburg)[1]†

Undated. Postmark: London, 9 [?] *June 1892*
69 Torrington Square W.C.[2]

Dear Berliner![3]

I shall only to give you the adresse of my residence, because I hope to hear by you upon your life and other circumstances in Hambourg [*sic*].

I myself am too tired and excited and not able to write a letter.

Only, that I found the circumstances of orchestra here bader than thought and the cast better than hoped.

Next Wednesday is the performance of *Siegfried* which God would bless.

Alvary: (*Siegfried*), Grengg: Wotan,[4]

---

[1] Letters 102 and 103 were both originally written in English by Mahler. See also Notes (K.M.).
[2] Between Gower Street and Woburn Square. The house no longer stands and there are University of London buildings on the site (K.M.).
[3] Translators' note: The exclamation mark after the addressee's name is merely German epistolary custom, with no emotional connotation.
[4] Max Alvary (1856–98), tenor, who came from Hamburg; Karl Greugg (1853–1904), baritone from Vienna (K.M.).

Sucher: Brünhilde, Lieban: Mime.[1]

This is the most splendid cast I yet heard, and this is my only trust in these very careful time.

Please to narrate me about all and am

yours,

Mahler

I make greater progress in English as you can observe in this letter.

103. *To Arnold Berliner†*

Undated. London, [9 June] *1892*

Bedford-Street [*sic*] S.O. [*sic*]

Postcard

Dear Berliner!

Siegfried—great success I am *myself* satisfied of the performance. *Orchestra: beautiful* [.] Singers: excellently—Audience: delighted and much thankfull.

Mittwoch:[2] *Tristan* (Sucher)

I am quite *done up*!

Yours,

Mahler

104. *To Arnold Berliner†*

Undated. London, [19 June] *1892*

Postcard

Dear B,

Now *Tristan* positively an even greater success.—Whole thing really capital. My position here: 'Star'! Poll.[3] very flexible: H.=O.[4] Wednesday *Rheingold*. Drop me a line again soon.

M

[1] Rosa Sucher (1849–1927), soprano, from Berlin; Julius Lieban (1857–1940), tenor, from Berlin (K.M.).

[2] Translators' note: i.e. Wednesday.

[3] Bernhard Pollini, director of the Hamburg Theatre (o.e.).

[4] To be read: H. equals nought. H. refers to Frau Schumann-Heink, whose outstanding gifts Mahler always acknowledged, but who often deliberately annoyed and exasperated him at rehearsals, though she was doubtless quite capable of appreciating his greatness. The equation seems to indicate that in London she gave Mahler no particular cause for annoyance (o.e.).

105. *To Arnold Berliner†*

Undated. London, [14 July] *1892*

Dear Berliner,

Yesterday at long last, after overcoming utterly incredible difficulties, *Götterdämmerung.*

Performances daily more mediocre—success all the greater!—'Me top again'!—On Saturday 23rd I leave here, going straight to *Berchtesgaden,* where I hope to see you.

What have you been doing all this time? How is 'Beethoven' getting on?[1]

A propos my performance of *Fidelio*—especially the *Leonora* overture[2] was violently attacked and condemned by half the critics here.—The audience, I must admit, gave me absolution for my blasphemy with a veritable *hurricane* of applause—indeed audiences here are positively overwhelming me with rapturous signs of approval. I actually have to take a bow after *every act*—the whole house keeps on yelling 'Mahler'—until I appear.—Hamburg papers are supposed to have said all sorts of things. Why don't you write me anything about it! Or are you too 'keeping accounts'—about letters and answers?

If you write a few lines by return, I shall still get them here.

Address: W.C. Alfredplace 22 [*sic*!]

Ever yours,
Mahler

106. *To Arnold Berliner†*

Undated. Postmark: Berlin, 27 August 1892

Dear Berliner,

On the point of leaving[3] I ran into Herr Bertram.[4] With chattering teeth he told me that he and several other members had cleared out—because of the terrible panic that had swept the city,[5] etc. etc.—

For the last fortnight I have been suffering from an acute intestinal infection, so I am seriously considering whether, in the circumstances, it would be

---

[1] See Notes.
[2] *Fidelio* was performed twice in London: on 2 and 20 July (K.M.). Mahler had introduced the *Leonora* Overture no. 3 immediately before the last scene, i.e. during the scene-shifting. Previously the Overture had always been played before the opening of Act II (o.e.). [According to contemporary reviews *Leonora* no. 3 was played between the acts (K.M.).]
[3] Returning to Hamburg at the end of his holidays (o.e.).
[4] Theodor Bertram (1869–1907), baritone at the Hamburg Opera during the 1891–2 season, who later joined Mahler in Vienna. He committed suicide in Bayreuth in 1907 (K.M.).
[5] The cholera epidemic in Hamburg (o.e.).

advisable to stay away from Hamburg a few days longer until my condition has somewhat improved. Please *telegraph me express immediately* at my expense, giving me your detailed advice—*all responsibility resting on me*! Your telegram would have to reach me by midday, so that I could still arrange to leave, which might well have to be that afternoon.

How are you? Are you unworried?

Kind regards and thanks,

Yours sincerely,
Gustav Mahler

107. *To Arnold Berliner*†

Undated. Berlin-W[ilmersdorf], *29 August 1892*
Kurfürstendamm 148

(. . .) Everything in life is somehow connected with everything else, and so now I link my lunch-hour by gaslight with Feld at that frightful old Hotel Royal[1] with a cosy chat over coffee with Lö-, Li- and Rosenfeld[2] in the sunshine on that verandah you doubtless know so well.—We are all amazed and delighted by your courage and far less concerned about ourselves than the times and circumstances would dictate.—I accept your invitation to stay with you in Uhlenhorst[3] for some time immediately after my return (about 10 September).

Today I hope to be introduced to your sister here, and tonight I chug off to Berchtesgaden again.—My sister seems to be almost beside herself with fear. Today she sent a telegram to Kapellmeister Frank, but in the end I managed to get hold of it.

Kindest regards,
Yours sincerely,
Mahler

---

[1] A small hotel (long since demolished) in Hamburg (Hohe Bleichen), where Mahler lodged during the 1891-2 season and where he made Berliner's acquaintance over lunch, the introduction being performed by the conductor, Leo Feld, of the Stadttheater (o.e.).

[2] Löwenfeld, Lilienfeld, Rosenfeld—three participants in the coffee-session. [Raphael] Löwenfeld later [1894] founded the Neues Schiller Theatre in Berlin (o.e.).

[3] Translators' note: A fashionable residential district on the Aussen-Alster, some distance from the inner city of Hamburg.

108. *To Friedrich Löhr* (Vienna)†

Undated. Berchtesgaden, [September] *1892*

Dearest Fritz,

Above all—regarding the first part of your letter—do not let it worry you; I have arranged everything with Justi; so do not bother about it any more.

In Munich I spent two days with Heinrich and some time with Gustl and Marie.—As you know, these are things one can only give an account of by word of mouth. (. . .)[1]

This dreadful thing in Hamburg! It is terrible. I do not yet know how much of it I shall have to contend with! The theatre opens again on the 16th—I have not yet made up my mind! Shall I go or not?—Well, that is a bridge I shall cross when I come to it (i.e. on the 16th)!

What a pity we have not yet managed to find a little time to be together! Could you not perhaps just manage to make it possible—somehow? Perhaps we could meet in Salzburg and spend a day together there! Think it over, old man!

Here, **always raining**—but we put up with it cheerfully, trudging around, urged on by **never failing impuls**[2] of our dear, merry old Natalie![3]

It really is a trial looking after Justi—she is always collapsing, she seems simply incapable of developing into a normal being.[4]

My greetings to Uda. Let me know instantly about the above!

Ever yours,
Gustav

109. *To Arnold Berliner*

Undated. Postmark: Berchtesgaden, 4 September 1892
Postcard

Dear Berliner,

Here I am again and here I shall spend this holiday that has been so harshly thrust upon me.—I shall, God willing, be back in Hamburg on the 12th.[5] If the epidemic has not died down by then, I shall gladly accept your invitation to

[1] What followed has nevertheless been omitted for reasons of discretion (F.L.).
[2] Words in bold type in the letters in English in the original (K.M.).
[3] Natalie Bauer-Lechner (o.e.).
[4] Justine Mahler had not recovered from the strain of nursing her parents (o.e.).
[5] Mahler did not return until the beginning of October, and he conducted his first opera performance of the season on 5 October (K.M.).

stay with you out in Uhlenhorst. Please let me know how you are getting on and what the situation is up there.

> Yours sincerely,
> Mahler

110. *To Emil Freund* (Vienna)

> Hamburg, 28 October 1892

Dear Emil,

You can imagine how worried I am.[1] Please see that Justi does not stay up at night, on any account. You *must* get a nurse.

Write every day, at least a postcard.

> In haste,
> Ever
> Mahler

111. *To Friedrich Löhr†*

> *Undated. Hamburg,* [December 1892]

Dearest Fritz,

I was overjoyed to hear from you again, old friend!—How I wish I had time to reply! But Bülow has just approached me again, for the third time, asking me to conduct his third subscription concert! This time it will probably work out, and I shall have to rush head over heels to learn it by heart!

If only I hadn't so many worries—with a cooler head I would easily be a match for Bülow!

So for today no more than my very best wishes—you are right, we must send short messages to each other every now and again—after all, many small strands can in the end be twisted into a rope—and many a prisoner has escaped from his dungeon by means of such a rope.

> Yours,
> Gustav

---

[1] The elder of Mahler's two younger brothers [i.e. Alois] was in bed with pneumonia at his sisters' house [in Vienna, Barthensteingasse 3] (o.e.).

1893

112. *To Gisella Tolney-Witt* (Budapest)†

[Hamburg] 7 February 1893

Dear Fräulein Tolney-Witt,

Although I am not easily persuaded to enter into 'correspondence', and my best friends bemoan my habits in this respect, there is a question in your letter that provokes an answer from me: 'why such a large apparatus as an orchestra should be necessary in order to express a great thought.' But there are a number of things I must say first if I am to make it clear to you how I see this problem.

You seem to have explored musical literature somewhat, and I assume that you are not unacquainted with very early and early music, up to the time of Bach. Have you not then been struck by two things?

First: that the further back you go in time, the more elementary the terms relating to performance are, i.e. the more the composers leave the interpretation of their thought to the performers—for instance in Bach's work it is very rare to find the tempo indicated, or indeed any other hint of how he intends the work to be performed—there are not even such crude distinctions as *p* or *ff* etc. (Wherever you do find them, they are usually put in by the editors, and mostly wrong, at that.)

Secondly: the more music evolves, the more complex the apparatus becomes —the apparatus that the composer produces in order to express his ideas. Just try comparing the orchestra that Haydn uses in his symphonies (i.e. it was not the way we see it at Philharmonic Concerts at the Redoute[1]—for many more instruments have been added, perhaps half of them) with the orchestra that Beethoven requires for his Ninth. To say nothing at all of Wagner and modern composers. What is the reason for this?—Can you suppose such a thing to be *accidental* or even an *unnecessary* extravagance, the result of mere whim, on the composer's part?

Now I will give you my view of the matter: in its beginnings music was merely 'chamber music', i.e. intended to be played in a small space before a small audience (often consisting only of those involved in the work). The feelings intrinsic to it were, in keeping with the time, *simple*, naïve, reproducing emotional experience only in bare outline: joy, sadness, etc. The musicians were confident that they knew their business, they moved within a familiar field of ideas, and on the grounds of clearly delimited skill, well grounded within

[1] The Redoutensaal in Budapest (K.M.).

these limits! Therefore the composers made no prescriptions—it was taken for granted that everything would be rightly seen, felt and heard. There were scarcely any 'amateurs' (Frederick the Great and others were, I am convinced, very rare cases). The noble and rich simply had paid performers, who had learnt their trade, to amuse them by playing to them in their chambers. That is why the compositions were not maltreated by lack of understanding! Usually, indeed, composers and musicians will have been one and the same person.

Within the Church, which was of course the chief domain of this art and whence it had come, everything was precisely ordained in advance by ritual. In short, the composers did not need to fear being misunderstood, and contented themselves with sketchy writings for their own use—without giving special thought to the fact that others would have to interpret them or might even interpret them wrongly.

In the course of time, however, they seem to have had such bad experiences that they began to concern themselves with making sure the performer had unambiguous directions as to their intentions. So a great system of sign-language gradually evolved, which—like the heads of notes indicating pitch—provided a definite reference for duration or volume. Together with this, moreover, came the *appropriation of new elements of feeling* as objects of imitation in sounds—i.e. the composer began to relate ever deeper and more complex aspects of his emotional life to the area of his creativeness—until with Beethoven the *new era* of music began: from now on the *fundamentals* are no longer mood—that is to say, mere sadness, etc.—but also the transition from one to the other —conflicts—physical nature and its effect on us—humour and poetic ideas—all these become objects of musical imitation.

Now not even quite complicated signs suffice—instead of requiring a single instrument to produce such a rich palette of colours (as Herr Aug. Beer[1] would say), the composer took one instrument for each colour (the analogy is apparent in the word 'tone-colour'). It was out of this need that the modern, the 'Wagnerian' orchestra gradually came into being.

Thirdly, I would now mention only one thing more, the physical necessity to enlarge the musical apparatus: music was becoming more and more common property—the listeners and the players becoming ever more numerous—in place of the chamber there came the concert hall, and from the church, with its *new* instrument, the organ, the opera-house evolved. So you see, if I may sum it up once more: We moderns need such a great apparatus in order to express *our* ideas, whether they be great or small. First—because we are compelled, in order to protect ourselves from false interpretation, to distribute the various colours of our rainbow over various palettes; secondly, because our eye is

[1] A noted critic for the Budapest newspaper *Pester Lloyd* (K.M.).

learning to distinguish more and more colours in the rainbow, and ever more delicate and subtle modulation; thirdly, because in order to be heard by many in our over-large concert halls and opera-houses we also have to make a loud noise.

Now perhaps you will object, as women will, being almost never convinced, at the most persuaded: 'Well, does that mean that Bach was less than Beethoven or that Wagner is greater than he?'—in reply to which I will tell you, you little 'tormenting spirit' (really a tormenting spirit, for I have been tormenting myself with this letter for almost an hour now)—in order to answer this question you must apply to One who can behold man's entire history at a single glance. We are the way we are! We 'moderns'. You too are that way! Supposing I now prove to you that you, little tormenting spirit, demand a greater apparatus for your life than the Queen of England did in the seventeenth century, she having breakfasted, as I read recently, on a pound of bacon and a tankard of beer, and having whiled away the tedium of her evenings in her boudoir by spinning, or the like, by the light of a tallow candle? What do you say now?—Away, then, with the piano! away with the violin! which are good for the 'chamber' when you are alone, or with some good companion, wishing to call the great masters' works to mind—as good, as a recollection, as, say, an engraving is as a reminder of the brilliantly colourful paintings of a Raphael or a Böcklin[1]—I hope I make my meaning clear to you—in which case I shall not be vexed at having devoted an hour of my life to you, who have shown such lovable trust in a stranger.

And now, since this letter has grown so long, I should be glad to know that I have not written it in vain, wherefore I ask you to let me know whether it reaches you safely.

With best wishes,
Gustav Mahler

113. *To Friedrich Löhr*

Hamburg, 18 May 1893

Dear Fritz,

There is nothing for it—you must come and spend at least a few days with me at the Attersee![2]—Perhaps I shall come to Vienna—but I cannot yet say for certain.

---

[1] Arnold Böcklin (1827–1901) (K.M.).
[2] A lake in Upper-Austria; Steinbach is situated on the eastern shore. Mahler spent the following three summer holidays there (K.M.).

Justi is here, taking up all one's attention as usual—so you must make do without a letter. Besides, you still 'owe' me an answer to my last.[1]

Write about the above matter.

Affectionate greetings to Uda.

> Yours ever,
> Gustav

114. *To Friedrich Löhr*†

> *Undated. Postmark: Berlin, 16 June 1893*
> *Postcard*

Dear Fr.,

We shall arrive about 10.00 p.m. tomorrow evening (Saturday the 17th) at the North-Western station. Please meet us at the station. Otto will also be there, to take Justi to Nina.[2]

> Yours,
> Gustav

115. *To Arnold Berliner*†

> [Steinbach] 21 June 1893

Dear Berliner,

Well, here we are, and it is splendid! You will be delighted when you come here in August! I have read in several newspapers including the *Hamburger Fremdenblatt*, that I have been engaged to go to *Boston*.

For various reasons it is *extremely important* that this report should be *denied*. Please be so kind as to have this done in the Hamburg and, if possible, also in the Berlin papers. The *démenti* should be quite brief, *without any further remarks*.

What do you think of the elections?[3] I thought about you! I have no news at all! I take to this life here like a duck to water. Please write *immediately* letting me know if you have been able to do anything in this matter and, if so, what. Do come *as soon as possible*!

My sister sends her regards and I mine.

> Yours,
> Mahler

Address: Steinbach am Attersee, Salzkammergut.

---

[1] No longer extant (F.L.).
[2] Frau Nina Hoffmann-Matscheko (1844–1914), wife of the painter Josef Hoffmann (o.e.).
[3] The election to the German Reichstag on 15 June. See also Notes (K.M.).

116. *To Friedrich Löhr*†

Undated. Postmark: Steinbach am Attersee, 4 July 1893
Postcard

Dear Fr.,

So it's **all right**! I shall expect you here on Saturday the 8th.—Please give me the exact time, so that I can meet you.

Yours,

G

1894

117. *To Arnold Berliner*†

Undated. Postmark: Hamburg, 30 April 1894

Dear Berliner,

I am sorry I offended you with my vehemence yesterday, and herewith apologize in case it is necessary. But you have a singular gift for driving me into outbursts.[1] This is really a case of p=qu. No reply yet from Weimar,[2] a bad sign.

Best wishes,
Yours sincerely,
Mahler

118. *To [Otto Lessmann* (Berlin)]†

[Hamburg] 15 May 1894

Dear Sir,

Please accept my warmest thanks for your kind offer.—It is, however, scarcely my intention to confuse a concert audience with musicological remarks —for it seems to me that that is just what would be achieved by giving them 'programme notes', forcing them to *read* instead of *listening*.

Certainly I think it necessary that the thematic patterns should be clear to every listener. But do you really believe that, with a modern work, making them

[1] There had been an argument about vivisection, Mahler supporting Richard Wagner's [opposing] view, Berliner disagreeing (o.e.).
[2] About acceptance of Mahler's First Symphony for performance in Weimar (o.e.).

acquainted with a few themes will suffice?—One can only know and appreciate a piece of music by making a *thorough* study of it, and the profounder the work, the harder this is and the longer it takes.—At a first performance, on the other hand, it is important for the listener to surrender himself to the work unreservedly, allowing its general human and poetic quality to make an impression on him; and if he then feels attracted by it, he should then go into it in more detail. But how does he set about it if it is the *man* he seeks to know, who is, after all, profounder and even better than his work? Where are the programme notes for that? What has to be done in that case too is to give plenty of time to him, attentively and lovingly endeavouring to understand his innermost being! Admittedly he grows and he undergoes transformations, whereas the work always remains the same.—But analogies are always lame.

Again, my warmest thanks. I look forward to seeing you soon in Weimar. I remain, in great haste,

Yours very truly,
Gustav Mahler

119. *To Friedrich Löhr*†

Undated. Hamburg, [Spring 1894]

My dear Fritz,

Just received your note.—Unless I sit down at once and at least answer your question I shall not get round to it for some time—for such a rusty old cart as our 'correspondence' is easier to set creaking than moving.

Here goes: I am not yet included in the great constellation of the planets. Several agents have in fact 'proposed' that I should 'accept' Richter's[1] post—but that is so much hot air. These gentry are making proposals without having been empowered to do so.—I believe you hit the nail on the head with your *reservatio.* The situation in the world being what it now is, the fact that I am Jewish prevents my getting taken on in any Court theatre.—Neither Vienna, nor Berlin, nor Dresden, nor Munich is open to me. The same wind is now blowing everywhere. In my present peculiar (by no means melancholy) state of mind it does not really upset me.—Believe me, German artistic life the way it is at present holds no more attractions for me. In the last analysis it is always the same hypocritical, corrupt, dishonest behaviour wherever one turns. Supposing I came to Vienna! How would I be treated in Vienna, with my way of going about things? I should only need to try once to convey my interpretation of one

---

[1] Hans Richter, conductor at the Vienna Court Opera and of the Philharmonic Orchestra (K.M.).

of Beethoven's symphonies to the famous Philharmonic Orchestra,[1] trained as it has been by the honest Hans,[2] to be involved forthwith in the most repulsive dog-fight. Haven't I had the same experience even here, where I hold undisputed sway by virtue of Brahms's and Bülow's utterly unqualified championship of me.

What a storm I bring down on my head whenever I depart from normal routine and try out some idea of my own.—I have only one desire: to work amid simple, ingenuous people in some small town where there are no 'traditions' and no guardians of 'the eternal laws of beauty', to my own satisfaction and that of a small select circle who can follow me.—If at all possible, no theatre and no 'repertoire'! But, of course, for as long as I must pant along after my precious brothers, always so daringly taking wing, and till my sisters are tolerably provided for, I have to continue my lucrative bread-winning artistic activity.

After all, I must count myself lucky in comparison with you, poor fellow, whom life has driven into a far tighter corner, subjecting you to the base demands of every day.—How deeply I feel that! I hear from Heinrich[3] now and again—things are going as badly as ever with him.

We must meet again this summer. At any rate you must come to stay at the Attersee with me! Perhaps I shall come to Vienna!

But it is still too early to make plans.

Brahm,[4] who won my unreserved admiration with his *Schiller*, which you can have from Justi, has become the director of a Berlin theatre! What a loss! He doesn't know what he is doing, either! But he'll be all finished with writing books! He is a splendid fellow, really intelligent.—Do not think I am in a 'bad mood'! On the contrary—I have achieved a kind of fatalism, which finally makes me regard my own life, whatever turn it may take, with a certain 'interest'—and even enjoy it. I have come to like the world more and more! {I} am 'devouring' an increasing number of books! They are, after all, the only friends I keep by me! And what friends! Heavens, if I had no books! I forget everything round about me whenever a voice from 'one of us' reaches me! They become ever more familiar and more of a consolation to me, my real brothers and fathers and lovers.

My very best wishes to yourself and Uda, and do write,

Yours,

Gustav

---

[1] The Vienna Philharmonic Orchestra (K.M.).
[2] Hans Richter (K.M.).
[3] Heinrich Krzyzanowski (K.M.).
[4] Otto Brahm (1856–1912), German actor and theatre director (K.M.).

120. *To Arnold Berliner*†

Weimar. 5 June 1894
Hotel Erbprinz

Dear Berliner,

By the same mail I am sending you two packages: my symphony,[1] i.e. the orchestral parts, and—my tailcoat and top-hat. Both to be kept for me. Please do acknowledge receipt—just a postcard to Steinbach am Attersee, Upper Austria, so that I know they have arrived safely. My experiences here can be summarized as follows: Humperdinck's *Hänsel und Gretel* is a *masterpiece*, and I treasure it as a delightful addition to dramatic literature. My symphony was received with a mixture of furious disapproval and wildest applause.—It is amusing to hear the clash of opinions in the street and in drawing-rooms.— Well, when the dogs bark, we know we are in the saddle! 'Me top again'! (at least in my own view, which will, however, scarcely be shared by more than a select few).—

His Serene Highness, Her Serene Highness, Their Serene Highnesses, were extremely gracious—also in the provision of excellent canapés and champagne.

Performance, after utterly inadequate rehearsal, extremely shoddy.— Orchestra retrospectively extremely satisfied with symphony as result of barrel of free beer, also their affections won by my style of conducting. My brother was there—extremely satisfied with demi-failure[2]—myself ditto with demi-success!

If you happen to see any reviews (*Voss*, etc.,[3]) please send them on to me in Steinbach.

I shall be going back there tomorrow!

With all good wishes,

Yours sincerely,
Gustav Mahler

121. *To Friedrich Löhr*†

Steinbach am Attersee, 29 June 1894
Postcard

Dear Fritz,

Beg to report safe delivery of a strong, healthy last movement to my Second.

[1] Mahler's First (o.e.).
[2] Otto Mahler had said that if the symphony turned out a success, that would simply prove it was no good (o.e.).
[3] The Berlin *Vossische Zeitung* whose music critic was Dr. Karl Krebs (K.M.).

Father and child both doing as well as can be expected—the latter not yet out of danger.

At the baptismal ceremony it was given the name 'Lux lucet in tenebris'.[1] Silent sympathy is requested. Floral tributes are declined with thanks. Other presents, however, are acceptable.

Yours,
Gustav

These are my birthday greetings to you!

122. *To Arnold Berliner*†

Undated. Steinbach, 10 July 1894

Dear Berliner,

I have just been reading *Eckermann*[2] and must copy out for you the following words of Goethe's, in remembrance of the excursion we made into aesthetics that night.

What *Goethe* says on the *meaning of the terms Classical and Romantic* is this: 'What is Classical I call healthy, what is Romantic sick.—Most modern work is Romantic not because it is modern but because it is weak, sickly and ill, and old work is not Classical because it is old but because it is strong, fresh, joyful and healthy.—If we distinguish Classical and Romantic by these criteria, the situation is soon clarified.' Eckermann's *Conversations*, Part II, page 63 (Brockhaus [Pub., Frankfurt/M,] 1876). The inner connection between my argument and Goethe's should be obvious.—At any rate something different from the nauseating platitudes one finds in encyclopedias.—

I am of course hard at work. The fifth movement is grandiose, concluding with a chorus for which I have written the words myself.[3]

Strictly in confidence between the two of us (the *whole* piece of news).—

The sketch is complete down to the last detail and I am just completing the score.—It is a *bold* work, *majestic* in structure. The final climax is colossal. At the beginning of *August* I shall be in Bayreuth. In Ischl I ran into *Brahms*. He was very interesting, I'll tell you about it when we meet. Birrenkoven[4] is causing quite a stir in Bayreuth, Cosima and the others not having had to do

---

[1] 'The light shineth in the darkness' (K.M.).
[2] Translators' note: Goethe's Boswell, as it were.
[3] The Second Symphony (o.e.).
[4] Willy Birrenkoven (1865–1955), German tenor, with the Hamburg Opera from 1893 to 1912. At the Bayreuth Festival he sang Lohengrin and Parsifal, alternating with Ernest van Dyck. See also Notes (K.M.).

anything more with him. By the way, *he* is singing in the opening performance, *not* Van Dyk! [*sic*]
  Do write!

Yours sincerely,
Mahler

123. *To Emil Freund*†

Undated. Steinbach am Attersee, Summer 1894?

Dear Emil,
  Many thanks for your message and all the trouble you have taken!
  I shall be here until 20 *August* and hope you will *really* come for a few days.—
  Please do *not* use the *money* in the way you suggest, but send it to my *bank* in Budapest as soon as you receive it, first having deducted 500 florins and giving them to old L.,[1] who has just asked me to lend him that sum. He will pay it back in September. It does not really matter to me when he repays, you can arrange that to suit *him*. Please send a line to say what you arrange and *when* you are coming.

Ever yours,
Mahler

124. *To Arnold Berliner*

Steinbach, 25 July 1894

Dear Berliner,
  Tomorrow I leave here for Bayreuth.—I can stay there only until 4 August at the latest, the very day you named as that of your arrival! Being very keen to spend at least one or two days with you and the *Behns*,[2] I herewith submit a humble application (which you are requested to convey forthwith to our friends as well) that you should make your departure from Hamburg somewhat earlier in order to arrive in Bayreuth on 3 August at the very latest. From there I shall send you my address, and then you can let me know when you are arriving. If I can, I shall meet you at the station; if not, I shall leave a note at your hotel saying where and when we can meet. Well then, until we meet, *au revoir*!

[1] Probably a reference to Siegfried Lipiner (K.M.).
[2] Hermann Behn (1859–1927), who lived in Hamburg, was well known for his brilliant adaptations for two pianos of classical and modern works; his arrangement of Mahler's Second Symphony was published in December 1895 (o.e. + K.M.).

Please give the *Behns* my *kindest regards* and be sure you come in good time!

Yours sincerely,

Mahler

The last movement (score) of the Second Symphony is finished! It is the most important thing I have done yet.

125. *To Friedrich Löhr*†

Undated. Postmark: *Steinbach, 19 August 1894*

Dear F.,

I arrive in Vienna at approximately 5.30 on Tuesday and should like you to pay us a visit between 8.00 and 9.00 that evening in the Igel[1] on the Wildpretmarkt (ground floor).—Shall be spending Wednesday and Thursday in Vienna and should like you to keep a full day if possible, at least an afternoon anyway—besides every night—free for me—

Yours,

G

126. *To Arnold Berliner*†

Undated. Postmark: *Hamburg, 19 October 1894*

Dear Berliner,

I cannot find it in me to write to Wolff[2] about your concert ticket and shall wait until he comes, which, so far as I know, should be within the next few days.—But then I shall instantly tackle the matter and if possible squeeze out of him a *free* pass to all his concerts.—Yesterday I had the *first rehearsal.*[3] It goes tolerably. Unfortunately there are a few *Marweges*[4] there again—headed by Herr *Bignell*,[5] who seems to mourn the passing of the purity of the classical principle.—But let's forget it! Do send a line soon! Did you hear *Hänsel und Gretel* at the Opera-House? and Strauss?[6]

Yours sincerely,

Mahler

[1] Der rote Igel (The Red Hedgehog) was a well-known public house in Vienna, often frequented by Brahms amongst others (K.M.).
[2] Herrmann Wolf (1845–1902), concert agent in Berlin. See also Notes (K.M.).
[3] For Mahler's first Philharmonic Concert on 22 October 1894 (K.M.).
[4] Friedrich Marwege (1841–191?), first violin when Mahler conducted one of the 'Bülow concerts', was outraged by Mahler's tempi, phrasing, etc. (o.e.).
[5] Robert Bignell, first violin, later conductor of his own string orchestra (K.M.).
[6] Richard Strauss had just been appointed conductor of the Berlin Philharmonic Orchestra, and had opened the season on 15 October 1894 (K.M.).

1895

127. *To Arnold Berliner*

Undated. Postmark: Hamburg, 31 January 1895

Dear Berliner,

I have just heard from Fr. Michaels that you are 'beside yourself' because I did not long ago tell you my Second is to be played in Berlin.[1]

Look, how do I know it really is going to be? Strauss did 'accept' it in a few non-committal words. But I am by no means convinced he is really going to do it.—If he does, you will get your information from the newspapers, just as I shall.—In that event I shall go myself, and we shall spend a few days together.—

My sister wrote and told you that I recently rehearsed the first three movements here.—

The effect is so great that one cannot describe it!—If I were to say what I think of this great work it would sound too arrogant in a letter.—But for me there is no doubt whatsoever that it enlarges the *fundus instructus* of mankind.

The whole thing sounds as though it came to us from some other world. And—I think there is *no one* who can resist it.—One is battered to the ground and then raised on angels' wings to the highest heights.—In these last few days I have known 'many a fate'—more of that (perhaps) when we meet!

Ever yours,
Mahler

128 *To Emil Freund*

Undated. Hamburg, 18 February 1895

Dear Emil,

On 4 March my Second Symphony is to be played at the Berlin Philharmonic Concert. If you are free and want to come to this première, you are cordially invited to be there. Natalie Bauer L. is also coming. But if you mean to come, let me know at once, so that I can have a good seat reserved for you. I ought long ago to have thanked you for your loyal help, but recently I have been so overworked that I have hardly had time to eat.

Hoping to see you in Berlin—more news then.

Yours ever,
Gustav

[1] Strauss had invited Mahler to conduct the first three movements from his Second Symphony at the 9th Philharmonic Concert on 4 March 1895 (K.M.).

129. *To Oskar Eichberg* (Berlin)

Hamburg, 30 March 1895
Parkallee 12.III

Dear Sir,

I only now find leisure to write a few inadequate words of gratitude for two kindnesses you have shown me, kindnesses of inestimable value to me. The first is your attitude to my work after my début in Berlin, and the understanding you showed in your judgement of it.—If henceforth I attain any degree of recognition in musical circles as a composer, it is you alone I have to thank for it.[1] The second—which matters to me far more—is the fact of having actually encountered sympathy for and understanding of my endeavours. If you could know my Calvary as a creative artist, if you could behold the ten years of continual repulse, disappointment and humiliation—having to shut away in a drawer work after work as each was completed, and, whenever, surmounting all obstacles, I succeeded in finding a public, it was only to meet with incomprehension—only then could you fully appreciate how heartfelt my gratitude to you is, and this, I think, is the reason for my long delay in writing.—I feel that such gratitude cannot be expressed in words.—If you do not think it sounds too arrogant, I should like to say: I feel confident that some day I shall be better able to do it: when I can point to the man who was the *first* and *only one*, of all those who were qualified to do so, who felt and understood what language was being uttered and what roads taken; and who, finally, proclaimed and testified to it in times that demanded *all* of a man's courage, faced with a flood of hostility and scorn.—Believe me, dear Herr Eichberg, *I needed* this experience in order to stand my ground and go on with my work.—I am now 34 years old and, *à la* Quintus Fixlein,[2] have written a small library, the 'readers' of which are still confined to my closest friends. Wings that are again and again paralysed can but fail at last. Now, perhaps, you will realize what it is I have to thank you for.

Please continue to take the sympathetic interest in my work that you have shown, and believe me when I say that I shall never forget what I owe you.

In deep obligation I am,
Yours faithfully,
Gustav Mahler

---

[1] Oskar Eichberg, music critic of the *Berliner Börsen Courier*, had written a favourable review of Mahler's Second Symphony (K.M.).
[2] Translators' note: The hero of a narrative work by Jean Paul.

130. *To Oskar Bie* (Berlin)

Hamburg, 3 April 1895
Parkallee 12. III

Dear Sir,

Only today do I find time to express my very deep gratitude for your warmly appreciative words about my work[1] and also for sending me the latest number of your journal,[2] in which those words are published. I was sincerely moved by the manner in which you gave my work notice.—

If you will not think it immodest of me, I shall venture to say that in your words I have found an intuitive awareness of the roads I had taken and the goals I had striven towards. I shall look forward to an opportunity of discussing the matter with you in greater detail.—

How much I regret having been able to offer no more than the exposition of a work to a man such as yourself—for exposition is what these three movements are, as you will scarcely have failed to realize.

What satisfaction I felt, how important, indeed how *necessary* it was to me, after so much misunderstanding and narrow-mindedness, to hear the voice of one who saw and understood, you will easily comprehend when I tell you that this was the first approval and encouragement I had received in all of ten years.

How paralysing it is, this continual tilting against windmills!—

I have long given up expecting any understanding from my 'colleagues'. I feel that those who will some day follow me are not to be found where music and the like is 'made'.

My music is 'lived'. What attitude should those take to it who do *not* 'live', who feel no breath of the rushing gale of our great epoch?—

I hope you will allow me to call on you when, before long, I pass through Berlin. I feel that within a few hours we should get to know each other much better.

Once again my cordial thanks, to which I add the plea that you will continue to manifest your kind interest in me.

Ever your most devoted
Gustav Mahler

---

[1] The Second Symphony, movements 1–3 (o.e.).
[2] The March issue of the magazine *Neue deutsche Rundschau* (Berlin, S. Fischer Verlag), containing an article, 'Kunst und Theater', by Professor Bie, discussing Mahler's work (o.e. + K.M.).

131. *To Friedrich Löhr†*

Undated. Hamburg, [Spring] *1895*

Dear Fritz,

The enclosed letter from (. . .) is the latest instalment (just arrived) in a correspondence that has again sprung up between (. . .) and myself.[1] This time, however (mainly as the result of a very seriously meant epistle, the completely unlyrical style of which is thoroughly characteristic of (. . .)), the intercourse has taken a more human turn, culminating in the enclosed letter.—

There's not much I can do for him here! Of course, I shall try everything! But I have too few contacts in that quarter. So it has occurred to me that in Vienna (Lipiner or someone like him) perhaps something could be done for him (Nina M.[2]—etc. etc. Spiegler).—Please, dear Fritz, do take the matter in hand. Spare no pains and do not let refusals dishearten you! Take his letter and mine to people you can show them to. Get something done for the poor chap. (. . .)

I last saw him in the summer (on my way back to Hamburg) (. . .) he seems to have been just in the midst of the crisis! 'The world' and 'life' have got him down. (. . .) All he wants is enough to live on, somehow! N.B. His needs are very modest, and I shall myself always be happy to make some small contribution to his upkeep.

I write in haste, but must just add that it is my most ardent desire that the 'correspondence in instalments', which you began so promisingly, should not lapse straight after the first instalment.

Begin somewhere—just plunge in—wherever you happen to be at the moment will do.

Yours ever,

Gustav

[Postscript above the letter heading] Please let me know something about (. . .) as soon as possible. Dash, dash around! Spare no pains! Get Natalie[3] to help you!

132. *To Arnold Berliner*

Undated. Postmark: Hamburg, *11 May 1895*

Dear Berliner,

Very many thanks for your 'prompt' package. The Behns have not yet arrived. Meanwhile I am residing quite happily in the Oberstrasse.

[1] This letter is almost certainly about Heinrich Krzyzanowski whose situation had become very precarious. See also next letter as well as Löhr's Note (K.M.).

[2] Nina Matscheko-Hoffmann (K.M.).

[3] Natalie Bauer-Lechner (K.M.).

I only today received (. . .)'s reply to my parcel and letter. I was deeply touched more by what was passed over in silence in his reply than by {what} was said. It is really high time something was done for the poor fellow. You would certainly seem to be best able to do something, with your academic contacts; I am really quite cut off from the world. (. . .) is now at the stage where one is ready to snatch at *anything*, and indeed there is hardly any type of job he would not accept so long as it brings him in some kind of living. Until then our monthly allowances should completely cover his extremely modest needs.

Please do something, and let me know as soon as you know anything definite.

I am deeply obliged to Professor Neisser;[1] I am almost ashamed of putting him to trouble. On 31 May I arrive in Berlin! I hope to see you before you leave. There is something very *interesting* I have still to tell you.

                                        In haste, ever yours,
                                        Mahler

133. *To Friedrich Löhr*

                              Undated. Postmark: Vienna, 2 June 1895
                                              Pneumatic postcard

Dear Fritz,

Just arrived in Vienna. Please stay at home! I shall be coming round to see you in the next few hours, and then we can work out the rest.

What I should like best is to spend this afternoon and evening alone with you.

                                        Yours ever,
                                        Gustav

134. *To Friedrich Löhr*

                          Undated. Postmark: Steinbach, 17 August 1895
                                                      Postcard

Dear Fr.,

Sorry, I can't come to see you—I have to leave tomorrow.—This summer has produced my Third—probably the most mature and individual thing I have done so far.

I shall send you the title on a second postcard.[2] I am eager to know what impression you gain simply from reading the title—i.e. whether I have suc-

---

[1]Geheimrat Albert Neisser, a dermatologist in Breslau. See letters 344 and 346 (K.M.).
[2]See letter 137 (F.L.).

ceeded in setting the reader on the road along which I want to travel with
him.—Please send me your impressions at once—to Bismarckstrasse 86,
Hamburg.

Yours ever,
Gustav

135. *To Arnold Berliner*

Undated. Postmark: Steinbach, 17 August 1895

Dear Berliner,
    In the next few days—probably on *Thursday*[1] evening—I shall be arriving
in Berlin. I am staying for about 3 days, and hope to spend a good deal of time
with you.
    My Third is almost finished.
    Quite peculiar!

Ever yours,
Mahler

136. *To Arnold Berliner*

Undated. Postmark: Steinbach, 17 August 1895

Dear Berliner,
    On the next page is the complete title of my new work. What I need is simply
to find out what impression this title makes on the listener—i.e. whether the
title succeeds in setting the listener on the road I wish to travel with him.
    We'll talk about it later

Yours,
Mahler

Die fröhliche Wissenschaft[2]
    Ein Sommermorgentraum
I.   Der Sommer marschiert ein.
II.   Was mir die Blumen auf der Wiese erzählen.
III. Was mir die Tiere im Walde erzählen.

---

[1] 22 August (K.M.).
[2] *The Gay Science.* A summer morning's dream. I. Summer marches in. II. What the flowers
in the meadow tell me. III. What the animals in the wood tell me. IV. What the night tells
me. V. What the morning bells tell me. VI. What love tells me. VII. The life divine.—
Mahler later abandoned these titles completely, the main title because of its resemblance to
Nietzsche's *Die fröhliche Wissenschaft* ('The Gay Science') (o.e. + K.M.).

IV. Was mir die Nacht erzählt.
V. Was mir die Morgenglocken erzählen.
VI. Was mir die Liebe erzählt.
VII. Das himmlische Leben.
(All finished except No. 1.)

137. *To Friedrich Löhr*†

Hamburg, 29 August 1895
Bismarckstrasse 86

Dear Fritz,
In great haste!
They say Krzyz.[1] really is engaged here from next year on. I have not heard anything from him personally for years. Nor has Pollini uttered a word about it; but then, that is his way.—It does not in the least affect my position at the theatre here—at most, I may find it pleasant to have such a colleague.

I have heard nothing about Vienna since my conversation with Besetzny.[2]

My new Symphony will take approximately 1½ hours—it is all in grand symphonic form.

The emphasis on my personal experiences (that is, what things tell me) corresponds to the peculiar ideas embodied in the whole work. II–V inclusive are meant to express the hierarchy of organisms, which I herewith list as follows:
II. Was d. Blumen m. e.
III. W. d. Tiere m. e.
IV. W. d. Nacht m. e. (human beings)
V. W. d. Morgenglocken m. e. (angels)
   the last two with words and singing.
VI. 'W. m. d. Liebe erzählt', a summary of my feelings towards all creatures, which develops not without deeply painful spiritual involvement, which, however, is gradually resolved into blissful confidence: *Die fröhliche Wissenschaft*. Finally, 'd. h. L.' ['Das himmlische Leben'] (VII), which, however, I have decided to entitle: 'Was mir das Kind erzählt'.[3]

No. I 'Der Sommer marschiert ein',[4] is intended to hint at the humorously

[1] Rudolf Krzyzanowski was appointed second Kapellmeister at the Hamburg Theatre for the 1896–7 season and he remained in Hamburg until the end of the following one (K.M.).
[2] Mahler was referring to his recent conversation with Dr. Josef, Freiherr von Bezecny (18 ?–1904), Generalintendant of the Vienna Court Opera (K.M.).
[3] 'Das himmlische Leben', originally conceived as a Lied in its own right (February 1892), eventually became the finale of the Fourth Symphony (K.M.).
[4] 'Summer marches in' was only composed the following year (K.M.).

subjective content. Summer is conceived in the rôle of victor—amidst all that grows and flowers, creeps and flies, thinks and yearns, and, finally, all that of which we have only an intuitive inkling (angels—bells—transcendental).

Eternal love spins its web within us, over and above all else—as rays flow together into a focal point. Now do you understand?—

It is my most individual and my richest work.

No. I is not yet done and must be left to some later date.—Send me a brief note to say whether you have now understood me.

Yours ever,

Gustav

I hear with great delight that you are going to take the examination! Please do not give up again!

What does the passage in your last letter about Waldvenusbrünnlein[1] mean? I simply cannot make it out!

[Enclosed quarto sheet]

Symphony No. 3

Die fröhliche Wissenschaft

EIN SOMMERMORGENTRAUM

I.   Der Sommer marschiert ein.
II.   Was mir die Blumen auf der Wiese erzählen.
II.   Was mir die Tiere im Walde erzählen.
IV.   Was mir die Nacht erzählt (alto solo).
V.   Was mir die Morgenglocken erzählen (female chorus with alto solo).
VI.   Was mir die Liebe erzählt.

Motto: 'Vater sieh an die Wunden mein!

Kein Wesen lass verloren sein!'[2]

(from *Des Knaben Wunderhorn*)

VII.   Das himmlische Leben (soprano solo, humorous).

All except No. I is already scored.

138.   *To Arnold Berliner†*

Undated. Hamburg, [September] *1895*

Dear Berliner,

First and foremost, the Beethoven portrait herewith enclosed. *Behn* will already have written to tell you that he has done a two-piano reduction of my

---

[1] 'Venus's woodland fountain'.
[2] 'Father, behold the wounds I bear!
Let no living being despair!'

symphony. I find it *first-rate*, and it is going to be published at once at B.'s expense.[1] Now his sudden and long-lasting silence is most pleasantly explained. —Just think: Lohse has really left, *I* am the *sole* conductor, and Pollini has not made the slightest attempt to find a replacement for L.[2] So I am actually conducting *every day*, since even the light operas, which indeed Pohlig might very well conduct, are handed over to me.—Cannot help wondering how long I shall be able to stand it.—Has my *fröhliche Wissenschaft* been having some slight effect on you, or are you still as misogynous as ever? When are you coming? Our little house is magnificent, and my whole life in it is a great source of energy.

Do send a line soon!

Yours sincerely,
Mahler

The 'himmlische Leben' will soon be in your hands.

139. *To Arnold Berliner†*

Undated. Hamburg, September 1895

Dear Berliner,

I hasten to send you two pictures[3] for Professors N. and D.;[4] I should add, to you privately, there is none left for *myself*, for I had only six made—I shall now order a further six.

Please tell Professor N. that I am very happy to be able to do him a favour, sincerely hoping I shall be in the same fortunate position more often.

On principle I shall *not* have *any more* copies made, so that the pictures will retain rarity value. Incidentally, I have strictly forbidden further copying.—I have not seen W.'s book![5] We had agreed to go shares in buying it. So please send me my half.—Perhaps it is like the Sibylline books, and half will be worth more than the whole—but for the opposite reasons, of course. So: please send it! I have not yet had a *single* free evening!

My address is: Bismarckstrasse 86.

[1] The publication of the full score of Mahler's Second Symphony, as well as the two-piano reduction, was paid for by Hermann Behn and Wilhelm Berkhan, a rich merchant in Hamburg (K.M.).

[2] Otto Lohse (1859–1925), second conductor in Hamburg (September 1893 to May 1895), had joined an American opera ensemble. See also Notes. Mahler actually conducted twenty-three nights during September 1895 (K.M.).

[3] The supposed portrait of Beethoven was in fact that of an unknown Viennese got up *à la* Beethoven (o.e.).

[4] Albert Neisser in Breslau and Georg Dohrn, conductor in Breslau (o.e.).

[5] Weingartner's draft of a mystery play, *Kain*, in three 'days', with its own festival hall, etc. (o.e.). See also Notes.

You could do me a favour. *None* of my letters to *Wolff*[1] has been *answered*—
Go and see him:
Karlsbad No. 19, and find out two things on my behalf.
I. Have the hall and the orchestra been definitely booked for 13 *December*?[2]
II. Which choir can I expect?
Here is your chance to get to know Wolff, which will be useful later on.

With best wishes, in haste,

Mahler

140. *To Arnold Berliner*

Undated. Postmark: Hamburg, 10 September 1895
Postcard

Dear Berliner,
You need not go to Wolff. He has already replied to me. I'm afraid everything is still undecided.—*Vederemo!*[3] Would it give you pleasure to have the *manuscript* of the 'Himmlische Leben' instead of a *copy*?

With all good wishes,

Yours ever,

Mahler

141. *To Friedrich Gernsheim* (Berlin)†

Undated. Hamburg, [12?] *October 1895*
Bismarckstrasse 86 (Hoheluft)

Dear Professor Gernsheim,
From Herr Wolff I have just heard to my very great joy that you might be prepared to lend your support to my project. You cannot imagine *how profoundly obliged* I should be to you. The part taken by the choir in my symphony[4] is certainly very important, but it is only of very short duration. It comes in only at the end of the last movement, and most of it is *a cappella*. If you would permit me to introduce myself and my work to you in person, I would come to Berlin for that purpose on *Monday* (the day after tomorrow) or *Tuesday*, calling on you at any time convenient to you in order to perform my work. As you know,

---

[1] Herrmann Wolff, concert manager in Berlin (K.M.).
[2] First complete performance of Mahler's Second Symphony (o.e.).
[3] An Italian expression ('we shall see') frequently used by Mahler (K.M.).
[4] The Second Symphony. Gernsheim was conductor of the famous Berlin choir Sternsche Singverein which sang at the first performance of Mahler's symphony (K.M.).

the first three movements were performed in Berlin last season, when, I have been told, I had the honour of your presence in the audience. I therefore venture to infer that you may feel some interest in me.

Permit me to repeat that your sympathetic support would make me deeply grateful to you and that I should consider myself fortunate if I were ever able to prove my gratitude to you.

It would be most kind if you would telegraph to let me know when it would be convenient to you for me to call.

With kindest regards, I am,

Yours sincerely,

Gustav Mahler

142. *To Arnold Berliner*

Undated. Postmark: Hamburg, 16 September 1895

Dear Berliner,

Can you lend me another 170 marks? If so, please send it *immediately*. When I have the chance I shall tell you of a shabby trick played on me by Pollini, which means I am temporarily greatly embarrassed.[1]

Please answer by return in any case.

Yours ever,

Mahler

143. *To Friedrich Gernsheim*

Hamburg, 17 October 1895

Bismarckstrasse 86

Dear Professor Gernsheim,

I was very happy to receive your message, and I am tomorrow sending the entire chorus material to the address you give. You can scarcely estimate the great favour you are doing me. Such readiness to support a colleague is something I account a particular honour in that it should be you, of all people, who sees your way to showing some interest in my work.

I shall never forget what you are doing and sincerely hope soon to be able to do something that will give expression to my gratitude.

---

[1] Mahler [had] provided for his four brothers and sisters without ever thinking of his own needs (o.e.). [At this point he was only taking care of the two sisters, Justine and Emma.]

I have secured Frau Ritter-Götze[1] as a soloist, and now await only your summons to appear with her for a rehearsal with the choir.

I am, with gratitude,

Your sincerely devoted

Gustav Mahler

144. *To Friedrich Gernsheim*

Hamburg, 29 October 1895
Bismarckstrasse 86

Dear Professor Gernsheim,

Thank you very much indeed for your letter. I have sent you parts for 30 *basses* and 30 tenors. Would it not be advisable to have more male voices? For all eventualities I shall be sending you some more in the next few days.

I have been studying your scores[2] with *great pleasure*. I find it difficult to decide in favour of any one more than another. I am firmly resolved to have one of them performed at the first opportunity. Meanwhile: thank you for sending them. The only question is: how long may I keep them? I should like to have your Third, at any rate, by me for a while longer. I would then bring it back in November, when we have our rehearsal.

With kind regards, I am,

Yours in gratitude,

Gustav Mahler

145. *To Anna v. Mildenburg* (Hamburg)†

Undated. [Hamburg, 21 November 1895]

(. . .) tell you personally about the last scene![3]

So glad, satisfied! None but myself (who draws every breath with you)

---

[1] Maria Ritter-Götze (1865–1922), mezzo-soprano at the Berlin Opera, but finally replaced by Hedi (or Hedwig) Felden from the Hamburg Opera (K.M.).
[2] Symphonies No. 1 (Op. 32: 1875), No. 2 (Op. 46: 1882), and No. 3 (*Miriam*, Op. 54: 1888). Gernsheim's Fourth Symphony was not published until 1896 (o.e.). Mahler never conducted any of Gernsheim's works (K.M.).
[3] Anna Mildenburg comments: Written after the Nile scene (3rd act of *Aida*). This letter and the following [152] refer to my first appearances as Aïda and Ortrud (*Lohengrin*). They date from my early days at the Hamburg Stadttheater (1895) and were sent to my dressing-room during or after the performance—usually in an unsealed envelope.
The première of *Aida* with Anna Mildenburg had been scheduled for 4 October but Fräulein Mildenburg excused herself and the performance was ultimately postponed until 21 November; it was conducted by Bruno Schlesinger (Walter) (K.M.).
6*

noticed that you were labouring hard in your singing this evening. The voice was *always* beautiful—the *p* very beautiful, poise and appearance capital. You are maintaining the standard you have achieved. Many passages were first-rate —*inter alia* particularly

uns ein neu – es   Le – ben die   höch - ste

The fact that the end of the aria did not go according to *our* plan is entirely Walter's fault for taking the whole preceding aria too fast, *rushing* it, so that you never had time to *breathe*; otherwise you would have been first-rate. So don't take it to heart. Tonight has given me the *certainty* that you can do it.

The audience as a whole is very enthusiastic. Most of the duet with *Amneris* you did beautifully. Likewise with Amonsaro. The first aria suffered rather because you were nervous—but still, it was *beautiful.* (Your kneeling down a second time at this point in the second scene was probably a lapse of memory.) It was all *sky-high* above your predecessors in this role.

So you can be very pleased! Sleep well! I am *very* satisfied with this evening! You have achieved another splendid, well-deserved success!

In December there *will* be *Le Nozze di Figaro*[1] for you; on 8 and 18 December *Rezia*.[2] So we shall have to do some more intensive *study*! Until *Saturday*, then. All right? Come *early*! Have a rest *tomorrow, not singing a single note*! (. . .)

146. *To Anna v. Mildenburg*†

Berlin, 8 December 1895

(. . .) At the end of the last movement of my symphony (the Second) what I need, as you know, is bell chimes, and that is something no musical instrument can produce.[3] So from the beginning I realized that only a bell-founder could help me. I have finally tracked one down; getting to his foundry takes about half an hour by train. It is near the Grunewald. I made an early start, and found a splendid fall of snow on the ground. The cold quickened my rather weary system, for the previous night I had again hardly slept. When I arrived in Zehlendorf (that is the name of the place) and tried to find the way amid pines and firs, all covered in snow, everything quite rural, with a pretty church gaily

[1] On 25 December (K.M.).
[2] In Weber's *Oberon* which was performed on 18 and 29 December (K.M.).
[3] Translators' note: In this and the following letters to Anna v. Mildenburg Mahler uses the second person singular, the intimate 'thou'.

sparkling in the winter sun, I left my troubles behind, seeing how free and happy man becomes as soon as he leaves the unnatural restless bustle of city life and returns to the tranquillity of nature. Having grown up in a small town, you must know what I mean. After a longish search I reached the foundry. I was received by an unassuming old gentleman with lovely white hair and beard, and with such calm, friendly eyes that I instantly felt as though taken back to the times of the old guilds. I found everything so charming and beautiful. I had a talk with him and, impatient as I am, I could not help finding him rather slow and long-winded. He showed me some glorious bells, including a magnificent big one that he had made to the German Emperor's order for the new cathedral. The tone was mysteriously vast. I had dreamt of something of the kind for my symphony. But the time has not yet come when only what is most valuable and significant will be just good enough to serve a great work of art. So I chose some rather more modest bells, which will still serve my purpose, and, having stayed about two hours, said good-bye to the dear old man. The return journey was just as glorious. But then to the Intendant's office, for more of that hanging about, cap in hand. Those faces! Those dry-as-dust people! Every inch of their faces bore the mark of that self-tormenting egoism which makes everyone so unhappy! Always 'I, I'—never 'thou, thou, my brother'! (. . .)

147. *To Anna v. Mildenburg*

Berlin, 9 December 1895

(. . .) Today I shall be having the first rehearsal—true, a preliminary one only, but at least a rehearsal. I have to drill the heavenly host. You wonder what that is, eh? One cannot explain in words (obviously, else I should not have put it into music), but when you hear the passage in the last movement you will probably remember these words, and then you will know what I mean. Last night I sat through my first dinner-party (really almost like a convict 'doing time'); one of the critics was also present, actually one who was most abusive last year. (. . .)[1]

148. *To Anna v. Mildenburg*

Berlin, 10 December 1895

(. . .) So everything went off well, beyond all expectation. The performers were so enthusiastic and so carried away that of their own accord they found the

[1] Read 'last season'—at the performance of movements 1–3 on 4 March 1895 (K.M.).

right expression for everything. If only you could have heard it! It sounds greater and mightier than it was ever heard before. (. . .)

149. *To Max Marschalk* (Berlin)†

Hamburg, 17 December 1895

Dear Sir,

I have just had the pleasure of receiving your esteemed letter. For some time I have been reading your articles in various journals, and your offer is in accord with my unspoken wishes. As far as the matter itself is concerned, nothing can be more welcome than your allowing me to waste no *words* on my aims, which I believe I have formulated clearly in terms of music. With you I know I am in good hands, and you will know how I felt without my having to utter a word. For have not even those who are now denouncing me again in the way we know all too well always lit upon *what really matters*, even though they have also insisted on assuring me most emphatically that it did not in the least matter to *them*?

The attitude I have adopted is entirely in keeping with my nature and with my conception of my art. I should regard my work as a complete failure if I felt it necessary to give men like yourself even the slightest indication of the emotional trend of the work.

In conceiving the work[1] I was never concerned with detailed description of an *event*, but at most with that of a *feeling*.—The *conceptual* basis of the work is clearly expressed in the words of the final chorus, and the sudden alto solo casts light on the first movements. The fact that in various individual passages I often retrospectively see a real event as it were taking its course dramatically before my eyes can easily be gathered from the nature of the music. The parallelism between life and music may go deeper and further than one is at present capable of realizing.—However, I am far from requiring everyone to follow me in this. I gladly leave the interpretation of details to each listener's imagination.—

Finally, I cannot suppress a deep sigh when I realize that the solid phalanx of the daily press will now, as always, block my way as soon as I appear on the scene with these poor works of mine, and that I shall probably once again have to wait a full year before making myself heard. I shall then come forth with a new work,[2] one that lies, almost completed, awaiting the day of its resurrection.—

Thank you, my dear Herr Marschalk, for being, as I believe, of one mind

[1] The Second Symphony (o.e.).
[2] The Third Symphony (o.e.).

with me. May the quickening breath and the strength with which approval and support ⟨of such men as you and Bie⟩ invigorate me prove to you in the future that I am not unworthy of it. I have just instructed my publisher to send you a piano reduction forthwith.

Yours sincerely,
Gustav Mahler

⟨Might I burden you with a request to send a copy of the essay you wish to publish?⟩

150. *To Max Marschalk*

Hamburg, 29 December 1895

Dear Sir,

Thank you very much indeed for your letter, above all for the attitude expressed in it. Believe me, the fact that you say *yes* to my work and that *you* credit it with 'actuality' is worth more to me than a favourable review published for all to read. Admittedly it would be of the greatest importance to me to see how my work is reflected in another personality and whether I have succeeded in finding a convincing form of expression for my ideas.—Naturally, a single hearing does not suffice. Even the most experienced and competent listener must first trace the interconnections between the various parts of the work; only then will the significance of the whole work reveal itself to him.

Well, I can wait (that is an art I have mastered). I shall await your article with calm confidence.

Thank you for your New Year greetings, which I cordially reciprocate.

Yours sincerely,
Gustav Mahler

151. *To Friedrich Gernsheim*†

Hamburg, 30 December 1895
Bismarckstrasse 86

Dear Professor Gernsheim,

I do not want to let this year pass, in which I have had so much to thank you for, without again expressing how deeply obliged I am to you. The knowledge that I can prove my gratitude is a source of great joy to me. I am grateful not in the limited, common sense of 'reciprocity', but in the happy knowledge that I have found a true ally, one who, despite the different paths we tread, is a congenial comrade-in-arms, pressing on, in his own way, towards the same goals as myself. I feel you will not take these words merely as empty phrases, but will accept in friendship and trust the hand I hold out to you.

I have not yet had an opportunity to express my gratitude to the Stern Society, and beg you to convey my sentiments should the occasion arise.

I shall never forget the times spent with you and your valiant colleagues.

My Hamburg plans are still in the balance. Pollini, who is *seriously ill*, cannot be seen by anyone at all. (Between ourselves, if the persistent rumours now circulating are to be believed, there are yet other reasons for his ominous state of mind). I cannot make any decision without consulting him. And so I cannot yet tell you anything more definite about the performance of your C minor.[1] I have it always on my desk, nibbling at it with real pleasure, re-living in spirit the happy hour in which you introduced me to this masterpiece of yours. I do not think I have forgotten any of the hints I picked up from your performance of it on the piano. Have you absolutely nothing choral that I could use for a Good Friday concert? Words in *German* will do perfectly well. The *sine qua non*, however, is that it should be religious in character.

With very best wishes for the New Year to yourself and your wife,

I remain

Your sincerely devoted

Gustav Mahler

1896

152. *To Anna v. Mildenburg*†

Undated. Hamburg [1 January 1896]

(. . .) Enjoyed it very much tonight![2]

In splendid voice: it sounded wonderful. Undoubtedly great success with the audience! Tone and poise surprisingly good. Enunciation almost always *clear*, great progress. Often, unfortunately, quite incorrect (causing you to 'wreck' quite a lot, especially: 'Zurück, Elsa', as in *Tannhäuser* too). Also did not notice much of our preparation. It was also too facile. We shall have a thorough go at it again before the next *Lohengrin*. The scene with Elsa was very good, but *too loud*, that was not the right colour for secretive, glittering, hypocritically

---

[1] Gernsheim's Third Symphony (o.e.).
[2] Written after the second act of *Lohengrin* (see also letter 145), which was performed on 1 January 1806, conducted by Karl Pohlig (K.M.).

humble Ortrud. Appearance in Act II in first costume wonderful—but not so good in the second because of careless *posture*. For heaven's sake make the most of your imposing presence in such roles. The running up the steps in front of Elsa was not right either. What was best, almost good, was jumping up from the steps. For sheer voice the invocation of the gods was really terrific. The whole audience would have burst into a roar of applause if just one had begun. All in all delighted to note still further *progress*. What a good omen for the New Year that begins tonight! Goodnight! See you soon! (. . .)

153. *To Friedrich Gernsheim*

Undated. Hamburg, end of January 1896

Dear Professor Gernsheim,

What in the world must you have been thinking of me when all this long time you have received no sign of life from me!—Alas, there is a (for me) very sad reason: the concerts planned for this season will now not take place at all.—Pollini has been gravely ill for months, and it is no use trying to get anywhere with him. *Between ourselves*, his condition is so critical that everything here is now really a sort of interregnum.—So my plan is one among various things of which nothing has come. I have decided to go on with my concerts next season —even if I have to do it on my own. Until then I shall have to postpone the idea, so dear to me, of performing your symphony and so blazing a trail for your gifts—but I do really mean *postpone*, not *cancel*!

I hope to look you up soon in Berlin! There I shall perhaps hear something about your 4th? How did it go in Mainz, I wonder?[1]

My most cordial greetings to you and to your wife,

Sincerely yours,

Gustav Mahler

154. *To Richard Batka*†

Undated. [Hamburg 1896?]

Dear Herr Batka,

Unfortunately we live in a time when a great deal is thought and written 'on' artistic creation.—That is in itself a sad symptom. But what I really cannot

---

[1] Gernsheim conducted the first three movements of his Fourth Symphony in Mainz on 21 January 1896 (K.M.).

reconcile myself to is your inquiry into what artists are working 'at'.[1] Doubtless only those who follow in our footsteps will be able to determine that, although even that is not very likely to amount to much, as art-historical and critical works of all periods prove. You do me the honour of including me among the 'creative'; but in my view these are the last people to be capable of answering such a question. Perhaps I speak only for myself. But I could no more tell you what I work 'at' than what I live 'on'.—'The living cloak of godhead'[2]—that might serve as an answer! But it would only make you go on asking questions, would it not?

When I have given birth to a work, I enjoy discovering what chords it *sets vibrating* in 'the Other'. But I have not yet been able to give an explanation of that myself—far less obtain one from others. That sounds mystical! But per-haps the time has again come when we and our works are on the point of once again becoming a little in-'comprehensible' to ourselves. *Only if that is so* do I believe that we work 'at' something.—Do forgive my brevity, but, as you can doubtless imagine, I have no more time to spare. Again kindest regards and best wishes for your enterprise.

Yours very sincerely,
Gustav Mahler

155. *To Max Marschalk*†

Undated. Hamburg, 5 March 1896
Bismarckstrasse 86

⟨Dear Sir,⟩

Many thanks for your package. By all means send me your work. We can easily fit a one-act opera into our repertoire.—May I make just one comment? Why did you change the title? *Flames* strikes me as a *very good choice*. It com-mands interest and give a very felicitous pointer to the contents. *Phanor und Phanette*[3] sounds stereotyped and—deters both theatre management and public.—

On the other hand, you are right to drop the description 'romance'. What I am saying is: do send me your work. I am always delighted to get to know anything of yours. I shall call on you the very next time I come to Berlin.—

---

[1] Reply to a questionnaire about artistic creativeness and the problem of the artist's par-ticipation in some common cultural task (o.e.).
[2] Quotation from Goethe's *Faust* (K.M.).
[3] *In Flammen* (or *Phanor und Phanette*) opera by Marschalk (1896) based on a text by Goethe, first performed in Gotha on 20 February 1897 (K.M.).

The symphony I am presenting this time, the First, is not the *new* one of which I wrote, but one written *before* the C minor.

I should not venture to conduct my latest work. People must first digest my older works, which is why I am pressing on as fast as I can to give them the opportunity.

My latest symphony goes rather beyond what caused the stir about the C minor and indeed about the *D major*, which is what is to be performed this time.[1] Nor is it yet finished.—

Since I shall be in Berlin at the beginning of next week, please postpone sending the package until I return to Hamburg, otherwise it would have to wait at the post office because there would be no one to collect it.—

With kind regards, I am,

Yours sincerely,

Gustav Mahler

The rehearsals start at 10 a.m. on Sunday and Monday. I look forward to seeing you there.

156. *To Max Marschalk*†

Hamburg, 20 March 1896

My dear Herr Marschalk,

Thank you very, very much for everything—above all for your under-standing.[2] You are right about the title (*Titan*) and the programme. At the time my friends persuaded me to write some sort of programme notes to make the D major easier to understand. So I worked out the title and these explanatory notes retrospectively. My reason for omitting them this time was not only that I thought them quite inadequate—in fact, not even accurate or relevant—but that I have experienced the way the audiences have been set on the wrong track by them. Believe me, even Beethoven's symphonies have their inner pro-grammes, and closer acquaintance with such a work brings understanding of the development of feeling appropriate to the ideas. It will eventually be the same with my works.—

As regards the third movement ('Marcia funebre'), I must admit that my inspiration came from the well-known nursery-picture (*The Burial of the Huntsman*[3]).—But at this point in the work it is irrelevant—what matters is

[1] Mahler's first three symphonies are thus: No. 1 in D major, No. 2 in C minor and No. 3 in D minor. On 16 March 1896 he conducted a concert in Berlin which included his Symphony No. 1 (four movements only), Symphony No. 2 (the first movement: 'Todtenfeier') and the first performance of 'Lieder eines fahrenden Gesellen' with Anton Sistermanns (K.M.).
[2] After the concert in Berlin on 16 March (o.e.).
[3] Woodcut by Moritz von Schwind (K.M.).

only the *mood* that has to be expressed, the mood from which the fourth move-- ment then suddenly flashes like lightning out of a thundercloud. It is simply the outcry of a heart deeply wounded, a cry preceded by the uncannily and ironi- cally brooding sultriness of the funeral march. 'Ironic' in the sense of the Aristotelian *eironeia*.—

The words of the songs are my *own*.[1] I did not give my name in the pro- gramme to avoid providing ammunition for adversaries who would be quite capable of parodying the naïve and simple style.

Thank you once again—I am so weary and apathetic at the moment. Oh, how heavy my heart is!

⟨Do let me hear something from you!

> Your sincerely devoted,
> Gustav Mahler

What has happened to the *Flammen?*⟩

157. *To Arnold Berliner*

> *Undated. Postmark: Hamburg, 20 March 1896*

Dear Berliner,

Riches (not meaning the proceeds from my concert) having just come my way, please let me know how deep 'in the red' I am with you; I have again forgotten, of course.

Apropos, I heard that your seat at my concert was right at the back.

I asked Wolff to send you tickets (10). I hope it was not he who gave you such a poor seat; that was far from my intention.

Please be so good as to tell me what happened.

> Yours sincerely,
> Gustav Mahler

158. *To Max Marschalk* (Berlin)†

> Hamburg, 26 March 1896

My dear Herr Marschalk,

Your interpretation of my work[2] is so consistent and profound that there is really none of it I would wish changed.

If you will permit me to make one comment, I should like to see it emphasized

---

[1] 'Lieder eines fahrenden Gesellen' (o.e.).
[2] The First Symphony (K.M.).

that the symphony begins at a point beyond the *love–affair*;[1] it forms the basis, i.e. it dates from earlier in the composer's emotional life. But the real-life experience was the *reason* for the work, not its content.

(Your interpretation of the third and fourth movements is *masterly*. It is all the more pleasing to me because it points to what is typical and universally valid in the world. I should be sorry to see a single word of it changed. Here you have really entered into my mind.) My slight suggestion does not amount to an objection, but it does bring us to the important question *how*, or perhaps even *why*, music should ever be explained in words at all. From a remark in your letter I gather that on this point we understand each other and are in agreement. Let me explain my standpoint briefly.

I know that, so far as I myself am concerned, as long as I can express an experience in words I should never try to put it into music. The need to express myself musically—in symphonic terms—begins only on the plane of *obscure* feelings, at the gate that opens into the 'other world', the world in which things no longer fall apart in time and space.—

Just as I find it banal to compose programme-music, I regard it as unsatisfactory and unfruitful to try to make programme notes for a piece of music. This remains so despite the fact that the *reason* why a composition comes into being at all is bound to be something the composer has experienced, something real, which might after all be considered sufficiently concrete to be expressed in words.—I am sure we now stand at a great parting of the ways, where the divergent paths of symphonic and dramatic music will soon become obvious to anyone with a clear notion of the nature of music.—Even now, if you compare a Beethoven symphony with Wagner's tone-poems, you will have no trouble in recognizing the essential difference between them.—True, Wagner has taken over symphonic music's *means of expression*, just as the symphonic composer, for his part, is completely justified in making whatever use he wishes of the means of expression with which Wagner has enriched music. In this sense all the arts, indeed art and Nature itself, are interconnected. But this is something to which no one has yet given enough thought. People are not yet able to see it in *perspective*.

Nor is this a 'system' that I have constructed, out of which to make my creative work. It is a purely personal view of things that I have come to have after having (with all attendant travailing) written several symphonies and time and again, insistently, come up against the same misunderstandings and problems.—

So it is on the whole just as well if in the early stages, as long as my way of doing things is felt to be disconcerting, the listener is provided with signposts

[1] With Johanna Richter in Kassel (K.M.).

and milestones on his journey—or rather, with a map of the heavens, so that he can get a picture of the night sky with all its luminous worlds.—But any such exposition cannot offer *more*.—People have to have something *already known* to refer to if they are not to lose their way. That is why I shall be grateful to you for publishing your article[1] (which I like better than anything else hitherto written about me). Of all possible interpretations yours seems to me the most appropriate because it is the most *straightforward*, corresponding closely to the incidental or exterior cause of the interior experience.

Having said all that, I now feel some misgivings, as you will appreciate, in setting out to say anything about the C minor symphony.—I called the first movement 'Todtenfeier'. It may interest you to know that it is the hero of my D major symphony who is being borne to his grave, his life being reflected, as in a clear mirror, from a point of vantage. Here too the question is asked: *What did you live for?* Why did you suffer? Is it all only a vast, terrifying joke?—We *have* to answer these questions somehow if we are to go on living—indeed, even if we are only to go on dying! The person in whose life this call has resounded, even if it was only once, must give an answer. And it is this answer I give in the last movement.

The second and third movements are intended as an interlude, the second being a *memory*! A ray of sunlight, pure and cloudless, out of that hero's life.

You must surely have had the experience of burying someone dear to you, and then, perhaps, on the way back some long-forgotten hour of shared happiness suddenly rose before your inner eye, sending as it were a sunbeam into your soul—not overcast by any shadow—and you almost forgot what had just taken place. There you have the second movement!—When you then awaken from that melancholy dream and are forced to return to this tangled life of ours, it may easily happen that this surge of life ceaselessly in motion, never resting, never comprehensible, suddenly seems *eerie*, like the billowing of dancing figures in a brightly lit ball-room that you gaze into from outside in the dark—and from a *distance* so great that you can *no longer* hear the *music*! Life then becomes meaningless, an eerie phantom state out of which you may start up with a cry of disgust.—There you have the third movement. What follows need not be explained to you!

What it comes to, then, is that my Second Symphony grows directly out of the First!

From now on, whenever I bring out a new work, I should like your permission to make you acquainted with it before it is first performed. That is

---

[1] Marschalk's article analysing Mahler's First Symphony appeared in *Die redenden Künste* (3rd vol., no. 13, Leipzig, 1896–7) (o.e.).

better than any programme! I am so delighted by your appreciation, you 'keeping up' with me! If only you knew how greatly I, a wayfaring man, need it, you would certainly never allow your interest in me and my work to slacken.— I beg that you will maintain your kindly, thoughtful interest in me and not mistake that plea for a sign of vanity. Very, very many thanks! Do send me your article as soon as it appears.

Your sincerely devoted,
Gustav Mahler

⟨Misprint:
  Not: 'wie mein Schatz Hochzeit macht'
  but: 'wenn mein Schatz Hochzeit macht'⟩

159. *To Albert Spiegler* (Vienna)†

Hamburg, 3 April 1896
Hohe Luft, Bismarckstrasse 86

Very dear Albert,

I send you this very fond, rosy greeting[1] and best wishes after a happy and, this time, indeed, very 'grand' journey here (the guard having taken me to his heart and for one mark let me go on travelling second class from Leipzig, whence I was supposed to travel third). In the proud consciousness of this I wish you many-many-many happy returns of your birthday! How much rather I would wish it you in person on Sunday, if only I could, like a bird or Baron Königs-warter,[2] be in two places at once. That is something Gustav would wish still more for himself, i.e. he wishes he were in one place and in Vienna (terribly, terribly, does he wish himself that, and to be with all of you!).

For the rest I found G. well and very hungry and immensely busy and work-ing hard as ever. I shall here have a chance of hearing all sorts of glorious things: Mozart's *Requiem*, and some of the *St. Matthew Passion*, and *Siegfried* and *Fidelio* next week.

We go for immense walks and the weather is pretty good.

Farewell! I am writing in the midst of everyone that's why it's so daft.

Natalie

Of course Natalie has written all over the paper. So I can't get a word in.

---

[1] The letter is on pink paper initialled G.M. The first part is written by Mahler's friend Natalie Bauer-Lechner (K.M.).
[2] Probably a reference to the noble family known as the Austrian 'Rothschilds' (K.M.).

Very best wishes to all of you on your birthday, dear Albert, and I only wish I could spend a little time with you all again.

Yours,

Gustav Mahler

At 7 on Sunday week I shall be at your place! Yours, Natalie.

160. *To Max Marschalk*†

Undated. Hamburg, 12 April 1896

My dear Herr Marschalk,

Your package arrived just when 'the rushing tide of life' was roaring its loudest all about me. I had to postpone replying, though all that is so purely human in your letter called for an immediate reply.—So you too have trodden the path of suffering that I too know so well.—There was indeed something in your face that made me sense it even before I received this confirmation.

Well, first and foremost: your opus,[1] which I should best like to go through with you at the piano. Here I shall confine myself to a few general hints that you will perhaps briefly consider.—What struck me most is the feature that you also emphasize in your letter: at present you are still going in very much for 'tone and colour'! This is the mistake made by all gifted beginners *now* composing. I could show you a similar phase in my own development.—*Mood*-music is dangerous ground.

Believe me: we must for the time being keep to the good old principles. *Themes*—these must be clear and *plastic*, so that they can be clearly recognized at any stage of modification or development—and then *varied* presentation, holding the attention above all through the logical *development* of the inner idea, but also by the *genuine opposition* of contrasting motives.

That is all still blurred in your work. Next, you must shake off the *pianist*! None of this is a movement for an *orchestra*—it is conceived for the piano—and then rearranged for orchestra without getting free of the trammels of that *instrument*.—

I suffered from *that* ailment once myself.—All of us nowadays start out from the piano, whereas the old master's origins lay in the *violin* and the *voice*.—

Of course I am now speaking only in crude generalizations. Not *everything* in your opera could be assessed by these criteria.—

I am firmly convinced that you are talented, and I very much look forward to hearing another of your works.—One other small point, by the way: you often write *long* passages with the same *rhythmic pattern*, sometimes even with

[1] The opera *Phanor und Phanette* or *In Flammen* (o.e.).

the same orchestration. That has a monotonous effect. *Variety* and *contrast*! That is, as it always was, the secret of *effectiveness*! By this means even shallow minds contrive for a while to disguise the lack of substance in their work.—

On the purely technical side there is a great deal I should like to discuss with you, but that can be done only by referring to the score, and personally! When I next pass through Berlin I shall call on you for that purpose.—Some nice bits of invention that I single out are:

Passages of string accompaniment such as

which drag on monotonously through large parts of your score, are of typical piano-character. One of these days we shall go into this in detail.—And now, most important of all: would a performance at our opera-house mean much to you? If so, I shall do everything in my power to arrange one. *Next season*, of course, since we close at the end of May.—[1]

I write this too in great haste, begging you to take the will for the deed—for the moment. Perhaps you will look me up in *Hamburg* one of these days? And play me something new! You are always welcome.

With warm regards,
Yours sincerely,
Gustav Mahler

161. *To Adele Marcus* (Hamburg)†

Undated. [Hamburg, April 1896]

Dearest,

I am becoming so modest in my demands that I shall be content to know whether you *slept* well.

My hand is so much better now that it hardly knows what the other one is

---

[1] Mahler's undoubted good intention to perform some of Marschalk's compositions was never realized (K.M.).

doing.—I shall now make the 'flowers tell me' something beautiful. Heavens, how stupid people are, not wanting to know anything of it. No one can imagine —even I hardly can—what beautiful sounds those are! So splendid—captive rays of sunlight, no less! It does cheer me up again. I only wish you could share the experience.

Well, and how did you sleep?

Yours ever,
Gustav Mahler

162. *To Max Marschalk*†

Undated. Hamburg, 21 April 1896

In haste!

My dear Herr Marschalk,

⟨I have only had a few glances at *Lobetanz*! But in what a *different* way this music struck me! I find it very captivating and interesting—this is *individuality* and one knows what you want!⟩ By mood-music I mean of course only the feeble, incoherent, highly-coloured manner peculiar either to youthful immaturity, which is still in ferment, or to creative impotence.

I myself went through a phase in which my over-lifesize sensibility dissolved everything into incoherence and I *could not preserve* my integrity. But all *creation* is essentially related to the face that the artist must struggle to achieve. —Well, so we are clear on that point now.—It is not just that there are 'tone and colour' in your *Flammen*, but that most of it is little else.

⟨I will tell you what I propose,—I am at present in the Wagner cycle and terribly overburdened with work. Yesterday I conducted for the *19th* time in succession.—That is the usual practice in *Hamburg*. I will afterwards have a good look first of all at Bierbaum's[1] poetry and then return to your score again.

Meanwhile there will be holidays. (End of May). Then I will be passing through Berlin and will seek you out straight away. Then we can get together immediately. In the meantime, be patient.⟩

I am so very glad I can write to you hopefully. I should not have wished to deceive you with flattery, and yet the liking I have come to feel for you person-ally would have made it painful to criticize your work adversely, so perhaps destroying a relationship that began so promisingly.—Now all is well!

---

[1] The German poet Otto Julius Bierbaum (1865–1910) (K.M.).

My very best thanks to you for your package ⟨and the *splendid* article⟩.
I hope to see you again soon.

Yours sincerely,
Gustav Mahler

⟨Herr Muck's criticism is too narrow even for a conductor!⟩[1]

163. *To Max Marschalk†*

Undated. Hamburg, 24 April 1896

Dear Friend,

In haste, another emendation! From the very beginning I assumed that any adverse criticism of your work on my part would not alter your opinion of my ability! And this being so, I should never have hesitated—whatever the risk—to open my mind to you with complete candour. But believe me, as a man of greater experience: a close relationship between two people is endangered in the long run if one of them has to take a negative, i.e. *uncomprehending*, attitude to the other's work. For what, basically, does 'I do not like it' mean other than 'I do not understand it'? Just as it is clear that your approach cannot be comprehensible to such a person as ⟨Muck⟩ (for whom I have always felt instinctive aversion, without ever having got to know him more closely), so too it is certain that what appeals to me in your letters and now in your music is a fundamental affinity—and this in a wider sense than you can perhaps yet imagine. Even the choice of your text (*Lobetanz* which I recognized, with a real joy bordering on astonishment, as being akin to my own inmost nature, like something *known to me of old*) strikes me as significant. It was positively as if I were once again hearing sounds from my own young days. My 'fahrender Gesell' must have been very instructive to you in this respect. Do you not find all the elements of *Lobetanz* gathered together there? Especially 'tone and colour'?—

What that dunce says about your instrumentation is wholly incomprehensible to me, coming as it does from such a stickler! Rest assured: your instrumentation is *good* and will sound capital! So far I have merely skimmed through it, but my red pencil is at your service, should it turn out to be necessary. I am sending you, as 'printed matter', copies of some songs of mine.[2] They date from before my D major symphony. Perhaps this is the best way to give you more intimate insight into my heart and soul and all my being.

It recently occurred to me that perhaps what you are meant to write is a

[1] Karl Muck (1859–1940), German conductor. Kapellmeister at the Royal Opera in Berlin 1892–1912 (K.M.).
[2] *Lieder und Gesänge* published in 1892 in three volumes by Schott in Mainz (K.M.).

fairy-tale. Perhaps I have a 'text' for you. I shall bring you something when I come to Berlin.

With cordial greetings,

Yours sincerely,
Gustav Mahler

164. *To Max Marschalk*†

Undated. Hamburg, May 1896

Dear Herr Marschalk,

Do not waste another thought on poor R![1] I have quite grown out of him by now. It was just one of those momentary impulses that caused me to look it out from among my papers for you. I can quite imagine that you—coming to it with a fresh eye—also cannot warm up to that flight of youthful fancy.—What impelled me mainly was the desire to find a subject for you.—At any rate, you know now why I had such a sense of affinity from first reading *Lobetanz.*—

I shall send your scores within the next few days.—I am very much looking forward to seeing you again. I shall be coming to Berlin on the first of June. If it suits you, we can meet in some tavern that evening. Perhaps you can drop me a line suggesting a suitable place.

Yours sincerely,
Gustav Mahler

165. *To Anna v. Mildenburg* (Malborghet)†

Steinbach am Attersee, 24 June 1896

(. . .) Just think, I left the drafts of my work (the Third Symphony) in Hamburg. I meant to work on them this summer, and I am utterly desperate about it. This is such an unfortunate mishap that it may cost me my holidays. Do you realize what it means? It is almost as though you had left your voice somewhere and had to wait for someone to send it on to you. (. . .)

166. *To Anna v. Mildenburg*

Steinbach am Attersee, 25 June 1896

(. . .) I can well understand your thinking so much about your poor Papa.

---

[1] *Rübezahl*, one of Mahler's earlier opera projects, see Notes (K.M.).

I feel the same whenever something lovely and good comes my way. It is so sad that precisely those who care for us most are those who rarely live to see the realization of what they wish for us. They accompany us a short way along the stony path, but then have to leave us; we must consider ourselves fortunate if they can catch even a distant glimpse of the shining goal. (. . .) Think also of the living and remember that the day must also come when it will be too late to put things right. It is at moments such as these that one most clearly feels the bonds holding a family together. (. . .)

167. *To Anna v. Mildenburg*

Steinbach am Attersee, 26 June 1896

(. . .) In the next few days I shall be making a short trip to Ischl, where for years I have been regularly meeting Brahms. Here I can really say as in *Faust*: It does me good to see the Old Man now and then! He is a gnarled and sturdy tree, but bears sweet, ripe fruit, and it is a joy to contemplate that mighty, leafy tree.—Admittedly we are not quite compatible, and the 'friendship' is maintained only because, as a young man, still developing, I don't mind treating the grand old master with due consideration and forbearance, showing him only the side of myself that I think he finds agreeable. (. . .)

168. *To Béla Diosy* (Budapest)

Steinbach am Attersee, 26 June 1896

My dear Diosy,

I must apologize for the long delay in replying to your kind letter. The chief reason is that I am up to my neck in work, which makes it simply impossible for me to think about anything else.—Apart from that I feel I am in a rather awkward position. What shall or can I reply to your well-meant arguments? I have already written to you saying I shall be glad to accept a post in Budapest if one is offered to me.—It depends *entirely* on the *terms* and *from whom* the offer comes.—But I have no wish to become involved in intrigues, or even to be the cause of them!

I shall be returning to *Hamburg* for *this winter*. If I am made an offer and am still free, I shall be *sincerely* glad to accept it. It must, of course, be made *officially*.—I myself believe that one will have to wait and see how things turn out. It is enough, after all, if the people in Budapest know I may possibly be 'available'. The rest is up to *them*, not to *me*! I am most grateful to you, my dear

Diosy, for keeping me so much in mind and for the really touching interest you have shown on my behalf. I hope eventually to be in a position to show that my feelings of friendship towards yourself are equally genuine. If you hear of any new 'development' in the situation, you will always find a very eager reader or listener in

Yours sincerely,
Gustav Mahler

Do you happen to know where Kössler[1] is?

169. *To Anna v. Mildenburg* (Malborghet)

Steinbach am Attersee, 1 July 1896

(. . .) ⟨You would like to know 'what love tells me'? Dearest Annerl, love tells me very beautiful things! And when love speaks to me now it always talks about you!⟩ But the love in my symphony is one different from what you suppose. The ⟨motto⟩ of this movement (no. 7) is:[2]

Vater, sieh an die Wunden mein!
Kein Wesen lass verloren sein!

Now do you understand what it is about? It is an attempt to show the summit, the highest level from which the world can be surveyed. I could equally well call the movement something like: 'What God tells me!' And this in the sense that God can, after all, only be comprehended as 'love'. And so my work is a musical poem that goes through all the stages of evolution, step by step. It begins with inanimate Nature and progresses to God's love! People will need time to crack the nuts I am shaking down from this tree for them. (. . .)

170. *To Bruno Walter* (Berlin)†

Steinbach am Attersee, 2 July 1896

Dear Friend,
This is going to be just a brief reply to your greetings and an invitation to come to us by about the 16th, unless, for some reason unknown to me, you have arranged your holiday differently. My sisters[3] will I think by now have mentioned in their letters that I have not been idle, and I hope that in a few weeks I

---

[1] Hans Kössler (1853–1926), composer, professor at the Budapest Conservatory (o.e.).
[2] The Third Symphony. See letter 137 in which Mahler—correctly—attaches this motto to the sixth movement (K.M.).
[3] Justine and Emma (K.M.).

shall have brought the whole of my Third to a happy conclusion.—I am already scoring it, the first sketch having turned out to be fairly clear.—I think the gentlemen of the press—*engagés* or otherwise—will be having bouts of the staggers again, whereas those who enjoy good fun will find the promenades I have laid out for them very entertaining. I am afraid the whole thing is again sicklied o'er with the notorious spirit of my humour, 'and there is frequent opportunity of pursuing my inclination to make a furious din'. Sometimes, too, the musicians play 'without taking the slightest account of one another, and here my savage and brutal nature reveals itself most starkly'. Everyone knows by now that some triviality always has to occur in my work. But this time it goes beyond all bounds. 'At times one cannot help believing one is in a low tavern or a stable.'—So come as soon as you can, and forearmed! Your taste, which has perhaps been purified in Berlin, will be thoroughly ruined again. Kindest regards, also to your family—looking forward to seeing you soon.

Yours as ever,

Gustav Mahler

⟨The titles of the first two movements, which of course are closely related, are

    1. Pan erwacht

attacca 2. der Sommer marschiert ein.⟩

171. *To Anna v. Mildenburg*

Steinbach am Attersee, 6 July 1896

(. . .) Well, to make up for that you are all going to get something quite beautiful. Summer marches in, all a-ringing and a-singing such as you just can't imagine! It bursts into bloom on every side. And now and again there are infinitely mysterious and sorrowful sounds, as of inanimate Nature in morose immobility awaiting the emergence of new life. This is something that cannot be expressed in words. (. . .)

172. *To Anna v. Mildenburg*

Steinbach am Attersee, 9 July 1896

(. . .) Such an odd thing happened when your letter came. As usual, I looked at the postmark, and this time, instead of saying Malborghet, as at other times, it consisted solely of the letters P.A.N. (followed by 30, but I didn't notice that until later). You see, for weeks I have been searching for a title for the whole of this work of mine, and finally I hit upon *Pan*, which, as you know, was the name of a Greek divinity that subsequently symbolized the essential nature of All Things (*Pan*, Greek for 'everything'). Well, you can imagine my surprise at seeing these three at first incomprehensible letters, which I ultimately deciphered as 'Postamt Nr. 30'. Isn't it droll? (. . .)

173. *To Anna v. Mildenburg*

Steinbach am Attersee, 10 July 1896

(. . .) I have been hard at work too! Heavens, what a sigh of relief I shall breathe when I have got this work, too, safely completed! Like the farmer when he has got all his corn into the barn. About another three weeks should do it! Then I shall shout Hurrah! now for a rest! And let's hope the weather will also give its blessing—at the moment it's behaving terribly! There isn't half an hour here without a downpour! It's so frightful, one really is justified in talking about the weather all the time. (. . .)

174. *To Anna v. Mildenburg*

Steinbach am Attersee, 18 July 1896

(. . .) But I did write and tell you I was engaged in a major work. Don't you realize it takes all a man has, and how one can be so deeply involved that one is almost dead to the outside world. But just try to imagine such a major work, literally reflecting the whole world—one is oneself only, as it were, an instrument played by the whole universe. I have often explained this to you before— and you must accept it if you really understand me. Look, everyone who has shared my life has had to learn this. At such times I am no longer my own master (. . .) The composer of such a work has to suffer terrible birth-pangs, and before it all assumes order in his mind, building up, surging up, he is often preoccupied, self-immersed, dead to the outside world. (. . .) My symphony will be something the world has never heard before! In it Nature herself acquires a voice and tells secrets so profound that they are perhaps glimpsed only in dreams! I assure you, there are passages where I myself sometimes get an eerie feeling; it seems as though it were not I who composed them. If only I can manage to complete it the way I intend. (. . .)

175. *To Anna v. Mildenburg*

Steinbach, 21 July 1896

(. . .) This time I really dread returning to Hamburg. Perhaps even Pollini himself has no notion how things will turn out there. But the situation is bound to become pretty explosive, with all those conflicting interests. Will Pollini succeed in driving me into clearing out? I really don't yet know what I should do then, since there is nowhere a vacant post I could accept. (. . .) My work is taking longer than expected! How relieved I shall be when I can write to you: I have finished! And yet it is a strange feeling, taking leave of a work that has been the very essence of one's life for all of two years! Can you understand that? Whenever I say something like that, it always seems to me that it may hurt your feelings. Does it? (. . .)

176. *To Friedrich Gernsheim* (Berlin)†

Undated. [Steinbach, Summer] *1896*

My very dear Professor Gernsheim,

When I sent your symphony[1] back to you, I thought I should be with you a few hours afterwards. I did in fact pass through Berlin on the way, but was unexpectedly called away by telegram.

At the end of August I shall be passing through Berlin again, and very much look forward then to making up for what I missed.

Until then, warmest regards,

Yours sincerely,
Gustav Mahler

177. *To Max Marschalk*†

Undated. [Steinbach, Summer] *1896*

My dear Herr Marschalk,

Recently I received a copy of *Die Welt*,[2] in which I found your splendid weekly review. (What you said about the 'Wagnerian' cult was after my own heart.) But alas—what I did not find was your article on my humble self! My dear fellow, my adversaries are legion—and all far too fond of the sound of their own voices!—My friends remain quite mum! How then am I to fare, poor

[1] No. 4 or possibly no. 3: cf. letter [151] of 30 December 1895 (o.e.).
[2] The Berlin weekly *Die Welt am Montag* (o.e.).

devil that I am (or let us say Mahler-devil, as one witty critic has put it)? Is this to continue for ever?

Please, dear, good friend, speak up! Your approval is worth far more to me than any slight benefit I can derive from a 'favourable review'.—But it is nevertheless necessary that *those who approve* should express their opinion, not only the others. I do beg, do not simply leave it at that this time!

I am now well into my 'Third'!

With warmest regards and in the hope that you will not take amiss some pressure from one who is under pressure,

I am,

Yours sincerely,

Gustav Mahler

Is Bie also keeping mum?

178. *To Max Marschalk*

Steinbach am Attersee, 6 August 1896

Dear Friend,

You would be quite wrong to assume that I do not feel justified in recommending your works for performance at our opera-house. On the contrary, now that it is clearly in accordance with your wishes, I shall do everything possible to have either *Flammen* or the fairy-tale [*Lobetanz*] performed on our stage. But I must not conceal from you that my influence there at the moment is not the strongest. I am on *bad terms* with Pollini—but that is in confidence. Still, I shall try to get our theatrical director[1] interested in *Lobetanz*, and hope to achieve more in that way than by a direct approach. Not only should I be pleased for your sake if I were successful, but it would also be interesting in itself to see what effect this very individual work would have. Please send me the libretto and music about the beginning of September, when I shall be back in Hamburg.—

My work is finished.[2] It has the following titles, from which you will be able to gather at least something about the contents.

Ein Sommermittagstraum

I. Abteilung.

Einleitung: Pan erwacht.

Nr. I: Der Sommer marschiert ein (Bacchuszug).

[1] Adolf Steinert (1864–1913) (K.M.).
[2] The Third Symphony (o.e.).

II. Abteilung.

Nr. II: Was mir die Blumen auf der Wiese erzählen.

Nr. III: Was mir die Tiere im Walde erzählen.

Nr. IV: Was mir der Mensch erzählt.

Nr. V: Was mir die Engel erzählen.

Nr. VI: Was mir die Liebe erzählt.

I refrain from commentary on this. You shall have a chance to know the work before I bring it to Berlin.

Your letter came into my hands only today, on my return from a longish walking-tour.

I hope this letter catches you in Berlin. If not, I suppose it will be forwarded. With all good wishes for your summer holidays,

Yours sincerely,
Gustav Mahler

I shall be back in Hamburg from 24 August on.

179. *To Friedrich Löhr†*

Undated. Hamburg, [Autumn] *1896*

My dear Fritz,

I am delighted by your essay! It's very well done (I should like to see a 'collection' of such essays) and puts into words what I think and feel. By a different route you arrive at my very own position.—You must do this sort of thing more often! People like yourself need to make themselves heard above the dreadful hubbub of voices in 'this day and age' (which reminds me of an orchestra's 'tuning up' before a concert).—

I'm knocking about the world quite a lot now. I assure you it is a fight, a real one, in which one does not notice one is bleeding from a thousand wounds. In the lulls one suddenly feels something moist, and only then realizes that one is bleeding. I find my 'successes' especially painful, for one is misunderstood before one has got out what one has to say.—I feel so homesick! Oh for a quiet corner at home! When shall I have earned that? I fear—only over yonder where all of us and all things shall be gathered together.

What a contrast it is for me—just now, when for a while I am seeing 'Rudolf'[1] beside me (do you understand these quotation marks?)—to see your voice again! We have not changed much, thank God! Worse luck that one has to be

---

[1] R. Krzyzanowski who was engaged as conductor at the Hamburg Stadttheater from September 1896 (K.M.).

7

so conscious of the fact. Fondest good wishes to you, my dear Fritz—do drop me a line! Regards to Uda and the family.

Yours,

Gustav

180. *To Bruno Walter* (Breslau)†

Undated. Postmark: Hamburg, 12 September 1896

My dear Walter,

Just a hasty note: *cheer up and keep a stiff upper lip!* The one thing that is clear to me is that ⟨Weintraub⟩ has supporters and 'connections' there, and that is why Löwe wants to stay on good terms with him—which I already knew anyway. Löwe himself hinted as much to me this summer. Further, that you are a thorn in ⟨Weintraub⟩'s side and that he would like to edge you out.— Now, you shall *not* oblige him, but *valiantly* stick it out. Do *not* lose your composure—be gay and friendly to everyone. After all, you have your marshal's baton in your knapsack, so whether today or tomorrow is all the same. If things get too hot, write to me: perhaps I can get something done through ⟨Löwe⟩. But hold your fire till the last moment. Besides, you always have me to fall back on: *I shall not let you down!* So bear up, old man.

Very best wishes,

Yours,

Mahler

Things are better here than I first thought!

81. *To Theodor Löwe* (Breslau)†

Undated. Hamburg, [Autumn] *1896*

Dear Löwe,[1]

I have been hearing strange things from Breslau—not altogether a surprise, I must say. May I be quite frank? When a young lion sets foot among those old donkeys (Messrs. ⟨Weintraub⟩ and Co.), of course they would dearly love to give him the proverbial kick. But that is likely to be a bit difficult so long as he is alive. Now, dear Löwe, for the time being do let him *live*, in other words, give him a task worthy of him, give him *a free hand*, and lend him your directorial protection into the bargain. *I vouch* for success. That ⟨Weintraub⟩ or

---

[1] This letter, addressed to Direktor Löwe [= 'lion'] in Breslau, was among Bruno Walter's papers. It must have been written soon after the preceding letter, but not posted, presumably because meanwhile better news had come from Walter (o.e.).

yours, together with his colleagues, is not worth so much as one of Walter's nail-parings. This is something I herewith emphasize *fortissimo*!

I hope you will yet be grateful to me for telling you.

With kindest regards,

Yours sincerely,

Gustav Mahler

⟨In haste! Please don't take amiss.⟩

182. *To Max Marschalk†*

Undated. Postmark: Hamburg, [27 September] *1896*

Dear Herr Marschalk,

I had already had a talk with *Steinert*, the theatrical manager here, about *Lobetanz*, so your packet arrived at the right moment. He will receive the book this evening, and I shall not fail to recommend it to him most warmly. When I looked at the score again I really could not help laughing at *Muck*'s pronouncement.—I assure you it will sound *splendid* and quite unusual. I should find 'doing' it *very interesting*.—What a breed they are, these Court conductors!—More about that next time!

I am afraid Nikisch is not conducting the whole work,[1] only the second part ('Was mir die Blumen erzählen'), which is the shortest, lasting only nine minutes.[2]

But I, poor wretch, not only have to put up with that, I have to be grateful into the bargain.

Yours sincerely,

Gustav Mahler

183. *To Max Marschalk†*

Undated. [Hamburg, 2 November] *1896*

Dear Friend,

At half-past nine in the morning, the day after tomorrow, which is Wednesday, I shall begin rehearsing the second movement of my symphony at the Philharmonie.—How I should like to have you there! Will you come?—I also have a favour to ask of you. The rehearsal finishes at 11.30 a.m. If you cannot

---

[1] The Third Symphony (K.M.).
[2] The performance took place at the 3rd Philharmonic Concert on 9 November 1896 in Berlin (K.M.).

come earlier, there will be *just under an hour* at my disposal before the train leaves at 12.30, and I should like to spend the time with you.

Hoping, then, to see you at the Philharmonie.—

Yours sincerely,
Gustav Mahler

184. *To Max Marschalk*†

Undated. Hamburg [1896?]

Dear Friend,

I have just got up after a horrid bout of influenza. That is why I am so late in replying to your letter.—

I have read the libretto.[1] I entirely agree with you: I find it moving, but doubt whether it would be suited to the stage and more especially to 'the opera', which has now come down so much in the world that one can no longer be sure the triumphant force of a poetic work will have any effect on the public. But what does such an opinion amount to?—If you, the composer, feel inspired by the material and the form, then by all means finish it.—First and foremost, the problem is very much whether *that sort of thing* isn't just what we are now in need of again. Mascagni led us into this briar patch, and I see no reason why someone else, you for instance, should not lead us out of it again. The main thing is *how you do it*! And if you want me to tell you frankly my main reason for encouraging you to finish it, it is this: it always upsets me very much to see anything that has been begun left unfinished unless there is some external necessity. Believe me, *finishing something* and getting something *accomplished* is an art in itself, and one that also has to be learnt.

But the next time you make a choice, consider carefully what you are doing! And always bear in mind that, especially as an opera-composer, you have to reckon with the degenerate taste of the public and the *cliché*-ridden minds of theatrical directors and of the critics.—You must achieve one *success*.

Afterwards you will be freer to do as you like! You may well think this is a piece of advice I myself ought to take to heart. But you know how easy it is to give advice to others.—I myself am incorrigibly unpractical, and I certainly have to suffer for it.—

When the *Wichtelchen* is finished, I should like to have a look at it as soon as possible. Perhaps I can get something done about it. But—it is not going to be easy! I have burnt my fingers often enough!

Yours,
Gustav Mahler

[1] *Das Wichtelchen* (The Pixie), one-act opera by Marschalk, libretto by Moritz Heimann (o.e.).

185. *To Richard Batka*†

Hamburg, 18 [November] 1896
Bismarckstrasse 86, Hohe Luft,

Dear Sir,

I have pleasure in supplying you with the information you require![1]—all the more so since I have for some time been wishing to establish a connection with your journal, which I have been reading with great interest and satisfaction since its first appearance a short time ago.

If you would like a detailed account of my life and work, written by someone well qualified and authoritative, I can recommend Max Marschalk, Steinmetz-strasse 20, Berlin I, who knows and understands my works and aims better than anyone else. But far be it from me to anticipate your own decision.

I was born in 1860, in Bohemia, and spent most of my adolescence in Vienna. Since I was twenty my external activities have all been connected with opera. For one year (1885–6) I was also Kapellmeister in Prague, as you may perhaps recall. My first public appearance as a creative artist was with the completion of Weber's *Die drei Pintos*, a work that was also performed in Prague at that period, under my direction.[2]

From earliest youth I have composed every sort of thing that one can compose. I regard my three big symphonies as my major works: the first two have been performed several times, but the last (3rd) only in part—this part (the 'Flower' piece) having 'got going'.—This last is now in demand among conductors at most concert establishments, a fact for which I doubtless have to thank the good 'notices', something with which I had not hitherto been over-whelmed. The fact that this short piece (more an intermezzo), torn as it is out of the context of the larger work, my most important and large-scale so far, is bound to give rise to misunderstanding cannot prevent me from allowing it to be performed separately. I simply have no choice. If I am at long last to get a hearing I must not be finicky, and so this modest little piece needs must often this season 'lie bleeding at Pompey's feet', introducing me to the public as a 'meditative', finespun 'singer of Nature'. Of course no one gets an inkling that for me Nature includes all that is terrifying, great and also lovely (it is precisely this that I wanted to express in the whole work, in a kind of evolutionary development). I always feel it strange that when most people speak of 'Nature' what they mean is flowers, little birds, the scent of the pinewoods, etc. No one knows the god Dionysus, or great Pan. Well: there you have a kind of

[1] R. Batka, editor of the *Prager Neue Musikalische Rundschau*, proposed publishing an informative and explanatory article on Mahler, and had approached Mahler with a request for biographical and other information. See also letter 188 (o.e.).
[2] As guest conductor, on 18, 21, 24, 29 and 31 August 1888 (K.M.).

programme—i.e. a sample of how I compose. Always and everywhere it is the very sound of Nature! This seems to be what Bülow once referred to, in speaking to me, as what he significantly called 'the symphonic problem'. I recognize no other kind of programme, at least for my works. If I have occasionally given them titles, it was in order to provide pointers to where feeling is meant to change into imagining. If words are needed, then we have the articulate human voice, which can realize the most daring intentions—simply by combining with the illuminating word! But now it is the world, Nature as a whole, which is as it were awakened out of unfathomable silence, to ring and resound.

To say more to anyone who does not know my music would only deepen the obscurity, as it may be thought, of my interpretation of what modern music should be. I leave it to you to find the appropriate terms for my meaning. If, however, you wish to use my own words for this purpose, do so by all means. In any case, I thank you very much for your kind interest and remain

Yours faithfully,
Gustav Mahler

I cannot at the moment lay my hand on a photograph of myself, but I shall get one as soon as possible and send it to you.

186. *To Bruno Walter* (Breslau)†

Undated. Hamburg [Autumn 1896?]

Dear Walter,

There is not the slightest chance of X's[1] getting away from here. Pollini would not dream of letting her go. She sings a great deal here, in every part there is.— Her popularity with audiences has grown considerably, and that, after all, is the decisive factor. Give my warmest regards to Direktor Löwe: I am glad everything is going as I wished and predicted. Keep on the right side of the press!— Go to see those gentry now and then! Just bear in mind that you cannot behave with dignity in a dog-house: all you can do is see to it that the curs leave you in peace.

Yours ever,
Gustav Mahler

Keep on sending me the notices.

---

[1] Probably Anna v. Mildenburg (K.M.).

187. *To Bruno Walter†*

Undated. Hamburg, [December?] *1896*

Dear Walter,

Take courage, and *stick it out* at any price! I remember it was once the same for me in *Prague* (just ask Elmblad), and afterwards everything was different. Do not forget, after all, I am still about. The main thing is that you should at long last get a chance to conduct, and that you surely will.

Yours as ever in great haste,

Mahler

⟨I have just had your card! My best greetings to [Johannes] Elmblad! Tell him he should remember my weeks of rehearsal for the festival[1] with Neumann [in Prague], and to give my greetings to *Liessel*![2]⟩

188. *To Max Marschalk†*

Hamburg, [2] December 1896

Dear Friend,

The enclosed letter[3] explains why I write.

Was it presumptuous of me to refer to you as 'the person who' in my reply?— If you want to accept, let me know *by return.* And return the enclosed, won't you? I can of course provide you with material. Please send me a questionnaire!

With warmest greetings,

Yours sincerely,

Gustav Mahler

Do you know Weingartner has accepted my Third for performance at the Royal Opera-House? I should be very much obliged if you could quite *briefly* give me your impression of *Zarathustra.*[4]

---

[1] Probably a reference to the concert on 21 February 1886 when Mahler conducted extracts from *Parsifal* and Beethoven's Ninth Symphony in which Elmblad participated (K.M.).
[2] Elmblad's second wife, the Swedish poet Sigrid Agnete Sofia Pettersson (1860–1926) (K.M.).
[3] An inquiry from Richard Batka [see letter 185]. The *Prager Neue Musikalische Rundschau,* vol. I, no. 15, contained an article on Mahler by M. Marschalk (o.e.).
[4] A reference to the first performance of *Also sprach Zarathustra* in Berlin on 30 November 1896 by Arthur Nikisch (K.M.).

189. *To Max Marschalk*†

Undated. Hamburg, [4] December 1896

My dear Friend,

First of all, why should you suppose I didn't 'care for' your article? Because I did not write to you about it? If I had not liked it, I would certainly have told you so. We are on such a footing, are we not, that I could have done so!—Quite the contrary: the way you write is completely to *my* taste! For goodness' sake let us not have any panegyrics! They *can only do harm*! What we want is not incense! Hang it all, we are sliding into such a whirlpool of personality-cults and galvanized ecstasy that 'a cool head and warm feet' are doubly necessary. How glad I am that there are also such people as you and—myself. That is just as I like it! Incidentally, I really do not know why you think your article so restrained. I do not see how anything could have been said about me that would have done me more honour. And, frankly, it was the first time that anything said about me really satisfied me and warmed the cockles of my heart.—Permit me to differentiate myself thoroughly from ⟨Strauss⟩—and to differentiate what you write about me from what the shallow Corybants say about that—forgive the harsh term—knight of industry! All the press's utterances about him reveal his knack of currying favour with his own kind.—No more about that sort of thing! So may it remain, and never let yourself be tempted into 'any other way'!—

I hope Sonne has written to you by now.—Herewith some biog. data: born in Bohemia, 1860. Spent youth at grammar school—learning nothing, but making music from the age of four, composing before I could even play scales.—At 17 went to the University in Vienna and instead of going to lectures (Faculty of Letters) spent time in the Vienna Woods.

Conservatory—piano—composition. Won various first prizes. Should I mention that? Then at 19 job in the theatre at 30 gulder a month! Wandered from one small theatre to the next for years. First major engagement in *Prague*. Then *Leipzig*, then *Budapest* as operatic director, and from there to *Hamburg*, where I have been for the last six years.

The first work in which I really came into my own as 'Mahler' was a *fairy-tale* for choir, soloists and orchestra: 'Das klagende Lied'. I number that work Opus 1. Faced the public for the first time as completer and arranger of Weber's *Pinto* sketches. I regard that work as far from obsolete and am convinced that it will be taken up again when this clamour for Realism has died down.

In Leipzig and Dresden it is still in the repertoire.—By the way, the première was in *Leipzig*, under my baton.

I regard the three symphonies, which you know, as my major works. In addition a large number of *humoresques*[1] for solo voice with orchestral accompaniment, in the manner of 'Lieder eines fahrenden Gesellen' which you have heard. One who is chained in that galley, the opera-house, cannot get as much music written as do the current matadors of the concert hall. He can only write on his 'day off'. But then his inner experience concentrates in *one* work. I cannot do anything but give myself *completely* to *each* new work.—

I explained my attitude to music and art in a fairly long letter last year, which you may remember. Besides, you know it better from those works of mine with which you are acquainted, better than I could ever explain it to you. A music-maker's life, after all, offers nothing in the way of external events—he lives *inwardly*. It is probably rather significant that musicians take little interest in the visual arts; it is their nature to try to get to the bottom of things, to go beyond external appearances.

I really do not know if there is anything else that ought to be mentioned. Perhaps you will 'ask' again!—I greatly value your opinion of *Zarathustra*. ⟨I was amused to find that 'Sträusschen' [Richard Strauss] has now also turned to the *E flat clarinet* and this has even been pointed out in some reviews as a bold innovation. Well!—I'll let him keep this honour. For really *what* you write has always seemed to me more important than what it is scored *for*.⟩

I am to conduct Beethoven's *Coriolanus* and Berlioz's 'Fantastique' in Leipzig![2] Perhaps you will come along? That would be very nice, and it would be a chance to see me conduct!

Well, warmest thanks for your labour of love.

I am, in the bitter cold of an easterly winter wind, in a room that has not yet warmed up,

Your almost petrified

Gustav Mahler

I must rush to the stove to warm up. I am afraid this letter may bear traces of my plight.

190. *To Max Marschalk*†

Undated. Hamburg, 6 December 1896

Dear Friend,

I have no idea how things are usually done on such occasions. Nor is it, I think, for me to inquire. Please bring something in any case, since there is no

---

[1] This was Mahler's title for his songs from *Des Knaben Wunderhorn* for voice and orchestra (K.M.).
[2] On 14 December. See letter 191 (K.M.).

time left now.—I was delighted to get the news about *Lobetanz*! If *Lobetanz can be staged*, then I am confident I can get *your music* performed in at least *several opera-houses* (Leipzig, Hamburg, Prague). By the way, has Muckchen[1] in Berlin given his verdict? If so, perhaps Weingartner can be got to pull his weight in the other direction. I shall set to work on him about it anyway. But only when I see him—letters are useless. You know, it really is always the same old story. The moment anyone is just *himself*—woe betide him! He will have to work it off, like a debt. And that mortal sin is forgiven him only after his death. Experience is no use to the world, for the thing always seems different, remaining 'everlastingly new'. Look at Strauss's case! This time these gentry are proudly thumping their chests for having put an end to the neglect of genius. Behold: no sooner doth he appear than we blow his trumpet! Hurrah! Henceforth genius will get paid cash down!—We must possess our patience. I repeat: rest assured: your *Lobetanz* is an *original* thing, and in my view the *music* is even better than the libretto. At any rate, only music *like yours* can provide the right 'milieu' for this type of thing, and we shall *see it through all right*! But let me *know at once* when the performance is settled.

Keep on sending me *your articles* as they appear! *Please do!* I never read news-papers (*let that be strictly between ourselves*). They annoy me too much!

Yours sincerely,

Gustav Mahler

What about Leipzig? Can you come? That would be capital!

---

191. *To Max Marschalk†*

Undated. Hamburg, 10 December 1896

Dear Friend,

I have just been seeing the producer.[2] Since reading the newspaper notice he is all agog, going so far as to claim he had already spoken to Pollini about it. I got it into his head at last that the play with Thuille's music (*Lobetanz*[3]) was stillborn, whereas your music was the really valuable part of the whole thing and the sole reason why I had recommended the work to him. I hope we can pull it off—above all, a *performance* here even *before* the Berlin première.

I shall just have to see how I can manoeuvre the work out of the Thalia Theatre[4] into the Stadttheater, the only place where the orchestral situation

[1] The conductor Karl Muck (K.M.).
[2] Adolf Steinert (K.M.).
[3] Thuille's opera was not produced until 1898 in Karlsruhe. When Mahler put it on three years later, in Vienna in 1901, it had only six performances (K.M.).
[4] This theatre was also run by Pollini (K.M.).

makes it really possible to stage your work. More about that next time. I am in a great hurry today—just leaving. By the way, at the pressing request of the Liszt Society I shall be conducting the first two movements of *my C minor*[1] instead of the 'Fantastique'!

$$\left\langle \frac{8 - 11}{XII} \ 96? \right\rangle$$

Yours sincerely,
Gustav Mahler

As a matter of fact, the reason why I rarely date my letters is that I generally don't know what the date is!

---

192. *To Adele Marcus* (Hamburg)†

Undated. [December 1890s]

Dear Adele,

First of all, here are the manuscripts, which I again almost forgot to return to you.—And also the autograph you asked for.

Today I can tell you officially that I shall be arriving in Hamburg at the beginning of January and that henceforth I shall not give you a moment's peace. I wish to be invited to breakfast, diner and souper. Bill of fare the *well-known* favourite dishes! Never *more* than *one* course on pain of damnation.—I magnanimously excuse you from breakfast. To make up for that, you are to keep me company on walks and see to it that other people do not bother me. Given under our hand and seal in the Winter Palace.

Gustav

---

193. *To Bernhard Pollini*†

Undated. Hamburg [December 1896]

Dear Sir,

I have several times asked Herr Bittong[2] not to arrange individual rehearsals for *The Water Carrier*,[3] since the individual parts are already well rehearsed.— On the other hand, I should be very glad of *ensemble rehearsals*.—Although these have been arranged every day, they have not been fully attended, since members of the cast are involved in other important rehearsals.

---

[1] At the Lisztverein's fifth concert in Leipzig Mahler conducted the first two movements of his Second Symphony (K.M.).
[2] Franz Bittong (1842–1904), chief stage manager at the Hamburg Stadttheater, later its director (K.M.).
[3] Opera by Cherubini; it was put on only three times during the 1896–7 season, on 5, 9 and 26 January 1897 (K.M.).

Such a rehearsal was again arranged for tomorrow; foreseeing that Frau Doxat[1] and other members would be unable to attend because of the orchestral rehearsal of *The Merry Wives*,[2] I have cancelled the arrangement and informed Herr Bittong accordingly. Since it has become necessary to inform you of the situation, I take the opportunity of drawing your attention to the completely unpractical procedure adopted by Herr Bittong when arranging rehearsals. Since I have been here, he has arranged *all rehearsals* without consulting a single conductor.—This procedure is totally unprecedented—and is particularly unsuited to the given situation, since Herr Bittong lacks any musical qualification that might enable him to assess the requirements of either casts or conductors.—

I draw your attention to two particular defects that are, I assure you, unique.

I. Every day members' names are put up for two—or indeed *several*—rehearsals taking place at the same time.—The individual singer has to choose between rehearsals.—

II. Every day individual rehearsals and ensemble rehearsals are held (the latter are usually cancelled, since as a result of this procedure the whole cast can never assemble at one time), which are simply a *waste of time* and, what is worse, a *waste of nervous energy*, for the members already know their parts perfectly.—On the other hand, many rehearsals are *urgently necessary*, yet Herr Bittong cannot be moved to arrange them.—

The reply I received in a conversation this morning would seem to indicate that little change can be expected; any objection is rejected out of hand with the words: 'These are the Herr Hofrat's orders.'

You yourself, Herr Hofrat, have been good enough on several occasions to assure me that the conductor's requirements in this respect are decisive.

I therefore beg you to be so kind as to have tomorrow's rehearsal for *The Water Carrier* cancelled as soon as possible and to request Herr Bittong to arrange rehearsals in a more practical and prudent manner.

I am, sir,

Your obedient servant,

Gustav Mahler

[1] The soprano Ida Doxat (1867–19??), from September 1896 a member of the Hamburg Stadttheater, was married to Rudolf Krzyzanowski (K.M.).
[2] Performed once, on 27 December 1896 under Krzyzanowski (K.M.).

1897

194. *To Max Marschalk*

Hamburg, 2 January 1897

Dear Friend,

My sister [Justine] and I send our warmest thanks for your good wishes, which we sincerely reciprocate. I am in the midst of quite unfathomable work.—Leipzig was frightful. Orchestra beneath criticism, and critics even beneath orchestra.— Belated thanks for all you did.[1]—Incidentally, on 15 January, in Dresden, the Royal Orchestra, there is to be a strange potpourri of selections from my works, for which I have just been asked my permission. Have granted same about as eagerly as Marsyas due to be flayed. What else can one do? Just listen to this: II. 2nd and 3rd movements, III. 2nd movement.[2] Currants from various cakes. On 21 January, in the Gewandhaus in Leipzig,[3] the 'Flower' piece!— Still, it does mean things are moving.

What are they saying in Berlin about the performance of *Lobetanz?*—You are not going to tell me the Berliners have become as taciturn as my informant here, whom I shall (at the first suitable opportunity) poke in the ribs again.

Yours sincerely,
Gustav Mahler

195. *To Friedrich Gernsheim* (Berlin)†

Undated. [Hamburg, January] *1897*

My very dear Professor Gernsheim,

It was a great joy to receive your letter.

I must say quite frankly that after my last visit to Berlin I was left with the impression that my compositions had had a repellant effect on you, with the result that our personal relationship had suffered.—Now all this has been most delightfully cleared up by your letter, and I am very glad indeed, since for my part I have come to have a warm and lasting interest in both your work and yourself.—Believe me, this would not be changed even if you were to tell me candidly that my nature and my approach as a composer had remained strange

---

[1] Marschalk had written the programme notes for the Leipzig concert (K.M.).
[2] This movement was replaced at the last moment by the fourth movement ('Urlicht') of the Second Symphony, sung by Irene v. Chavanne. The concert was conducted by Ernst v. Schuch (K.M.).
[3] At the 13th Gewandhaus Concert conducted by A. Nikisch (K.M.).

to you, perhaps even uncongenial. Your kind remark about my songs now makes me hope that here too a bridge may yet be built. Be that as it may, my affection for and delight in your work as an artist will remain unchanged.

I shall have my songs copied and shall send them to you. I am already eagerly looking forward to the performance of your Fourth by Nikisch, for which I shall certainly come to Berlin.[1] For my part, I shall take the first opportunity of finding an audience for your works.—From one passage in your letter I gather that some of your experiences have been very unfortunate. If you can, take a little comfort from my fate.—There are times when I am disheartened and feel like giving up music completely, thinking of ultimate happiness as an obscure and tranquil existence in some quiet corner of this earth. What crushes my spirits is this terrible treadmill of the opera-house. Is it really impossible to find a post at some concert establishment? Perhaps you can think of something.

I shall be passing through Berlin at the beginning of June and shall give myself the pleasure of descending on you for an hour or so. What are you planning now? I am quite agog to see what your Fifth will be like. With kindest regards to both your wife and yourself, and very best wishes also from my sisters,

I remain

Your devoted

Gustav Mahler

196. *To Max Marschalk*†

Undated. Hamburg, 14 January 1897

My very dear Friend,

I despair of carrying out the task you have set me. With the best will in the world I cannot think of any little stories to tell about myself. Have forgotten everything, the 'good' and the 'bad' things I have been through. Opposition has dogged me ever since I set foot in this world.

So—*questionnaire*, please! I promise to answer as conscientiously and speedily as I can.

Tomorrow I go to Dresden, where Schuch is putting on a motley programme: 2nd, 3rd and 4th movements of the C minor plus the 'Flower' piece.[2] He insists on my being there. On the 21st the 'Flower' piece is being done at the *Gewandhaus*, and on 9 March Weingartner will be conducting two or three extracts from my symphony.[3] So I hope to have a few hours to spend with you again.—

[1] On 11 January 1897 (K.M.).
[2] Dropped at the eleventh hour by Schuch. See letter 194 (K.M.).
[3] The Third Symphony of which only movements 2, 3 and 6 were performed (K.M.).

By the way, there is 'something going on' here. I have managed to get my resignation through *here*, which means I shall be leaving my present job at the end of May.—They need a director in Vienna and have come to the conclusion that I am the right man for the job.—But the great stumbling-block—my being a Jew—lies in the road and may well barricade it. I am really half-thinking of settling in Berlin for a while. Do you think I can get pupils for 'lessons' there, or something of the kind? Please do not forget to let me know what you think. Perhaps you can give me some idea of the situation! About *Lobetanz* I shall soon be writing to you again. I shall *not give up*! I may possibly stop in Berlin on my return journey from Dresden.

Would you have time to spend a few hours with me (on Sunday)? I shall send you a telegram in time to let you know when I am coming; and perhaps I may have a line from you in Dresden if you cannot be free that day! I shall be staying at the Hotel Europa in Sendig.

With best wishes,

Yours,

Gustav Mahler

Right! At any rate—please, my dear fellow—do not touch on the 'Fahrenden Gesellen' episode in my life. (The connection with the First Symphony is purely artistic.)

197. *To Max Marschalk*†

Undated. Hamburg, January 1897

My dear Marschalk,

So it is fixed: 9 March in the Royal Opera-House: 'Flowers', 'Animals', 'Love'.[1]

When the time comes I shall see that you come to know something, at any rate, about these pieces. I hope you will come to some of the rehearsals. Perhaps I shall see you beforehand at *Chenier*,[2] which has been provisionally fixed for 5 February.—The fact that I am leaving Hamburg has become common knowledge—I do not know how—and any discretion in this respect has become superfluous.—

How is *Wichtelchen* coming on?[3] Do bring it to Hamburg!

Yours,

Gustav Mahler

---

[1] The Third Symphony, 2nd, 3rd and 6th movements (K.M.).
[2] Hamburg première of Umberto Giordano's opera *Andrea Chenier*, conducted by Mahler (o.e.).
[3] *Das Wichtelchen*, opera by Marschalk. See letter 184 (o.e.).

198. *To Arnold Berliner* (Berlin)†

Undated. Hamburg, [January] *1897*

Dear Berliner,

I have always wanted to become a capitalist—or have publishers queuing up on my doorstep; but I simply cannot get it to happen. In the last few days, however, something else has happened, which may be of interest also to you, to make me 'put my house in order', and so I come again to my account with you, my dear Berliner, which should have been settled long ago. I hope it does not make you think too badly of me and that you will give me the opportunity of doing as much for you, which I shall always gladly do. The 'event' I refer to is this: driven to it by a series of circumstances, I handed in my resignation here a few days ago, and it was accepted.—I have not yet found another post.—I have had a succession of offers from Munich, Vienna, etc.—But everywhere the fact that I am a Jew has at the last moment proved a block over which the contracting party has stumbled. And so there is a possibility of my having to live by free-lancing in Berlin next winter.—Weingartner is to rehearse my Third with the Royal Orchestra in the Autumn;[1] he seems very enthusiastic about it.

Well, very best wishes from

Mahler

199. *To Arthur Seidl* (Dresden)

Hamburg, 21 January 1897
Hoheluft, Bismarckstrasse 86

Dear Herr Dr. Seidl,

Thank you very much indeed—above all for the very perceptive critique of the performance of my work, from which to my great joy I think I can deduce not only a flattering assessment of my artistic personality, but also approval based on truly deep understanding of what is characteristic of me. This realization is one of the most precious things I have gained from Dresden. Indeed, hardly anything else counts beside it. How on earth was it that, knowing only these three movements,[2] which actually amount to no more than an interlude in the work as a whole, you could arrive at such a comprehensive understanding of my nature, correct on all major issues? I can only assume—what would be very precious to me—that you were guided by some inner affinity such as I

[1] This performance never materialized (K.M.).
[2] The three middle movements of the Second Symphony. [See letter 194] (o.e.).

have already sensed in your articles. I have long been reading them with interest and sympathy, even though I have not yet come to know you personally.

I hope you have received the piano reduction and have found confirmed and elaborated in the work as a whole what is hinted at and promised in these three interim movements.—Frankly, the cornerstone movements can hardly be appreciated without actually being heard.—But perhaps, with the aid of your imagination and the excellent reduction, *you* can do the impossible and form a fairly clear picture of the work as a whole. I should be vastly grateful if in your own good time you could let me know what you make of it.—And now yet another request! Weingartner is conducting 3 main movements of my 3rd *Symphony* in Berlin on 9 March. Would you not come over from Dresden for the evening? You see, you belong to the 'public' I compose for—and thank heaven it is not *always* 'outside time and space'.

Let me have a line so that I can reserve a seat for you. It seems they are in short supply.—

The two tickets you sent solved a puzzle, for I had not been able to find a hole in any of my pockets.

Again, very many thanks. I hope soon to have the pleasure of making your acquaintance in person. Please excuse my writing in such great haste.

With kindest regards,
Yours sincerely,
Gustav Mahler

200. *To Friedrich Löhr†*

Hamburg, 5 February 1897

My dear Fritz,

How very nice of you to have had a 'boy'![1] See to it that he remains one! (For that is something that one must not only be, but also are![2])

Who knows, I may come in March and take a good look at him for myself! As I am something of an expert in that field, you can rely on my judgement!— In case you still have any doubts by then!—I do not like it here any more! If it were not for this wonderful snow outside my windows, which are patterned with frost, really and truly I should like nothing about it at all. But it is very nice of the Lord always to send one something more or less worth looking at. If it is

---

[1] Dr. Clemens Löhr who was born on 28 January 1897 and died on 25 June 1974 (K.M.).
[2] A favourite expression of Mahler's (o.e.). [Translators' note: The above is a literal translation of the obscure German original: 'Denn das muss man nicht nur sein, sondern auch sind!']

not a fragrant summer's day, then at least a glittering winter's day!—Agreed
then—we shall make it up with Him!

But really, do write again soon! After all, you must be as pleased as Punch—
aren't you?

Very best wishes to Uda! A grand job she has done!

And warmest best wishes to you too, old fellow, and stay young in spite of
your boy!

Yours,
Gustav

201. *To Anna v. Mildenburg*†

Undated. Hamburg, [February 1897]

(. . .) Hail to you there in Bayreuth![1] Soon you will be in what was the abode
of one of the most glorious spirits in the history of mankind. Awareness of it
must remove any uneasiness you may experience on meeting the present
occupants. Just keep on thinking: he would be satisfied with you, because he
looks into your heart and knows all you can do and strive for. Well, you are
setting forth on your road equipped as few women have been! So be of good
cheer! (. . .)

202. *To Bruno Walter* (Breslau)

Undated. Hamburg, approx. beginning of 1897

My dear Walter,

Now you will *have* to be patient! Nothing can be done at the moment! But
that may change any day now! I have had to go through it too! After all, you
are still so young! Just do not do anything rash, but lie low.—As soon as anything crops up we shall set the wheels turning! So don't lose heart!

Yours ever,
Gustav Mahler

---

[1] Anna Mildenburg had gone to Bayreuth to study the role of Kundry (*Parsifal*) with Frau
Cosima Wagner (o.e.). She sang Kundry at the 1897 Bayreuth Festival (K.M.).

203. *To Bruno Walter†*

Undated. Hamburg, [February] *1897*

Dear Walter,

In great haste! So that's agreed. I shall put at your disposal the 1,200 marks you need, sending you 100 marks on the first of each month for twelve months from a given date. I think this is best. I beg you to be as thrifty as possible so that you manage on that. I fear this amount will stretch my resources to the limit. It is the *best* way. See that you get your call-up as soon as possible! Write again soon.

Yours ever,
Mahler

204. *To Max Marschalk†*

Undated. Hamburg, 17 February 1897

Dear Friend,

Let me keep *Lobetanz* for a while—and just stop thinking about it. I am very glad to hear you are 'in the thick of things'; that is what matters, after all. Your time will come, and if I can do anything to help it on, I am always on hand. My departure from here will mean losing my chief means of applying pressure.— Still, I should not give up hope too soon.—Perhaps I shall still be able to do something for you when something has been settled about my immediate future. And if not here—then '*there*'!

I hear that seats for Weingartner's final rehearsal and concert are sold out; Weingartner has to resort to Suchers[1] to get seats for my sister[2] and myself.— How will *you* get in? Perhaps via the newspaper? It is really too bad, isn't it, that that should turn out to be a problem too?—Well, I am so sceptical that I shall not believe this concert will be given until I see the printed programme.

At any rate I shall be coming to Berlin for a few days at the beginning of March. Looking forward to seeing you then!

Yours sincerely,
Gustav Mahler

The score of my Second is published at long last. I have told them to send you a copy.—Please let me have a card saying whether you have received it or not!

---

[1] Probably the conductor Josef Sucher and his wife, the celebrated soprano Rosa Sucher, both attached to the Royal Opera in Berlin (K.M.).
[2] Justine Mahler (K.M.).

205. *To Arthur Seidl* (Dresden)†

Hamburg, 17 February 1897
Bismarckstrasse 86

My dear Dr. Seidl,

I was overjoyed and greatly stimulated by your kind and deeply thoughtful letter. It is extraordinary how you have been able to explain me to myself in a number of ways. You have defined my aims, as distinct from those of Strauss, quite accurately. You are right in saying that my 'music *generates* a programme as a final imaginative elucidation, whereas with Strauss the programme is a set task.'—I believe that there you have touched on the great conundrums of our age, at the same time enunciating the *either–or* of things.—Whenever I plan a large musical structure, I always come to a point where I have to resort to 'the word' as a vehicle for my musical idea.—It must have been pretty much the same for Beethoven in his Ninth, except that the right materials were not yet available in his day.—For Schiller's poem is, in the last resort, inadequate; it cannot express the wholly new, unique idea he had in mind. Incidentally, I recall R. Wagner's somewhere saying the same thing quite baldly. In the last movement of my Second I simply had to go through the whole of world literature, including the Bible, in search of the right word, the 'Open Sesame'—and in the end had no choice but to find my own words for my thoughts and feelings.

The way in which I was inspired to do this is deeply significant and characteristic of the nature of artistic creation.—

I had long contemplated bringing in the choir in the last movement, and only the fear that it would be taken as a formal imitation of Beethoven made me hesitate again and again. Then Bülow died, and I went to the memorial service. —The mood in which I sat and pondered on the departed was utterly in the spirit of what I was working on at the time.—Then the choir, up in the organ-loft, intoned Klopstock's *Resurrection* chorale.—It flashed on me like lightning, and everywhere became plain and clear in my mind! It was the flash that all creative artists wait for—'conceiving by the Holy Ghost'!

What I then *experienced* had now to be expressed in sound. And yet—if I had not already borne the work within me—how could I have had that experience? There were thousands of others sitting there in the church at the time!—It is always the same with me: *only when I experience something* do I compose, and only when composing do I experience!—I know you will understand this without my enlarging on it. After all, a musician's nature can hardly be expressed in words. It would be easier to say what is *different* about him than about others.—But what this difference is he himself would perhaps be least able to say. So it is the same too with his *aims*! He moves towards them like a sleep-walker—he does not know what road he is taking (perhaps past yawning abysses), but he heads towards the distant light, whether it be the ever-radiant star or a seductive will-o'-the-wisp! I was very pleased by what you said about 'productive' criticism. I have always sensed that in you—in everything I have heard or read about you.

Happy the artist who has such a 'critic' as an ally!—I cannot but regard our having met as a rare stroke of luck. I hope you do not take this as flattery or *quid pro quo*! The fact that you cannot come to Berlin is a drop of salt in my cup of joy. I say 'cup of joy' because I am still unaccustomed to 'being performed'. You cannot imagine how often I have been seized with agony of mind when putting score upon score into my drawer, no one taking the slightest notice of the work I was producing (despite frantic efforts on my part).—I shall never cease to be thankful to *Strauss* for setting things going, and in what a truly high-minded way! Let no one suggest that I might regard myself as a 'rival' (as unfortunately happens so often nowadays).—I must repeat that I cannot regard two such people as 'rivals'. Apart from the fact that my works would doubtless have earned me a reputation as a freak if Strauss's successes had not paved the way for me, I number it among my greatest joys that I found among my contemporaries such a comrade-in-arms, such a comrade in creation. Schopenhauer somewhere uses the image of two miners digging a shaft from opposite ends and then meeting underground. This seems fittingly to characterize my relationship to Strauss.—How lonely I should feel and how hopeless my efforts would seem if I could not divine future victory from these 'signs and wonders'. When you refer to us, in a way so flattering to me, as the 'opposite poles' of the new magnetic field, you express a view I have for a long time held in secret, and only when you come to know the scores I have written since my Second will you realize, I think, how profoundly intuitive your way of putting it is.— Forgive the sloppiness of this letter. I am writing in a great hurry in the midst of preparations for a tour of several weeks, which will take me to Moscow, Petersburg, Munich, Budapest, etc. The fear of not being able to reply to your kind letter for weeks compels me to dash off these hasty lines. Finally, my warmest gratitude for the touching care with which you have collected notices of my appearance in Dresden. As yet, nothing definite can be said about *Vienna* and the directorial crisis there. *Between ourselves*—this crisis cannot be resolved until the *autumn*, and the choice now seems to lie between *Mottl* and my humble self.

Candidly, I do not know whether I really want to be offered the post, which might perhaps *divert* me from my essential aims. But I am really fatalistic about that, for the present not giving the matter a thought, simply waiting to see what happens.

With kindest regards, and once again many thanks—not for what you have done for me, but for what *you are* to me: it is an enrichment of my whole life and work.

In sincere friendship,
Gustav Mahler

I shall be staying on in Hamburg until 5 March, after which I shall be 'on the road'.

206. *To Anna v. Mildenburg* (Hamburg)†

Undated. [10] *March 1897*
[In the Berlin–Moscow train?]

(. . .) Well, yesterday I fought both my battles (last rehearsal and concert[1]) and must regretfully inform you that the 'enemy' prevailed. There was great applause, but also great opposition. Hissing and clapping! In the end Weingartner did bring me on to take a bow, and it was then that the uproar really started. I am pretty sure the press is going to tear me to shreds. (. . .) Justi seems terribly upset by this failure in Berlin! For my part, I have stopped thinking about it and in a certain sense am even proud of it! In ten years' time these 'gentlemen' and I shall meet again. (. . .)[2]

207. *To Max Marschalk*†

Moscow, 13 March 1897

My dear Marschalk,
What a whirl it has been! On Tuesday evening in Berlin I was a crashing failure, and today here I am—and it is all just like a dream. I have not seen a Berlin newspaper yet, having left the following day. Only the *Börsen Courier*! Granted, from that I could tell I was going to be so walloped and battered that no tailor could 'iron me out' again. What I do want to know is whether *you* understood me! That evening I had to put up with so many stupid remarks from friend and foe alike that it left me feeling quite stupefied. Please send what you have written to me in *Munich*, care of Dr. Heinrich Krzyzanowski, Schellingstrasse 70.

[1] Weingartner's performance of Mahler's Third Symphony (the 2nd, 3rd and 6th movements) on 9 March in Berlin, with the Royal Orchestra (o.e.).
[2] Oddly enough, Mahler's prediction proved right: the next time his Third Symphony was heard in Berlin was when he conducted it in its entirety in January 1907. But the situation had not yet changed in Mahler's favour (K.M.).

I shall be arriving there on Thursday 18th. *Here* there is a concert on Monday[1]—I find the city quite *intoxicating*! Everything is so different, so exotically beautiful! Perhaps in the end it will all turn out to be a dream, and when I wake—I shall find myself really living on Mars!

Yours,

Gustav Mahler

208. *To Anna v. Mildenburg*

Moscow, March 1897
[Hotel Continental]

(. . .) Moscow makes a weird and wonderful impression. First impression: no clatter of wheels—nothing but sledges. And my fur coat is a real blessing; without it the cold would practically have prevented my making the short trip from the station to the hotel. There are only open sledges! I have not eaten for two days, and am beginning to feel quite weak. I can imagine the looks you would give me! But any attempt to eat meets with unequivocal rejection from my stomach. (. . .)

209. *To Anna v. Mildenburg*

Moscow, 15 March 1897

(. . .) Nikisch arrives here this evening; he is soon to give a concert too. I shall be able to speak German again at long last. I stroll around all day. The city is splendid to look at, only the people are almost as temperamental as southern races! But incredibly bigoted. Every two steps there's an icon or a church, and every passer-by stops, beats his breast, and makes the sign of the cross as is customary in Russia. (. . .)

210. *To Anna v. Mildenburg*†

Moscow, [16] March 1897

(. . .) By now I am tremendously looking forward to leaving. A city as foreign as this weighs too heavily on one's feelings. As far as I can judge, the concert

---

[1] 15 March. The programme consisted of works by Beethoven, Wagner and Schumann (K.M.).

went very well. Audiences here, I must say, are really quite disorderly, and not very attentive. The concert began at 9 p.m. and finished at midnight. It was 4 a.m. before I got to bed. Now I am dreading the three-day journey to Munich, where I shall arrive on Friday. Today is Tuesday. (. . .)

211. *To Adele Marcus* (Hamburg)†

[Moscow, 16] March 1897

Dearest Adele,

It would be the height of ingratitude if I were not to send you one of these letter-cards.—And from Justi you have, I dare say, received my brief orders of the day? So all I need add is that the concert yesterday seemed to go very well.— Right in the middle of the *Siegfried Idyll* it occurred to me that for the first time in my life I was making music simply for money. That too is part of this year's progress! So now it won't be long before I achieve bourgeois respectability!

With warmest regards,

Yours sincerely,

Gustav Mahler

212. *To Anna v. Mildenburg*†

[Vienna, end of] March 1897

(. . .) Just think, on the journey from Moscow to Warsaw two trains collided shortly before mine came—we suddenly had to halt in the midst of open country and wait until the shattered coaches had been cleared out of the way. But don't say a word about this to Justi; she is too nervous, it might keep her from sleeping until I get back.

Well, yesterday we had the first rehearsal.[1] Sheer torture for the composer. Now the second is due—I hope it compensates me for yesterday's agonies.

My Berlin début still seems to be causing a stir. Today I am sending Justi an account of it, from the *Allgemeine Zeitung* here, which greatly amused me. These gentry never change their spots! Thank God my journeyman years are drawing to an end. (. . .)

---

[1] For a concert in Munich on 24 March with the Kaim orchestra. The programme consisted of works by Beethoven, Berlioz and Wagner (K.M.).

213. *To Friedrich Löhr†*

Undated. Postmark: Vienna, 26 March 1897

Dear Fritz,

Keep tomorrow (Friday) free for me. I shall let you know time and place later!

I am in a great hurry and have to watch every minute.[1]

Ever,
Gustav

214. *To Friedrich Löhr†*

Undated. Budapest, 31 March 1897

Dear Fritz,

I am arriving in Vienna tomorrow (1 April) afternoon, and shall be with you during the afternoon.[2]—Arrange for me to see your family in the course of the afternoon or evening.—I should like to spend the evening alone with you, if you have time. If you cannot be at home, leave a message for me.

Yours ever,
Gustav

N.B. I shall stay on over the following day—but shall not have a moment to spare.

215. *To Ludwig Karpath* (Vienna)

[Vienna], 3 April 1897

Dear Karpath,

You cannot imagine what bad luck I had. His Excellency von B.[3] waited for me until eleven (evidently I was given *that time* by mistake), then had to go out. He came back at twelve, but was so busy that he could not see me, with the result that I must wait, in desperation, until tomorrow.

Perhaps I shall again see you at *breakfast* in the *Europa*[4] at 8.30.

Yours in haste,
Gustav Mahler

[1] During this visit to Vienna negotiations were opened between Mahler and the management of the Court Theatre, which finally led to his appointment at the Vienna Opera House; this is also the background to the following letter (o.e.).
[2] Mahler conducted a concert in Budapest on 31 March. See Notes (o.e.).
[3] Baron von Bezecny, Generalintendant of the Vienna Court Theatres (o.e.).
[4] The former Café de l'Europe (o.e.).

216. *To Ludwig Karpath†*

[Vienna, 4] April 1897

Dear Karpath,

Decision due *tomorrow*. Things are said to be still *favourable*.[1]

I am sorry, a telegram just received compels me to hasten back! Please send everything of *interest* to Hamburg, Bismarckstrasse 86.

I hope to see you again soon.

Thank you very much for all your kindness.

Yours sincerely,
Gustav Mahler

217. *To Emil Freund* (Vienna)†

Hamburg, 9 April 1897

Dear Emil,

Please send me the *Wiener Abendpost* and all the morning papers in which my appointment is announced! By return if possible!

Yours ever,
Gustav

218. *To Ludwig Karpath*

Hamburg, 11 April 1897
Hoheluft, Bismarckstrasse 86

In haste,

My dear good Karpath,

My warmest gratitude to you for your loyal endeavours and above all for your *discretion*, without which everything might have fallen through at the last moment.—You have earned a lasting claim on my confidence and my friendship. —Confound it! I have just heard of Bezecny's *resignation*.[2] *It has come too soon!* (This, actually, was the serious crisis at which I hinted to you and by which my appointment, already *decided on* by Prince Liechtenstein,[3] was so suddenly and unexpectedly delayed.)—I wonder whether the anti-semitic papers will not

[1] This refers to the impending decision whether to engage Mahler as conductor at the Vienna Court Opera (o.e.).
[2] Bezecny did not, however, retire until the following year, on 14 February 1898 (K.M.).
[3] Prince Rudolf, von und zu Liechtenstein, the Emperor's Lord Chamberlain, at the same time Supreme Director of the Court Theatres, an office of even greater authority than that of the Generalintendant (o.e.).

make capital out of this. By implying, for instance, that *my* engagement forced him to go! *That* is something we should anticipate and prevent! My dear fellow, please keep an eye open and let me know, frequently and quickly, how things are going. Perhaps you will try to give me some guidance as to the attitude I should take.

Pollini will be back today or tomorrow, and I shall try to get immediate release from my engagement.

Very cordially, in haste,
Gustav Mahler

219. *To Ludwig Karpath*

[Hamburg,] 15 April 1897

Dear Karpath,

Many thanks for your news! The cutting from the *Allgemeine Zeitung* [Munich], which I have just received, speaks of 'utterances' I am alleged to have made: 'Re-organization—forced retirements—new appointments!' *That* sort of thing will not do me any good—only set all the members on my back.

Heavens—what a wasps' nest I have stirred up! For now only this in this confidence: I shall be in Vienna by 27 *April*. The only people I have told are Bezecny and Wlassak,[1] and it must be left to *them* to make what use of it they will.—

Is it true that *someone else* is to be appointed alongside or 'over' me?

Yours in haste,
Gustav Mahler

220. *To Friedrich Löhr*

Undated. Postmark: Hamburg, 15 April 1897

Dear Fritz,

This witches' sabbath is driving even me mad.—The main thing is that I shall be in Vienna on 27 April, and shall take the bull by the horns. Admittedly the start does not seem very obviously promising!—But I do what is right, and fear no one. And if these gentry do not take to me, they can—do the other thing. Rabble! Friend and foe!

Yours ever,
Gustav

[1] Hofrat, Dr. Eduard Wlassak (1841–1904), Director of the Secretariat of the General-intendanz (o.e.).

221. *To Max Marschalk*†

Undated. Hamburg, 20 April 1897

My dear Marschalk,

⟨I am sending you your poor *Lobetanz*, for which I could alas find no home here.—It is fortunate for this and your other children that I am going to 'better' myself, and I promise you that as soon as I myself am 'at home' I will take up the cause of the orphans as far as I can.⟩

I just do not know whether I did the right thing in accepting Vienna! I face the immediate future with great anxiety. For the time being all I ask of Providence is not to be kept from my 'vocation' for too long. You know of course that what I most feared was being made a director, which is precisely what has now happened. But: *vederemo!* Do write again soon. Above all, never let the bonds between us break. I shall need all your forbearance in the near future. I shall have my hands full, and mind and heart as well. Perhaps you will come to see me in Vienna!

Yours,
Gustav Mahler

Letters addressed to me at the Imperial Opera-House, Vienna, will always find me.

222. *To Friedrich Löhr*

Undated. Postmark: Hamburg, 20 April 1897

Dear Fritz,

Wait! Hold everything till I get there! I shall be in Vienna next Tuesday (27 April)! I can hardly believe it!

I shall have to be prepared for quite a dance, but shall try to make it go to my tune!

Till then—
Yours,
Gustav

You can tell V.[1] and prepare them, anyway!

[1] The Baronesses Vesque-Püttlingen, whose interest Löhr had engaged on Mahler's behalf (o.e.).

223. *To Bruno Walter*†

Undated. Hamburg, [April] *1897*

Dear Walter,

I have recommended you *most warmly* to Direktor Rudolph in Riga, hoping he will engage you if there is in fact a vacancy. Quite apart from that, you do not need to worry at all about what ⟨Harder⟩¹ has told you. And my recommendations will carry more weight from now on. All right, then!—What have you got to say to Vienna? ⟨I shall tell Herr Löwe what I think when I get the chance.⟩

Yours ever,
Mahler

224. *To Arnold Berliner*

Undated. Postmark: Hamburg, 22 April 1897

Dear Berliner,

Just a hurried note to thank you for your letter. I must expressly say what pleasure it gave me, since you began by doubting that it would. All that my Vienna appointment has so far brought me is immense uneasiness and expectation of struggles to come. It remains to be seen whether the post suits me. I have to reckon with bitterest opposition from unwilling or incapable elements (the two normally coincide).

Hans Richter especially is said to be doing his best to make things hot for me.² But: *vederemo*! This has not been exactly a bed of roses either, and recently, in particular, I have had to put up with really degrading treatment.

Another new chapter now begins. But I am going *home* and shall do my utmost to put an end to my wanderings so far as this life is concerned. I hope I shall see you in Vienna one of these days, so that we can chat again just as in old times. I am in a terrible hurry and must close.

With all good wishes,

Yours,
Gustav Mahler

---

¹ Karl Harder, concert-agent in Berlin (K.M.).
² Mahler had told Berliner of a correspondence with Richter that fully justifies this surmise (o.e.).

225. *To Ludwig Karpath*†

[Hamburg, between 18–23] April 1897

Dear Karpath,

A brief note to thank you for your messages. I have my hands full, with work.
—My farewell concert will be on Saturday,[1] and on *Sunday* off to Vienna, where
I arrive on Monday. I shall get in touch with you the moment I arrive. Perhaps
on Monday we can lunch together?

Looking forward to seeing you! Oh, who wrote the article in the *Fremden-*
blatt—really charmingly agreeable! And so 'well informed'![2]

Yours ever,

Gustav Mahler

226. *To Camilla von Stefanovic-Vilovska*†

Undated. Postmark: Hamburg 25 [April] 1897

Dear Frau Stefanovic-Vilovska,

Your very kind letter finds me on the point of leaving—I might almost say,
on the point of boarding the train! How much it delighted me—just like yourself, I remember my youth and my youthful experiences fondly! My greatest
joy is not that I have reached a position of great worldly prestige, but that I have
found a home—*my home.* That is: if the gods will guide me. For I have to
reckon with a grim struggle ahead.

Do not fail to look me up when you come to Vienna! That would really please
your old friend and 'colleague'. Perhaps we can *play* together again, as in old
times.[3] And I promise to 'bully' you again as I always used to. Agreed?

Please give my kindest regards to your husband. I hope some day I shall have
the honour of making his acquaintance.

With all good wishes,

Yours very cordially,

Gustav Mahler

[1] On 24 April. This concert, which was also Mahler's annual benefit concert, consisted of
Fidelio preceded by a performance of Beethoven's 'Eroica' Symphony, and took place at the
Stadttheater (K.M.).
[2] Karpath got this article published through the good offices of his friend Julius Stern, editor
of the *Wiener Fremdenblatt*: Karpath provided the material, and Stern wrote the article (o.e.).
[3] The lady to whom this letter is addressed is the violinist who became well known in the
1880s under the stage-name Milla von Ott. She had been friendly with Mahler from the time
in Iglau and throughout his years of study at the Conservatory in Vienna (o.e.).

VI
VIENNA (1)
1897–1901

1897 continued

227. *Unknown Addressee*[1]†

[Vienna], 29 April 1897
Hotel Bristol

I herewith beg to inform Your Highness that I have arrived in Vienna and should be glad of permission to call.

May I ask Your Highness to have the kindness to appoint a time?

With deep respect,
Gustav Mahler
Conductor at the Imperial-Royal Court Opera-House

228. *To Ludwig Karpath*†

Undated. [Vienna, beginning of May] 1897

Dear Karpath,

When I went to see Jahn I had to wait, since he happened to be closeted with *Hans Richter*.—When I was admitted, Jahn came up to me in the most amiable way, instantly sending for Wondra[2] to meet me. What he offered me for my début was *Don Giovanni*, which of course I had to accept. For my second work *I* asked for *Tannhäuser*, for the following Tuesday, whereupon he proposed *Hans Heiling*[3] for the third work. It seems that the management intends to make a public pronouncement; so please 'await' that.[4] I cannot yet 'see' the situation

---

[1] Draft, probably addressed to either Prince Liechtenstein or Alfred Prince Montenuovo (1854–1927). It is most likely that the former is the intended recipient because he was Montenuovo's superior (K.M.).
[2] Hubert Wondra, chorus master at the Court Opera from 1888 to 1908. As Jahn's nephew he had some influence at the Opera (K.M.).
[3] Opera by Heinrich Marschner (K.M.).
[4] Karpath had known from the very first of the Court Theatre management's negotiations with Mahler, but at Mahler's request made no journalistic use of the information before the official announcement (o.e.).

clearly. Frankly, I should really prefer something other than *Don Giovanni*—
but I could not possibly refuse.[1]

When shall I see you?

Yours in very great haste,
Gustav Mahler

229. To *Emil Freund* (Vienna)†

Undated. [Vienna, Spring] 1897

Dear Emil,

Please let me have the loan of *200* florins for a few days.—Adler[2] has just
written to say that if he does not receive my *curriculum vitae* within the next
two days everything will have to be put off till the autumn!

So send it off *this instant*!

To: Prof. Dr. G. Adler, Prague-Weinberge.

Yours ever,
Mahler

230. To *Anna v. Mildenburg* (Hamburg)

Vienna, 17 May 1897

(. . .) Yesterday and the day before I had no chance to write you so much as a
line. There was a tremendous whirl of congratulations, visitors, etc.! All my
troubles are over now, thank God! The whole of Vienna hailed me with out-
and-out enthusiasm! Next week we have *Walküre, Siegfried, Le nozze di Figaro*
and *Zauberflöte*. There can no longer be any doubt that I shall become director
before long. (. . .) Do tell me how things are with all of you in that theatre
(that penitentiary) of yours! (. . .) It's all going famously! The whole company
are very taken with me, and my position is an exceptional one, quite
splendid. (. . .)

<hr/>

[1] Mahler actually made his first appearance in Vienna conducting *Lohengrin* on 11 May
(K.M.).
[2] Guido Adler. See Notes (K.M.).

231. *To Ludwig Karpath*

Vienna, 1 June 1897

Dear Karpath,

Yesterday I finally had an abscess on my tonsils opened! If you are not afraid of infection, do visit me for a quarter of an hour. I am still confined to my room today.

With best wishes,
Yours,
Mahler

232. *To Anna v. Mildenburg†*

Vienna, [4] June 1897

(. . .) I shall be conducting *Fliegende Holländer* again tomorrow and *Lohengrin* the following night. You would be delighted to see the position I have here! And how the whole company likes me! One really does feel as though one had escaped from prison! (. . .)

233. *To Anna v. Mildenburg*

Vienna, 12 June 1897

(. . .) My throat is still in a dreadful state, and I fear I am going to have to put up with one or two more abscesses. It appears, from what the surgeon says, I have a neglected catarrh of the nose and throat and I have to undergo daily treatment with silver nitrate. When I come back in August I have to undergo another radical operation. Such is the delightful information I should gladly have spared you. It's not that it is at all dangerous, but it is painful and wearisome. And now I am to see whether mountain air (800 metres) will do me any good. I have rented a cottage in Kitzbühel in the Tyrol. I am going there tomorrow. I hope to be in Bayreuth in mid-July for the opening of the Festival. (. . .)[1]

---

[1] Anna v. Mildenburg made her début at Bayreuth in the role of Kundry (*Parsifal*) on 19 July 1897 (K.M.).

234. *To Adele Marcus* (Hamburg)†

Kitzbühel, 18 June 1897

Dear good Adele,

Things are happening again! And there is always something!—I hereby notify you that once again we are on the point of packing, to go in search of new lodgings.—Down in the village an epidemic of scarlet fever has broken out, so we have no choice but to move on a bit.—You can picture the state we are in. We are bearing it in the best of spirits—in the well-known Mahler manner.

I hear my star is rising again in Hamburg, and that Fräulein Sans[1] is even said to be seriously considering making me conductor of the Philharmonic. If this sort of thing continues, even Marwege[2] will one day consider me quite a passable conductor.—

How ever could you be so silly as to keep on your rooms in the Heimhuder-strasse when we were already in the process of finding you a pleasant flat in Vienna? Advertise your flat in the papers instantly! And come to us in Vienna as fast as you can!—

Incidentally, what do you think of the change of climate in my favour there? My 'popularity'? At the moment I have only *three enemies* in Vienna: Jahn, Richter and Fuchs! All the others think me a delightfully charming person to know! Ugh! They *will* get a surprise!

The weather is simply terrible, and all of us have to go out house-hunting. We shall write again when we have found something.

With very best wishes to you and your family,

Yours as ever,

Gustav Mahler

My special regards to your Mama, whose hand I kiss.

235. *To Friedrich Löhr*

Kitzbühel, 4 July 1897

My dear Fritz,

Since our birthdays have come round again, it is only right that we should overcome our ghastly reluctance to put pen to paper and wish one another many happy returns. This year we have especially good reason to do so, since there is a good chance that from now on we shall be able to spend our lives

[1] Frl. Elizabeth Sans was a pianist (amateur) and a composer on a small scale. I believe she belonged to the circle of Mahler's Hamburg friends. She had nothing to do with the Philharmonic Orchestra in Hamburg (K.M.).
[2] Violinist, see letter 126 (K.M.).

near each other again in the old friendship that has never been ruffled by even the slightest disagreement.

Such a friendship, dating from one's youth, is after all something one is not likely to come by a second time, and we have been clever enough to preserve ours; may it remain intact until, I hope, a blissful end.

I hear you are going to set up your summer establishment just outside Vienna? If that is so, I should wend my way there quite frequently in August, and we could again listen to many tales from the Vienna woods—or we could tell them some. Please let me know more about this.

> Very best wishes from your old friend
> Gustav

---

236. *To Wilhelm Hesch*

Undated. July 1897

My poor dear Hesch,

I simply cannot describe how I sympathize with you.[1] We are all stunned. In such misfortune consoling words are of no avail; indeed, I have none to write. But one thing I know is of comfort to someone so sorely tried—that is the knowledge that a friend's sympathy is genuine and comes from the heart.— And you do know, my dear Hesch, that in me you have a friend who feels for you like a brother! How dearly I should wish to be with you to lend you my support. But it will not be long—by the end of the month I shall be back in *Vienna*, and the first thing I shall do is to seek you out, if you are there. Do write to me in full about everything, I beg of you. To me it is an enigma. How are the children, and how are you going to arrange things now? *And above all, how are you?* My dear friend, this misfortune was sent *by God to try you*, and you will *not be found wanting*—for you are both a *man* and *an artist*! The main thing now, as our Prince Liechtenstein is always saying, is to '*pull yourself together*'. Promise me, my dear Hesch, that you will be *sensible*—if not for God's sake, then for the sake of your children and your friends. If only I were already with you. Where will you go? Who will look after you? Please write and tell me all about everything! In fact, now you must write to me more often. And about everything that concerns you.

For today I shall press your hand, my poor, afflicted friend.

All of us here send our greetings and heartfelt wishes for your welfare.

> Your old friend,
> Gustav Mahler

[1] On the death of Hesch's wife (o.e.).

237. *To Friedrich Löhr†*

Undated. Postmark: Vienna, 31 July 1897

Dear Fritz,

I have lost your address! When can we meet? I think I could be free in the afternoon of Thursday the 5th.

Ever yours,
Gustav

238. *To Wilhelm Hesch*

Undated. Vienna, August 1897

My dear Hesch,

I was tremendously glad to get your latest news. God grant that the improvement may be maintained and progress steadily. We all (but especially I) are longing to see you.—It would be very good if you would send me a few lines again, letting me know how you are getting on. I am again up to my eyes in the rush of work—as usual at the beginning of the season. It is unbearably hot here, and you may be thankful you are still miles away from the city.

Heartfelt greetings, my dear Hesch, from

Your ever faithful
Gustav Mahler

239. *To Bruno Walter* (Berlin)†

Undated. Vienna, August [?] 1897

Dear Walter,

You are mightily mistaken if you think an opera-house like Mannheim would engage you for *one* year. In my opinion it is now high time for you to do your year's military service. Your qualms about not being sufficiently accomplished, etc. are utter *nonsense*! I can vouch for your being as accomplished as anyone need be. Supposing you could get Mannheim in '98, everything would break down if you had to do your military service in '99.[1] The same goes for *Riga*. I recommended you so warmly to *Rudolph*[2] at the time that I have no doubt he will engage you as soon as there is a vacancy.—My advice then is: *do your year*. Nonetheless I shall write to Direktor W.[3] if you think it will do any good. But

[1] Walter apparently never did his military service (K.M.).
[2] Julius Rudolph, Director in Riga (see letter 223, (K.M.).
[3] The manuscript says Western. It is not clear whether Mahler is referring to the director of the Stadttheater at Reichenberg (Bohemia), Emmanuel Western (K.M.).

what do you ultimately gain? From now on my recommendations will have increasing weight (if I stay alive). If I become director in Vienna (and *entre nous*, there are excellent prospects of my reaching that position in a very short time),[1] I shall not for some time be able to engage you myself, but I shall certainly have ample opportunity to do something for you.—Unfortunately I am still very poorly. Illness really has a firm hold on me now! Please put up with these abrupt lines from a convalescent who is just about to take to his bed again. ⟨(My sisters don't yet know about it.)⟩

Yours sincerely,
Gustav Mahler

The letter to W. goes by the same mail!

240. *To Ludwig Karpath*†

Undated. Vienna, August [1897]

Dear Karpath,

I have twice tried, in vain, to get you on the telephone.—Generalmusik-direktor Schuch, of Dresden, has been to see me. He would very much like the Viennese newspapers to take note of the celebrations at the Dresden Court Theatre from *1 September*, marking the completion of twenty-five years of his activity there. So you would oblige me by writing something in appropriate taste, perhaps also getting a few other papers to follow suit.—

You know what to say. *Distinguished conductor*. Outstanding man of the theatre. High honours and decorations. Champion of dramatic art and its modern exponents. About to receive further great honours and acclaim.—*Can I count on you?*

With best wishes,
Yours in great haste,
Mahler

241. *To Ludwig Karpath*†

Undated. [Vienna, August] *1897*

Dear Karpath,

⟨Enclosed, the required box ticket.⟩

Very distressing notice in the *Tagblatt*.[2]

[1] Mahler was then still only conductor at the Vienna Court Opera [though he had become deputy director on 21 July]. See also Notes (o.e.).

[2] What is referred to is the *Wiener Tagblatt*, not the *Neues Wiener Tagblatt*. The report, which was totally unfounded, concerned Hans Richter (o.e.).

That sort of thing does more harm than good. I can't understand these people! I hope we shall meet again soon.

In haste,

Mahler

⟨What has happened to the article on Schuch?⟩

242. *To Ludwig Karpath*†

Undated. [Vienna, August 1897]

Dear Karpath,

You *have* done a magnificent job.[1] I shall remain a client of yours. Warmest thanks, hoping to see you soon,

Yours,

Mahler

243. *To Bruno Walter* (Berlin)†

Undated. Vienna [September 1897]

Dear Walter,

First of all, go *straight* to X.[2] and ask him from me if he would care to sign a very favourable contract as first tenor at the *Vienna Court Opera*, and, if so, *from what date he will be available.* If necessary I myself or my delegate would come to B.[3] to arrange everything. I should just like to know in principle how he feels about it, in order to know whether it is a practical possibility or not.

I suppose you will already have given him some idea of what I am like, and so he will know that an engagement with us is a guarantee of his artistic career for his whole future.—

I should even be prepared to *accept any more or less reasonable conditions.* Between ourselves, my appointment should be definitive before the end of this month, but I am already transacting business with full directorial authority.[4] ('What a change wrought by Divine intervention!') I shall discuss your affairs another time. Keep your chin up. Nothing can go wrong for you *now.* Reply *at once*, by *telegram*; then send a letter with further details.

Yours,

Mahler

[1] Karpath's article on Schuch's jubilee (o.e.).
[2] The manuscript says Kraus, i.e. the tenor Ernst Kraus (1863–1941). Kraus had just been taken on at the Royal Theatre in Berlin, and Walter had coached him during the preceding summer; he declined Mahler's secret offer (K.M.).
[3] Berlin, according to the manuscript (K.M.).
[4] Mahler was officially appointed on 8 October 1897 (K.M.).

244.   *To Max Marschalk†*

Undated. Vienna, [Autumn] *1897*

My dear Marschalk,

⟨Of course you guessed correctly. I could not bring myself to send off your work without looking at it. But with the best will in the world I cannot find the time, and anyway after so long I do not have the right to continue to withhold the score from you. At some less busy time I shall ask you for it again.⟩ I am as 'swamped' as only a theatrical director can be. A dreadful, consuming life it is! All my senses and emotions are turned outward. I am becoming more and more of a stranger to myself. How will it all end?

Warmest regards, and remember me as one usually remembers those who have died.

Yours,
Gustav Mahler

My sisters send their regards!

245.   *To Ludwig Karpath†*

Undated. [Vienna] *Autumn 1897*

Dear Karpath,

I am dead and done for!

Yours ever,
Mahler

1898

246.   *To Nanna Spiegler†*

Vahrn, Carinthia, 1 August 1898

My dear Nina,

I must not leave Vahrn without having sent you at least a line. I am not yet quite well—the pain comes on every morning (and is of course borne with incomparable heroism). I have worked at some little things from *Des Knaben Wunderhorn,* just to provide evidence of 'keeping going'! Tomorrow, alas, I am off to Vienna. That really hurts! But it has to be! The pain usually lasts

8*

from about half-past nine until two in the afternoon, or even 3 or 4 (Albert
wants to know). Very best wishes to both of you from

your
incredible hero
Gustav

247. *To Albert Spiegler* (Engelberg, Switzerland)†

Undated. Postmark: Vienna, 27 August 1898
Imperial-Royal Directors' Office
Imperial-Royal Court Opera-House

Dearest people,

My condition persistently remains the same; general health excellent. Pain
stationary, of course now with the addition of moral wrath and annoyance with
the powers of the underworld. I am now *touché* (by means of Dr. Boer[1])!
Gersuny[2] is not here, and there is nothing for it but simply to go to 'someone
else'.

I am writing in greatest haste in the office.

Ever yours,
Gustav

248. *To Bruno Walter* (Riga)†

Vienna, 28 October 1898

Dear Walter,

What I write today is in the *strictest confidence*!

⟨Richter⟩ and ⟨Fuchs⟩ are *leaving*!

I herewith ask if you are able and willing to accept my offer of an appointment
at the Vienna Court Opera. If so, I would send you a contract to become opera-
tive from the termination of your engagement in Riga; and we would then see
how to get you out of Riga as fast as possible.—What I should like best is for
you to start with us next autumn.

⟨Do not talk to anyone at all about this and tell me by return post⟩ the first
day from which you are free!

Yours,
Mahler

[1] Ludwig Boer, although not mentioned in the official annals of the Vienna Opera, is said to
have treated all the singers, besides being Mahler's personal doctor (K.M.).
[2] Dr. Robert Gersuny (1877–1927) (K.M.).

249. *To Bruno Walter*†

Undated. Vienna, [November] *1898*

My dear Walter,

What is all this beating about the bush? If I make you an offer, I do really know what I am doing. I need an *adjutant* here, one who carries his marshal's baton in his knapsack. (I am at present conducting everything myself, and am by now *exhausted*.)—What concern of yours is it whose *successor*[1] you are, and for that matter what concern of the public's is it? Besides, you will not be a 'finished' conductor in two or even ten years. If we are anything at all, we are always *learners*. You yourself will not be able to say where at present you could learn more than with me. So strike while the iron is hot. Leave the rest to me and your own endeavours. It would be very important to me to have you before 1900, because I shall be dead by then if things go on the way they are going on now. So let me have another word from you—*by return*, and no excuses! You will be getting *5000* florins to start with.[2]

Yours,

Mahler

1899

250. *To Friedrich Löhr* (Vienna)†

Undated. Vienna, 3 [April] *1899*

Dearest Fritz,

You should have the concert ticket by now. The full rehearsal is on Friday, at 2.30.[3] I should like you to be there, and to dine with me afterwards. At such a time, when I take off these accursed directorial boots—as it were—I'm sure we shall have lots to talk about. I should also like to have there those few people for whom this work was written. So be sure to come, won't you? My dear fellow, do.

Yours,

Gustav

[1] Walter had made it a condition that he was officially introduced to Vienna as Richter's successor (K.M.).
[2] Walter remained in Riga. He intensely regretted causing Mahler a grave disappointment (o.e.).
[3] For the performance on 9 April of Mahler's Second Symphony in Vienna, Mahler conducting the Vienna Philharmonic Orchestra. The soloists were Lotte v. Barenfeld and Marcella Pregi (K.M.).

251. *To Ludwig Karpath*†

Undated. [Vienna, 11] *April 1899*

My dear Karpath,

Where on earth are you? I have been searching for you for two whole days.
I was really delighted by your notice.[1] I do congratulate you. It would be a
credit to the most celebrated of your colleagues, it is so very good both in content
and in form.

I believe it will cause a general stir.—But now please do put in an appearance
again.

I did not see the article in the *Pester Lloyd*,[2] but could not help laughing
heartily over what you wrote on it. You *did* give it to them hot and strong!
Well! *habeant sibi!*

Yours,
Mahler

252.   *To Siegfried Lipiner*†

Undated. [Aussee, June 1899]

Dearest Siegfried,

Just a line to let you know that your *Adam* has this minute arrived. What a
joy! At last!—I have just finished the first act! Outside there is a southerly
gale raging! It is strange how it has been blowing in concert with your verse,
always in tune and on time.—

This is a truly Dionysian work! Believe me, no one else alive today, except
me, will understand it. There is some affinity with it, to my mind, in Euripides'
Bacchae. Only Euripides always has too much talk about things instead of the
things themselves —*What* ever is it that delivers all living creatures into the
power of Dionysus? Wine intoxicates, intensifying the drinker's condition.
But *what* is wine?—No visual representation has ever yet succeeded in capturing
what flowers spontaneously from every note of music. *This* music lives and
breathes throughout your poetry in this work of yours. It is really unique.—
Instead of telling of wine or describing its effects, it *is* wine, it *is* Dionysus! It
seems to me, incidentally, that what Dionysus personified to the ancients was
simply *instinct*, in the grandiose mystical sense in which you have interpreted
it. In your music, as in the myth, those in ecstasy are driven forth to become

---

[1] After the Vienna première of the Second Symphony (o.e.). Karpath's review appeared in
Neues Wiener Tagblatt on 10 April (K.M.).
[2] According to Karpath the article was abusive and irrelevant (K.M.).

one with the animals.—I do thank you, dear Siegfried. I shall always honour your work. But it is just as well that it is *I* who have it. I need it, and it needs me!

Yours ever,

Gustav

253. *To Siegfried Lipiner*

Undated. [Aussee, July 1899]

Dearest Siegfried,

I was on the point of setting out to visit you when your sweet letter came. Yes, I too am quite paralysed by this awful weather.—However, I have meanwhile settled all cosily into your *Adam* and have realized that life begins only in those lofty regions. The trouble is adjusting oneself again to the nether regions. I have known the higher ones for so long that I can stand the arduous travelling to and fro better than most people.—

I can well imagine your wanting to begin on something else meanwhile. It is sure to be on the same lines, and I should love to get a glimpse of it.—If you are by now up to coping with *earthly remains* (*asbestos* ones, admittedly), without being made miserable, send me a wire, and I shall sally forth to see you. There is a lot in *Adam* that you will have to explain (or rather: confirm) to me. The fact is, it is one of those works that have to be read backwards after one has reached the summit.—I really can't tell you what pleasure it has been giving me. 'Kaspar stands as solid as a house!'[1] The material has all been really and truly resolved into pure form. It is some loftier phenomenal world, in which the types have become individualities. The interpretation of the Biblical fable is original and grandiose, and everything conceptual has been *rendered visible*! Such delicate touches as, for instance, having the famous 'Am I my brother's keeper?' uttered casually and simply in the first act are characteristic of the way the whole work is handled.—That—and much else besides—everyone would doubtless have wanted to do. It strikes me as especially important in relation to the spread over four evenings. I pick this out of course merely as one *example*. I could cite countless similar ones. Even from this work one realizes there is a long road ahead. There is nothing in it, not even the slightest touch, of what one might call mere poetic prattle. The serpent bites its own tail. —Justi is now copying it all out.—

So when can I come? All the same, don't go and let yourself be carried away

[1] Beethoven's comment on Kaspar in Weber's opera *Der Freischütz* (o.e.).

into asking me to come if you are, even in the slightest degree, in a creative mood! In that case it is better to deny oneself everything!

Very best wishes to yourself and Klementine,[1]

Yours,

Gustav

It's too bad, but I have to be in Vienna by 1 August, because that master-hand of Fuchs's[2] had an accident while bottling wine. Another sacrifice to Dionysus!

254. *To Friedrich Löhr*†

Undated. [Aussee,] *4 July 1899*

My dear Fritz,

Tomorrow you will be entering your forties. I recall this day so dear to me, as every year, sending my very very best wishes to you and your family. It is an odd turn of fate that we have become as close to each other, in terms of space, at the beginning of our forties as we were in our youth, and yet actually more separated from each other, seeing less of each other than when one of us was in the north and one in the south. But I hope you too regard this separation as a purely local—or rather, temporary—one. For, believe me, that is all it is. But we two cannot consort with each other the way others do. Since at present I do not belong to myself, I cannot belong to you either. But this I will say: wait but a little while, and then this directorship and other farcical things will be among the shades in Tartarus and we shall behold each other face to face again in the golden light.

From my heart, my dear Fritz,

Yours,

Gustav

255. *To Nanna Spiegler*†

Undated. Postmark: Alt-Aussee, 14 July 1899

My dearest Nanna,

What a terrible fellow I am, not yet to have written to you (which I have been meaning to do day after day), and remain a terrible fellow, for even today I am merely informing you that I do not intend writing to you, only sending you very

[1] Lipiner's wife (o.e.).
[2] The conductor Johann Nepomuk Fuchs. This accident led to his death on 5 October of the same year. See also letter 255 (K.M.).

best wishes and telling you that my thoughts are often with you all. Things have gone very badly with me this year. In the midst of everything all my threads broke, and I can't get hold of them again. I feel quite wretched about it, as if I had something heavy weighing on my conscience. Alas, it is all the fault of the resort's music and the horrible water. A stove in the new room might well have become my Muse! But one cannot write tunes with frozen fingers! Admittedly that is poor consolation!

On 1 August I must return to the struggle, Richter being in Bayreuth and Fuchs's maestro-hand being in no fit state as a result of a broken wine-bottle (the only connection the worthy man has with Dionysus). Oh! Oh! Oh! Ah! Ah! AAAAAAA!

There, how I wail to you! And you, poor thing, have perhaps more cause than I! Lipiner's *Adam* is quite magnificent! I have taken it utterly to my heart and am very happy about that! Greetings to you always, and to Albert from your

hanged
Gustav

256. *To Ludwig Karpath*

[Aussee] 17 July 1899

Dear Karpath,
Thank you very much for the kind attentions. Do give my warm regards to our friend Hesch, who is, I hope, in as good health as he is in spirits.[1]

Yours,
Mahler

257. *To Bruno. Walter* (Riga)

Undated. Vienna, 1899?

Dear Walter,
You have completely misinterpreted my silence.—You know how lazy I am when it comes to writing letters—but now every line is a sacrifice! Well—I have long since forgiven you, if there was anything to forgive. I cannot even remember what it was all about.—There was nothing more to be done here on your behalf because things had taken a fresh turn. So—water under the bridge— we're friends again, aren't we? You might have sent me word of yourself

[1] Karpath and Hesch had sent Mahler a picture-postcard from Karlsbad, and Karpath had also sent Karlsbad wafers and biscuits (o.e.).

occasionally. I did not even know where you had got to! Make up for it now, dear Walter, and do not take offence at my brevity. That is, I dare say, how things will have to remain for as long as I am director.[1]

With best wishes,
Yours in haste,
Mahler

258. To Bruno Walter

Undated. Vienna, approx. Autumn 1899

Dear Walter,

I am on *no* terms *at all* with Berlin. In the present circumstances any efforts would be futile, in any case.—Put up with it all as best you can! It has to be the way it is, and so all will turn out for the best! Nothing in our relationship has changed in the slightest. Do your best to get on.—These 'chaotic moods' are quite normal at your age and at {your} stage of development, they do not perturb me in the least. Besides, it is no misfortune to become Berlin Court conductor when one is still so young.[2]

Yours as ever,
Mahler

1900

259. To Bruno Walter (Berlin)†

Undated. Vienna, [early Spring] 1900

Dear Walter,

In *strict confidence*! Please, in no circumstances breathe a single word of this letter to anyone.—There is a possibility of my being able to engage you at the Court Opera in place of X.[3]—Will you now come *sans façon*? Will you and can you become and be to me what I need? Without standing on ceremony—all

---

[1]This evidently in reply to a letter from Walter trying, by once more justifying his refusal of Mahler's offer, to dispel the resentment he still believed Mahler felt (o.e.).
[2] Walter signed an interim contract with the Royal Opera in Berlin in the early autumn of 1899 and took up his post the following autumn (K.M.).
[3] 'X' = Hans Richter who left the Vienna Opera on 15 April 1900. Early in June Walter was in Vienna and had a confidential talk with Mahler. The latter promised to keep Richter's post open until the end of the coming season. Finally they agreed on a salary of 6000 florins (K.M.).

from the point of view of the brilliant *future* that opens up before you here—
if so, accept, and the thing is settled. As a starting salary you would have *5000*
florins, which would in time rise considerably.—Please reply at once!

Yours in haste,

Mahler

260. *To Nanna Spiegler*†

Undated. Paris, [20] *June 1900*

Vienna delivery postmark: 22 June 1900

Dearest Nanna,

   Although I am now in the Austrian Embassy, thus, so to speak, representing
Austria,[1] I am deigning to write in this condescending way to you from Paris,
the main thing being, do you hear from Natalie, whose letter I enclose? All this
wild uproar all around me—how boundlessly inappropriate to be playing music
for the French *at this time*, with the World Exposition going on—is so distasteful
that I cannot even enjoy this beautiful city, Paris. There is simply no way of
conveying how utterly *everything* is mere phrases, poses, lies! At five on Friday I
shall still be conducting the *Fliegende Holländer* overture, and by eight I shall be
in the train. I simply do not know how to wait for it. There is really only one
word for it all: Pah!—though for the first few days (before the first concert)
it was not so bad. I wandered about the countryside outside Paris—it is really
so lovely and full of memories of the various Louis and Napoleons that there is
perhaps nowhere else where one has so strong a sense of transience. But now
there is a concert every day, and I cannot get out of town. So far I have held
aloof from official welcomes, banquets, etc., and hope to do so until I leave!
Actually all that seems to be what counts most! I assure you, dear friends, it
could all be done without any music-making, and *la gloire* would not suffer
in the least. I positively feel like laughing when I take up my baton.

O! O! O! O!

My love to you and Albert. On Sunday morning, I hope, I shall be bathing
in the Wörthersee. Heaven knows when I shall get rid of this sense of disgust!
I feel as if I had prostituted myself!

Yours,

Gustav

---

[1] During the Paris Exhibition the Vienna Philharmonic under Mahler's direction gave three
concerts, on 18, 20 and 21 June (K.M.).

261. *To Nanna Spiegler* (Engelberg)†

Vienna, 18 August 1900
Court Opera, Vienna

My dear Nanna,

I was so delighted to receive your sweet letter—why don't you write a word about *how you are?*

This summer, for me, has been so glorious that I feel myself really and truly braced for the coming winter.

If I can keep this up in future—managing to get mental and physical repose in the summer—then I shall be able to lead a human sort of life even here in Vienna. *Only mind that all of you soon come to spend the summer near by, so that we can be together more often.*

In this coming winter I shall myself make the fair copy of my work;[1] and this will give me a foothold in all the stress of life, a foothold such as I have needed particularly in these recent years.

One feels so utterly desolate when one has to survive without what is sacred to one. I particularly feel unhappy and have to assume a mask—one that does, I dare say, often grin at you all rather oddly. Last winter, even, when I had to leave my work, the very one that I have completed this year, at a stage when it was in its most frail, truly embryonic beginnings, I could not imagine that anyone would be capable of picking up such frail threads again and continuing to work them. But it is singular. The moment I am in the midst of nature and alone with myself, everything trivial and commonplace vanishes away, leaving no trace. In such days *nothing can harm me*; and that helps me again and again.

Now, I must admit, it comes rather hard to be here again, taking up the old struggle; I am still half living in the world of my Fourth.—This one is quite fundamentally different from my other symphonies. But that *must be*; I could never repeat a state of mind—and as life drives on, so too I follow new tracks in every work. That is why at first it is always so hard for me to get down to work. All the skill that experience has brought one is of no avail. One has to begin to learn all over again for the new thing one sets out to make. So one remains everlastingly a *beginner!* Once this used to make me anxious and fill me with doubts about myself. But since I have understood how it is, it is my guarantee of the authenticity and permanence of my works. And so for the first time I look towards the future without the worst doubts—though I should never dare to be confident. For it is and always will be a gift of God—one that, like every loving gift, one cannot deserve and cannot get by asking.

I embrace you and send love to Albert.

Yours, Gustav

[1] The Fourth Symphony, which Mahler completed in the summer of 1900 (K.M.).

262. *To Siegfried Lipiner†*

[Vienna] 19 August 1900

My dear Siegfried,

Today I simply have to sit down and thank you for your glorious, profoundly moving *Hippolytos*.[1] What actually kept me so long from writing to you about it was awareness of how inadequate all words are when one is faced with such a work, and my deep-seated conviction that silence is the only language befitting such an encounter.—On the other hand, I know from my own experience how much the creative artist needs response, how he needs to get a resounding echo of his work from the hearts of those to whom he has given it, and I know I *must tell* you what I feel lest you misunderstand. There is still a lot I have to ask you about—perhaps I shall be able to produce many of the answers myself. (For I am still reading and living in it—thank heaven this summer has so buoyed me up that all the wretched turmoil of the theatre is not quite submerging me.) Just one thing I must tell you: on my first reading of the second act I was rather disconcerted by the motivation of Phaedra's end. It struck me as a weakening of the naïve myth, rather the way I always feel it is weakened in Grillparzer's *Argonauts*.[2] It seemed to me this 'toning down' of the apparently brutal solution was sentimental (in Schiller's sense of the word). But then I resorted to your proven method—approaching a work of art in a *mindless* state—turned to it a second time without any preconceptions, and thereupon instantly understood what you meant. In fact, now I could hardly imagine any other solution.—Well, so there is a question I have been able to answer for myself.

Then there is something else that has become grandly clear to me about your essential nature: a new and deep connection between your creativeness and the musical side of your being. I am coming to understand more and more your occasional semi-humorous complaints that the gods did not endow you with the gift of music. My dear Siegfried: you do make music! No one will ever be able to understand you better than a musician, and I may specifically add: than *myself*. It sometimes seems to me quite a joke how closely my 'music' is related to yours. This has become particularly clear to me from *Adam*, which I am still steadily assimilating. Another qualm that I must confess to (but one that likewise disappears as soon as I throw my 'preconceptions' overboard) is of a more technical nature. The priest, who is of such an individual stamp, struck me as

[1] One of Lipiner's dramas (o.e.).
[2] The second part of Grillparzer's trilogy *Der Goldene Vlieses* (1819). In 1878 Mahler began composing an overture to *Die Argonauten* which he entered *pro forma* and unsuccessfully for the coveted Beethoven prize. The manuscript has been lost, but according to the *Geschichte der Gesellschaft der Musikfreunde in Wien* (1912) a thematic outline still existed at the beginning of the century (K.M.).

being rather the 'confidant' of old-fashioned drama. In that respect I dare say I may have been somewhat demoralized by Ibsen and the rest of those modern gentry. I simply don't know whether that could have been avoided. There is always something rather contrived about creating a figure to say something for the sake of the development. What do you think about this? Are you cross? But I am only thinking of something on similar lines to Goethe's Natural Daughter. The moment one replaces a generic term by a personal name, it all seems quite different! Anyway, I should like to hear your views.—Which reminds me: when are you coming back? It seems ages since we talked to each other. About *Adam* again—I can't help feeling that the fourth drama in your *Christus* cycle is the barrier you are still finding it so hard to get over. I often have the same problem—the fourth movement, or perhaps some other one, simply will not take on form, and if I decide to do all the others first the 'arithmetical error' very often comes to light at the end, and then I find the cause of the deadlock. It always arises from the fact that {I} have at that point taken the wrong path. So then, when I can see the three completed movements there before me, it all becomes so clear that I almost automatically, in logical progression, find the right path out of the wilderness. I keep on thinking to myself: Couldn't you do the *Magdalene* and *Judas* without taking the fourth evening into account?—Good Heavens, when I consider what is here being bestowed on mankind! *Adam* 'stands as solid as a house' (a remark of Beethoven's about *Der Freischütz*), and even if you write no more of it, it is one of the finest things in the world. But of course if one does read it in the context of what is yet to come, its stature becomes still more gigantic! Do get at least the *Magdalene* on to paper! All I am asking you to do is to take one step after the other—that is the only way of making progress—every strenuous mountain-climb teaches me that. When, exhausted, I gaze upward towards the summit, my strength fails and I lose heart, but then I let the summit be and just press on, step by step—and finally reach my goal.—I still think it will be hard for you to get beyond the fourth drama, which it is so hard to come to grips with and give definitive form to. Just write the *Magdalene* and then *Judas* and after a while *John* will suddenly stand revealed before your eyes. *That too has happened to me*—I have suddenly realized that a last movement was *beyond the limits of the work*. What I mean might be explained in a metaphor: one often stands in a big hall with a mirror at the end of it, and one is entirely mistaken about the form; it is only when one comes to the borderline that one realizes one has been tricked by the mirror and therefore has been aiming for the wrong thing. I don't know whether I have made myself clear.

And now very best wishes to you, my dear Siegfried. All day long the deeply stirring conclusion of the third act has been haunting me! (I read it only this morning.) Please tell Klementine I should like to keep *Hippolytos* a little longer; I shall return it to her the next time she comes.

That glorious finale! Till now I never realized one could also do that sort of thing in words.—You will drop me a line, won't you, to say how you are getting on? And when you are coming.

Best love also to Klementine. Oh yes, I *have* finished my Fourth. And during the winter I shall make the fair copy.

Yours ever,
Gustav

263. *To Siegfried Lipiner*

Undated. [Vienna] *August 1900*

Dearest Siegfried,

By *development* (*re* 'confidant') I didn't mean development of the *action*, but development of the *character* of one of the protagonists. You see, it always seems clumsy if something essential, something the audience must be informed of, is conveyed by an unimportant figure (obviously brought in solely for that purpose).—This sort of figure is always to be found in Racine and his like, and 'confidant' is simply the technical term for that role.—But fundamentally all that doesn't matter a damn. If all confidants had such glorious words to speak as your priest I would accept them.—And after all why shouldn't one make one of one's figures utter such an account of what is going on, if otherwise one might need perhaps as much as a whole act to express the whole thing in an unobtrusive way?—I regard the *potion* in *Götterdämmerung* in the same light, and such things simply pertain to the *liberty* and courage of the artist.

Yours in great haste, ever,
Gustav

264. *To Siegfried Lipiner†*

Undated. [Vienna] *Autumn 1900*

Dearest Siegfried,

Well, if you really insist—though I can't understand why—I shall send you your *Hippolytos*. As things are at present, I should have had time to read some more of it. Later, when you come back, I shall again be up to the eyes and shall not be able to return to such a sublime world.—I think I have now grasped the conflict that prevails in earthly life between maidenly and womanly love

(Artemis–Aphrodite), which also manifests itself in young men. In your *Hippolytos* it is the other way round, as usual—Phaedra, the woman, is purified by Hippolytos's reluctance, and it is wonderful to feel that this sublimity is the insoluble contradiction in life as a whole, one that takes on its most decisive and most fateful form only in the lives of lovers. That is why the lovers have to die—not in atonement for their tragic guilt—but because a wonderful, mystical connection between love and death brings everything to fruition and completion in them.—What is peculiar, something I have found in no other poet, is how in your works concepts merge into each other—the strange relatedness, indeed unity, of all life and creation suddenly becoming clear as it does only in music.— If I should not have understood aright, do please enlighten me.—Such a great work is of course not simply wound on to the spool of some kind of 'idea', and its essence can as little be expressed by such as can the essence of the universe.—

Warmest wishes,

Yours ever,

Gustav

265. *To Bruno Walter* (Berlin)†

Undated. Vienna, [early Autumn] *1900*

Dear Walter,

Now you are on the spot you will be able to assess the situation.—I shall have to make my decision sooner than expected; otherwise I should fall between two stools—or, rather, between an armchair and a stool (you would be the armchair!). Please let me know by return what you think of our project and when you will be able to tell me the result.

Yours in haste,

Mahler

The Fourth has arrived.

266. *To Ludwig Thuille* (Munich)†

Undated. Vienna, [November] *1900*

Dear Herr Thuille,

Your *Lobetanz*[1] is now definitely fixed for the beginning of February (this because of Schoder,[2] who has to appear in Weimar in January, during her official leave of absence, which would mean a break in the performances, and

---

[1] Première in Vienna on 18 March 1901, conducted by Franz Schalk (o.e. + K.M.).
[2] The soprano Maria Gutheil-Schoder (K.M.).

in our experience that might easily be detrimental to the work's future at our Opera).

I shall of course keep you posted.

Thanks very much for your information about the second performance of my work.[1]—Yes, our friends the conductors have an unfortunate habit of 'getting things wrong'.

But good heavens—why should things be better for 'us' than for the great masters, who had to put up with that sort of thing year in, year out, century after century? Luckily piano reductions do gradually work their way into people's minds and feelings, and concert audiences finally begin to set their imaginations to filling in what is missing.—If it were not so, Beethoven's symphonies would still seem monstrosities to this day.

With best wishes,
Yours sincerely,
Mahler

1901

267. *To Friedrich Löhr*†

Undated. Vienna [February 1901?]

My dear Fritz,

Enclosed is a ticket I instantly reserved for you. So I was rather taken aback to hear you had almost bought one.—Actually the entire hall, down to the last, least seat, is taken by season-ticket holders.[2] So you can see I am now 'in fashion'.

Ever,
Gustav

Been quite tormented and feeling low.[3]

---

[1] The Second Symphony was performed by Mahler in Munich on 20 October, and repeated by Bernhard Stavenhagen on 8 November (K.M.).

[2] Probably this was for the first performance of 'Das klagende Lied' in Vienna on 17 February. It was a Singverein concert which was reserved for season-ticket holders (K.M.).

[3] Mahler suffered from haemorrhoids in early February 1901 shortly before the first performance of 'Das klagende Lied' (K.M.).

268. *To Bruno Walter* (Berlin)†

Undated. Vienna, February 1901

Dear Walter,

On 17 February, at half-past noon, my 'Klagende Lied' will be performed for the first time: here, myself conducting. Could you and would you be there? Try to get the day off. *One day* will suffice if you travel through both nights. It really is essential that you should hear it, since, in the event of there being performances outside Vienna, I propose designating you conductor! Reply at once! Pfitzner's opera interests me very much.[1] Is it really impossible to get a piano reduction out of Elberfeld? That really would be too much of a joke! Well, do what you can in that quarter, too. Hoping to see you on Friday,

Yours,
Mahler

269. *To Emil Freund* (Vienna)†

Abbazia, 30 March 1901

Dear Emil,

Together with this letter you will be receiving a parcel containing another manuscript, which I should like you to keep together with the rest. Let me know *at once* on a postcard when you have received the package.

I am getting on famously! I shall be back in Vienna on Easter Sunday, and hope to see you soon.

Yours ever,
Gustav

270. *To Bruno Walter*†

Undated. Vienna, [May] *1901*

Dear Walter,

Where not writing letters is concerned, I am forced to outdo you.—I am so glad you have safely entered harbour—something my ship is no longer likely to do. I have no doubt that you have chosen well and have entered into happy bondage.[2] My best wishes go out to you and your betrothed, whom I much

---

[1] *Die Rose vom Liebesgarten* (The Rose in the Garden of Love) was first performed in Elberfeld on 9 November 1901. The Vienna première took place on 6 April 1905 (K.M.).
[2] Walter had married the singer Elsa Korneck on 2 May (K.M.).

GROSSER MUSIKVEREINSSAAL.

Sonntag, **17.** Februar, halb 1 Uhr Mittags:

Ausserordentliches Concert der Wiener Singakademie.

Zur ersten Aufführung gelangt:

Das
klagende
Lied

für Soli, gemischten Chor und grosses Orchester

von

Gustav Mahler

unter persönlicher Leitung des Componisten.

Mitwirkende:

Frau **Elise Elizza**, k. k. Hofopernsängerin.

Fräulein **Anna v. Mildenburg**, k. k. Hofopernsängerin.

Fräulein **Edith Walker**, k. k. Hofopernsängerin.

Herr **Fritz Schrödter**, k. u. k. Kammer- und Hofopernsänger.

Das **k. k. Hofopernorchester**, verstärkt durch einen **Bläserchor**.

Die Mitglieder der „**Wiener Singakademie**" und des „**Schubertbund**".

Das Concert wird eingeleitet mit:

R. Wagner, Eine „Faust"-Ouvertüre.

Sitze à fl. 5, 4, 3, 2 und 1.50, Entrées à fl. 1.

Alexander Rosé, Concertbureau, I., Kärntnerring Nr. 11.

Fig 3. Announcement of the first performance of *Das klagende Lied*, Vienna, 17 February 1901

look forward to meeting during some summer visit. There is only one copy ⟨
the Fourth[1] in existence, which I shall show you in the summer. Tell Pfitzn⟨
to send me his opera.[2] *Der arme Heinrich*[3] is at present out of the question f⟨
my Viennese.

Very best wishes,
Yours in haste,
Gustav Mahler

271. *To Bruno Walter†*

Undated. Vienna, [early June] *190⟨*

Dear Walter,

Oh, capital! I am leaving for the Wörthersee this evening, but have arrange⟨
that as soon as your definite acceptance is received you shall be sent a two-yea⟨
contract, to run from 1 July, with an annual salary of 6000 florins. (The perio⟨
has been kept short so that your salary can be raised when the contract i⟨
renewed.) Everything else can be settled between ourselves, by letter.

My address is: Maiernigg am Wörthersee, near Klagenfurt.

Perhaps you will come and see me there in August?

One thing is most important. Your appointment must *not* be made know⟨
before you arrive in Vienna. I have very good reasons for this. *Nor in Berli⟨
either!*—It will be best for you to make your first appearance in Vienna wit⟨
something new. I am thinking of *Hoffmanns Erzählungen*[4] and *Puccini's Bohèm⟨*
for a start.[5] I hope you will now *really* enter harbour. With best wishes, in grea⟨
haste, just leaving—

Yours,
Mahler

The season opens on 18 *August.* So you can have a real rest beforehand.

272. *To Nanna Spiegler* (Vienna)†

Undated. Posted from Klagenfur⟨
Arrival postmark: Vienna, 21 June 190⟨

All this, as you see it on this card,[6] is the view as it usually is here. I am

---

[1] Mahler's Fourth Symphony (K.M.).
[2] *Die Rose vom Liebesgarten* (o.e.).
[3] Opera by Pfitzner; it was not performed in Vienna until 1915 (K.M.).
[4] *The Tales of Hoffmann*, opera by Offenbach (K.M.).
[5] Walter made his début with *Aida* on 27 September (K.M.).
[6] See Plate 7.

ending it although you do not otherwise share my views. Perhaps you will
when you read it!

Since there's an inch to spare I'll not flinch, but scribble, at a pinch, a nibble
of rhyme—hoping you don't find it too fibble!

> This line I am writing simply and purely
> Because it fits in architecturely!
> I am in a café,
> sending my love,
> your constant
> G.

And at the same time to Natalie![1]
Alas, alack, she's fallen in the lake!
That's her portrait![2]

273. *To Max Kalbeck*†

Maiernigg am Wörthersee, 22 June 1901

Dear Herr Kalbeck,

I have been on holiday for a fortnight now, and received your kind letter
yesterday.

I am really glad you find the work worthwhile, and am now doubly glad
that at the eleventh hour I abandoned *Hoffmanns Erzählungen*—which is in
any case little more than rhyming prose—in favour of *The Queen of Spades*,
which I regard as Tchaikovsky's most mature and artistically solid work.

As regards the fee, I have already taken the usual steps with the management;
my only fear is that it may take some time to go through because of the holidays.
If you would prefer the matter to be settled speedily, please drop me a line.

Scarlet fever is not very noticeable here by the lake; and even if it were—
'y reste! You can see that too is an article of faith with me; though it is also
knowledge that a man's real enemies are not outside him, but within himself.—
Actually I cannot understand how it comes that you—with a musician-poet's
soul—do not possess that faith-knowledge. What is it then that delights you
when you hear music? What makes you light-hearted and free? Is the world
less puzzling if you build it out of matter? Is there any explanation to be got
from your seeing it as an interplay of mechanical forces? What is force, energy?
Who does the playing? You believe in the 'conservation of energy', in the
indestructibility of matter. Is that not immortality too?

[1] Natalie Bauer-Lechner (K.M.).
[2] See top left corner of Plate 7 (K.M.).

Shift the problem to any plane you choose—in the end you will always reach
the point where 'your philosophy' begins to 'dream'.

I shall be {back} in Vienna at the end of August.

You are likely to be travelling then, so, when the translation is finished
please convey it to:

Herrn Graf,[1] Director's Office.

But do deliver it to Herr Graf in person, since otherwise it might easily get
lost, this time of year being what it is.

With kind regards to yourself and your wife,

I am,
Yours sincerely,
Gustav Mahler

274. *To Bruno Walter†*

Undated. Maiernigg, [June] 190

Dear Walter,

Hurrah! Your appointment has been approved, from 1 *July*—providing your
resignation has gone through in Berlin. So you will begin receiving your salary
this month. And that will help you to get a really decent holiday.—Well, so
you can enjoy unlimited leave until the Imperial assent is given, even if it takes
until the autumn. Do write soon.

Yours,
Mahler

275. *To Bruno Walter†*

Undated. Maiernigg am Wörthersee, [July] 190

Dear Walter,

This is just a scrawl to put your mind completely at rest, at the same time
expressing my delight about the happy solution of the problem—in the midst
of 'ordinary' vacation work. My secretary will be sending you all the details.
The moment you get the Imperial assent, send me a wire. Then we can work
out final arrangements.—Please don't yet breathe a word to anyone! In the
interests of your future in Vienna. It would be a good thing if we could meet in
August, before the season starts.

[1] Ferdinand Graf (K.M.).

One last question: What are the *Kroll Hall* acoustics like? Strauss wants to conduct my Third there! Orchestra on the stage! Can it be done?

In haste,

Yours ever,

Mahler

276. *To Bruno Walter*

Undated. Maiernigg, August 1901

Dear Walter,

For all eventualities I just want to tell you to take things easy as long as you need to. After all, you have nothing to lose here, and I want a thoroughly *fit* Walter, not a nervous wreck.—Don't worry about anything!

Best wishes,

Yours in great haste,

Mahler

277. *To Nanna Spiegler*†

Undated. Postmark: Klagenfurt, 20 August 1901

Dearest Nanna,

So here at last is the holiday letter! The fact that Natalie is so valiantly keeping you posted makes it easier for me to wait until I have finished my homework in the cottage up there on the hill. Otherwise I should surely be a better correspondent.—This year's vintage is *tantum quantum* quite satisfactory. Perhaps there will be something left over for you in the winter.

Of course the *old* complaint is the same as ever: too much rush—too little time! And I always have to leave off something when I am in the middle of it. Well, I have gradually become calmer about it since discovering that the creator can interrupt his travail quite without injury to the child, continuing later at some convenient time. Or perhaps like hens, zealously hatching the egg—and running off now and then for food.

But you are not behaving at all well, are you! I tell you both: protect yourselves from rain and cold in summer. What a pity you can't see our refuge here. I am sure you would follow our example. On Friday or Saturday I shall be going to Vienna. Justi will be staying for about three weeks longer. The poor girl is badly in need of it, I'm afraid, and will need taking great care of in Vienna this winter. At the moment she has gone off and away. My expeditions this year were not so good as last year. Weather anything but favourable Consequently it was impossible for me to spend my last moments thinking of you, let alone send you a picture-postcard before I left. In pelting rain, with thunder and lightning, I rushed up and then down the Drei Bärenhütte,[1] unable to think of anything but my boots, which had a hole in them, which let the wet in.

My Fourth will probably be on the programme in Vienna in October,[2] and then you will glimpse an aspect of me that you do not yet know. All I fear is that that aspect will please you most so that henceforth you will look at me only from one side.

Since I shall not be conducting the Philharmonic any more this year, there will be no more celebratory suppers, and I want you both to think of some way of making up this loss to me I should also like to ask for somewhat gentler treatment on such occasions—as befits my arrogance. This summer again I have read as good as nothing, being far too busy professionally. It is ten years now that this has been going on And so there will be nothing left for me to do but, like Quintus Fixlein, to write books for myself. Well, for that I shall expect a memorial tablet on my woodland cottage: Here every morning the once so famous G.M. would sit. All I beg is that no mistake should be made and that the tablet should not be affixed to the neighbouring little annexe, where it would be still more appropriate but, as an expression of piety, comprehensible solely to Natalie and myself. Well! So the holiday letter is written, leaving me only just enough space to give you a big hug, with love to Albert and the children.

Yours,
Gustav

278. *To Henriette Mankiewicz* (Gmunden)†

Undated. Maiernigg, just leaving, [approx. 21 August] *1901*

One always has to begin letters to you, my dear Henriette, by saying 'thank you'. If one writes one of the sort I am writing today, one doesn't even know how to begin to begin.

Your Japanese[3] arrived yesterday. I must confess I have as yet no idea how I shall use them to the best advantage—I should need your imagination for that—but since they come from you I know even now they will adorn my house

---

[1] Probably near Maiernigg (K.M.).
[2] The Fourth Symphony was not performed in Vienna until 12 January 1902; the première took place in Munich on 25 November 1901 (K.M.).
[3] Japanese roses (o.e.) [probably a piece of embroidery].

better than anything my gardener or any painter could do. Even if they were quite ugly and unknown to anyone except myself, they would still be precious and beautiful to me—because they come with your greetings and will bloom on your behalf. Well! There you are, this is a love-letter! Even if perhaps not in *optima forma*—that is something I have by now forgotten how to do.

Today I leave here, with a *heavy heart*! It is sad to realize one has to wait a whole year.

And also because I have had to break off right in the middle of work—as usual. How fortunate mothers are—they cannot be forced to interrupt their birth-pangs—and perhaps it is a blessing for the children too. I'm afraid, my dear Henriette, I shall not be able to keep my promise to visit you in Gmunden in September. Those ill-begotten children of mine at the Opera have seen to that, misconducting themselves to such an extent that I have to work here absolutely flat out in order to bring them to their senses with all speed. My succeeding in this, if I do succeed, is the precondition for my doing what I so *dearly* wish to do—visit you in Gmunden—for it is bound to take me three days, how ever I look at it. I can't spend two consecutive nights travelling. In Vienna I shall play you what I have done (chips from the workshop) this year. There are some things—some young shoots that you will harbour and cherish in your loving and understanding heart. In my songs I always think quite personally of someone dear to me, to whom I should like to sing whatever it may be; and this time I chose you. I can think of *no one more dear to me.* Well! I began my letter with a declaration of love, and I close with one. This added in haste, for letter-writing is and always was my bane!

May all go well with you, my dear, and do send me a card via G., to Vienna, every now and then, letting me know how you are, as I now find it quite difficult to get anything out of N.

Yours ever,
Gustav

Greetings to Gretchen and Frl. N.

279. *To Arnold Berliner* (Berlin)

Vienna, 29 August 1901

Dear Berliner,

I was delighted with your letter. It gives me a welcome opportunity to say that my feelings towards you have not changed and that I recall our old relationship with undiminished affection. I have always seen the cause of our separation as simply—the separation itself. I can really remember no other cause. Nor could any momentary discord and its consequences have any lasting effect—such a thing would be out of proportion, out of character, as regards both of us. My life being what it is, I cannot maintain relations with close friends over long distances; I simply lack the sheer physical time. It is in the nature of things that such friendships then petrify into 'memories'. But just come and spend a few days with us, and those memories will be instantly transformed into 'the present'.

Even this quarter of an hour in which I am writing to you is time I cannot really spare.—I hope to come to Berlin in the course of this winter.[1] Then I shall certainly look you up, and I am convinced we shall find each other unchanged. For me the genesis of our relationship is sufficient guarantee of that; for it was a shared outlook and cast of mind that brought us together, not merely some feeling or mood, such as brings very young people together. You will, I hope, forgive my brevity.—

I must get back to work.

When you think of me here, do so quite without diffidence, and as for those last days in Hamburg (which I now find more ridiculous than embarrassing), wipe them clean out of your memory and rest assured that he who lives here now is, in unchanged deep affection,

Your old friend,
Gustav Mahler

280. *To Bruno Walter* (Vienna)

Undated. Vienna, Winter 1901

Dear Walter,

I hear you are in despair over the second act.—There is really no need at all for you to be upset. If that goose ⟨Elizza⟩[2] makes a mess of things and ⟨Slezak⟩[3] is slovenly, then it simply means the ensemble can't be got to work. Don't worry yourself to death about it.

Best wishes,
Yours,
Mahler

---

[1] Mahler went to Berlin to conduct his Fourth Symphony on 16 December (K.M.).
[2] Elise Elizza (1870–1926), soprano, member of the Court Opera 1895–1918 (K.M.).
[3] Leo Slezak (1873–1946), tenor, member of the Court Opera from 1901–1912, and from 1917–1934 (K.M.).

PFARRKIRCHEN

. The first page of Letter 10: see p. 63, where the three small crosses, one on the view of Pfarrkirchen and two over the word *Schmeissefliegen* in the text, are explained in a footnote

2. (*above left*) Mahler in Iglau, 1881

3. (*above right*) Mahler in 1889 with members of the opera house orchestra in Budapest

4. (*opposite*) Kassel, Obere Karlsstrasse 17, where Mahler lived from 22 August 1883 to 1 September 1884

5. Mahler in 1902, from an etching by Emile Orlik

6. Mahler in Vienna with his sister Justine, 1899

7. Postcard to Nanna Spiegler, summer 1901 (see Letter 272)

8. Wiener Hofoper, *c.* 1902

9. Natalie Bauer-Lechner, *c.* 1905

10. Maiyernigg, 1905. Mahler with Alma and their two daughters

11. Mahler in Vienna, 1907

12. Mahler at Fischleinboden, 1909

13. (*opposite*) Josef Steiner at the time of his friendship with Mahler

14. (*below left*) Josef Krug–Waldsee

15. (*below right*) Friedrich Gernsheim

16. (*above left*) Karl Goldmark

17. (*above right*) Geza Zichy

18. (*opposite*) Siegfried Lipiner

19. The Löhr family, *c.* 1918. *Left to right*,
Friedrich, Uda, Maja and Clemens

20. Toblach, taken in 1974

281. *To Karl Moll* (Vienna)†

Undated. Vienna, [early December] *1901*

Dear Herr Moll,

I have just received your card and could not help laughing heartily. Dignity is something I utterly lack, as you well know. Apart from that, your request will not put me to any great trouble. I shall see to it in your name and in mine.— Since I should like to reserve seats tomorrow for you for *Zauberflöte*[1], please telephone, as you did recently, to let me know whether you will still be here over the week-end. Schoder is singing Pamina—it is one of her finest achievements.— Kindest regards to your charming family, whom I hope to see again on Sunday evening, if only from a distance.

Yours most sincerely,
Mahler

282. *To Anna Moll* (Vienna)†

Undated. Vienna, [9] *December 1901*

My dear friend,

(You will, I hope, permit me to use this form of address, which I should like to claim as a delightful privilege—one, it is true, that I have not yet earned, but which has been so magnanimously conferred upon me.)—Well, this parenthesis has turned out almost longer than my letter! What this blunder in 'declension' may end by doing is to bring down Fräulein Alma's scorn upon me.—This evening I am leaving—and alas, for longer than I thought. You see, I have been urgently requested also to assist at the rehearsals of my Second, which is due to be played in Dresden on 20 December.[2] So it will be a full fortnight before I see you all again. May I confess to you that this separation seems very long and quite upsets me? That in this short time I have come to feel so close to you all, have become so devoted to you and your family, that I feel the time away from you as a deprivation? I speak so frankly because I feel you will accept this confession as warmly as it is made; and that you too no longer regard me as a stranger. May all go well with you and may you remain well disposed to me.

Your very devoted
Gustav Mahler

The contents of the little package are to be shared, according to hallowed ritual, between mother and daughter.

[1] The performance on Sunday, 8 December by Mahler (K.M.).
[2] Conducted by Ernst von Schuch (K.M.).

9

VII

VIENNA (2)

1902–1907

1902

283. *To Mysa Wydenbruck-Ezsterhazy* (Vienna)†

Undated. Vienna, [January] *1902*

Dear Countess,

Thank you very much indeed for your kind and cordial words.[1] The newspaper item was most inopportune. It is so embarrassing to have such an entirely personal matter dragged into the public eye. But the fact that such valued friends as yourself, dear Countess, share in my happiness makes up for much. I am delighted that you will continue to give me your friendship in this new life of mine; rest assured that I shall always reciprocate from the depths of my heart.

Yours sincerely,
Gustav Mahler

284. *To Karl Goldmark* (Vienna)

[Vienna,] 16 January 1902

My dear Goldmark,

Please forgive my delay in writing to thank you for your good wishes on my engagement and your kind remarks about my latest work.[2] I trust you will not have misinterpreted my silence. I scarcely need to assure you that of all the congratulations I have received none was more precious to me than yours.—The stir that such an event causes in one's life continues, compelling me to write no more at the moment.

With kindest regards and once again many thanks,

I am,
Yours sincerely,
Gustav Mahler

---

[1] Mahler was thanking her for her congratulations on his engagement to be married (o.e.).
[2] The Fourth Symphony, first performed in Vienna on 12 January 1902, with Mahler conducting and Margarethe Michalek as soloist (o.e. + K.M.).

285.   *To Max Kalbeck†*

Undated. [Vienna, January 1902]

My dear Herr Kalbeck,

On Sunday you acted as 'audience'.[1] Today it is my turn! And so you will have to put up with my *applause* and shouts of *Bravo*! I am constantly amazed at all sorts of things you say and am always wanting to ask—how on earth do you know that?—But I enjoy it—and you can see how right I was not to provide a programme.—

Everyone will eventually get on to the right track, just like you. *From Beethoven onwards* there is no modern music that has not its inner programme.—But any music about which one first has to tell the listener what experience it embodies, and what he is meant to experience, is worthless.—And so once more—*pereat*—every programme!—One simply has to come provided with ears and a heart and—not least—give oneself up *willingly* to the rhapsodist. A residue of mystery always remains—even for the creator!—

Thank you very much for bringing three good things with you!

Yours sincerely,
Mahler

In haste. I really have a lot more to say.

286.   *To Alfred Roller* (Vienna)†

Undated. Vienna [end of May 1902]

Dear Professor Roller,

My wife and I shall be very glad if you will lunch with us tomorrow at one o'clock. Moser[2] will also be there. I particularly hope you can come, so that we can talk a little about *Tristan* before I leave (on Saturday[3]). Messrs. Lefler and Brioschi[4] have been given my instructions (no name being mentioned), and they are putting a good face on it.[5]

With best wishes,

Yours in haste,
Mahler

[1] Probably a reference to the performance of Mahler's Fourth Symphony in Vienna which Kalbeck reviewed very favourably (K.M.).
[2] Koloman Moser (1868–1918), Viennese painter and art designer (o.e.).
[3] Probably 31 May when the Mahlers went to Krefeld where Mahler conducted the first complete performance of his Third Symphony on 9 June (K.M.).
[4] Heinrich Lefler (1863–1919), and Anton Brioschi (1855–1920), both at the Court Opera in Vienna—the former from August 1900 to 31 May 1903 as chief stage designer and the latter, from 1886 until his death, as a scene painter (K.M.).
[5] Mahler had not yet officially announced his intention of commissioning Alfred Roller to design the new production of *Tristan* (o.e.).

287. *To Alfred Roller*†

Undated. Vienna [between 10 and 13 June 1902]

Dear Professor,

We have just returned from our trip, and I can hardly wait to see your models.[1] When can I have them collected? It would be very nice if you could come to lunch at the Hohe Warte[2] on Sunday—we could have a little chat.

Meanwhile very best wishes and thanks from

Yours,

Mahler

288. *To Alfred Roller*†

Undated. Vienna [June 1902]

My dear Professor,

I am quite delighted with your colour-sketches, which I have just received. They far excel even my very high expectations.—I suppose the modifications in Act III (regarding the layout) had to be made in view of the prevailing difficulties?—I am sending your sketches straight off to Herr Lefler, in accordance with your wishes, and am already keenly looking forward to our working together next season, which will, I hope, lead to much future collaboration. Again thanking you, my dear Professor, most warmly, with best wishes from my wife and myself,

I remain,

Your sincere admirer,

Mahler

289. *To Mysa Wydenbruck-Ezsterhazy*†

Undated. Vienna, 21 June 1902

Dear Countess,

I am on the point of going away, and must beg you to pardon my 'brevity'.

1. I have engaged Herr Kafka for a living wage, and he is continuing his studies under Prof. Ress. He will soon be given a chance to show whether his undoubtedly attractive gifts suffice to justify thorough training. On that it depends whether I can offer him a permanent engagement.

[1] For *Tristan* (o.e.).
[2] 'The Watch-Tower': a hill in the northern part of Vienna where the Moll Family lived first at Steinfeldgasse no. 8 and later at no. 5 (K.M.).

2. I am certainly always prepared to do something for Herr Reiter,[1] as far as lies in my power.—It is *not* in my power to produce his opera as a favour to him, since the Court Opera is not my personal property, but a public institution, as the director of which I bear great responsibility. I doubt whether his opera is worthy of a stage performance, but my judgement is not yet final, and it is my custom to go through works once again even after I have rejected them. I am beside myself about our little friend la Schoder—regarding her happiness as a calamity for our opera-house.[2]

With kindest regards and all good wishes,

Yours sincerely,

Gustav Mahler

290. *To Wilhelm Hesch*

Undated. [Maiernigg] *July 1902*

My dear Hesch,

I was tremendously delighted by your letter. Thanks be to God you have got it over. I had a few lines a few days ago from Dr. Boer about the result of the operation; he was very reassuring. We are all very glad it went so well; let us hope that now at long last you will recover *completely*.[3] Still, I do think you will have to have a *thorough* convalescence and not rush straight back to work. Take it easy for as long as you need to. I shall not let you appear again until the doctors give their approval. What luck that you were in such good hands. Quite apart from his immense skill, Professor Hochenegg is very *human*: a combination that is, I'm afraid, but rarely met with in his profession.

Do let us hear from you again! You can imagine how I long for news from you.—As soon as I arrive in Vienna I shall come and see you!

Very, very best wishes from,

Your old friend,

Mahler

---

[1] Josef Reiter (1862–1939), Upper-Austrian composer whose opera *Der Bundschuh* (The Laced Boot) was performed under Mahler's direction on 13 November 1900 and whose choruses were very popular (o.e.).
[2] Frau Marie Gutheil-Schoder was expecting a child (o.e.).
[3] After a long illness Hesch died on 4 January 1908 (o.e.).

291. *To Nanna Spiegler* (Engelberg)†

> *Undated. Postmark: 28 July 1902. Arrival postmark: 31 July 1902*
> *Maiernigg am Wörthersee*

Dearest Nannerl,

You must all forgive me! I am up to my eyebrows in *work*—really with scarcely time to breathe. I am in low spirits over your bad behaviour. Here am I joyfully sending you news of all good things that befall me: you know all my wishes and expectations are focused on whether I see myself getting a better chance to work, or not! And the latter is in high degree the case, as ever it was. From this you may infer that everything is wonderfully well with me! Whenever I can breathe again, in this headlong rush, and look around me, I shall write again. But you, Albert, do please, write to me a tiny bit more fully! With love to both of you from your old

Gustav

292. *To [Franz Wüllner]* (Cologne)†

> *Undated. Maiernigg am Wörthersee, [Summer] 1902*

Dear Sir, Revered Maestro,

I have already written telling Herr Direktor Hofmann[1] that I shall accept your invitation with pleasure.[2] The times and the number of rehearsals you have suggested are quite satisfactory. But may I {draw} your attention to the fact that in Krefeld apart from the strings a number of additional wind and percussion players participated.—Further, in one movement there is a part for *Flügelhorn*. The player was brought from Cologne, but did a very poor job.—I think it should be easy to find someone proficient on this instrument in the army.—Finally, may I remind you that a female choir and a boys' choir are used in one number (5).—I know I shall be in safe hands when I ask you to be so good as to see to this too. The intonation in the passages for female voices is not without pitfalls (mainly in some of the *a cappella* bars). What is particularly difficult is the *entry* of the boys' choir, since they have to begin the number without any guidance whatever. At this point in Krefeld my heart was in my mouth.

May I conclude by saying how much I look forward to making your

---

[1] Julius Hofmann (1840–1910), director of the opera-house in Cologne (K.M.).
[2] For a performance of the Third Symphony which did not materialize (K.M.).

9*

acquaintance in person at long last?—something that a peculiar concatenation of events has hitherto prevented.

With kind regards,

I am, highly esteemed Herr Doktor,
Your obedient servant,
Mahler

One thing I must say candidly: I am not quite happy about exposing my symphony to the acoustics of a theatre (one, moreover, that has evidently not yet been tried out).[1] I should much have preferred it if you, revered maestro, had put my work on one of the usual Gürzenich programmes. However, I shall assent to all your decisions.

293. To Josef Krug-Waldsee (Magdeburg)†

Undated. 1902

Dear Herr Krug,

I was very surprised and even more delighted by your letter. So you have the audacity to tackle my monster,[2] have you? Please accept my very cordial thanks, together with the sincere wish that you may derive some little pleasure from it.— Now to answer your question. Those titles were an attempt I made at the time to provide non-musicians with a clue and a guide to the thought, or rather mood, of the individual movements and to the relationship between the movements and their place in the whole. Only too soon, alas, did it become clear to me that the attempt had failed (indeed, it can never succeed), leading merely to misinterpretations of the direst sort. It was the same fate that had overtaken me previously on similar occasions, and I have now finally given up trying to comment, analyse or provide any aids whatsoever! These titles, which Nodnagel[3] gave (they are correct apart from the first, which should read: Introduction to the first movement: Pan awakens, Summer marches in (Bacchanale)), will certainly convey a good deal to you *after* you have got to know the score. They will also give you some hint of how I imagined the constantly increasing articulation of feeling, from the muted, rigid, merely elemental form of existence (the forces of Nature) to the delicate structure of the human heart, which in its turn reaches further still, pointing beyond (to God).—

Please do express this in your own language, without citing the utterly

[1] The new Stadttheater in Cologne, inaugurated on 6 September 1902 (K.M.).
[2] The Third Symphony which Krug-Waldsee conducted in Magdeburg on 22 October 1902 (o.e. + K.M.).
[3] Ernst Otto Nodnagel (1870–1909), composer and writer on music (K.M.).

inadequate titles, and you will then have acted in my sense. I am *very* thankful you consulted me; it is of no little importance for the future of this work of mine, and of my creative work as a whole, how it is presented to the 'public'. May the seriousness of your temperament enable you to set an example to others.

Once again warmest thanks for everything.

Yours sincerely,

Mahler

294. *To Arnold Berliner*†

Undated. [Postmark: Vienna, 29 December 1902]

Dear Berliner,

In great haste: I cannot give any thought to Frau Götze.[1] We are already well supplied in that particular line. Give her my kindest regards. I was expecting a visit from you this past autumn. I was very much looking forward to welcoming you here. I hope you will carry out your intentions next year.

With very best wishes,

Yours sincerely,

Mahler

You might have added a word about how you are and what you are doing. How is the *Handbook of Physics*[2] coming along?

1903

295. *To Alfred Roller*†

Undated. Vienna [February 1903]

My dear Herr Roller,

How you have put me to shame! For days I have been wondering how to thank you for all the great and wonderful things for which the Opera-House and I owe you thanks.[3]—And I have come to the conclusion that instead of trying to put anything into words, I should simply remain silent.—I know we

---

[1] The contralto Marie Ritter-Götze (1865–1922) who wished to leave Berlin (o.e.).

[2] In 1903 Berliner published his *Lehrbuch der Experimentalphysik in elementarer Darstellung*, 857 pp. (K.M.).

[3] Probably written after the première of Roller's new production of *Tristan* on 21 February (K.M.).

are similar in one respect: in our completely unselfish devotion to art, even if we approach it by different roads. And I was also fully aware that you would not think me unappreciative or undiscerning if I {did} not try to put anything into words about what you have achieved and what you have come to mean to me.

And I should be very sad, as though it were some kind of farewell, over our saying such things to each other now, were I not joyfully certain that our collaboration hitherto is only a *beginning* and an indication of things to come. In this spirit I send my very best wishes, hoping to see you very soon (before the second night of *Tristan*). Could you not dine with us on Friday? If I do not hear from you I shall take it that you are coming. Best wishes also from my wife.

Yours most sincerely,
Gustav Mahler

296. *To Franz Bartolomey* (Vienna)†

Undated. [Vienna, March 1903]

Dear Herr Professor,

It was only during the rehearsal that I learnt of the terrible misfortune[1] that has befallen you, and I thank you from my heart for making the great sacrifice of taking part in the rehearsal despite your great sorrow.

Let me assure you that I well appreciate what selflessness and moral courage it took to carry out one's duty at such a time. Please accept my deepest sympathy and my warmest thanks, dear Herr Bartolomey.

I shall never forget this.

Yours very sincerely,
Gustav Mahler

297. *To Julius Buths* (Düsseldorf)†

Vienna, 25 March 1903

Dear Professor Buths,

I am in full agreement with everything you suggest and beg you to do just as you see fit in every respect.[2]

---

[1] Mahler learned only by chance of the illness and death of Bartolomey's child, in spite of which this excellent clarinettist at the Vienna Court Opera took part in rehearsals for Charpentier's *Louise*. The first night was on 24 March 1903 (o.e.).
[2] Regarding a performance of Mahler's Second Symphony conducted by Buths in Düsseldorf on 2 April 1903 (K.M.).

Well then, this would mean that the main interval in the concert would come between the fourth and fifth movements. I marvel at the sensitive intuition with which you (in contrast with my own arrangement) have recognized the natural break in the work. I have long tended to this view, and all the performances I have hitherto conducted have reinforced the same impression.

Still, there really ought *also* to be a lengthy pause for recollection after the first movement, because the second movement does *not* have the effect of a *contrast*, but simply of a discrepancy after the first. This is my fault, not inadequate appreciation on the listener's part. Perhaps you have already felt this after rehearsing the two movements consecutively.—The andante was composed as a kind of *intermezzo* (as the echo of *long* past days in the life of the man borne to his grave in the first movement—'when the sun still smiled on him'—).

While the first, third, fourth and fifth movements are related in theme and mood, the second stands alone, in a certain sense interrupting the strict, austere sequence of events. Perhaps this is a weakness in the conception of the work, but you will certainly see my intention from the above indication.

It is quite logical to interpret the beginning of the fifth movement as a development from the first, and the long pause before the fifth will make the listener aware of this too.—

May I offer you some advice based on my own experience with the *a cappella* chorus in the last movement?

I have hitherto observed that it is impossible to avoid an unbearable disturbance when the choir *stand up* to make their entry, as they usually do. The audience's attention has been aroused to the highest pitch by the trumpet fanfares, and now the mysterious sound of human voices (which should begin *ppp* as from a great distance) should come as a *surprise*.—My advice is to make the choir (who have presumably been sitting down so far) remain *seated*, making them stand up only at the E-flat-major passage: 'Mit Flügeln, die ich mir errungen' (basses). This has always been astonishingly effective. It is also very important to have a well-balanced array of horns and trumpets for the 'great roll-call'. The horns and kettle-drums must be kept together and, if possible, facing the trumpets, but these again should sound well away from one another. The flute and bass clarinet[1] must play with such accuracy and polish that they hardly need the conductor, so that you need not *beat time* during the whole passage.—My choice would be to have a special rehearsal for this passage; I consider it the most difficult in the whole work. The two solo voices 'O Schmerz, du Alldurchdringer—o Tod, du Allbezwinger' must be

---

[1] There is no bass clarinet in this passage; Mahler must be referring to the piccolo, and the transcriber must have misread the word (K.M.).

heard very *strongly* above the orchestra, which has to observe the greatest discretion in order to avoid '*drowning*' the singers.

As I feared, to my great regret I shall not have the privilege of being with you on 2 April.

May I offer my best wishes from afar, expressing my deep gratitude for your efforts and your whole approach, which I find both elevating and heart-warming.—I shall be thinking of you frequently in these days.

Yours most sincerely,
Gustav Mahler

298. *To Emil Freund* (Vienna)

Undated. Maiernigg am Wörthersee, August 1903

Dear Emil,

I have just received the enclosed letter from *Peters Editionsverlag* in Leipzig (one of the most important international firms).

Please give me a tip how to tackle this.

1. To do as well as possible for myself.

2. To avoid acting contrary to my obligations towards Stritzko.[1]

N.B. I should like at least 10,000 florins for my work.[2]—Would it not be best for me to approach Stritzko first, asking whether he will pay me that amount—perhaps letting him understand that otherwise I should like to accept some other publisher's offer?

Yours in haste,
Gustav

Send the letter back.

299. *To Bruno Walter*†

Undated. [Maiernigg, Summer 1903]

Dear Walter,

Luckily I have just reached an amicable settlement with my publisher and *can now dispose my works freely*! I shall therefore be happy to negotiate with P.[3]

---

[1] Josef Stritzko, director of the music-engraving firm Josef Eberle in Vienna. Up to now this firm had printed all Mahler's symphonic works and sold them through various music publishers (K.M.).

[2] The Fifth Symphony which Peters Verlag finally published in September 1904 (o.e. + K.M.).

[3] According to the manuscript 'P' stands for Peters Verlag and 'B' for Gustav Brecher. The contract with Peters was finally settled on 4 Oct. 1903 (K.M.).

if he can offer really decent terms. Write and tell B. this, thanking him for his loyalty and hard work on my behalf. Looking forward to your 'proper' letter, I send best wishes to you and your wife.

Ever yours,
Mahler

In haste, thank heaven!¹

300. *To Karl Goldmark†*

Undated. [Maiernigg, Summer 1903]

My dear Goldmark,

The matter cannot be settled as fast as Karpath thought. It came as such a surprise to me, and I had already made all my arrangements for the season, which cannot now suddenly be changed, since they are all closely inter-connected. On the other hand, for me it *goes without saying* that if you have something new we must get down to it *as soon as possible*.—First of all I must think it over.—It would be a great help if you would send me the revisions—and I shall distribute the parts for study as soon as I have a clear idea who will be available—which is rather a problem now, at the beginning of the season. We have some new people, some of whom can obviously be considered for *Merlin*.²—

Meanwhile in haste my kindest regards—and please do let me know what you think of my proposal.

Yours most sincerely,
Gustav Mahler

Please remember me to all at the Berghof!³

301. *To Julius Buths* (Düsseldorf)

Vienna, 12 September 1903

My dear Professor Buths,

So you mean to try to do the Fourth?⁴

This persecuted step-child that has so far known so little joy in the world.

---

¹ i.e. Mahler was in the midst of composing (o.e.).
² Goldmark had extensively re-worked his opera *Merlin* and had asked Karpath to offer it to Mahler (o.e.).
³ A country house near Unterach am Attersee, where friends of Mahler's (Ignaz Brüll and his brother and sister, Richard Specht, etc.) were spending the summer (o.e.).
⁴ Buths conducted Mahler's Fourth Symphony in Düsseldorf in May 1904 with Marcella Pregi as soloist (K.M.).

I am tremendously glad you like the work, and I can only hope that an audience educated by you will feel and understand as you do. My own experience in general has been that humour of this type (as distinct from wit or good humour) is frequently not recognized even by the best of audiences.

I am happy to be able to inform you before anyone else that my Fifth will be published shortly (as soon as I can find a publisher).

Warmest thanks for all the happiness you are giving me.

Yours most sincerely,
Mahler

Pregi should be most suitable, and I thank you also for this devoted and meticulous choice.

I open the envelope again to inform you that I have made a few slight but very important alterations to the instrumentation in the first movement.

Perhaps it would be best for you to send me your score so that I can enter them immediately.

302. *To Arthur Seidl* (Munich)

Undated. [Vienna] *23 September 1903*

Dear Herr Doktor,

I was most interested to receive and read your articles and was particularly pleased by the way that that quick-change artist, the composer and critic, was taken down a peg or two. I much regret having missed you in Munich. I did not even receive your card.—You will be interested to hear that my Fifth is just being copied out. I do not yet know where it is to be published or performed.— Nikisch would like to have it for Berlin, but I do not wish to take the risk because of the unfavourable attitude the press there have adopted towards me, as you know.[1]—After all, I should not care to let the same thing happen to me with this work as happened to the First, Second and Fourth, all three of which at their first performance there were slaughtered in the bloodthirstiest way, as a result of which they have not been 'in demand' anywhere else.

What do you advise?

Kindest regards and warmest thanks,

Yours very sincerely,
Mahler

---

[1] Nikisch performed the Fifth Symphony in Berlin on 20 February 1905 (K.M.).

303. *To Willem Mengelberg* (Amsterdam)

Undated. Vienna, October 1903

Dear and revered friend,

Enclosed, as promised, a wad of scores 'arranged' by ourselves. May I take this opportunity of saying once again how much I enjoyed the delightful days in the company of yourself and your wife, and that I feel Amsterdam has become a second home to me, thanks to your kindly hospitality and your profound artistic understanding?[1]

Once again my warmest and most sincere thanks for everything.

Your ever devoted

Gustav Mahler

My kindest regards to Diepenbrock,[2] who has also found a special place in my affections. As soon as I have a chance, I shall reply to his most kind letter, which I found in the roll of pictures only after my return to Vienna.

304. *To Hugo Reichenberger* (Munich)

[Vienna] 8 November 1903

Dear Herr Kapellmeister,

The vacancy I mentioned is linked with the appointment to be made in Karlsruhe. If the applicant here for that position is not appointed, there will be no possibility of a change here for a long time. I beg you to take this, above all, into account, and in view of the extremely vague prospects regarding Vienna not to feel under any obligation in this direction. *If a vacancy occurs here* and you are available, then you are assured of the post, and I can promise you would have a free hand (for I conduct only very rarely).[3] If you are offered the job in Karlsruhe and it suits you, then do certainly accept! Going on the information I have, I do not really think the applicant here has much chance.—It would, besides, be worth considering whether you might not find a very congenial sphere of activity in Munich—if Fischer really is leaving.[4] Munich does need

---

[1] Mahler had been to Amsterdam for the first time in October 1903 and directed two performances of his Third Symphony (on the 22nd and 23rd) and one of the First Symphony (on the 25th) (K.M.).

[2] Alphons Diepenbrock (1862–1921), Dutch composer and conductor (o.e.).

[3] Reichenberger was conductor in Munich where he remained until 1905 when he went to Frankfurt. Only in September 1908 did he take up an appointment at the Vienna Court Opera where he stayed until 1935 (K.M.).

[4] Franz Fischer (1849–1918), conductor in Munich since 1880. It had been rumoured that he was leaving several times but he held the post up to his death (K.M.).

two first conductors, and Mottl is, after all, not so young as he was and doubtless likes to take things a little easy—besides, he is away on tour a great deal.—

If I were you, *I* should not consider *Cologne.*—The situation there could not be congenial to a young man who wishes to make his way. Please treat this information and these views of mine as confidential.

Yours very sincerely,
Gustav Mahler

305. *To Hugo Reichenberger*

[Vienna] 21 November 1903

Dear Herr Kapellmeister,

It is not impossible that next year a vacancy will occur here. I therefore beg you to inform me, for all eventualities, if you should be about to sign a contract.

In haste,

Yours very sincerely,
Mahler

306. *To Karl Goldmark*†

Vienna, 2[?] December 1903

My dear Goldmark,

I am preparing a production of *Saba* for Christmas,[1] with Slezak as Assad and Schubert[2] as the Queen. On this occasion I also intend including the opening duet of Act IV. *Merlin* can be performed only with Slezak, so the note was definitely premature. Please make your decision about Frankfurt regardless. On the contrary, I should be in favour of a first performance in Frankfurt, since one could turn it to good account for the performance here.

With kindest regards,

Yours most sincerely,
Gustav Mahler

[1] Goldmark's opera *Die Königin von Saba* (1875) did not finally open with the new cast until 25 May 1904 (K.M.).
[2] The soprano Betty Schubert (K.M.).

307. *To Karl Goldmark*

Vienna, 6 December 1903

My dear Goldmark,

I shall follow your instructions to the letter. I am very glad to hear you are satisfied with our cast. I hope to have finally found an Assad who is equal to his task.

But *how hard* it was to wrench the part away from Herr Slezak! With kindest regards, in great haste,

Yours most sincerely,
Mahler

1904

308a. *To Max Kalbeck†*

Undated. Vienna, January [1904]

Dear Herr Kalbeck,

This time I have meddled with your trade and must therefore crave absolution.[1] I dare say you would like to know before the performance on Saturday of the changes I have made in the libretto and (in part—perforce) in the music. —I have arranged the piano reduction for you in such a way that all the differences in relation to the general run of performances are immediately obvious. You will therefore not have to waste any time finding your way about.

I should be happy if this were of a little help to poor *Euryanthe*, whom I dearly love, and enable her to make—if not a princely living on the stage, at least a tolerably decent one. She deserves it if only for the sake of her very considerable progeny.

With all good wishes,

Yours sincerely,
Mahler

[1] For certain changes Mahler had made in Weber's *Euryanthe*, produced on 19 January 1904 (K.M.).

308b. *To Max Kalbeck*

Undated. Vienna, January [1904]

To prevent any misunderstanding, dear Herr Kalbeck, may I remark further to my letter of yesterday that the two insertions, 1. in the duet between the two women in the second [third] scene of Act I, and 2. in the duet between Adolar and Euryanthe in the first scene of Act III,[1] are written in by hand simply for the reader's convenience. In the *printed* version they are in the appendix, having been omitted by Weber himself after the first performance in Vienna.—

I found that restoring these two parts of the score suited my adaptation, and I have included them *as they stand*.

With best wishes,

Yours in haste,
Mahler

309. *To Richard Specht†*

Undated. 1904

Dear Specht,

I think it was Walter's laconic attitude that gave you such a fright.[2]—Well—I have emended only a few tiny details; the passage on p. 11 where you touch on one of the most important psychological problems might well have been expanded and given more weight, for I believe that that is how it is with all human values.

On p. 16 I have indicated the 'literary' version.—The repetitions of certain words came about only in the course of setting to music.—

The reference to my parents as 'publicans' seems to be a rather trivial example of extreme accuracy. I think it would be adequate to describe my father simply as a businessman.—

Finally, I should like to thank you most warmly for your sympathetic treatment, from which alone (as you correctly observe) understanding can come about—and vice versa. Despite my sporadic successes (which I perhaps owe only

---

[1] It is the *third* scene of Act I to which Mahler refers, the recitative between Euryanthe and Eglantine, 'So einsam bangend finde ich dich?', and the recitative and duet, 'Hier weilest du? hier darf ich ruh'n?'. Mahler's version is discussed by G. Adler in an article in *Zeitschrift der internationalen Musikgesellschaft*, No. 7, 1904 (K.M.).
[2] Specht had written a little book on Mahler, which appeared in a collection of short biographies published by Gose & Tetzlaff (Berlin, 1905). Mahler had remarked to Bruno Walter that he would like to see certain changes made, and Walter conveyed this to the author so abruptly that it appeared to constitute rejection of the whole piece of writing. The above letter is the reply to Specht's letter to Mahler (o.e.).

to attendant external circumstances) there still seems to be a long hard road ahead for my works—and for my future ones perhaps even more so!

The time therefore seems to have come when there is need of such a brave pioneer to tell it all over again.—

My Sixth will pose conundrums that only a generation that has absorbed and digested my first five symphonies may hope to solve.

Yours sincerely,

Mahler

The whole thing was immensely to my liking; and I am astonished by how deeply you have penetrated into my essential nature. And your understanding is doubly precious to me because it has proceeded from the works to their creator.

310. *To Willem Mengelberg* (Amsterdam)†

Vienna, 12 June 1904

Dear, good friend,

Many thanks for your news, which has given me very great pleasure. Glad tidings indeed—that at long last you are *master* in your own house! I had—quite frankly—been greatly worried about you, and had already been working towards getting you here. (The position of Director of the Musikverein has become vacant, and only a temporary appointment has been made.) And only the fact that the *salary* is so disproportionately small (approximately 8,000 crowns) made me hesitate.—I kept this back door open in my mind for you, should the worst come to the worst...But the way everything had turned out is so much better and, let us hope, for ever!

I am all the more delighted to accept your invitation to conduct my Second and Fourth Symphonies in Amsterdam in November, since it will be a very pleasant opportunity to see you and your wife again and to consolidate and strengthen our recently formed friendship. Those days in Amsterdam are among the happiest times I have ever spent together with a fellow-musician.

Of course I agree to the same fee.—If it were possible, however, for the concerts again to be put on as early as *October*, I should be very grateful, since I am to conduct my new symphony (5) in Cologne on *18 October*[1] and could then very conveniently proceed to Amsterdam, whereas otherwise I should have to make the whole long journey (which, as you know, I find so terribly disagreeable) a second time. Whether before or after Cologne makes no difference to me, so long as both can be connected.

[1] '1 October' in G.E. but the manuscript clearly and correctly states '18 October' (K.M.).

But ⟨similarly⟩, if that cannot be done, I shall also be available in November. But I should have to know something definite *soon*, so that I can make my arrangements at the Opera. This time I shall bring my wife along, in the hope of extending our relationship so that our wives become as good friends as we three are already.

Regarding ⟨Leuwen⟩[1] and ⟨Willeke⟩[2] I shall do everything possible to send you both, for I feel *your position* will be *strengthened* if you bring your countrymen back home again—⟨particularly the outstanding ones like van Leuwen; Willeke on the other hand is *not so* first rate as van L., he hasn't sufficient maturity or routine. However I believe he will feel more at home in a concert than in opera, where his long years of experience are in fact a disadvantage.⟩

In any case, I would ask you to *telegraph* immediately to let me know if you definitely want both, so that I can then take the necessary steps. Since we close down here on 22 June, everything would have to be arranged by then. Of course I do not yet know what the two gentlemen themselves think about it.

If you decide to take ⟨Willeke⟩ and would like to get rid of ⟨Mossel⟩[3] I shall be glad to have him (I think we shall be able to cut him down to size here). I enclose a slip listing the conditions to be conveyed to him so that he can say if he accepts. I should, however, like you to await my reply to the telegram I shall be expecting from you. I am very reluctant to lose ⟨Leuwen⟩; yet it will be of *such great advantage to you* that I shall console myself with that thought.

Many greetings to your dear wife ⟨and to your esteemed neighbours and friends the Boissevains⟩, and kindest regards to yourself from

Your most devoted

Gustav Mahler

311. *To Arnold Berliner*

Undated. Postmark: Vienna, 19 June 1904

Dear Berliner,

I cannot spare a single day of my summer. On Wednesday I am off to Maiernigg. My wife gave birth to a daughter on the 15th,[4] and will have to stay here for at least three weeks. I am leaving her in the care of her mother,

---

[1] The flautist Ary van Leeuwen, member of the Vienna Court Opera Orchestra from October 1903–September 1920: Mahler incorrectly spelt the name 'Leuwen' (K.M.).
[2] The cellist Wilhelm Willeke, member of the Vienna Court Opera Orchestra from July 1903–August 1907 (K.M.).
[3] Mossel, cellist, member of the Concertgebouw Orchestra in Amsterdam (K.M.).
[4] Anna Mahler (K.M.).

going to the lake all on my lonesome. You know why. It is simply a duty, and the Neissers will understand that. The first performance of my Fifth is being given on 15 October in Cologne. Perhaps I shall see you there?

Very best wishes, in great haste,

Yours sincerely,

Mahler

Alma is as well as can be expected, and so is the little wench.

---

312. *To Friedrich Löhr*

Undated. [Maiernigg] *6 July 1904?*

Dearest Fritz,

From the presence of a cake before me I gather it's my birthday tomorrow! So today must be yours.[1]—Neither yours nor mine means very much to me any more. For me every day on which we 'get on' a little is a birthday. In reality *that* is the one we notice least. At any rate, today provides a welcome occasion to send you my greetings. Now you too will soon be leaving.[2] Do let me know where for! I find it difficult to write, having for so long written nothing but music. Again I have some things to be brought forth into the light of day![3]

Ever yours,

Gustav

---

313. *To Bruno Walter*†

Undated. [Maiernigg, Summer 1904]

Dear Walter,

Many thanks for your letter.

Yes, I do indeed see what Wagner means in the utterance you quoted. I cannot see where you find a mistake in it. One must not throw out the baby with the bath water! After all, there is no denying that our music involves the 'purely human' (and all that goes with that, including 'thought'). As in all art, it is the pure means of expression, etc. etc., that matter. If one wants to compose, one must not want to paint, write poetry, describe. But *what* one composes is, after all, only the whole man (i.e. man feeling, thinking, breathing, suffering). There would be no objection to a 'programme' (even though it is not precisely

[1] Correctly would read: 'yesterday must have been' (F.L.).
[2] This no doubt refers to my journey—for the purposes of study—to Germany, Brussels and Paris in the summer of 1904. That would date the letter (F.L.).
[3] The Sixth Symphony was completed in the summer of 1904 (K.M.).

the topmost rung of the ladder)—but then it must be a *musician* expressing himself in it, not a man of letters, a philosopher, a painter (all of them contained in the musician).

In short: anyone who is not a genius had better leave it alone, and anyone who is, need not worry about tackling anything he likes.—All this theorizing about it strikes me as being like a man who has fathered a child and only afterwards begins to wonder whether it really is a child, whether he generated it with the right intentions, etc.—He has simply loved and—*proved himself*! Basta! And if one does not love and *cannot* procreate, then there is no child. Basta again! And as the man is and according to his abilities, *so* too the child will turn out accordingly. Once again—basta!

My Sixth is finished. I think I *have proved myself*! A thousand times basta! With very best wishes,

> Yours ever,
> Mahler

Wife and children as well as can be expected. My regards to your wife.

314. *To Arnold Berliner*

Undated. Postmark: Vienna, 9 September 1904

Dear Berliner,

Anyone coming with an introduction from you will of course be received most warmly. So tell the lady to produce your card when she calls.—I am again in the thick of things. We were very pleased to hear of your promotion. But you *really must* come to Cologne (10 October).[1] My Sixth is finished—and so am I!

Very best wishes,

> Yours ever,
> Mahler

On *4 October* the new *Fidelio*![2]

315. *To Arthur Seidl* (Dessau)†

Undated. [Vienna] *September 1904*

My dear Herr Doktor,

I must not fail to inform you that my Fifth Symphony is to be performed for the first time in Cologne on 18 October.—I have not yet found out what the

---

[1] The first performance of the Fifth Symphony, postponed, however, until the 18th (K.M.).
[2] The new staging by Roller, also postponed, but only for three days (K.M.).

people there are like.[1] But naturally I should like to have such people as yourself there on that occasion. Perhaps I shall be lucky and you will be both free and sufficiently interested to come. That would be a great pleasure to me, and—I must admit—a great *relief*. Cologne is, after all, rather off the beaten track, and it is all too easy for some catch-phrase to be coined that determines the attitude taken to a work for quite a long time. My Fourth long suffered as the result of a formula produced by unperceptive scribblers in the daily press. Well then—I take heart and ask you to come!

Yours sincerely,
Mahler

316. *To Willem Mengelberg†*

Undated. Vienna, November 1904

My dear Mengelberg,

Now that I am back at home and somewhat recovered from the strenuous journey, my thoughts turn to those wonderful days in Amsterdam.[2] Everything I have to thank you for in this respect—your youthful, purposeful energy, your congenial interpretation and penetrating understanding of my works—all these are among those things of which we said once among friends, on the occasion of a symposium, that one could feel them deeply, but not utter thanks for them.

And so in spirit I press your hand in friendship, asking you always to preserve the same feelings towards me, feelings all the more precious to me in that they are rarely found, and all the more admirable since only from them springs that living art in which I know you to be the enthusiastic adept.

The main purpose of this letter is to ask you to convey my gratitude to your wonderful choir and your glorious orchestra.

What they achieved during those few days can be assessed only by myself and —you. It is solely that unique *élan*, that profound seriousness, to which I owe a truly exemplary performance of my most difficult work, and I beg you to tell all concerned that I shall never forget their moving eagerness and invigorating energy.

With kindest regards to your wife and yourself,

Yours most gratefully,
Gustav Mahler

[1] A strange remark considering that Mahler only six months earlier, on 27 March, had conducted his Third Symphony in Cologne (K.M.).
[2] In October Mahler had given three concerts there: on the 23rd he conducted his Fourth Symphony twice in the same evening, and on the 26th he conducted his Second Symphony, repeating it the following day (K.M.).

PROGRAMMA

VAN HET

BUITENGEWOON CONCERT

TE GEVEN DOOR DEN HEER

GUSTAV MAHLER

MET MEDEWERKING VAN

MEVROUW OLDENBOOM-LUTKEMANN

EN VAN

HET CONCERTGEBOUW-ORKEST.

ZONDAG 23 OCTOBER 1904 — 8 UUR.

---

1. **Symphonie No. 4 (G-dur). . Gustav Mahler.**

IN 4 DEELEN.

   I. Heiter, bedächtig.

   II. Scherzo. In gemächlicher Bewegung. (Todtentanz).

   III. Adagio.

   IV. Sopran-Solo. (Das himmlische Leben").

DE SOPRAAN-SOLO VOOR TE DRAGEN DOOR MEVROUW

ALIDA OLDENBOOM-LUTKEMANN.

(EERSTE UITVOERING.)

--- PAUZE. —

2. Herhaling van de Symphonie No. 4 (G-dur). . . Gustav Mahler.

Fig 4. Programme of the concert in Amsterdam on 23 October 1904, in which
Mahler conducted his Fourth Symphony twice (see Letter 316)

317. *To Rudolf Kastner* (Berlin)

Undated. [Vienna] *approx. November 1904*

My dear Herr Kastner,

I have just returned from Amsterdam, where my 'Fourth' was performed twice running at one concert—(a splendid idea, don't you think?)—to find your letter and your article in the *Münchener Neueste Nachrichten.*[1]

You have given me really very great pleasure.

I believe you understand me as only a very few others do, and I can't help wishing you would some time write something more about the whole nature of my music. The world has need of it!! Does one always have to be dead before people will let one live?

Thank you again, do let me hear from you soon, and if you come to Vienna I count on seeing you.

With kindest regards,

Yours sincerely,
Gustav Mahler

1905

318. *To Alexander v. Zemlinsky* (Vienna)†

Undated. Vienna, [January] *1905*

Dear Herr von Zemlinsky,

Won't you look me up some time? Our project[2] must be talked over personally. Perhaps you would care to have coffee with us this afternoon.

If so, please come at about 2 o'clock.

With all good wishes,

Yours,
Mahler

Perhaps together with Schönberg.

---

[1] Of 21 October, on the première of Mahler's Fifth Symphony (K.M.).
[2] The first performance of [almost] all of Mahler's orchestral songs (including the 'Kindertotenlieder') at one of the concerts organized by the Vereinigung schaffender Tonkünstler [Society of Composers in Vienna], of which he was honorary president (o.e.).

319. *To Ludwig Karpath†*

[Vienna] 2 March 1905

Dear Herr Karpath,[1]

To the best of my knowledge only some of the individual songs from *Des Knaben Wunderhorn* have been set to music. So my situation is really rather different: up to the age of forty I took the words for my songs—in so far as I did not write them myself (and even then they are in a certain sense related to the *Wunderhorn*)—exclusively from that collection.—But I think it would be idle to claim any priority in this respect.—

Another difference is that I have devoted myself heart and soul to that poetry (which is essentially different from any other kind of 'literary poetry', and might almost be called something more like Nature and Life—in other words, the sources of all poetry—than art) in full awareness of its character and tone.[2]

And there can be no doubt that it is I, who for many years was mocked for that choice of mine, who did, after all, set the fashion going. But it certainly is comical, in the circumstances, that precisely my settings of these songs have still not been performed, down to this day, whereas my imitators are already very famous and their songs frequently sung.

With many thanks and best wishes,

Gustav Mahler

I must avail myself of your undertaking not to name me as your informant in this matter.—

320. *To Ludwig Karpath†*

[Vienna] 7 March 1905

Dear Herr Karpath,

I was not aware of any way in which you might be supposed to have offended me—nor, for that matter, that your last letter required an answer.[3]

Thank you very much for your kind offer *re* Lauterbach,[4] but I see no reason for adding yet another applicant to those who have already come forward.

Apart from anything else, I do not at all care to have the matter made public.

[1] The altered mode of address may be traced to the fact that Mahler's relationship with Karpath had gradually cooled off (o.e.).
[2] Karpath wrote an article on this subject, published in *Signale für die musikalische Welt* [no. 21, 15 March 1905], whose Vienna correspondent he was at that time (o.e.).
[3] Karpath, who was sometimes upset by things Mahler said, in this case thought he himself was in the wrong, and wrote to Mahler to that effect, whereupon he received this reply (o.e.).
[4] Lauterbach & Kuhn, music publishers in Leipzig (o.e.).

You can bury the 'hatchet' with a perfectly easy mind! I did not take your opposition too seriously anyway, and certainly did not bear you any particular grudge for it. As you know from experience, I am pretty hardened to that sort of thing.

When anyone has such a clearly preordained path to follow as I have, neither unjustified fault-finding nor uncritical praise can throw him off balance. For the rest, believe me, I am much more capable of understanding and forgiving all the anger I arouse than my opponents are of understanding and forgiving my equanimity. So let us regard everything as all right, shall we (and if possible let it *remain* so)—only please do not expect correspondence from someone as harassed and overworked as

Yours, with best wishes, and as always in great haste,

Mahler

321. *To Max Kalbeck*†

Undated. [Vienna, 14 June 1905]

Dear Herr Kalbeck,

I have read the enclosed pamphlet with profit. You will perhaps be interested in glancing through the chapter 'Score and Libretto', if you do not happen to know it already.

I am leaving tomorrow evening, wishing you a pleasant summer and both of us a *Don Giovanni* that will live, that will outlive us.[1]

If you would still like to see the sketches, Roller will show them to you at your convenience. He is staying on for a few days.

With very best wishes,

Yours most sincerely,

Mahler

322. *To Emil Freund*

[Maiernigg] 6 July 1905

Dear Emil,

Please be so good as to reply to the enclosed and tell me what this is all about now! Is there no end to this pre-existence?[2] Damn it all!

Yours ever,

Mahler

[1] Allusion to the new production of *Don Giovanni* with Roller's staging, given for the first time on 21 December 1905 (K.M.).
[2] Mahler is almost certainly referring to some sort of trouble with the tax authorities. Freund used to help Mahler in these matters (K.M.).

323. *To Alfred Roller†*

Undated. *Maiernigg, Summer* [1905]

Dear Roller,
I must send you the enclosed bad news[1] at once. (In your last letter you forgot to give your address. I wanted to write to you, but only today thought of the obvious expedient: having my letter forwarded to you by the office in Vienna.)
The best thing would be for us to *talk* the matter over, since you will, I hope, soon be here (and staying for quite a while).—But if you do not intend to come till later, you would have to state your case as soon as possible with reference to this charming 'announcement', which, quite candidly, does not really surprise me at all after our last application.
Very best wishes from my wife and myself. Looking forward to seeing you here *soon*.

Yours,
Mahler

324. *To Max Kalbeck†*

Undated. *Vienna, Autumn 1905*

Dear Herr Kalbeck,
Would you be kind enough to send me the words of the Basilio and Figaro aria in the last act? I have worked through the whole of it and gladly accept your truly inspired, quite exquisite translation. I should like to keep only a very few numbers in the old familiar form. First, those that have established themselves by reason of their popularity (on the principle we observed in *Don Giovanni*), and also various details that strike me as being, if not so poetic, at least more *drastic* in the old version—a factor of great importance in the libretto of a comic opera. I have also worked thoroughly through the recitatives.—The final version will of course, as usual, take on shape only *during rehearsal.*—
As soon as I have a complete piano reduction I shall send it to you for checking. We are going to have a glorious time—I am looking forward to it with quite childish delight!

Yours very sincerely,
Mahler

---

[1] Rejection of application for funds for production of *Die Walküre* (o.e.).

325. *To Willem Mengelberg†*

Undated. Vienna, [November or December] *1905*

Dear Mengelberg,

I am again sending you the enclosed letter, which I have reclaimed from the Post Office. May I again remind you that I shall be conducting my Fifth in Antwerp on 5 March?[1] Immediately afterwards I could be at your disposal. But I must now beg you to send me the full score of the Fifth *by return*, as I have made very extensive and important revisions, and then you will have time to have them entered into the instrumental parts. From where you are you can easily work out how long it will take me to get from Antwerp to Amsterdam, and you can arrange rehearsals accordingly. Please let me know the exact timetable.

With warmest regards and my congratulations on your American triumph. Perhaps the Amsterdamers will now gradually begin to realize what a treasure they have in you.

Yours very sincerely,
Mahler

Very best wishes to your wife!

1906

326. *To Willem Mengelberg†*

Undated. Vienna, [January] *1906*

Dear friend Mengelberg,

I too am looking forward tremendously to our meeting again—to seeing you and your wife and all our good friends. But the rehearsals, as you have proposed them, are a bit on the short side. I definitely ought to have three rehearsals for the symphony! Would it not be possible for me to squeeze in *one* rehearsal somehow on the *Tuesday*?[2] Perhaps in the morning, if I can catch an early-morning train or a night train from Antwerp? Besides, dear Mengelberg, the Fifth is *very, very difficult*. Please hold thorough *preliminary rehearsals*, otherwise we shall have a *shambles*! I shall be hissed if the performance is not *brilliant*. If you mean to do the songs, I would recommend *Messchaert*, who is

[1] After the concert in Antwerp Mahler conducted two concerts in Amsterdam: on 8 March, the Symphony No. 5 and 'Kindertotenlieder', and on 10 March a performance of 'Das klagende Lied'. On 11 March Mengelberg conducted a repeat performance of the latter work (K.M.).
[2] 6 March (K.M.).

having a *Mahler* evening here in January,[1] so probably enjoys singing them. Perhaps on the same evening as 'Das klagende Lied': for an overture only, or something of the kind would be suitable after the symphony, enabling me to have the rehearsals exclusively for the symphony.—Enclosed is the score with a multitude of *revisions*, all of which are extremely important.

Very best wishes,

Yours ever,

Mahler

327. *To Alexander v. Zemlinsky†*

Undated. Vienna, [17 April 1906]

Dear Zemlinsky,

Would you agree that we should first play through the piano reduction[2] alone? If so, please come to my office at 6 p.m.

We shall go to our house afterwards. Schönberg will call for us.

Best wishes,

Yours in haste,

Mahler

328. *To Alexander v. Zemlinsky†*

Undated. Vienna [17 April 1906]

Dear Zemlinsky,

I have gone and made a muddle. Would it inconvenience you to come *tomorrow*, Wednesday, instead of this evening? For this evening we have *Lehmann's* first appearance in *Traviata*.[3]

So I just have to be there!—

In any case, do please come to my office at 6 o'clock.

In great haste,

Yours,

Mahler

Perhaps you could let Schönberg know.

---

[1] On 18 January Johs. Messchaert gave a recital in Vienna at which he sang six songs from *Des Knaben Wunderhorn* (K.M.).
[2] Zemlinsky's piano reduction of Mahler's Sixth Symphony, arranged for four hands and published in May 1906 by C. F. Kahnt in Leipzig (o.e. + K.M.).
[3] Lilli Lehmann appeared in *La Traviata* on Tuesday, 17 April 1906 (K.M.).

329. *To Frau Albert Neisser* (Breslau)†

Undated. Vienna, [Spring] *1906*

Dear Frau Geheimrat,

I shall do my utmost to arrange a few performances worth your seeing and hearing in the *first week of May.* (How would you like a Mozart cycle? Interspersed perhaps with something by Wagner?)

But afterwards I shall have to sit tight in Vienna, working, for *Essen*[1] will swallow up a fortnight of my time.—Do bring our friend Berliner along, so that I can dream once again the lovely dream of the Fürstenstrasse. How lovely it was! With all very best wishes to you and your husband (of whom, during the Stettin days, I thought with furious friendship—*tout comme chez nous*) from

Yours in great haste,
Mahler

EDITION PETERS

Mahler
Fünfte Symphonie
☞ 20 *Aufführungen in 2 Jahren.*

Fig 5. Advertisement for Mahler's Fifth Symphony, October 1906 ('20 performances in 2 years')

330. *To Ludwig Karpath*†

Undated. [Vienna, June 1906]

Dear Karpath,

Thank you very much for your kind letter. Enclosed is a copy, inscribed for you, of the miniature score.[2] You can easily get a copy of the piano reduction

[1] Mahler conducted the first performance of his Sixth Symphony in Essen on 27 May 1909 (K.M.).
[2] Of Mahler's Fifth Symphony (o.e.).

10

(which is excellent) from the publisher. I have none myself.—I gave up reading the reviews after the first one (Leopold Schmidt[1]).

These gentry are always the same. Now all at once they like my first five symphonies. The Sixth must just wait until my Seventh appears.

Yours ever,
Mahler

331. *To Josef Reitler* (Paris)

Undated. June 1906

Dear Sir,

I received and read your letter with much pleasure.[2] My heartfelt thanks to you for your very kind words and your interest in my work. For the present I must be satisfied with the knowledge that there are small groups of connoisseurs here and there with whom my works count for something, to whom they have perhaps even become precious. The prime obstacle to performance is everywhere the expense involved. But above all it is the forms of expression, which are markedly different from what people are accustomed to, and which only very few people at present feel originate in the composer's nature and not in his whim or caprice.

I honestly doubt whether Paris is at present a suitable milieu for my music and the thought of going to Paris to force upon people a kind of music that is found disconcerting even in my native country has, quite frankly, never occurred to me, and I cannot yet say whether I should advise such a venture even if you, dear Herr Reitler, were to undertake the quite thankless task of preparing the ground for me.

In principle this is what I think: if I am offered full orchestral facilities (by which I also mean a *sufficient number of rehearsals*) in Paris at a time when I can absent myself from Vienna (as you know, my work there is almost indispensable), then I shall be only too glad to offer my services. You would, as you have been good enough to say, relieve me of all the organizational side.—

Be all that as it may—whether you succeed or not—your words have given me infinite joy; I sometimes feel I shall not live to see 'my time'; and then an

---

[1] Writer on music and professor of music history; from 1897, music critic of the *Berlin Tageblatt*. Published three volumes of criticism (K.M.).
[2] Reitler was then living in Paris, as a music critic and had in spring 1906 suggested a performance of one of Mahler's symphonies. Mahler was almost completely unknown there at that time (o.e.).

echo from an unknown world comes just as the right moment; so perhaps after all *legor et*—(something of which I am certain) *legar*!

With heartfelt thanks,

> Yours very sincerely,
> Gustav Mahler

332. *To Alfred Roller*

> *Undated. Maiernigg, early June 1906*

My dear Roller,

The 20th, which on your splendid postcard shines upon the just and unjust here below, now draws nigh, and I can say nothing better to you than: sail forth with a high heart to that land still unknown to you, who have no notion yet what courage is needed to discover and to inhabit it.—We, your friends, can for the time being only watch and wave to your frail bark from our safe shore.—So when next we meet (and I hope it will be *soon* and *here* in Maiernigg) we shall both wear the knowing look of the *haruspex*, about whom you will recall the old saying: *haruspex ridet, si haruspicem videt*.—But what I hope (and please pass this on to Fräulein Milewa) is that we shall remain 'the same as ever', having become *richer*. For your wife will now be included *legaliter* in our bond of friendship. So now we are a company that can hold its head up anywhere. It would be very nice if you could include the Puster valley in your tour of the Tyrol and spend a few days with us (completely undisturbed whenever you may wish it so). Very best wishes, my dear Roller, and please convey my regards and heartfelt good wishes also to your fiancée.

> Yours as ever,
> Mahler

333. *To Friedrich Löhr*

> *Undated. Maiernigg, 21 June 1906*

Very urgent!

Dear Fritz,

1. Translate the following for me:

> Qui paraclitus diceris
> Donum Dei altissimi,
> Fons vivus ignis caritas
> et spiritalis unctio.

2. How does one stress (or scan) paraclitus diceris?

3. Translate the following for me:

> hostem repellas longius
> pacemque dones protinus
> ductore sic te praevio
> vitemus omne noxium.

4. It is all from '*Veni creator spiritus*'. Is there a good (preferably a rhyming) translation of it?

Please reply *at once, express*! Otherwise it will be too late. I need it both as creator and as creature!

Yours,
Gustav

---

334. *To Friedrich Löhr*†

Undated. Postmark: Klagenfurt, 18 July 1906

Dear Fritz,

In great haste, as the spiritus has really taken hold of me—I sent you 100 Spiesse[1] today for H[einrich Krzyzanowski].—

I am beginning to think this wretched liturgical tome from which I took the words of 'Veni creator' is not entirely reliable.—Please send me an authentic text of the hymn as written by St. Francis.

> Infirma nostri corporis
> Virtute firmans perpeti?

Is perpeti right? How is it to be translated?

> Per te sciamus da Patrem
> noscamus atque filium.

Is that right? What do you make of the syntax?

Ever yours,
Gustav

---

[1] Slang for Gulden. See footnote to letter 6, p. 60 (K.M.).

335. *To Josef Reitler*

Undated. Maiernigg am Wörthersee, July 1906

My dear Herr Reitler,

I have planned a walking-tour for the first half of August, so cannot have the pleasure of welcoming you here during my summer holiday.—Perhaps, however, it will suit you to visit me between 16 and 20 August in Salzburg, where I shall be conducting *Le nozze di Figaro* at the Mozart festival, which takes place during that period.—

I shall be very pleased to make your acquaintance in person.

In this agreeable hope I remain,

Yours sincerely,
Mahler

336. *To Josef Reitler*

Undated. [Maiernigg] *July 1906*
Telegram

As informed you letter Paris am setting out on two weeks walking-tour therefore suggest if convenient to you meeting Salzburg 16–20 August

Regards Mahler

337. *To Friedrich Löhr*

Undated. Summer 1906
Picture-postcard: Lago di Misurina

Very many thanks for philological assistance. The sanctus spiritus conveys its gratitude to you.

Afraid I have to be in Salzburg in mid-August, which I find particularly tiresome this year. Here for two days' rest.

Very best wishes, also to Uda.

Ever,
Gustav

338. *To Willem Mengelberg†*

Undated. Postmark: Maiernigg am Wörthersee, 18[?] August 1906

My dear, good Mengelberg,

Thank you very much indeed for your kind letter. It was very important to me, and a great consolation, finally to hear something so fully understanding and deeply perceptive, after so much confused drivel (even from quarters from which one might have expected something sensible about the nature of the work, not merely superficial technical observations).[1]

What a pity you made your remark concerning the 'hammer'[2] so late. It was no longer possible to do anything about it, as my 'imprimatur' had been given weeks earlier. But you are *quite right*. I did feel it too, but then forgot about it. At any rate we can try *your* method in Amsterdam, perhaps adding a supplementary sheet to the score.—I am greatly looking forward to spending a few days with you again, and most certainly intend to bring my wife with me this time too. But, my dear friends, please do not go to any trouble about accommodation. We shall simply stay at the Hotel Amstel, spending the whole of the day with you. Agreed, then—I shall come to Amsterdam direct from Frankfurt and shall conduct my Sixth on the 24th.[3]—

The Cologne horn-player whom I had for my Fifth was *magnificent*. If he is the same one (do ask him), then he is unreservedly to be recommended.—The one from *Berlin*, on the other hand, is said not to be very good.—I am *very* much looking forward to hearing *your work* composed for the Rembrandt celebrations.[4] Can you not send it to me? I am convinced anything written by you cannot be bad. I shall cast around from Vienna for a second conductor and possibly horn-players. Here I am *up to my neck in calamities*! I have just finished my Eighth—it is the grandest thing I have done yet—and so peculiar in content and form that it is really impossible to write anything about it. Try to imagine the whole universe beginning to ring and resound. These are no longer human voices, but planets and suns revolving.—More when I see you.

With kindest regards to you and to your wife, and also to the Diepenbrocks.

Your very devoted

Mahler

You and your wife must come and visit me here some time.

---

[1] About the Sixth Symphony (o.e.).

[2] The original score of the fourth movement of the Sixth Symphony calls for a hammer at three climatic moments, without saying what it was to strike. Various experiments were made for the first performance, including a specially constructed drum of Mahler's own invention. The obvious inaudibility of the 'blows' may have caused Mengelberg to suggest a new and better method to make them clear. In which way we shall probably never know. Soon after the première of the symphony Mahler cut out the third hammer blow. Mahler never conducted his Sixth in Amsterdam, and the score does not mention any alteration regarding the execution of the 'blows' (K.M.).

[3] Nothing came of this tour to Amsterdam which should have taken place in January 1907 (K.M.).

[4] Entitled *Improvisationen über ein Thema für Orchester nach Radierungen von Rembrandt*; it was never performed by Mahler and only once apparently by Mengelberg (K.M.).

339. *To Josef Reitler†*

Undated. [Maiernigg] *August 1906*

Dear Herr Reitler,
   Try at any rate to make Colonne do the Third, because I myself have had second thoughts about the suitability of the more recent symphonies for this occasion. You are quite right. In Paris one *must* begin with the earlier works. But on no account would I advise the First; it is very hard to understand. Even the Sixth or Fifth would be preferable. But the words to the Third are not translated. Weinberger[1] is confusing it with the Second, which was played in Brussels and Liège.[2]
   So the translation will have to be made.—And I ought in any case to approve it first.
   I am writing in the haste of departure for Vienna. Kindest regards from
                              Yours sincerely,
                                   Mahler

340. *To Josef Reitler*

Undated. 1906

Dear Herr Reitler,
   So far I have been corresponding only with Herr *Astruc*.[3] But his second letter was worded in such a way that I felt no urge to reply. I may now say as much of Herr Colonne's invitation.[4]—I will in no circumstances agree to a reduction in the size of the orchestra. The very suggestion fills me with disgust, and I beg you to abandon the whole thing.—
   Getting away from here involves such great difficulties that it is only in quite exceptional circumstances—above all, only if I am assured of all the artistic requirements for perfect realization of my intentions—that I could bring myself to go to Paris. And—believe me, the time is not yet ripe! Let us wait another one or two years! In any case, it has been a pleasure *to* make your acquaintance, and I hope we shall meet again in the near future.
                              Yours very sincerely,
                                   Mahler

[1] The publisher (K.M.).
[2] The Belgian conductor Sylvain Dupuis had performed Mahler's Second Symphony in Brussels in April 1902 and in Liège in March 1898 (K.M.).
[3] Gabriel Astruc (1864–1938), director of the Théâtre du Châtelet in Paris and head of the concert agency Maison Astruc (K.M.).
[4] Eduard Colonne (1838–1910), French conductor and founder of the 'Concerts Colonne' in Paris (K.M.).

341. *To Willem Mengelberg*†

Undated. *Postmark: Vienna, 12 September 1906*

Dear Mengelberg,

I shall be conducting a few *concerts* again shortly and need my *revised* scores
Please ask your wife to be so kind as to get together those of my scores that
are at your house and send them to me.—You can of course have them back at
any time.—I also want to enter in my copy the revisions to my Fifth that I made
at your house and which have proved so successful. I therefore beg the loan of
your copy for some time.

From the midst of this accursed theatrical turmoil, which I shall not be
able to bear much longer, warmest regards to yourself, your wife and the
Diepenbrocks.

Your devoted
Mahler

342. *To Arnold Berliner*

Undated. *Postmark: Vienna, 4 October 1906*

Dear Berliner,

   1. I shall arrive in Berlin on Sunday morning, about six, and shall expect
you at my hotel, the Habsburger Hof, between seven and eight-thirty. If this
is too early for you (I take it you get up late), I shall be at the Philharmonie
from ten onwards for rehearsals.[1]

   2. Repertoire [in Vienna] 10–20 October:
   Wednesday 10th: *Fidelio* [The Polish Jew][2]
   Friday 12th: *Figaro*
   Sunday 14th: *Seraglio*
   Wednesday 17th: *Zauberflöte* [Il Trovatore][2]
   Friday 19th: *Tristan*
Providing all goes smoothly and no changes are needed.

   3. I shall arrive in Breslau on the morning of Sunday 21 October, staying
until the late evening of the 24th.[3] I have it in mind to bear you off on formidable
walks.

---

[1] Mahler attended the rehearsals for the first Berlin performance of his Sixth Symphony,
conducted by Oskar Fried in the Berlin Philharmonie on Monday, 8 October (o.e. + K.M.).
[2] The works in square brackets were those actually performed on the relevant days. *The Polish
Jew* is by C. Erlanger (1863–1919) (K.M.).
[3] Mahler conducted his Third Symphony on 24 October 1906 at the Orchesterverein,
Breslau (o.e.).

4. Have received the Erler reproduction.[1] He seems to have done a bit of touching up from memory after my departure—too bad!

5. Frau X.'s letter is a *factum humanum* in the history of civilization. The good lady has gradually developed from Pope Gregory into Leo the Tenth. All the Church in (. . .) will need soon is a Tetzel. The Borgia, I dare say, is already quite at home.

Until then—get in some good nights' rest, so that you will be able to withstand the rigours of 7 and 8 October (I shall be leaving late at night, after the concert).

Yours ever,
Mahler

343. *To Willem Mengelberg*

Undated. Postmark: Vienna, 15 October 1906

My dear Mengelberg,

By the same mail, with very many thanks, the scores of the Fifth.—I have also received my other scores. If you want them back, please drop me a line. You can have them whenever you like.—My Sixth seems to be yet another hard nut, one that our critics' feeble little teeth cannot crack. Meanwhile it is struggling along after a fashion through the concert halls. I am looking forward to the performance in Amsterdam.—Shall I bring the *cow-bells?*—You seem not to have received a fairly long letter from Maiernigg, in which I told you my Eighth was finished this summer.[2]

Warmest regards to *everyone*

Your friend
Mahler

⟨P.S. Do you still have my score of the *Manfred* Overture?[3] I couldn't find it in the parcel.⟩

344. *To Albert Neisser* (Breslau)†

Undated. [Vienna] *October 1906*[?]

My dear Geheimrat,

So I shall be arriving in Breslau on Sunday morning.—Now here is my

---

[1] Of Fritz Erler's portrait of Mahler, dating from 1905 (o.e.).
[2] Probably letter 338 (K.M.).
[3] Robert Schumann's Op. 115, the instrumentation of which Mahler had retouched, as he had with other scores by Schumann, Beethoven and Schubert (K.M.).

10*

earnest request: that no one shall meet me at the station or expect me at your house (at such an early hour). It definitely does not help me to feel at home if I disturb anyone's sleep by arriving on their doorstep at the crack of dawn, and you did promise me I was to feel at home in your house and not a 'visitor'.— So I beg you to allow me to arrive in the Fürstenstrasse entirely on my own. There a maid or a manservant will let me in and take me to my room, where I intend to beautify myself within the limits permitted by nature. I shall thereupon proceed most yearningly to the breakfast-room, where with my own fair hands I shall help myself to coffee and rolls, subsequently, with a cigar and something to read, awaiting further events.

Now promise to be a good chap and take *no notice at all* of my arrival, coming down to breakfast at your usual time. I am quite on tenterhooks to hear what you will have to tell me about *Salome*,[1] which I regard as Strauss's most important work. Greatly looking forward to seeing you and your wife again, I am,

Yours very sincerely,
Mahler

My symphony, the Fifth, plays about three-quarters of an hour [*sic!*].

---

345. *To Josef Reitler†*

Undated. [Vienna, 1906?]

Dear Herr Reitler,

Thank you for the information. Please just let Colonne go on his own sweet way. It has just occurred to me that, should he approach you again, my Fifth, which requires a relatively *normal* orchestra, would be better suited to his purpose. And then too it is more appropriate as an introduction than my Sixth.[2] —Both are hard nuts for the Parisians to crack.

All good wishes,

Yours in haste,
Mahler

---

346. *To Albert Neisser†*

Undated. Vienna, [October or November] *1906*

Dear Neisser,

Thank you immensely for everything. I am still enjoying all those good meals

---

[1] R. Strauss's opera was first performed in Breslau, on 28 February 1905; the Breslau ensemble also introduced the opera to Vienna in May 1907 (K.M.).
[2] After Mahler had given up the idea, it was Colonne who was set on getting the Sixth Symphony performed. He did not succeed (o.e.).

in the spirit and still smoking in the flesh.—Once again the reviews leave me dumbfounded. I really do believe that in time I shall become Breslau's national composer.—What a pity Dohrn[1] cannot do that sort of thing again. For that is really what counts most if one is to be understood. But as things are, it is really better not! So I too shall take up quarters in the Jahreszeiten.[2] With all my love and more love for all the love you have shown me, all good things to yourself and your wife

Yours,
Mahler

1907

347.   *To Willem Mengelberg*†

Undated. Postmark: Frankfurt-am-Main, [17] *January 1907*[3]
[Hotel Imperial] am Opernplatz

My dear Mengelberg,

I myself am terribly sorry. Spending a few days with you every year is something I have come to look forward to very much, and this year I shall miss them *greatly*. But on Monday I have to be in Vienna (orders from above).— So I think it best *not* to expect me this year. You know, don't you, that with you I feel not only personally but also artistically in good hands, and so it would, I think, be the best solution if this year you did my Sixth without me. I am sending you the cow-bells. Please send me your score (the full one). I want to put in for you a very important *revision* in the last movement.[4] I hope you will be able to make use of me next year (perhaps for the Seventh).

Many, many heartfelt greetings to you and your wife

from your friend
Mahler

---

[1] Georg Dohrn (1867–1942), conductor of the Breslau Orchesterverein and Singakademie (K.M.).
[2] Probably a reference to Hotel Vier Jahreszeiten (Four Seasons) in Munich where Mahler stayed in November 1906 in connection with the performance on the 8th of his Sixth Symphony (K.M.).
[3] Mahler had been in Berlin on the 14th to conduct his Third Symphony, was in Frankfurt on the 18th for a concert which included his Fourth Symphony and in Linz two days later to conduct his First Symphony which he had also given in Reichenberg on the 7th (K.M.).
[4] See pp. 207 and 209 in the revised score, Lindau, 1963 (K.M.).

348. *To Richard Horn* (Vienna)†

Undated. Frankfurt, [between 16 and 18] *January 1907*

Dear Herr Dr. Horn,

Further to our discussion a few evenings ago I am sending you the enclosed article (*Kölnische Zeitung*) on 'Matter, Ether and Electricity', which I have just read. What do you think now of the immutability of scientifically based views?— What will 'description' be like once our experience in this obscure field is as well ordered as, for instance, our views on astronomy are today?—And even my dictum (approximately) 'the laws of nature will remain the same, but our views about them will change', I must further add that even that does not strike me as certain. It is conceivable that in the course of aeons (perhaps as a result of a natural law of evolution) even the laws of nature may change; that for instance the law of gravity may no longer hold—does not Helmholtz even now assume that the law of gravity does not apply to infinitely small distances? Perhaps (I myself add) not to *infinitely great* distances either—for instance very distant solar systems. Just think that through to its logical conclusion.

Yours in haste,
Mahler

349. *To Julius v. Weis-Ostborn* (Graz)

Undated. Vienna, April 1907

Dear Herr Finanzrat,

Please forgive my not replying earlier to your kind letter, which was awaiting me on my return from Rome.[1] I found what you had to say most interesting, and there is a good deal I should like to say in reply, which I hope to do in person one of these days.

Perhaps on the occasion of a performance of *Iphigenie*, which you and our friend Decsey should not miss. I think it the best thing Roller and I have achieved so far.[2] Anyway we have advanced a fair distance along our road. This season it will be performed on Sunday 5 April, probably for the last time. Well then! Shall I be seeing you? In haste and with kindest regards,

Yours sincerely,
Mahler

[1] Mahler had conducted two concerts in Rome, at the end of March and the beginning of April (K.M.).

[2] The première was on 18 March; thereafter it was performed only on 13 and 18 April, and finally on *Sunday, 5 May*. Mahler probably refers to the latter date, as 5 April was actually a Friday (K.M.).

350. *To Arnold Berliner*†

Undated. Postmark: Vienna, 17 [June] *1907*

My dear Berliner,

It is all quite true. I am going because I can no longer endure the rabble. I am not leaving for America until the middle of January, and I shall stay until the middle of April.[1] I hope before then to see you a number of times in Berlin and in Vienna. For now just very best wishes in very great haste from,

Yours ever,
Mahler

351. *To Arnold Berliner*

Undated. Postmark: Klagenfurt, 4 July 1907[2]

Dear Berliner,

My contract[3] has been drawn up by a lawyer; I shall send it for you to have a look at as soon as everything is settled. Your mind can be quite at rest! It has all been very carefully thought out. The most I risk is being rather miserable for *three months* in the year, to make up for which I shall have earned 300,000 crowns *clear* in four years.

That is the position. We have had frightful bad luck! I shall tell you when we next meet. Now my elder daughter has scarlet fever—diphtheria![4] Shall we see you in the summer—in August? Do write again soon.

With all good wishes,

Yours,
Mahler

352. *To Arnold Berliner*†

Undated. Vienna [September (?) 1907]
Postcard

Dear Berliner,

To me, to us, it goes without saying that you can never come at a wrong

[1] Mahler's departure from Vienna depended on finding a successor as director of the Court Opera. At the end of August 1907 Felix Weingartner was appointed from the beginning of January 1908. During that autumn Mahler conducted only once at the Opera, a performance of *Fidelio* on 15 October, and he left Vienna on 9 December 1907 (K.M.).
[2] On the back of the envelope: 'Sender: Mahler, Maiernigg am Wörthersee' (o.e.).
[3] With the Metropolitan Opera (K.M.).
[4] Maria Anna ('Putzi'), born 3 November 1902, died on 12 July (K.M.).

time. Though you will sometimes have to keep yourself amused without me, because I am, as I shall explain when we meet, no longer so 'fit and active' as you remember me from earlier times.

I shall be away from 5 until 11 October.[1] Either before or after that we shall be delighted to see you.

Best wishes,

Yours in haste,
Mahler

353. *To Alexander v. Zemlinsky* (Vienna)†

Undated. [Vienna, November?] *1907*

Dear Zemlinsky,

We do want to say goodbye to you.[2]—Couldn't you and Schönberg drop in again for a while? I'm afraid we are engaged every evening, so it would have to be in the afternoon.—Preferably *at 4 o'clock*, when we are always in.—Please also bring my score (Seventh Symphony). You can have it back on my return.

All good wishes,

Yours,
Mahler

354. *To Max Kalbeck*

Undated. Vienna, probably December 1907

My dear Kalbeck,

Your kind letter gave me great pleasure. I sense that its tenor was dictated by a personal feeling reaching beyond the conventional. Our relationship is, alas, a fragment for which all the themes are doubtless extant, their 'development',[3] however, for many reasons, for ever falling short of 'realization'.[3]

I sincerely hope this new shape my life will take will also draw you into the circle of all that is dear and precious to me, for I have long regarded you as a friend, an elective affinity.

With kindest regards to yourself and to your good lady,

I remain,
Yours sincerely,
Gustav Mahler

[1] Mahler gave a concert in Wiesbaden with works by Beethoven and Wagner on 9 October 1907 (K.M.).
[2] Before leaving on first American tour (o.e.).
[3] A pun on the musical term 'Durchführeng' (development) and the present participle of 'durchführen' (to accomplish) (K.M.).

GESELLSCHAFT ⚜ MUSIKFREUNDE
IN ⸰ WIEN

Sonntag, den 24. November 1907, mittags halb 1 Uhr
===== im großen Musikvereins-Saale =====

I. AUSSERORDENTL. GESELLSCHAFTS-KONZERT.

o o o o o

Zur Aufführung gelangt:

GUSTAV MAHLER ═══
ZWEITE SINFONIE (C-MOLL)
=·= für Soli, Chor, Orchester und Orgel. ═══

1. Satz: ALLEGRO MAESTOSO. (Mit durchaus ernstem und feierlichem Ausdruck.)
2. Satz: ANDANTE CON MOTO.
3. Satz: SCHERZO. (In ruhig fließender Bewegung.)
4. Satz: „URLICHT" aus: „Des Knaben Wunderhorn".
5. Satz: FINALE.

MITWIRKENDE: ═════

Frau ELISE ELIZZA, k. k. Hof-Opernsängerin.
Fräulein GERTRUD FÖRSTEL, k. k. Hof-Opernsängerin.
Fräulein HERMINE KITTEL, k. k. Hof-Opernsängerin.
Fräulein BELLA PAALEN, k. k. Hof-Opernsängerin.
Herr RUDOLF DITTRICH, k. k. Hoforganist.
Der SINGVEREIN DER GESELLSCHAFT DER MUSIK-
FREUNDE.
Das K. K. HOF - OPERNORCHESTER.

DIRIGENT: DER KOMPONIST.

Preis dieses Programmes 20 Heller.

Fig 6. Mahler's last concert in Vienna, 24 November 1907

355. *To Anna v. Mildenburg*†

Undated. [Vienna, 7 December] *1907*

Dear old friend,

I have just composed a screed[1] to the 'dear members', which will be put up on the notice-board. But while I was writing it it occurred to me that you were not among those addressed and that for me you are a being *quite apart*. I have kept on hoping to set eyes on you during these days. But there it is, you are at the Semmering (where it is of course much nicer to be). And so on leaving the Opera, not Vienna, where I shall go on living, I can only send you these few heartfelt words and press your hand in spirit. I shall always watch your progress with affection and sympathy, and I hope calmer times will bring us together again. In any case, you know that even from afar I shall remain a friend on whom you can rely. I write this in the midst of frightful turmoil. May all go well with you. And be of good heart.

Your old friend,
Gustav Mahler

356. *To All Members of the Court Opera Company*†

Vienna, 7 December 1907

The hour has come that brings our work together to an end. Departing from the place of work that had become so dear to me, I herewith bid you farewell.

What I leave behind me is not such as I dreamt, something whole, something complete in itself, but fragments, things unfinished, as is man's lot.

It is not for me to judge what my activity has meant to those to whom it was dedicated. But at such a moment I may say of myself: I have always tried to do my best, always aimed high. My endeavours could not always be crowned with success. No one is so exposed to 'the resistance of the material'—'the malice of inanimate objects'[2]—as the executant artist. But I have always exerted myself to the limit, subordinating myself to the cause and my inclinations to duty. Never sparing myself, I have been able to demand that others too should give all that was in their power to give.

In the thick of the skirmish, in the heat of the moment, neither you nor I have remained unscathed or been immune from error. But whenever a work was accomplished, a task fulfilled, we forgot all the toil and effort, feeling

[1] Mahler's farewell letter to the company on leaving the Vienna Court Opera. See next letter (o.e.).
[2] Trans.' note: *die Tücke des Objekts*, a familiar quotation referring to e.g. the tendency of a dropped collar-stud to roll under the wardrobe.

richly rewarded—even when the world failed to accord us its approval. We have all made progress, and with us the Opera-House for the sake of which we have striven.

My heartfelt thanks now go out to all of you who have supported me, aided me, struggled on with me, in my difficult, often thankless task. To all of you my sincerest wishes for your further journey through life and for the prosperity of the Court Opera, the future destinies of which I shall always follow with the keenest sympathy.

Gustav Mahler

357. *To Bruno Walter†*

Undated. [Vienna, December] *1907*

My dear Walter,

Thank you very much for your sweet letter. Neither of us need waste words on what we mean to each other.—I know of no one who understands me as well as I feel you do, and I believe that for my part I have entered deep into the mine of your soul. Enclosed is the picture your wife asked for. Best wishes to both of you. Hoping to see you again in May.[1]

Ever yours,
Gustav Mahler

---

[1] Mahler had left the Vienna Opera. Bruno Walter was greatly upset by the parting of their ways and had written to say so (o.e.).

VIII

THE LAST YEARS
1908–1911

1908

358. *To Alfred Roller* (Vienna)†

New York, Evening of 20 January 1908
Hotel Majestic

Dear Roller,

This in great haste to give you notice (quite official) of the imminent visit of Mr. *Cottenet*, an influential member of the management of the Metropolitan Opera, who is tomorrow embarking for Italy, whence he will proceed, a few days after you receive this letter, to Vienna.—He is going to Vienna for the sole purpose of seeing you, in the hope of obtaining your services for the opera here.

The following for your guidance:

In general.

As a result of the *absolute* incompetence and fraudulent activities of those who have for years had control over the stage in matters of business and art (managers, producers, stage managers, etc.), almost all of whom are immigrants, the situation at the Opera is bleak.—

The audiences here, and all the factors affecting the artist—not least the board themselves (most of whom are multi-millionaires)—though corrupt and misguided are—in contrast with 'our people' in Vienna (among whom I also include the Aryan gentry)[1]—unsophisticated, hungry for novelty, and in the highest degree eager to learn.—

The position here is as follows: *Conried* has long been quite discredited here. —He has put himself beyond the pale mainly by being unfair and tactless.— The management (i.e. the millionaire board) has sacked him.—At the same time it was planned to appoint me in his place—this even before I arrived.—My (to me incomprehensible) resounding success evidently gave the whole affair impetus.—As you have guessed, I quite decisively refused. But I expressed my

---

[1] Translators' note: 'our people' (*unsere Leut*), sometimes used by Jews in reference to other Jews: cf. the English class expressions, 'one of us' and 'our sort'.

willingness to continue assisting the management, in some capacity, in artistic matters, and in any case to continue conducting and producing.—I'm afraid in these circumstances I have little influence on future developments.—The management plan, first of all, to appoint the present director of *La Scala*,[1] manager of the Metropolitan Opera, and to appoint *Toscanini*, a *very well-thought-of* conductor, to take charge of Italian opera, and hand, as it were, German opera over to me.—But this is all still in the air. For my part, I shall first have to decide how it all appeals to me.—

But now the main thing!

I have proved to the management (or rather, to one of them, the prime mover) beyond doubt that it is *above all* the *stage* here that needs a new master, and that I know only one man with the artistic and personal ability to clear up the mess.—At the same time I assured them (and I am still working on these lines) of the necessity of handing over the stage, and everything to do with it, lock, stock and barrel, to this man. Rather the way I always saw our position in Vienna.—I could write much more about this. Personally, I must tell you you will find here the *most ample* funds and the finest company—no intrigues—no red tape.—In a word, the most splendid sphere of activity I could wish for you. If I could take over the directorship, I shouldn't waste a word. But since you would have to deal with someone about whom I know nothing at all (the Italian from La Scala—or whoever it may be), I must advise caution.—Above all, should you receive an official offer—which is not yet certain—you must secure yourself complete freedom of action and authority over everything concerning the *stage*.

At least the position you have in Vienna.—You must above all insist on coming over here as soon as possible to see to everything for yourself and inform yourself while the season is still on. (The management will meet your every wish, if they see you are serious about it.)

For your information, you would have a season of approximately five months here—and could use some of the holiday for your preparations. **Last not least** —I think you can demand a salary of 15,000 dollars (75,000 marks). But to be on the safe side—in all these matters plead ignorance of the conditions and ask for time to think things over. You could perhaps ask the management to conduct all negotiations, on your behalf, with me personally here, since I am by now thoroughly familiar with conditions here and also with your needs and expectations.—Regarding the 15,000 dollars—if this point is raised, do not be too *firm*. The fact is I don't yet know exactly how far we can go, because the position you must demand does not yet exist at this opera-house.—It would be best if you could arrange to hand over negotiations on this matter *to me* on the

[1] Giulio Gatti-Casazza (K.M.).

grounds that only I am *in a position* to deal impartially with both your interests and conditions —and that you know too little of conditions here.

Seize the opportunity, my dear fellow, if you receive an offer and if there is nothing to detain you in Vienna.—The people here are tremendously unspoilt— all the crudeness and ignorance are—*teething troubles. Spite* and hypocrisy are to be found only among our dear immigrant compatriots. Here the dollar *does not reign supreme*—it's merely easy to earn. Only one thing is respected here: *ability* and *drive*! Well, I hope I've now given you all the information you need on that score.

Everything here is generous, healthy—but ruined by the immigrant *canaille* —I am writing in wild haste—it is only half-an-hour ago that I was authorized to write this letter, and the ship leaves tomorrow morning.

My wife has been confined to bed for the last week (poor thing). She sends her affectionate regards. We received your card today. Very best wishes, old friend, and keep a very cool head when Mr. Cottenet comes. What impresses these people most is what you have in high degree: *resolution*—calmness without chill.

Yours,
Mahler

I almost forgot something *important*. You have been given a bad name by those dubious gentry who guessed I was going to propose you. They say you 'squander millions' and there would not be enough for you in New York.—

I explained to the management that you spent great sums of money in the *right place*, which in fact meant you were *very economical.*

The (*very munificent*) board found this entirely plausible.

But in discussion it is essential to present yourself as shrewd and capable in financial matters. This will put their minds at rest, and then here it will be all the easier for you to ask for whatever you need. *Once again:* None of this is yet settled. My own refusal may yet bring about some quite unforeseen situation.

But *in any case,* before tying yourself down in any way in *Vienna,* let me know *first.*

359. *To Emil Gutmann* (Munich)†

Undated. New York, early 1908

Dear Herr Gutmann,

As a result of Conried's resignation and my refusal to take his place, I'm afraid everything here is now in a state of flux, so I do not yet know whether and, if so, for how long I am to return here next season. In any case, I believe

I shall be free during October, and I should therefore suggest that you arrange for the tour to start at the *beginning* of October. In that event I should be available on the terms given. I should of course have to have adequate rehearsals for two programmes before starting out on the tour. In the circumstances I should almost prefer another *first-class* orchestra to one that is still being formed, which will, after all, need more time to fuse into a whole than I shall have available.

Should my proposal to start at the beginning of October not suit you, you would have to be patient with regard to my acceptance until the position here is clarified. I think that by 1 April I shall be in a position to make arrangements for my next season.

Yours sincerely,
Mahler

If you accept the beginning of October, please send me a short *cable*, to which I shall wire back as briefly, whereupon we can regard the matter as fixed.

360. *To Emil Gutmann*†

Undated. New York, [early] *1908*
Hotel Majestic

Dear Gutmann,

Further to my letter of yesterday: I wonder would you consider it desirable to have the *first performance*[1] of my latest symphony, the Seventh, for the projected tour?

The ensemble is, I think, also suitable, since only *four horns* and *three trumpets* and *moderate* percussion are required. Only quadruple woodwind and a *guitar and mandoline*. It is my *best* work and preponderantly cheerful in character. I beg for a *reply* to this suggestion too by 1 April, because otherwise I shall have to accept other offers.

Yours sincerely,
Mahler

Of course only if I can have an ensemble that is in every respect excellent.

---

[1] The first performance of the Seventh Symphony was given in Prague on 19 September 1908, Mahler conducting (o.e.).

361. *To Josef Reitler*

New York, 4 February 1908
Hotel Majestic

Dear Herr Reitler,

I have just received your kind letter and hasten to thank you, even if briefly. (For unless I do so immediately I shall certainly not find time later.)

I found your news most interesting,[1] and if you had not taken pity on me, I should still not know how my successor's great work had been received. Admittedly, learning that my work has not been immediately forgotten, though it has been handed over defenceless to the destroyer, is a cup of joy filled only with gall.—To be quite frank, I was *deeply grieved* that it should be precisely *Fidelio* that had to suffer the ravages of time, for I had hoped it would *long* outlive me there.[2]

That I turned down the offer here you will of course have realized from my having once told you my main reasons for giving up my position in Vienna. And I am so firm in this belief that I must not tie myself down that even the incredible allurements that New York has to offer—*unlimited* funds and a salary that would sound fantastic in Vienna (300,000 crowns for six months plus some extras)—could not sway me.[3]

Once again warmest thanks for your repeated proof of friendship, and kindest regards from,

Yours very sincerely,
Mahler

362. *To Willem Mengelberg* (Amsterdam)†

Undated. New York, February 1908

My dear old friend,

You will soon (I hope) be receiving from Boston a letter asking you to take over that (splendid) orchestra, as successor to Muck.—*Schelling,*[4] with whom I discussed the matter yesterday, did say you were not very inclined to accept the position. As I can easily imagine your reasons, it is perhaps as well if I give

---

[1] An account of the first performance on 21 January 1908 of *Fidelio* under Weingartner (o.e.).
[2] Mahler's production of *Fidelio* was restored by Direktor Hans Gregor, who succeeded Weingartner from 1911–1918 (o.e. + K.M.).
[3] Mahler had been offered the post as director of the Metropolitan Opera (K.M.).
[4] Ernest Henry Schelling (1876–1939), American pianist, conductor and composer (o.e. + K.M.).

you a little information, so that you get a clear picture of conditions here, to avoid making too one-sided a decision.

The position in Boston is the finest any musician could wish for.—It is the *first* and *highest* in this whole continent.—A *first-class* orchestra. A position of absolute authority. A social position that no musician can ever attain in Europe. —A public more eager to learn and more grateful than any European can imagine. Your New York experiences are no criterion. Here in New York the theatre is the centre of attraction, and concert-going is confined to a small minority.

And now to what must also help to tip the scales for you: the salary.

If you are approached, ask for 20,000 dollars (approximately 50,000 guilders, indeed, slightly more). You can live very comfortably indeed on 6000 to 8000 dollars, putting the rest aside. If I were you I should not hesitate to accept the offer, for the most important thing for an artist is the instrument at his disposal and the response that his art awakens.

Please let me know by return what you think about it and if you wish me to go on using my influence in the matter. I shall be meeting *Higgins*[1] at the end of March (I have only had correspondence with him so far) and could then discuss everything on your behalf, perhaps settling a number of things that are difficult to deal with by letter.—It would be wonderful for me to have you nearby again. I shall probably also be spending the next few years here in America. I am quite entranced with this country, even though the artistic satisfaction to be got out of the Metropolitan is very far from what it might be.

I write in great haste, wanting you to have this letter as soon as possible. Please answer immediately, even if quite briefly.

Remember me very kindly to your wife and all friends in Amsterdam, and to yourself (all good wishes) from

Your old friend
Gustav Mahler

My wife, who is here with me, sends her best wishes.

363. *To Alfred Roller*†

New York, 15 February 1908

My dear Roller,

Meanwhile events here have been taking their inexorable course. The new management has been set up and the situation has clarified to the extent that

---

[1] Major Henry Lee Higginson (1834-1919), founder and manager of the Boston Symphony Orchestra (K.M.).

those whose views will be immediately decisive in future, i.e. the representatives of the proprietors of the Opera-House (millionaires), then Dippel, to whom the administration has been entrusted, and yours truly, who has so far been hovering as a kind of spirit over the waters and will probably continue to do so in future if circumstances remain unchanged, are now seriously discussing your appointment. I hope you will be receiving a telegram within the next few days, i.e. even before this letter arrives, suggesting that you should, to begin with, come here on an exploratory visit in the near future, that is, as soon as you can get away. During this visit everything is to be discussed and, I hope, also settled. First of all, whether you are willing and able to accept the position, what attitude you take towards the situation you find here, and what influence you can exercise over future developments. It has been agreed between me and the powers that be that you should be engaged as *chief stage manager* in charge of all stage and theatrical matters, with complete authority within your own sphere— responsible only to the board.—From the way negotiations have been going I hope to get you a salary of 12,000 dollars (60,000 crowns) per annum. To judge from all the inquiries I have made, you will easily be able to save 7000 dollars a year.—Whatever arrangements Mr. Cottenet is meanwhile making with you are already superseded, and you should act solely on this information from me. The best thing would be for you to take your holidays in April, arranging your trip to America so that you could return to Europe with us on 23 April, spending at least a *fortnight* here seeing exactly what your appointment will involve.— But what about your Vienna contract? Have you received it yet? If so, what are its terms? You will, of course, have to take that into consideration.—Let me know about that by return of post so that I know just where I stand! Fräulein Uchatius, who lives here and often visits us, says she could not imagine a more splendid place for you and that you would find it immensely stimulating and satisfying here. I think so too. There is still everything to be done here, and you will be coming at just the right moment. It would be delightful if we could be together again, yet I cannot conceal from you that I shall be able to enjoy your company for only a short time. I do not intend to stay here long; but at least for next season, if I am still in good health.—However, this is *just between ourselves*! Very best wishes (in great haste) also to your wife, who, as far as I can judge, would be very happy here.

Yours as ever,
Mahler

364. *To Paul Hammerschlag* (Vienna)

Undated. Postmark: New York, 17 February 1908

Dear Hammerschlag,

It is rather awful of me not to have given you any sign of life before this. After a performance of *Don Giovanni*[1] with Italian singers, among whom you probably know only Bonci (Ottavio) and Sembrich (Zerline), I thought of you intensely, regretting not having the faithful companion of my Mozart experiences beside me. *And in spite of the fact* that the singing was almost unsurpassable, I yearned for my Vienna production, which Mozart too, I think, would have liked better.

But if I were young and had the energy I squandered during ten years in Vienna, something might perhaps be brought about here that we groped for, as an ideal, in Vienna: the exclusion of any commercial consideration whatsoever. For the decisive bodies here are *so* fair and the means at their disposal are so unlimited. You will already have heard that the stockholders (i.e. the owners of the Opera) offered me the directorship with absolute authority, and that I firmly rejected it. I have not changed my views on the nature of the whole institution. Five years ago, however, I should not have been able to resist such an alluring offer. The climate, the people and the extremely generous conditions suit me extraordinarily well.—On Thursday my wife and I shall for the first time descend upon your cousin, who has been extremely obliging. My wife was indisposed most of last month and confined to her room. But she is pretty well now, and I hope she will be able to catch up with what she has missed.

I am also pretty well—as well as can be expected in the circumstances.—I look forward from day to day to my return and to seeing old friends again in Vienna. The *Neue Freie* [*Presse*] is sent to me occasionally (only very irregularly, alas) and from it I gather time and again that my successor's position is doubtless not a bed of roses either, and then I think myself lucky to have escaped from that nightmare (which still often plagues my dreams). But I look forward to having a 'real good old gossip' with you again. When you receive this, there will be two more months to go.

Kindest regards to you and your wife, and please forgive this very unsatisfactory letter. I do not plead lack of time, but confess frankly I am a very poor correspondent—in that respect perhaps also too much a child of our time. But perhaps you will find time to drop me a line.

Yours very sincerely,
Gustav Mahler

[1] Mahler conducted this opera in New York on 23 and 26 January, on 12 February and on 3 April 1908 (K.M.).

My wife is not at home at the moment, otherwise she would certainly enclose a line of greetings. Please remember me also to your brother Albert.[1] I am following his instructions to the letter.

365. *To Alfred Roller*

New York, 27 February 1908

Dear Roller,

Things have taken a turn that I cannot yet entirely assess. This much seems clear to me: that someone has put a spoke in my wheel.—What is striking is that the change I think I observe has occurred since Cottenet's visit to Vienna.— What happened there? Did he come and see you? And did he see anyone else? I have not yet been able to find out anything about it (which in itself is very suspicious), but have noticed a considerable cooling off on the part of the powers that be. I thought I could trump all their aces, hoping to have you here for *Fidelio*.[2] Unfortunately this is not possible, as I see from your telegram. And so we have lost the only opportunity of presenting positive grounds to strengthen our cause.—I no longer believe an offer will be made to you. The only thing I have been able to achieve is that you should be sent an invitation to spend one or two weeks here in April (at the company's expense, of course) to discuss this very matter (which I regard as settled in the negative).—I am putting this so bluntly so that you should have no illusions. If you think there is any point in coming here to have a look round—as an artist {you} would find it tremendously stimulating—let me know at once and I shall arrange everything. But do take into account the talk there will be in Vienna and the fact that such a journey (if it does not lead to your being engaged here) will expose you and make your position more difficult.—In any case, please reply immediately—also about Cottenet's visit—so that I am informed.—And how about your contract in Vienna? etc. Please do be a bit explicit. I must now be fully informed in order to act at once and with certainty if the occasion arises.— I am convinced that Mr. Cottenet—a very feeble character and an adherent of the Italians—has been thoroughly 'informed' about you and me by our dear compatriots.—

I advise the following: if you are interested in seeing America and can *disguise* your holiday *so well* that no one can in *any* circumstances interpret or construe it as an unsuccessful attempt to find a position here, accept the offer

[1] Dr. Albert Hammerschlag (1863–1935), physician in Vienna (o.e.).
[2] Performed three times that season under Mahler: on 20 and 26 March, and on 16 April (K.M.).

and let us know at once when you will be arriving. And it would be best to arrange your return journey so that you can travel with us on 23 April.—But if it is impossible to avoid arousing suspicion over there—(and I think it impossible)—please send me your refusal (by letter) at once. But do write instantly about everything so that I have a clear picture and may perhaps just be able to seize the last shred of hope.

Yours with very best wishes,
Mahler

366.   *To Anna Moll* (Vienna)†

Undated. New York, [March] *1908*
Hotel Majestic

Dearest Mama,

Almschi kept the letter to Karl, instead of posting it, to read it first—and so I am taking the opportunity of enclosing a few more hugs and kisses for you. You just can't imagine how much we both miss you and Karl. We are always thinking of both of you and talking about you—and nothing tastes quite the way it should because you are not with us.—If I manage to get a contract for next {year} the way I want it, then you must certainly come and stay with us for a month (to return with us) and Karl too must come for a week—he should surely be able to snatch that amount of time.

By then we shall have established ourselves and shall be able to help him in every way. Almschi is on top of the world again, thank goodness—fit as a fiddle —and has picked up a Viennese girl (Fräulein Uchatius)[1] with whom she gets on very well. Take good care of yourself so that we can have a really good time this summer. By the time you read this letter it will be only eight weeks until we are together again.

Every time Weingartner does something silly I can't help thinking how amused you must be, and I share the fun of it with you.

Fondest greetings from

Your
Gustav

---

[1] Marie Uchatius (1882–19 ?), painter (arts and crafts) (o.e.).

367. *To Anna Moll*†

Undated. New York, [end of] *March 1908*
Hotel Majestic

Dearest Mama,
    In frantic haste as usual.
    Here I am sending you a 'news-paper'. Not only because it really lays itself out (and you enjoy that, I know), but because it gives a very clear picture of the present situation. *Fidelio*[1] was a total success, completely altering my prospects from one day to the next. I am moving, or rather 'things' are moving, towards the formation of a Mahler Orchestra[2] entirely at my own disposal, which would not only earn me a good deal of money, but also give me some satisfaction. Everything now depends on the New Yorkers' attitude to my work.—Since they are completely unprejudiced I hope I shall here find fertile ground for my works and thus a spiritual home, something that, for all the sensationalism, I should never be able to achieve in Europe. A tree needs such ground if it is not to die. I feel this very strongly. Anyway, Almschi and I are leaving with joyful hearts (our joyfulness is considerably heightened, dearest little Mama, by knowing we shall soon have you and Karl with us again) and we shall make the most of a good summer.
    Fondest greetings to you, my dear ones,

from
Your
Gustav

368. *To Mysa Wydenbruck-Ezsterhazy* (Vienna)

Undated. New York, 17 April 1908

My very dear Countess,
    I do feel I must send you my greetings before once again setting foot in Europe, and tell you how deeply pleased and touched I was by your kind words. By the time you receive this letter I shall be happily afloat, and even at this very moment I no longer have any peace: either for sitting down or for writing. The homesickness that has tormented me all the time (I'm afraid I shall never be anything but a dyed-in-the-wool Viennese) is changing into that excited yearning which you too doubtless know.—I send you a thousand greetings (I almost

---

[1] New York première on 20 March 1908 (K.M.).
[2] Mahler had been invited by a newly-formed committee to conduct four Festival Concerts at Carnegie Hall during the autumn of 1908. See Notes (K.M.).

said: a thousand hugs); soon we shall see and speak to each other again. Please only regard this scrap of paper as a 'picture-postcard'.

Yours in devoted friendship,
Gustav Mahler

369. *To Alfred Roller*†

Undated. Vienna [June 1908]

Dear Roller,

If Dippel keeps his word he will be calling on you in the next few days, asking you to take over *Tristan* and *Figaro* for New York. I should like to discuss the matter with you in detail. (And in any case to see you again before my impending departure for Toblach.)

For today I want merely to draw your attention to the fact that in any discussion with Dippel it would be quite in order for you to bring up the matter of the fee that is still outstanding for your production of *Fidelio*. So don't forget about that.

What are you doing tomorrow (Saturday) evening?—I can't bring myself to set foot in the opera-house, so I shall be free.—Would you care to join us on a little spree?

Very best wishes,

Yours,
Mahler

370. *To Karl Horwitz*†

Undated. Postmark: Toblach, 27 June 1908

Dear Herr Doktor,

Figaro was published by *Peters*,[1] simply described as 'Vienna Arrangement', without any rights reserved, and is therefore free. So you can make use of it anywhere you like, and without any qualms. I fear, however, that the personnel of such a small theatre as that in Gablonz will *not* be adequate—for *Figaro* is one of the most difficult works to perform. Would it not be more to your advantage to keep to more modest works there, saving up *Figaro* for some later time when you can command sufficient resources? I have already heard of the *Walküre* affair.[2] To such a remote observer as myself the whole thing is totally incom-

[1] Mahler was referring to his and Kalbeck's arrangement of Mozart's *Figaro*. See also letter 324 (K.M.).
[2] An allusion to Weingartner's cuts (20 minutes) in a performance of *Die Walküre* on 16 June; these had angered not only the audience but also the critics (K.M.).

prehensible. W[eingartner] seems to regard not only myself but also R. Wagner as 'predecessors'. With best wishes, always delighted to hear from you,

Yours sincerely,

Gustav Mahler

371. *To Arnold Berliner*

Undated. Postmark: Toblach, June 1908

Dear Berliner,

A rumour has been going the rounds that you have robbed someone—well and truly. The postman has just delivered a whole library to me.—So it is true, and for the remission of your sins you are now doing good works, spreading culture among your friends.—Actually, Alma pulled a face when she saw all those books (a prize-giving ceremony at which she was afraid of being left empty-handed)—but then, when the miniature edition of Goethe's works came to light, her face smoothed out and brightened and she forgave you.

Now in haste my warmest thanks. I shall intercede for you in Heaven—that your sins be forgiven you. Alma will be giving you all other news.

Very best wishes from

Yours ever,

Gustav Mahler

How about nipping across here into the Dolomites? Say from Prague?[1]

372. *To Bruno Walter*

Undated. Toblach, Summer 1908

My dear Walter,

I have been trying to settle in here. This time it is not only a change of place but also a change of my whole way of life. You can imagine how hard the latter comes to me. For many years I have been used to constant and vigorous exercise—roaming about in the mountains and woods, and then, like a kind of jaunty bandit, bearing home my drafts. I used to go to my desk only as a peasant goes into his barn, to work up my sketches. Even spiritual indisposition used to disappear after a good trudge (mostly uphill).—Now I am told to avoid any exertion, keep a constant eye on myself, and not walk much.[2] At the same time

[1] i.e. after the first performance of Mahler's Seventh Symphony on 19 September (K.M.).
[2] Mahler had been told of his heart trouble and the change in his way of life this necessitated (o.e.).

the solitude, in which my attention is more turned inward, makes me feel all the more distinctly everything that is not right with me physically. Perhaps indeed I am being too gloomy—but since I have been in the country I have been feeling worse than I did in town, where all the distractions helped to take my mind off things.—So I have no very comforting news for you, and for the first time in my life I am wishing my holidays were over.—It is wonderful here. If only I could have enjoyed something like this once in my life after completing a work!—For that, as you know for yourself, is the only moment when one is really capable of enjoying things. At the same time I am noticing a strange thing. I can do nothing but work. Over the years I have forgotten how to do anything else. I am like a morphia-addict, or an alcoholic, who is suddenly deprived of his drug.—I am now exerting the sole remaining virtue I have: patience! Most probably I have chosen the worst possible time to be alone. Anyone in my state of mind, of course, is in need of diversion from outside himself. And so I can't help bemoaning the end of the opera season, which means I am now cut off from my main source of entertainment.—For today just very best wishes, also from my wife, who doesn't intend going to Lahmann[1] until September, and I shall probably go with her. Please talk to Dr. X and ask if he can't take both of us on as patients. Do also tell him what my condition is, so that I know whether it is at all advisable for me.

Best wishes to your wife and your charming little girl.

Yours, as ever,
Mahler

373. *To Karl Moll*†

Undated. Toblach, [Summer] *1908*

My dear Karl,

From afar, as though through mist or veils, I see all kinds of confusion in the 'swaying figures'.

For a time, as you know, things with us were in a very great whirl, and the high jinks seemed to have become a permanent institution, then various bouts of heart trouble and generally jangled nerves etc. etc. crystallized.—But now the air seems to be fairly clear.—*And even if it were not,* the two of you really ought to know that your presence is *never* a disturbing element so far as we are concerned. Quite the contrary, it even helps us to bear all the unpleasant things there are.

[1] Dr. Heinrich Lahmann (1860–1915). Walter had taken a cure at Lahmann's health resort in Dresden early in July (K.M.).

So I particularly ask you, and Mama as well, not to come a day later than you are able to or intended to.—We are already eagerly looking forward to seeing both of you, and friend Nepallek[1] (I have only just learnt of his letter) was only, in his sensitive way, excessively cautious and considerate. Almschi is fairly active again, thank goodness, and so I am hoping for (at long last) a restful and pleasant summer.—Wire to say when you are arriving.

Have you been so kind as to go to my flat and make sure that the *iron* strong-box is really locked? I can't remember if I locked it. ⟨You will probably bring hose—socks—with you.—If it's no trouble, please bring *100* Regalia Favoritas from the specialist tobacconist.⟩

With best wishes,

Yours,

Gustav

Please do come as soon as possible.

374. *To Emil Freund*†

Undated. Alt-Schluderbach, [Summer] *1908 or 1909*

Dear Emil,

I'm afraid neither of the pens suits me.[2] They are so fine. I need it mainly for writing music! Please have a similar—red—one sent at once, express, but with a broad nib. And as *soft* as possible.

How can it be that a pen you obviously ordered on Monday morning—doesn't reach me until Wednesday morning?—This is always happening with packages from Vienna—it's really sickening.—Please have the pen you will be ordering tomorrow morning sent on the evening train (about 7 p.m.), so that I have it the following morning.

I am terribly frustrated.

I shall immediately return these two pens, which are no use to me. Or rather, write and tell me whether I should do so immediately or will it do if I bring them to Vienna myself at the end of August.

Best wishes,

Yours in great haste,

Gustav Mahler

---

[1] Dr. Richard Nepallek, neurologist (o.e.).
[2] Gold-nibbed fountain-pens (o.e.).

375. *To Bruno Walter*

Toblach, 18 July 1908

My dear Walter,

As you see, I am still writing from here, and nothing came of the Scandinavian journey! I am so grateful for your kind, wonderful letter. I couldn't help smiling because I seem to notice that you are turning my own weapons against me. Heaven knows what you hit, but certainly not the 'enemy'! What is all this about the soul? And its sickness?[1] And where should I find a remedy? On a Scandinavian journey? The most that could have done for me would have been to provide me with some distraction. But it is only here, in solitude, that I might come to myself and become conscious of myself.—For since that panic fear which overcame me that time, all I have tried has been to avert my eyes and close my ears.—If I am to find the way back to myself again, I must surrender to the horrors of loneliness. But fundamentally I am only speaking in riddles, for you do not know what has been and still is going on within me; but it is certainly not that hypochondriac fear of death, as you suppose. I had already realized that I shall have to die.—But without trying to explain or describe to you something for which there are perhaps no words at all, I'll just tell you that at a blow I have simply lost all the clarity and quietude I ever achieved; and that I stood *vis-à-vis de rien*, and now at the end of life am again a beginner who must find his feet.—Is this a spiritual disposition that must be fought with a psychiatrist's weapons, as you imply? And where my 'work' is concerned, it is rather depressing to have to begin learning one's job all over again. I cannot work at my desk. My mental activity must be complemented by physical activity. The advice you pass on from doctors is of no use to me. An ordinary, moderate walk gives me such a rapid pulse and such palpitations that I never achieve the purpose of walking—to forget one's body. I have recently been reading Goethe's letters—his secretary, to whom he was in the habit of dictating, fell ill, and this so put him off that he had to suspend work for a month.—Now imagine Beethoven having to have his legs amputated after an accident. If you know his mode of life, do you believe he could then have drafted even one movement of a quartet? And that can hardly be compared with my situation. I confess that, superficial though it may seem, this is the greatest calamity that has ever befallen me. What it amounts to is that I have to start a new life—and there too I am a complete beginner.—

But now, in order not to end so dolefully, I want to assure you that I have

---

[1] Bruno Walter remarks: I suppose I had suggested that Mahler should read Feuchtersleben's *Dietetics of the Soul* (1838); his rejection of it is only too understandable in the light of his nature.

succeeded relatively well in discovering how to enjoy myself and life. Also that physically, on the whole, I am not doing too badly. It is wonderful here! I am sorry you are drifting around at the opposite end of the Continent, else I would have insisted on your visiting me here. My symphony (Seventh) will now be performed for the first time on 19 September in Prague—if the Czechs and the Germans have not come to blows by then. Make the most of a beautiful summer and do go for walks (for me too)! You don't realize how wonderful that is.

Very best wishes to you and your wife,

Yours ever,
Mahler

376. *To Emil Gutmann* (Munich)†

Undated. Toblach, Villa Alt-Schluderbach, *23 July 1908*

Dear Herr Gutmann,

I am at your disposal on 5 November for a concert in Munich. I cannot yet decide what to have in the programme. If the Seventh is a success, I shall be happy to include it.[1]—If not, I suggest my Fifth, which would likewise be new to Munich. I must however make the basic condition that the orchestra should be really excellent—above all first horn, first trumpet—and that I have the requisite number of rehearsals.—That would be of the order of five rehearsals.—

If that is not possible, I am prepared to conduct a concert with a classical programme. In that case I need only three rehearsals.

My fee is—as in all future cases, even if it should not be explicitly agreed between us—1500 marks. I am now looking forward to your decision, as I also have to make decisions regarding certain projects.

With kind regards,

Yours sincerely,
Mahler

377. *To Adele Marcus* (Hamburg)†

Toblach, August 1908

Dearest Adele,

During the last few days I could not help thinking of our recent conversation (in the Heimhuderallee).[2] I was reading *Eckermann*, as I usually do in summer, and found Goethe himself taking up the conundrum that was exercising your

[1] Mahler performed his Seventh Symphony in Munich on 27 October 1908 (K.M.).
[2] Adele Marcus's address in Hamburg (K.M.).

mind.—Of course I find his solution not merely 'better informed', but also more fitted to illuminate the mystery for you. Admittedly there is a residue, a something unresolved, that—despite all rational explanation—always remains in such things, bordering as they do on the origin of all things—the 'primal light'.—I cannot resist sending you the book, my dear. I have been reading bits of it here and there, again and again, for decades, and I can say it is one of my dearest possessions.—See what you can extract from it in the course of your life. At every stage of one's life one comes to this book as a different person.—Please excuse the paper—I have run out of writing-paper. (. . .)

I am on new terrain this summer. It is marvellous here, and the peacefulness and seclusion of this little spot allows me once again to become wrapped up in my work as of old. What is booming around in my heart and head here will one day resound in your world.—

In token of old friendship,

Your ever devoted

Gustav Mahler

I almost forgot the most important thing: the passage I refer to is (in this edition[1]) volume 2, pages 2–5.

Whenever Eckermann says anything you can normally read 'Goethe' instead; for the former became so deeply involved in the thoughts and style of his master that the latter seems to speak through his mouth.—

378. *To Bruno Walter†*

Undated. Toblach, [September] *1908*

My dear Walter,

I am now preparing for the journey.—I shall be arriving at the Südbahnhof on the morning of the 5th (probably about 8.30), but I'm afraid I have to dash away again almost at once—at 6 o'clock in the evening—for Prague. But perhaps we could lunch together and so manage to have a chat.

I have been hard at work (from which you can tell that I am more or less 'acclimatized'). I myself do not know what the whole thing could be called. I have been granted a time that was good, and I think it is the most personal thing I have done so far.[2] Perhaps more about that when I see you. Remember me to your wife—and very best wishes to you from

Yours ever,

Mahler

(I have to work through to the last day to finish it.)

[1] Published by Diederichs, Jena, 1908 (o.e.).
[2] Mahler is referring to *Das Lied von der Erde* which he had sketched during the past few months (o.e. + K.M.).

379. *To Alfred Roller*†

Undated. Toblach, September 1908

Dear Roller,

I shall be arriving in Vienna on the morning of the 5th, leaving again the same afternoon. As usual I have to work until the last moment in order to get my harvest safely in. If you have no prior engagement (if so, please do not go to any trouble), I should very much like to see you and have a word with you. I suggest your meeting me between 9.30 a.m. and 10.30 a.m. for breakfast in the Café Schwarzenberg.

We might also meet for lunch at 1.00 p.m. in the Hotel Meissl und Schadn. But I suppose you too will prefer the morning, since we shall not be alone at noon. I shall be lunching with Karl and Walter.[1]

Hoping to see you then, *if you have no prior engagements.*

Best wishes,

Yours,

Mahler

380. *To Emil Gutmann* (Munich)†

Undated. Vienna, [October] *1908*

Dear Herr Gutmann,

Further to my telegram of today I send you the following details:[2]

1. the ensemble is as follows:[2]

4 flutes ⎫	1 tenor horn	2 harps
1 piccolo ⎭	4 horns	1 mandolin
3 oboes ⎫	3 trumpets	1 guitar
1 cor angl. ⎭	3 trombones	4 timpani
1 E♭ clarinet ⎫	1 bass tuba	tam-tam ⎫
3 B♭ (or A) clarinets ⎬	in addition	bass drum
1 bass clarinet ⎭	a 1st trumpet	triangle
3 bassoons	(must be first class)	side drum
1 double bassoon	2 horns (ditto)	tambourine
		cow-bells[3] ⎭

(*in addition ... 2 horns (ditto)* marked "for reinforcement"; *tam-tam ... cow-bells* marked "3–4 players")

I should like to have the first two rehearsals separately: strings, harps, mandolin and guitar, wind and percussion, to be followed by five full rehearsals.—I can hold only *one* of these full rehearsals a day.—The above-

---

[1] Karl Moll and Bruno Walter (K.M.).

[2] For the Seventh Symphony conducted by Mahler in Munich on 27 October (K.M.).

[3] Mahler has forgotten the cymbals, glockenspiel and bells (K.M.).

mentioned special rehearsals might perhaps both be held on one day.—On the day of the concert *no* rehearsals, please, because the symphony is very strenuous for the wind section and they must have time to *rest.*—

So I shall be available in Munich on Tuesday 20th. Providing rehearsals can be held every day, including Sunday. Otherwise I should have to come a day earlier, which would be quite awful for me. Please put my mind at rest by confirming all this. For the material you must get in touch with Lauterbach & Kuhn, Rosstrasse, Leipzig, who are the publishers. I shall bring some of the instrumental parts that I had with me in Prague. The rest I am having copied with all speed here in Vienna.

Best wishes,

Yours sincerely,

Mahler

N.B. First trumpet, first horn and timpanist must be *really first class.*—The timpanist must have very good pedal-tuned drums.

Please book me an especially quiet room in a *pleasant, quiet* hotel.

1909

381. *To Anna Moll* (Vienna)†

Undated, New York, January 1909

My dearest little Mama,

I am never there when Almschi posts letters to you! But we are always thinking and talking of you. Simply to add 'greetings' strikes Almschi as too formal.

I need every ounce of strength this year, for this really takes it out of me. But I am being very careful, and I feel fine.

We are eagerly looking forward to your arrival, for you really are coming, aren't you? Arrange things so as to make the return trip with us in grand style, in your own state-room.

Karl will then come to meet us in Paris, where we shall have a few days' spree together.

I am making an extra 500 dollars, by the merest fluke. We'll spend them there.

A thousand hugs to you and Karl. And don't forget I talk to you every day, even if I don't write.

The fact is, my head and hands are full.

Your faithful

Gustav

⟨If he brings me any cigarettes, Dr. Haberfeld should declare them and put them down specially. There is no duty on around 300. [G.M.].
I'd rather it was in February—then I'd see you sooner.

Goodbye, Mum,
Alma⟩

382. *To Bruno Walter* (Vienna)†

Undated. New York, beginning of 1909

My dear Walter,

A letter from Herr ⟨Reitler⟩[1] reminds me that I still have not answered you, although I often have conversations with you in my head. One question I must not fail to answer immediately: the Philharmonic did once perform the symphony[2] under my baton, and it would be best for you to use the same material, which, including the score, must all be in the possession of the *Musikverein*. ⟨Schalk⟩ will certainly make it available to you.—There is much too much to write about myself, I couldn't even begin to try to begin. I am experiencing so infinitely much now (in the last eighteen months), I can hardly talk about it. How should I attempt to describe such a tremendous crisis! I see everything in such a new light—am in such a state of flux, sometimes I should hardly be surprised suddenly to find myself in a new body. (Like Faust in the last scene.) I am thirstier for life than ever before and find the 'habit of existence' sweeter than ever. These days of my life are in fact like the Sibylline Books.

I find myself less important every day, but am often baffled by the fact that in day-to-day life one keeps on in the same old humdrum way—in all the 'sweet habits of existence'.

I can't help thinking very often of Lipiner. Why don't you ever write anything about him? I should like to know whether he still thinks the same way about death as he did eight years ago, when he told me about his very peculiar views (at my somewhat importunate request—I was just convalescent after my haemorrhage).

How absurd it is to let oneself be submerged in the brutal whirlpool of life! To be untrue to oneself and to those higher things above oneself for even a single hour! But writing that down like this is one thing—on the next occasion, for instance, if I now leave this room of mine, I shall certainly again be as absurd as everyone else. *What* is it then that *thinks* in us? And what acts in us?

[1] Josef Reitler (K.M.).
[2] Mahler's Third. The performance Mahler refers to took place in Vienna on 14 December 1904 and was repeated on 22 December. Walter conducted the symphony in Vienna on 25 October 1909 (o.e. + K.M.).

11*

Strange! When I hear music—even while I am conducting—I hear quite specific answers to all my questions—and am completely clear and certain. Or rather, I feel quite distinctly that they are not questions at all.

Now instead of repaying like with like, do write to me again.—The permanent orchestra here really seems to be in formation. *If it does come to something, could you recommend a young musician of real talent as a conductor*, and with *general musical experience*, who would come here as my **assistent** [*sic*] **conductor**?

For this would be the condition on which I should be prepared to enter into a contract for yet another year. I must have someone to do the preparatory work for my rehearsals and also take over a concert for me every now and then.

Very best wishes to you, dear Walter, and to your wife.

If you see Lipiner, and Nanna,[1] remember me to them warmly.

Yours ever,

Mahler

383. *To Bruno Walter†*

Undated. New York [February 1909]

Dearest Walter,

In greatest haste! Please *find out* at once whether the *splendid* trumpeter of the Konzertverein, by whom we were so much struck that time, *is* still in *Vienna* and if so look him up and see if he would be willing to come to me in New York? If he is no longer in Vienna, find out where he is now and immediately cable me his *name, address*, and if he can come—just those essentials.—Be so kind as to go to this expense on my behalf. I shall definitely be taking over the orchestra in *New York*.[2] More about that soon. If you receive an offer in the near future, don't do anything final without asking me.

Affectionate greetings,

Yours,

Mahler

Very urgent! ⟨Ask [Franz] *Dreyer* and [Johann] Schnellar[3] whether they would be able to take up an offer from me. Perhaps even add it very briefly to the *cable*.⟩

---

[1] Nanna Spiegler (K.M.).

[2] Mahler left the Metropolitan Opera in order to take charge of the New York Philharmonic Orchestra (o.e. + K.M.).

[3] Both musicians. Dreyer (trombone-player) and Schnellar (timpanist) remained in Vienna as members of the Vienna Philharmonic Orchestra (K.M.).

384. *To Bruno Walter*†

Undated. [Postmark: Toblach (—date illegible)] *1909*[1]

My dear Walter,

I have been put under extreme pressure, having to deliver 24 programmes for next season within a fortnight! Please *write* something for me—and send it soon. Surely you haven't been upset by the newspaper-riff-raff's jabber? It all seems completely trumped up!

Yours ever,
Mahler

385. *To Alfred Roller*†

Undated. New York, [February] *1909*

My dear Roller,

I am really ashamed of not replying sooner to your sweet letter, which was a relief to me in more than one respect.—My first reaction was to sit down at once and tell you how happy your news had made me. It was really the first cheerful day I have had this winter.—Knowing you to be in that wilderness has been a constant nightmare to me since my departure, and I have been incessantly worrying about how you could free yourself from that web of inner and outer difficulties.[2]

But it has turned out in every way better than could have been expected. A *new* life (not the 'old one') is now beginning for you.—I am sure you have not been through all of it in vain. And I do not even believe you are saying goodbye to the theatre. Anyone who has a vocation for it, as you have, cannot give it up— and it certainly *will not give you up*! Perhaps it is only now that your work will become truly worthy of you, now when you are liberated from all petty considerations and can work purely as an artist.—One can write about 'expectations' and send congratulations, but 'expecting' is something about which one may remain silent. And yet I was perhaps more pleased by that short allusion of yours than by anything else. I always found it downright incomprehensible that you, who have so much love for children and understanding of what they are like, should yourself be deprived of that blessing. I believe it is only now that your wife too will come to full maturity—high-falutin though this may sound!

It seems to me that you need it only for your happiness—but your wife perhaps for her very life.

[1] See note on p. 448.
[2] On Roller's resigning from the Vienna Opera (o.e.).

About myself I have only good news to send. I am in relatively good health, as also is my family. My work is at least not degrading and not completely distasteful. I staged a really rather good production of *Figaro*[1] (entirely in the Lefler[2] *spirit*) and a magnificent *Bartered Bride*[3] (Lefler above, Mahler below); am definitely leaving the theatre this season and taking over a concert enterprise as from next year.—Your *Wilhelm Tell* was *miserably* ruined under Baumfeld—this was hardly his fault, merely the result of niggardliness and gross lack of understanding on the part of the producer; it did, however, cause a great stir and gave the theatre its first box-office success.

I learn about Vienna from random issues of the *Neue freie Presse*—being used to deciphering the code between the lines of that newspaper.—I am looking forward to soon being able to have a good old gossip with you about everything. Please accept for today this summary report, which I have as it were wrung from myself in the midst of this turmoil—which is just inseparable from the American way of life.

My very best wishes to you, dear Roller—remember me also to your wife and to Walter.

Yours sincerely,
Mahler

386. *To Karl Moll*

Undated. New York, 1909
Savoy Hotel

My dear Karl,

I hope you have by now received my last letter. Today I have to ask a favour of you! The moment you receive this letter, send 300 crowns to ⟨Hr. Dr. Heinrich Krzyzanowski, 18 Bezirk [Vienna] Dittesgasse 14^{III}⟩ (in my name). He is an old friend of mine and I hear he is in very grave financial difficulties.

Fondest greetings,

Yours,
Gustav

---

[1] Between 13 January and 26 March 1909 Mahler conducted *Figaro* six times (K.M.).
[2] Heinrich Lefler (b. 1866) was Roller's predecessor as chief stage designer at the Vienna Court Opera from 1900 to 1903 (K.M.).
[3] First performed on 19 February and repeated four times, lastly on 17 March (K.M.).

387. *To Karl Moll*

Undated. New York, 10 March 1909
Savoy Hotel

My dear Karl,

I am dragging myself out of insurmountable disinclination to write in order to send you a few lines.

Fortunately our return is so close that I can be brief.

1. A thousand thanks for sending dear little Mama to us. It did all of us a world of good, and by now I suppose she is back with you, busily unpacking.

2. And that is the reason for my heroic effort: Mama will certainly have told you of her consultation with Dr. Fraenkel. I should like to summarize the matter briefly—since it is of such importance—in order strongly to back up the new approach and *encourage* you all in it to the utmost.

Fraenkel is a genius of a *diagnostician*, and I urge you to have confidence in him for all you are worth.—So it is Mama's *kidney*—the heart trouble is only secondary.

If Mama follows his instructions to the letter for several *months*, *never* swerving from the right diet, she will recover *completely*. If she does not do this, serious kidney trouble is inevitable within two or three years.

Fraenkel's message to Mama is that she should consult one of the capable younger Viennese doctors (not a 'professor'), who is sure to confirm his diagnosis and who should keep an eye on her.

He recommends the following:

Mannaberg, Wilhelm Schlesinger, Paal [en] or one of Noorden's assistants (*not Noorden himself*, as he is too busy), for instance, *Falta*.

Milk must be her staple food. Please keep a watchful eye on her. She is very good, but one's loving friends never can bear it if one doesn't eat and drink properly at their houses.

Alcohol and *spices* are strictly forbidden. Anything fattening—puddings, bread, etc. are to be reduced to a minimum. *Red meat* forbidden. *White meat only in moderation. Vinegar* forbidden. Please be *meticulous*, dear people, and then dear little Mama will be well and young again in six months' time. Do not let anyone interfere. Our friend Nepallek will also help. I hope Mama arrived back all the better for her trip. Here, as usual, she was the youngest of all.

Fondest greetings and hoping to see you soon.—Alma is very well. ⟨About her *present state* she has doubtless written to you herself. She has been relieved of her *burden*. But this time she actually regrets it.[1]⟩

Yours,
Gustav

[1] It seems that Alma had had a miscarriage, and the last sentence implies that it was not the first one she had had (K.M.).

388. *To Willem Mengelberg*†

Undated. [Vienna, May 1909]

Dear Mengelberg,

Very many thanks for your news.—Please expect me on *3 October*, if that suits your arrangements. I could hardly get away before then. Let us still leave the Sixth this time. If you also want me in Frankfurt on 8 October, I am at your disposal then too.—Only I should have to have your final decision before the end of *July*, in order to make the necessary arrangements.

The symphony is being published by Bote & Bock.[1] Please be good enough to get in touch with them so that you receive everything in good time.—You will, I am sure, not object to our using *transcript* parts in Amsterdam (they will later be replaced by printed ones), so that I shall still be able to correct any mistakes. We can then perhaps take the material along to Frankfurt.

I have just written to the publishers saying that the material must be in your hands by 10 September at the latest, so that you can hold preliminary rehearsals with your people both in Amsterdam and in Frankfurt. I dare say this will be necessary, and I am counting now, as always, on your devoted care and attention.

It would be most delightful if this made it possible for us to be under one roof again for a little while! Please send your next letter to me at Villa Alt-Schluderbach, *Toblach* an der Südbahn, Tyrol, where I shall be going on 9 June, intending to stay until the middle of September.

Please also send the score of the Sixth to that address.

Very best wishes to you and your wife. I rejoice every time I read of your growing success. By now I suppose even those gentry in Amsterdam believe it?

Yours sincerely,

Gustav Mahler

389. *To Josef Reitler*†

Undated. Vienna, [Summer] *1909*

Dear Herr Reitler,

I should be very pleased if you could come to see me some time at home.— You are most likely to find me in around 11 o'clock in the morning. But it is the friend I shall be expecting, not the journalist.

With all good wishes,

Yours,

Mahler

[1] Mahler's Seventh Symphony which he conducted three times in Holland in October 1909 (K.M.).

Moderne Orchesterwerke

aus dem Verlag

Lauterbach & Kuhn, Leipzig.

Gustav Mahler

„Siebente Sinfonie" für gr. Orchester (neu).

H. G. Noren

op. 30 „Kaleidoskop". Variationen und Doppelfuge für grosses Orchester (neu).

Max Reger

op. 90 „Sinfonietta" für grosses Orchester (von 33 Orchestern angekauft).

op. 95 „Serenade" für grosses Orchester (von **54** Orchestern angekauft).

op. 100 „Variat. u. Fuge" über ein Thema von Joh. Ad. Hiller (im ersten Jahre v. 40 Orchestern angekauft).

Leo Weiner

op. 3 „Serenade" f. kleines Orch. (im ersten Jahre von **25** Orchestern angekauft).

op. 5 „Fasching". Humoreske f. kleines Orch. (neu).

Hugo Wolf

„Penthesilea". Sinfonische Dichtung für grosses Orch. (von 45 Orchestern angekauft).

„Ital. Serenade" f. kleines Orch. (von **148** Orch. angekauft).

Die Partituren stellen wir den Herren Dirigenten zur Ansicht gern zur Verfügung.

Fig 7. October 1908. Lauterbach & Kuhn's advertisement for the Seventh Symphony, published in 1909 by Bote & Bock

390.   *To Friedrich Löhr*

Undated. Postmark: Vienna, 8 June 1909

My dear Fritz,

Warmest thanks for the photograph,[1] which brought back happy memories of the old days.—I was quite surprised to see how like you your boy is; I thought at first it was a photograph of him. I am off to Toblach today, where I shall spend the summer.—My address there is simply: *Toblach an der Südbahn.*

If you should happen to be anywhere within striking distance, I should love to pay you a visit, or to have you there.

But in any case we shall see each other on my return in September. I shall then explain my long silence after receiving the photograph.

For today just best wishes to you and the family from Alma and

Gustav

Please take the enclosed joke in the right spirit![2]

391.   *To Emil Freund*†

Undated. Alt-Schluderbach, June 1909

Dear Emil,

Please get in touch immediately (if they have not already got in touch with you) with Direktor Hertzka of Universal Edition (continuation of Wipplinger-strasse) and discuss—or draw up—the contract for the publication of my Eighth Symphony, the terms of which I have already laid down in detail with Hertzka (I think that is his name).[3]

The terms are:

1. I relinquish the *copy*right.
2. I receive 50% of all gross earnings.
3. They engrave the score and the piano reduction for two hands, together with the words, and copy the orchestral and chorus parts.
4. A statement of account will be rendered to me once a year, on a given date, and I have the right to examine the books at any time.
5. The piano reduction is to be engraved at once: score and parts immediately after the first performance (première).

---

[1] *Löhr:* 'The one and only print of a photograph of myself as a young man had unexpectedly returned to my possession, so I had some copies made and sent one to Mahler.'
[2] Postcard photograph of Mahler on the deck of the steamer going to the United States. *Löhr* adds: 'I received by the same post another letter saying the same. Mahler had mistakenly thought he had lost the first before posting it.'
[3] The contract is dated: 'Toblach, 26 June 1909' (K.M.).

6. I expressly reserve to myself rights to the first performance.

7. Performing rights remain mine. However, Universal Edition is entitled to a share in royalties accruing from performances in the same proportion in which royalties are divided by the Berlin Society[1] (Rösch etc., I don't remember the name) between author and publisher.

Please have the contract sent as soon as possible for my signature, as there are certain reasons why I have to make a decision before mid-August. When are you coming?

It would suit me best, if it's all right for you, from 4 to 9 July.

Please bring a remedy called *New skin* (Albi[2] will give you the details—it's a kind of liquid adhesive plaster).

Very best wishes,

> Yours,
> Gustav Mahler

Write soon.
Your idea about wholemeal bread was a stroke of genius!

392. *To Arnold Berliner*

Undated. Postmark: Toblach, 20 June 1909

Dear Arnold,

I am a grass-widower at the moment (Alma is taking the cure in Levico). So I must do my correspondence with my own hand. As you can imagine, I particularly want news of you just now. For, knowing your psychological make-up, I am convinced 1. that you are expecting to starve to death in the near future, 2. that you therefore have no inclination to be communicative. Just at a time when one needs a friend most.—But, apart from that, I absolutely must know now how things are with you, how your professional affairs have been doing, and what prospects, what plans, you have for the future. I am all on my lonesome in a big house with innumerable rooms and beds. What a pity all our plans for the summer have so miscarried! Above all: when are you coming to stay with us? You will always find a good bed in a pleasant room and wonderful books that will be completely new to you.—For hours of depression and suicidal thoughts complete privacy is guaranteed. Afternoons and evenings will be spent talking, eating and going for walks.

I don't know when Fraenkel is coming or where he is. I wrote to him in Paris, care of the Crédit Lyonnais. Is that the address I have heard mutterings about?

---

[1] 'Society of German composers' founded by Richard Strauss, Friedrich Rösch and Hans Sommer (K.M.).
[2] Albert Spiegler (K.M.).

It is marvellous here and is certain to restore you in body and soul. I guarantee you bread and butter and sound boots for the entire rest of your life. I shan't even begrudge you ham. So: chin up! Or at least chest out (then your stomach will have to be drawn in and will take less filling). Please drop a line to let me know how you are and when you are coming.

Affectionately, in haste,

your

old Mahler

393.   *To Emil Freund*†

Undated. Alt-Schluderbach, [26] *June 1909*

Dear Emil,

Signed letter enclosed. With regard to some details very important to me, I shall get in touch personally with Direktor Hertzka, of whose good manners I have the most pleasant evidence, when I return from the country. Chief among them are two points: 1. The production of an edition of the score for purposes of study, as cheap as possible and in *convenient* format.

2. The price of the piano reduction for two hands, which should be kept as low as possible in the interests of diffusion of my work and indeed also in the financial interest of the publisher. Please in the meantime have my copy of the contract sent to Toblach, as I should like to let my wife (who, as you know, is not here with me at the moment) have a look at it.

My timetable has meanwhile changed in such a way that I should like you to arrive here on 2 or at least 3 July. I hope to have a chance soon to tell you in person why this is.

Very best wishes,

Yours,

Gustav Mahler

Please give my kindest regards to Direktor Hertzka.

394.   *To Theodor Spiering*

Undated. Postmark: [Toblach] *3 July 1909*

Dear Herr Spiering,

Thanks very much for your kind letter.

You have stated your wishes so clearly, and I find your views so completely justified, that I shall act in complete accordance with your wishes.

Please indicate which of the following concertos you would prefer.
1. Beethoven. 2. Mendelssohn. 3. Brahms.—Also what you would like besides
(to *start with*). Only I must confess I regard it as essential for you to start with a
true master, not a display-piece in the olde worlde style, Bruch, etc.[1]

Incidentally, I gather we are slightly restricted in our choice by the engagement of Herr Kreisler and of Maud Powell. I shall nevertheless seek to promote
your interests in the matter, since I myself have no obligations to anyone.—

So I shall now draw up the programmes, letting you know the result. I too
am glad to have you as a travelling-companion.

Please also be so good as to let me know—what I forgot to ask—whether you
need an advance and whether I should see to having your passage paid from
New York.—Please tell me frankly. We musicians are under no obligation to be
capitalists—all we have to do is conduct well, play the fiddle well. . . .

With very best wishes, and to your wife, even though we have not yet made
her acquaintance, also from my wife.

Yours very sincerely,
Gustav Mahler

395.   *To Anna Moll*

Undated. Toblach, Summer 1909
Postcard

Well, dearest Mama, if I am to burden you with a list of wants, I would ask
for the following: 1. a small jar of *real* honey (not that disgusting liquorice
syrup that Agnes has served up to me today). 2. A small bottle of fountain-pen
ink. 3. Two key-chains. 4. A little peppermint-oil or the like for a mouth-wash
after meals.—Almschi has been sending me thoroughgoing letters of lamenta-
tion, from which I deduce that she is finding the cure very strenuous. Besides, I
know being alone isn't the right thing for her at present. It is lucky she at least
has Gucki with her. If only all of us were together here again!

Love and kisses

from

Gustav

⟨I nearly forgot something else: an extinguisher to put out the candles. When
they are blown out, they make a 'plash'.⟩

---

[1] Mahler had appointed Spiering as leader of the New York Philharmonic Orchestra, and the
latter introduced himself to New York with Bach's E major Concerto on 10 November 1909
(K.M.).

396. *To Karl Moll*†

Undated. Toblach [July 1909]

Dear Karl,

Here are, I hope, the keys to the flat. By following Almschi's directions I managed to trace them in one of the 150 drawers.

Mama was kind enough to offer me cigarettes. A few would be very welcome —then tipped, please. I was tremendously pleased to get her letter; not having heard anything since I left, I had begun to worry a little. It's wonderful here! Especially now! You should come here some Sunday, just to see what it's like. I cannot think a painter could fail to find something in this glory. I am pretty well. As you know, I can take as much solitude as a drinker can take wine. Indeed I believe everyone could do with it once a year. A sort of purgatorio— or, say, a purging of the mind—both are right.

Thank you very much indeed, my dear people,

Yours,
Gustav

Please return the keys.

397. *To Julius v. Weis-Ostborn* (Graz)†

Undated, Toblach, 25 July 1909

My dear Herr von Ostborn,

A thousand thanks for your kind letter. While our friend Decsey was here your ears must often have been burning.—The idea we had about my Second was merely a flight of fancy, such as one sometimes indulges in when one is in high spirits. Of course I agree with you that such a plan should only be carried out at a favourable opportunity. If you mean to perform 'Das klagende Lied' next year, that will be quite enough for the worthy public to get their teeth into. Frl. Kittel and Fr. Elizza have sung the solo parts splendidly, and I can warmly recommend both ladies.[1]

Please forgive this scrawl.——I have so little inclination to write letters in summer, but do not wish to leave you completely without an answer. So I venture to send you this sloppy salutation in the hope that you will take the will for the deed.

With most cordial greetings to you and Dr. Decsey, also from my wife,

Yours very sincerely,
Gustav Mahler

[1] Weis-Ostborn performed 'Das klagende Lied' in Graz on 14 March 1910 with local artists (K.M.).

398. *To Emil Freund*

Undated. Alt-Schluderbach, 8 August 1909

Dear Emil,

I think we shall now have to let the matter[1] slide, if there is really any risk that the higher authorities might take a harder line. For the rest I shall leave it to your wisdom whether anything else should be done or not. I shall be leaving my flat, for which I have a tenant from *1 November*, at the beginning of October!

Could this perhaps lead to a revision of the official assessment? Do as you think best. I am *working very hard*—so do leave all details until we meet in Vienna.

Please let me know in any case what you intend to do in this matter.

> Very best wishes,
> Yours,
> Gustav Mahler

The Semmering honey is marvellous!

399. *To Bruno Walter†*

Undated. [Toblach, August] *1909*

My dear Walter,

You must never believe I have taken offence at anything you, or indeed anyone else, have said or done. But even if I were so petty-minded, I should not be able to find the slightest grounds for offence after your kind and beautiful letter. Quite the contrary, it gave me the most intense pleasure. You did guess the real reason for my silence. I have been working very hard and am just putting the finishing touches to a new symphony.[2] Unfortunately my vacation is also nearly finished—and as always I am in the tiresome position of having to rush back to town still quite breathless from composing, and to start work again. Well, that just seems to be my lot. The work itself (insofar as I know it, for I have been writing away at it blindly, and now that I have begun to orchestrate the last movement I have forgotten the first) is a very satisfactory addition to my little family. In it something is said that I have had on the tip of my tongue for some time—perhaps (as a whole) to be ranked beside the Fourth, if anything. (But quite different.) As a result of working in frantic haste the score is rather a scrawl and probably quite illegible for anyone but myself. And so I dearly hope it will be granted to me to make a fair copy this winter.

---

[1] Tax affairs (o.e.).
[2] The Ninth Symphony. [See also letters 407 and 415] (o.e.).

Now very best wishes, dear Walter—why don't you write anything of Lipiner? (When writing you should never fail to tell us all you know of him.) I shall be coming to Vienna at the beginning of September and shall see you as soon as I get there.

Yours ever,
Mahler

400. *To Theodor Spiering*†

Undated. Postmark: Toblach, 15 [August ?] *1909*

Dear Herr Spiering,

I assume I have received all your letters.—

So far as I recall, they were replies to my queries.—I have meanwhile embarked on a fairly large-scale work, in which I am quite immersed. Please forgive me on that account for not having written all this time.

The first programme is:[1]

Beethoven: *Weihe des Hauses*

      „   : *Eroica*

Liszt: *Mazeppa*

Strauss: *Till Eulenspiegel*

The second evening is for the first historical concert—do please play Bach's violin concerto. A piano part (continuo) would, however, have to be arranged for it, for I find one does really violate Bach's and Handel's works if one does not include a continuo.

Do you happen to know if such an arrangement exists?

I shall be staying on here until the end of August—then in Vienna.

I am greatly looking forward to seeing you again, at the 'Kaiser Wilhelm'. With all good wishes,

Yours sincerely,
Mahler

401. *To Alfred Roller*†

Undated. Toblach, [August] *1909*

My dear Roller,

Following up my wife's telegram of this morning I want to say I was about to give you some sign of life when your telegram came. I was indeed thinking that

---

[1] This programme was given on 4 November 1909 in New York (K.M.).

taking up a new position[1] would scarcely leave you time to catch your breath. And I, meanwhile, have been 'happy' in my own way. But it is now time for you to come and see us. Letters are really a very poor expedient. Do come soon! The Redlichs have announced their arrival for the week-end (but not to stay in the house). That will surely not bother you. Besides, Karl is paying. Strauss and his wife will also be coming in the next few days (probably on Tuesday).

Hoping to see you soon

Yours ever,

Mahler

Remember me kindly to your wife. Why don't you mention how your offspring is doing? *I take great interest* in it!

402.   *To Friedrich Löhr*

Undated. Postmark: Vienna, 17 September 1909

Dear Fritz,

Forgive my non-appearance all this time. I've been meaning to come and see you, every day, but have simply been so rushed that with the best will in the world I couldn't manage it.—We'll meet next week!

Till then best wishes,

Yours,

Gustav

403.   *To Friedrich Löhr†*

Undated. Postmark: Vienna, 25 September 1909
Pneumatic post

Dear Fritz,

Expect you five o'clock this afternoon in Café Central.

Best wishes,

Yours,

Gustav

---

[1] As principal of the Vienna School of Arts and Crafts (o.e.).

404. *To Emil Gutmann* (Munich)†

Undated. Vienna, [September] *1909*

Dear Herr Gutmann,

I too shall be embarking in Bremen on 12 October. I therefore deeply regret that this time I shall not be able to offer my services to the gentlemen in Nuremberg. I should otherwise have taken great pleasure in doing so. If they still intend to carry out their plans, I would suggest their inviting Herr Hofkapellmeister Walter, of the Vienna Court Opera, who is more fitted than anyone else to take my place.

Best wishes,

Yours sincerely,
Mahler

You misunderstood what I meant about the cyclical concerts. I meant that they should begin in autumn 1910 (instead of spring 1910), because I am fairly free of engagements about that time and could also offer a quite important new work, whereas both this and indeed my participation at all in such a comprehensive programme might be doubtful in the spring (after a strenuous autumn season). G.M.

405. *To Emil Freund*†

Undated. [New York, October 1909]

Dear Emil,

I am very worried indeed by the enclosed letter.

I myself gave the score to Direktor *Hertzka* before leaving, doing so in the presence of *Herr von Wöss.* As far as I can remember, the latter took it with him to make the piano reduction during the holidays.[1]

Please look into this at once, for it is of the greatest importance to me. I can only assume that the letter was written in Herr Hertzka's absence.

Please telegraph at once.

In haste,
Yours ever,
Gustav Mahler

[1] Josef V. v. Wöss was preparing the vocal score for the Eighth Symphony (K.M.).

406. *To Paul Hammerschlag* (Vienna)

Undated. Postmark: New York, 19 November 1909

Dear Hammerschlag,

⟨I have just learnt from Herr Altschul of the new position you have taken up.[1] I venture to see this as a 'promotion' and send you my heartiest [congratulations]. I had already heard rumours about it in the Summer.⟩ I am quite content with my position here. We have had many a concert that I would dearly have liked you to hear. I had great fun recently with a Bach concerto,[2] for which I transposed the *basso continuo* for organ, conducting and improvising—quite in the style of the old masters—from a very rich-toned spinet specially adapted by Steinway for the purpose.—This produced a number of surprises for me (and also for the audience).—It was as though a floodlight had been turned on to this long-buried literature. The result was intenser (also in terms of tone-colour) than any modern work. But I am dreadfully busy, worse than ever. Kindest regards to you and please remember me to your wife.

Yours ever,
Mahler

⟨Does this mean you have taken the first step to becoming a millionaire? Just like me!⟩

407. *To Bruno Walter*†

Undated. New York, [19] December 1909

My dear Walter,

I hope you have not been worried by my silence. The only reason for it is a tremendous burden of work (reminding me of Vienna days), which allows for only four things: conducting, writing music, eating and sleeping. I see by now that I am incorrigible. People of our kind cannot help doing thoroughly whatever they do at all. And that, as I have come to realize, means overworking. There it is, I am and remain the eternal beginner. And the little bit of routine I have acquired serves at best to increase the demands I make on myself. Just as I should like to publish revisions of my scores every five years, so too when I am conducting other men's works I need to prepare afresh every time. The only consolation is that I have never yet really had to change direction, but have always had to continue in the old one.—But of course that means one does

---

[1] Paul Hammerschlag had been appointed President of the Society of Austrian Banks and Bankers (K.M.).
[2] Mahler arranged four movements from Bach's orchestral suites (BMW 1067 and 1068) which he performed for the first time on 10 November 1909 in New York and repeated about twenty times during the following seasons. The score was published in 1910 by Schirmer (K.M.).

depart so far from paved roads that in the end one has to resort to pick and shovel like the settlers in some new continent—and that also explains the impassioned opposition I have to contend with in whatever I undertake.— My orchestra here is the true American orchestra. Untalented and phlegmatic. One fights a losing battle. I find it very dispiriting to have to start all over again as a conductor. The only pleasure I get from it all is rehearsing a work I haven't done before. Simply making music is still tremendous fun for me. If only my musicians were a bit better! Your news of your performance of the Third[1] was a great joy to me! How very glad I am, above all for you, that it was such a great success. Judging from the unanimity of the notices, the performance must have been quite outstanding.

These are the bright moments in our lives. How typical that those gutter-snipes have passed you over again and appointed ⟨Schalkchen⟩![2] I hope you aren't letting it upset you! They have now damned themselves. After all, your paramount position is something no one can take away. Just keep *calm*! You are bound to reach your goal. The day before yesterday I did my First here![3] Apparently without getting much reaction. However, I myself was pretty pleased with that youthful effort! All of these works give me a peculiar sensation when I conduct them. A burning pain crystallizes: what a world this is that rejects such sounds and patterns as something antagonistic! Something like the funeral march and the storm that then breaks out seem to me like a burning denunciation of the Creator. And in each new *work* of mine (at least up to a certain period) this cry again and again goes up: 'Not their father art thou, but their tsar!'[4] That is—what it is like *while I am conducting*! Afterwards it is all instantly blotted out. (Otherwise one just could not go on living.) This strange reality of visions, which instantly dissolve into mist like the things that happen in dreams, is the deepest cause of the life of conflict an artist leads. He is condemned to lead a double life, and woe betide him if it happens that life and dream flow into one—so that he has appallingly to suffer in the one world for the laws of the other.—Oh, something has just occurred to me, and I must interrupt myself lest I forget it. Please send me Slezak's transposition in *The Queen of Spades*—from the passage leading up to it right to the end.— I am to conduct this opera at the Metropolitan, and they are paying so much money that I shall probably be unable to resist.[5] Please also tell ⟨Hohmann⟩[6]

[1] In Vienna on 25 November (K.M.).
[2] Franz Schalk (K.M.).
[3] On 16 December and repeated on 17 December (K.M.).
[4] Conclusion of the 'Improvisation' in Mickiewicz's *Todtenfeier* ('Funeral Rites'), translated into German by S. Lipiner and published in 1887 (o.e. + K.M.).
[5] The première was on 4 March 1910 and it was performed on three further occasions during March (K.M.).
[6] Albert Hohmann, timpanist, member of the Wiener Konzertverein (K·M.).

that I should awfully like to have him. But there are disgusting difficulties with the *union* here.—They don't allow musicians to be imported. That is, anyone who comes with his contract in his pocket *will be rejected*. There is therefore only one thing for ⟨Hohmann⟩ to do—that is, come *without* a contract, spend six solid months here, not breathing a word to *anyone* about working for me (people gossip terribly, and if a complaint is made he will be thrown out at once and will not be allowed to play—that happened to me last year with a drummer). Can Herr ⟨Hohmann⟩ *remain silent* for six months or *longer* (for the persecution would start at once, even retrospectively)? And will he agree to come on no more security than my word? If so, everything would be settled between us. But I know this is a great deal to expect.—If ⟨Hohmann⟩ should find this acceptable, please send me the following cable:

> Mahler New York Hotel Savoy
> Agreed ⟨Hohmann⟩

I shall then cable back:

> ⟨Hohmann⟩ settled Mahler

But he must also *write* to me *instantly* so that I know for certain where I stand. All this must be done at once! Please do always tell me how Lipiner is (*exactly*), and also what his wife and the others are doing. By now I am immensely looking forward to the time when I can be together with everyone again! Oh that I may yet be granted that for a span of time!

The audiences here are very lovable and relatively far better mannered than in Vienna. They listen attentively and sympathetically. The superiors[1] are the same as anywhere else. I don't read any of them, but sometimes receive reports of what they say. (*I can recommend the same practice to you*—what they write sounds far less aggressive when reported.)—Well now, very best wishes, and do write soon, including whatever happens to be going through your mind. In the near future I hope to be starting work on my Ninth.

> Yours,
> Gustav Mahler

---

[1] 'Superiors' was what Mahler called the critics (o.e.).

1910

408. *To Guido Adler* (Vienna)

Undated. New York, 1 January 1910

Dear Guido,

You seem to have gravely misunderstood my last letter.—I gather this from lots of letters I have been receiving from Vienna during the last few days,[1] from which it appears that completely false and (I must confess) even offensive interpretations have been made. Now first of all as regards my letter: I often go to bed after rehearsals (it was from Richard Strauss that I first heard of this useful practice), because I find it marvellously relaxing and it does me a world of good. In Vienna I simply had no time for that sort of thing.—I have a great deal to do, but by no means too much, as in Vienna. By and large this work and this mode of life keep me feeling fitter and better than I have felt for many years.— Do you really believe that anyone as accustomed to work as I am could feel easy as a 'pensioner'?

I absolutely have to have some practical outlet for my musical abilities to counterbalance the tremendous inner upsurgings that go on when I compose: and it was my lifelong desire to have my own concert orchestra. I am glad to be able to enjoy this for once in my life (apart from the fact that I keep on finding it *very instructive*, for the technique of the theatre is totally different, and I am convinced that many of my previous inadequacies in instrumentation arose from my being accustomed to hearing music in the totally different acoustic conditions of the theatre). Why did neither Germany nor Austria offer me this? Can I help it if Vienna chucked me out?—Besides: I need a certain degree of luxury, a degree of comfort in my daily life, that my pension (which is all I have gained from almost thirty years as a conductor) would not permit. So I welcomed the chance of the American offer, which provided me not only with an occupation suited to my tastes and abilities, but also with a good salary that will soon enable me to spend what years remain to me in a manner befitting one's human dignity. And now, closely connected with this, I have to say something about my wife, to whom your views and remarks did a great injustice. You may take my word for it that she has *nothing* but my welfare in mind. And

---

[1] During the last winter Mahler spent in America there was a great deal of gossip in Vienna about the way he was thought to be overworking in a position not worthy of him, and so on. On hearing of these rumours, Mahler wrote the above impetuous letter (o.e.). Interestingly, Adler, after Mahler's death, claimed that he had never received this letter. See Edward R. Reilly, *Gustav Mahler und Guido Adler*, Vienna, 1978, p. 56 (K.M.).

just as during the eight years she spent at my side in Vienna she never let herself be dazzled by the worldly brilliance of my position nor ever, despite her temperament and the allurements of Viennese life and one's 'good friends' there (all living beyond their means), let herself be tempted to indulge in luxury of any kind, such as would have been in keeping even with *our* social position, so too her sole and earnest endeavour is at the soonest possible date to bring to a conclusion my efforts (which, I must repeat, do not constitute *over*-exertion, as in Vienna) to achieve the independence that only my creative work can provide. You should know her well enough by now! *When* have you ever found her guilty of extravagance or selfishness? Do you really believe she could have been so utterly transformed since you last saw her? I enjoy driving a motor-car just as much as (indeed, far more than) she does. And are we seriously supposed to live on the Vienna Court Opera's charity in an attic in Vienna? Is it not better that I should take the opportunity offered me to earn a decent living by honest work as an artist? I must once more assure you that my wife is not only a courageous, faithful companion who shares all my spiritual interests, but also (a rare combination) a sensible, level-headed manager of our domestic affairs, enabling me to save in spite of all the comforts of our physical existence, the person whom I have to thank for all the prosperity and orderliness, in the true sense of the word, of my existence. I could prove all this to you by giving you figures. But to my mind that is unnecessary. With a little good will (and recalling your own knowledge of us) you will be able to tell yourself all this.— Forgive my scrawl, and attribute my going into such detail to the respect and friendship I shall always have for you, and to the wish that you should not do my wife, and consequently myself, a grave injustice as a result of misinterpreting something said in a letter.

With all good wishes to your family and yourself from

Yours,

Gustav Mahler

409. *To Alfred Roller*

Undated. New York, 6 January 1910

My dear Roller,

For many weeks I have been on the point of writing to you.—But there are so many outer and inner obstacles that my good intentions are never fulfilled; and that is a miserable situation. This situation has been ended by a very sweet letter, which I have just received, from your wife (I hope it is not indiscreet of me to tell you). She herself forbade me to reply, and so I must ask you to convey my gratitude to her for her kind words.

Letter-writing long ago ceased to be anything I cared for. And two people brought and—kept—together by such a richly pouring life and who experience so much with and through each other have no use for the wretched surrogate.— Yet all I wish for and want to maintain is: from time to time to raise a sign so that if only from afar one may learn where the other is roaming or resting.— About me you know everything—because everything is always just the same. But from you I should like to hear how you are settling into your new house. Those gentry in the Opernring have seen to it that the empty space in your life has quietly filled; I suppose you feel as I do—the very thought of that place is like a bad dream. But the main thing is that there should be something to fill the empty space. Is that the case with you? And have you now a sphere of activity that suits you, in which you can find a degree of satisfaction? For me the theatre days have sunk into the abyss—they are as utterly remote as if I had been walking in seven-league boots.

I must add, though, that the whirl of events and of my inner life has prevented me from coming to my senses yet. It is the same here as it was there: every minute is chock-full, and the hours are too few.—I see with satisfaction the distance that I still have to cover here becoming less and less and, God willing, I hope that in about a year I shall be able to achieve a fairly human way of life. To have a home somewhere and be allowed to live and work there (instead of vegetating and working) and to be, I hope, near enough to my few friends to be able to see them from time to time. Although Alma and I play a new game every week about our future—Paris, Florence, Capri, Switzerland, the Black Forest—extend this list according to your knowledge of geography— I think we shall before long arrive somewhere not far from Vienna, where the sun shines and beautiful grapes grow, and that we shall not go away again. This is *not a real letter*, for I should really be writing about entirely different things; but it is the best means of putting an end to my (as I said at the beginning) miserable situation.

Very best wishes to you and your wife, and do let me know something about your new position.

Your old friend,
Gustav Mahler

410. *To Emil Freund* (Vienna)

Undated. New York, 3 February 1910

Dear Emil,

Greetings! (**How do you do,** as they say here.) I am getting on famously—I can stand all the strain without being any the worse for it.—Please give the newspaper company[1] a sharp prod, since it has for years been neglecting its contractual obligation to send me a statement (but this request is not my reason for pulling myself together and sending greetings to you).

So drop me a line to say how you are getting on.—Please make do for now with what amounts to no more than a postcard.

Very best wishes from

Your old
Gustav Mahler

411. *To Emil Gutmann*†

Undated. New York, [Jan. or Feb.] *1910*

Dear Herr Gutmann,

Just a hasty note. Even in the most favourable circumstances I cannot be in Munich by 8 April.—If I am able to leave here (on the *George Washington*) on 30 March, and if the weather is *favourable*, I shall be in Paris on the 8th and can be in Munich on the 9th. If the weather is bad, I shall be in Paris on the 9th and in Munich on the 10th. It would therefore be unwise to expect me in Munich before 10 April.—Also, I should like Casella[2] to deal with the Paris matter, as he alone knows my relations with Countess Grefullhe's agent; I have already (last spring) made a contract with her. Perhaps he can disentangle this tangled skein. About Vienna I know nothing at all. Nor, for that matter, have I time to make plans for next year.—{For} Herr Schalk I have paid 2,000 crowns, for Herr Schnellar[3] 200 crowns. If any other bills have been run up in Munich, please do send them to me.

In haste,
Yours sincerely,
Mahler

---

[1] Josef Eberle & Co. in Vienna; they had engraved and printed Mahler's early symphonies (K.M.).
[2] Alfredo Casella (1883–1947), the Italian composer and conductor who made the piano duet arrangement of Mahler's Seventh Symphony (K.M.).
[3] Franz Schalk, the conductor at the Court Opera. Johann Schnellar was a well-known percussion player and member of the Court Opera Orchestra (K.M.).

412. *To Emil Gutmann*†

Undated. New York, [27 February] *1910*

Dear Herr Gutmann,

About six weeks ago you cabled:

Conditions met cancellation impossible.[1]

A letter followed, in which the Vienna Singverein was guaranteed and Mengelberg named as a probability.—My chief conditions were that the choirs should begin to work on 1 January and that the conductors should personally vouch for their being ready in time. This is very difficult, because we are approaching summer, when the choral societies do *not* work, and so forget the little they have learnt.

Now I receive a letter telling me that *Ochs*[2] has expressed his willingness to rehearse the choirs himself. The Vienna Singverein has already *started* work.— On the next page you ask me to press Universal Edition into at long last producing the piano reduction, so that work can begin.—A few days later a telegram arrives, informing me that the Riedelverein[3] in Leipzig has taken over the new choir.—You will appreciate that I am now a little confused. I thought of cabling to you: *Consider performance impossible in present circumstances.* But I know you would have cabled back: Conditions met cancellation impossible.—My dear Herr Gutmann, I cannot assess the situation from here.— *I think it impossible* for the choirs to be ready in time! And I *strongly advise* you, in the most amicable way, to find a plausible excuse for cancelling the performance (perhaps, if you wish, substitute another of my works).—Otherwise you will find at the last moment, or eleventh hour, that we shall have to cancel it, and you don't need me to tell you what a blow that would be not only to you but also to *me.*—Hertzka sent me the proofs at the *end of January,* mentioning that printing was held up for a fortnight in Vienna because the printer had to finish other jobs first.—I could not set to work in January because I was ill and yet still had to conduct so as not to lose too much money. So that was another fortnight's delay.—I do not know how far the piano reduction has progressed. But it is obvious that the whole thing cannot be rushed through in this way.—[4]

Two full rehearsals are *quite insufficient.*—However, I can judge all the details only when I am back in Europe. I am conducting my Second on 17 April for

---

[1] This refers to preparations for the first performance of the Eighth Symphony in Munich on 12 September 1910. A repeat performance took place the following day (o.e. + K.M.).
[2] Siegfried Ochs (1858–1929), composer and conductor of the Berlin Philharmonic Choir (K.M.).
[3] Choral Society, conductor Georg Göhler; it participated in the performance in Munich (K.M.).
[4] The vocal score was published in April 1910 (K.M.).

Colonne! Perhaps I shall see you there. *Take my advice* and abandon the performance! The longer you leave it, the more unpleasant it will be.

In the most appalling rush,

Yours sincerely,

Mahler

413. *To Anna Moll†*

Undated. New York, [March] *1910*

Dearest little Mama,

May I send you a list of wants? Please bring to Paris for me a hundred cigar-holders, the sort with Nachtmann's filters, which I have for years been buying from the import tobacconist in the Kohlmarkt. Also a packet of filter wadding (Nachtmann's), and thirdly a few tipped cigarettes (not too many, otherwise you may have trouble at the customs). About fifty will see me through the short time. I think of our meeting in Paris every day.

I have weathered this year very well, without actually sparing myself. Of the three of us, I have actually been the only one who was always fit.

Undoubtedly Almschi has had a far better winter than for many years.—A few colds, but only very slight ones, which didn't keep her in bed long. The climate does not seem to suit Guckerl so well. She has now, thank God, got over a rather persistent catarrh (even with some fever). Now she is in the best of spirits and again looking splendid.

By the time you get this letter, it will be little more than a fortnight until we meet. Believe me, I am simply twitching all over with impatience.

Is there no prospect at all of finding a country house somehow like Göding[1] etc. . . . the sort of thing I discussed with Karl?

Fondest greetings, my dearest Mama, also to Karl and Maria.

Yours,

Gustav

414. *To Alexander v. Zemlinsky†*

Undated. Philadelphia [and New York, March 1910]

Dear Zemlinsky,

A completely unexpected quarter of an hour of leisure and solitude during a

---

[1] Small town situated about 65 miles north-east of Vienna. Residence of the Redlich family, visited by Mahler the previous summer (K.M.).

12

'guest'-tour gives me a chance to send at least a cordial greeting in reply to your delightful and interesting letter.

I'm afraid the news of your adventures with the new régime did not come as a surprise to me. Still, I should not have thought W.[1] would so blatantly flout his *promise* to produce your opera[2] before anything else.

This is a serious blow to you, as I can see for myself. Altogether I feel I too am very *much to blame*, even though 'not guilty'. And I very often have a bad conscience. But—who could have foreseen all this?

What I think now is that you must do everything possible to get your work produced at the Jubiläumstheater.

What are you and Schönberg doing? I should be glad of some news. But don't reply to this letter—I shall be arriving in Vienna at the beginning of May and shall come and see you at once.—This scrap of a letter has been in my dress-coat pocket for a week now—the coat in which I conducted the matinée in Philadelphia[3] and into which I put the envelope when I was interrupted in the middle of writing—and I am only posting it because this illustrates the life I lead here better than anything I could *say*.

I live literally from day to day, conducting, rehearsing, dining, going for walks—according to the dictates of the timetable that my wife keeps beside her. I am not exerting myself at all, am doing very little, and have never had so little time as now. You will know this from your own experience.—I am eagerly looking forward to seeing Vienna and my old friends again. Next winter I shall be back here. We have both come to like this country very much; we are very much attracted by all the freshness, soundness and straightforwardness of the way things are done. There is a *future* in everything. More about this when we meet. For today just very best wishes to you and Schönberg in all the haste of idleness.

Yours sincerely,
Mahler

415. *To Bruno Walter†*

New York, 1 April 191

My dear Walter,

   (. . .) Perhaps we should consider a mezzo-soprano in Vienna after all, so

[1] Felix Weingartner (K.M.).
[2] *Der Traumgörge*, written in 1904-6 and accepted the following year by Mahler for performance at the Vienna Court Opera. It was, however, never performed there (o.e. + K.M.
[3] Mahler gave two concerts here during spring 1910: on 17 January and 14 March (K.M.

that we can at least get the four women together there.—I could perhaps ask M[ontenuovo] to intervene—but really I would much rather not.

So there is still the baritone to be settled. I should think one ought also to find one among the many Telramunds or Wotans in the German provinces.—

I should especially like to have a clear, sweet voice for the Mater Gloriosa, but it should be easy to arrange that at the last moment.

This is all purely academic, for I still don't believe the performance will come about.—I find it all so confused.—Are the choirs studying their parts yet?—And will they be together in the summer? Can they be ready in time? I don't believe it.—As you will remember, I made the stipulation above *all else* that the material was to be ready by 1 January and that the choir was then to begin work. Today, on 1 April, I have still not been informed whether the choir has yet begun work, or, indeed, who will be singing. I shall *ruthlessly* cancel the whole thing if all artistic conditions are not met to my satisfaction. I shall be staying at the Hotel Majestic from 12 to 17 April.

A thousand thanks and greetings from

Yours ever,

Gustav Mahler

The fair copy of my Ninth is finished.

416.   *To Bruno Walter†*

Undated. New York, [beginning of April] *1910*

Dearest Walter,

Until today I have been fighting inwardly and outwardly against this catastrophic Barnum-and-Bailey performance of my Eighth in Munich. When X. took me unawares in Vienna that time, I didn't stop to think of all the to-do that goes with such 'festivals'.—Now, from all I hear, it seems the utterly inadequate is about to materialize. At least, I fail to see how I can escape my obligations. Of course I am today stipulating, as always, that the choirs must meet my requirements.—When I arrive in Europe and have carried out my commitments in Paris and Rome,[1] I shall see with my own eyes (and hear with my own ears) how things stand. If it should actually come to the point, the problem of the soloists must be solved satisfactorily, and this is where I rely entirely on your friendship. Please do take the matter in hand.—I still maintain that the main contingent should be supplied by *Vienna*; otherwise I don't know how homogeneity can possibly be achieved among the soloists. After all, X, Y, etc.

---

[1] Mahler had scheduled two concerts in Rome: on 28 April and 1 May. The latter was however abandoned by Mahler owing to disagreements with the orchestra (K.M.).

will not be indispensable in Vienna (and whether they are at all suitable is something only you can judge). Please drop me a line about all these things— to Paris—Hotel Majestic—where I arrive next week, staying until 17 April. Thence to Rome.—I am physically quite fit. My happiness would be complete if only I had not become entangled in Herr Emil Gutmann's meshes.

Very best wishes to you and your wife from

Yours—in great haste on the point of leaving

Gustav Mahler

417. *To C. F. Peters Verlag* (Leipzig)†

Vienna, 1 June 1910
Hohewarte, Wollergasse 10

Dear Sir,

In the course of the time during which I have been conducting my Fifth Symphony in various cities it has been necessary for me to enter in my score such a great number of alterations that I regard it as essential, in the interests of the work, to prepare a new edition of the same. It goes without saying that the costs of this revised edition will be met by myself alone.[1]—According to my entirely amateurish calculations at least a third of the plates will have to be freshly engraved. But what is most important to me is that I am rehearsing my revised score in connection with a performance to be given in New York in the coming season.[2] For this purpose I would beg you to be so good as to let me have my orchestra parts, into which I shall have all my alterations entered. This will of course be without prejudice to the publisher's rights, which means that the institution concerned will buy the material from you and obtain it from you. Meanwhile I shall use my corrected score for one of the rehearsals and, if the alterations meet with my approval, shall embody them in the performance. This collated material can then be used in preparing any future edition, should such be required. My present urgent request is therefore that you should send me, by return, for *my* private use a score and complete orchestral parts for:

10 I ⎫
9 II ⎬ violins
⎭
8 violas
8 'celli
6 double-basses.

[1] The revised score was only published in 1964 by C. F. Peters Verlag, in collaboration with the International Mahler Society (K.M.).
[2] This performance came to nothing (K.M.).

In the course of the next season I shall then take the liberty of sending you the necessary information.

I am, with kind regards,
Yours faithfully,
Gustav Mahler

418. *To Emil Freund*†

Undated. Niederdorf im Pustertal, 15 June 1910

Dear E.,

Regarding the contract about to be made with U-Edition,[1] don't forget that this extremely tiresome but, above all, disgraceful clause, which stipulates that I must always give them an option when I have finished anything, must be *dropped*. It is probably only an academic point, for I do not intend ever to leave U.E. But even so, it irritates me every time I think of it.

Just imagine, I have only just received the letter you sent to Tobelbad.[2]

Yours ever,
G.

419. *To Karl Moll*†

Undated. Munich, June 1910
Regina-Palast Hotel

Dear Karl,

What with all the rehearsals[3] and the parts to correct, I don't know whether I'm on my head or my heels. But Gutmann is doing a splendid job, and everything has gone admirably so far. I hope it is going to be a real treat for you in the autumn. I have just written to Pollack.[4] Please do not force him to remain in Grado. He *should* not extend his stay beyond 2–3 weeks, as it is said to be very exhausting for someone in his condition. Find him a sanatorium for consumptives somewhere in the Vienna Woods or on the Semmering, where he can *learn* what to eat and what sort of life to lead. I have just written to him on

---

[1] Mahler signed an exclusive contract with Universal Edition in Vienna that summer (K.M.).
[2] A small town near Graz. Alma Mahler took a cure there during June and July (K.M.).
[3] For the Eighth Symphony (o.e.).
[4] Dr. Theobald Pollack, Hofrat in the Ministry of Railways (o.e.).

these lines, hoping it will be effective. One simply has to keep this great baby in reins.

Fondest love to Mama—I can't make time to write.

In greatest haste,

Yours,

Gustav

420. *To Karl Moll*†

Undated. Munich, June 1910

Dear Karl,

Please be so kind as to have the enclosed pattern made up with all speed, so Almschili can have it on her birthday (30 August[1]).

More soon, my dear Karl,

Yours,

Gustav

The best seats are *boxes* and the circle (as I think it is called). The stalls are without exception hopeless. ⟨For the rest, any friends should mention my name at Gutmann's. That may possibly be of some use.[2]⟩

421. *To Theodor Spiering*†

Undated. Postmark: Munich, 21 June 1910

My dear Spiering,

So here I am in Munich, rehearsing my Eighth with might and main.— *You* are just the person I need. The leader is tolerably good, but his understanding does not go very deep and he does not really lead the orchestra. I hope to see you here in September.

I have had no news at all from America. As you know, after urging from me a proper manager was appointed, but to my considerable dismay he proposes 65 concerts, maintaining that success cannot be guaranteed without this vast increase in the work-load.—For such a colossal amount of extra work I then asked for a small increase in my fee (by contract I am committed to no more than 45 concerts), but this request was rejected by the committee, so that I shall now simply have to insist on the rights and obligations laid down in the contract.

[1] Actually on 31 August (K.M.).
[2] For admission-cards to the première of Mahler's Eighth Symphony (K.M.).

I informed the committee of this intention, but I have heard nothing from them since.

Very best wishes to you, and do thank your wife for her kind letter. I hope to make her acquaintance this year. My wife also sends her regards.

Yours very sincerely,
Gustav Mahler

---

422. *To Anna Moll†*

Undated. Munich, June 1910
Regina-Palast Hotel

Dearest Mama,

I am so perturbed by Almschi's letters, which have such a peculiar tone. What on earth is going on?

I mean to leave for Toblach on Sunday. But please drop me a few lines at once saying whether you think I had better go to Almschi in Tobelbad. I should prefer it, and it would be better for me, to have peace and quiet for a while in Toblach, because the strain here is really terrific. (Six hours of rehearsals every day.) However, if Almschi's condition so requires, I shall certainly go straight to Tobelbad (via Vienna). If you think this advisable, please wire. If not, a card will suffice. Then be an angel, won't you, and make sure I find a bed, butter and spinach, etc. in Toblach when I get there.—I shall get bread, etc. in Vienna.— I am pretty satisfied with the way rehearsals are going.—I hope in the autumn you will enjoy it.

I have wired to Karl for my score (copy) of the Eighth, of which I am desperately in need here. If only I were not so disquieted about Alma. It makes me quite miserable.

Love, my dearest little Mama, to you and Karl,

Yours,
Gustav

---

423. *To Karl Moll*

Undated. Munich, June 1910
Regina-Palast Hotel, Maximilianplatz

Dear Karl,

From the enclosed letter you will see my surmise that the climate would be too much for Pollack has proved correct. What must be done now is make sure he chooses the right place, stays there long enough and then does not on any account return to Vienna, but stays in the country well into the winter. One can then perhaps bring up the big guns: 1. a drastic statement about his condition and how dangerous it is, 2. my appointment in Vienna.

This morning (Wednesday) the score has still not arrived.

Greetings to you, dear Karl, in haste,

Yours,
Gustav

424. *To Emil Gutmann*†

Undated. [Munich, 26 June] 1910

Dear Gutmann,

This evening I leave for Toblach, where I hope to hear from you soon. Do see to it that *Maikl*[1] gets his holiday *before* he is billed, for otherwise the gentlemen of the Intendanz will be up in arms.—When the alto in Munich[2] has finished her part, send her to Toblach so that I can see how well she does it.

Did *Fried*[3] send my letter to *Senius*? This is important, because we should keep this 'second iron' in the fire.

Yours with best wishes,
Mahler

425. *To Alfred Roller*

Undated. Toblach, Summer 1910

Dearest Roller,

Your delightful letter filled us all with joy and envy. How I should have liked to dash straight off to be with you (and not only to see the house)—but I am in a very complicated situation, which makes it impossible for me to plan even an hour ahead. I am tremendously looking forward to our meeting in Munich, which will of course be more a meeting in the spirit. And especially afterwards in Vienna, where I shall be going immediately after the performance, I shall re-experience in memory the resonance of all that will merely roar and blow past in the vortex.

Very best wishes to you and your family.—Whenever you come this way, the

[1] George Maikl (1872–1951) did not get his holiday from the Vienna Opera but was replaced by Felix Senius for the performance of the Eighth (K.M.).
[2] Anna Erler-Schnaudt (K.M.).
[3] Oskar Fried (1871–1942), conductor and composer (K.M.).

whole household will be overjoyed to see you. But please *wire* beforehand—for this summer I am a restless wanderer.

I intend staying here until 2 September.

Your friend,

Gustav Mahler

426. *To Emil Freund*

Undated. Alt-Schluderbach, July 1910

Dear Emil,

I have just received your letter.

The [Universal] Edition matter was right enough. However, the clause ('touching up') must be formulated more precisely. Edition must agree 1. to make any changes on all plates (score and orchestral parts); 2. to enter any changes I require in the relevant scores or orchestra parts for as long as they offer the material for sale (but at *their expense*—not passing on half of their costs to me). (Please tell Direktor Hertzka, *privatim*, in case I should forget, that this is to be done in black, not in red, ink, for it has happened almost every time that the blockhead of a copyist has felt obliged to follow my example in the original, with the result that the orchestra could not play from it in the evening because red ink can't be read by lamplight.) 3. that the vocal compositions are to be treated as hitherto. I am to receive half of the earnings from these *without* any deductions whatsoever.

On these conditions I am prepared to accept Edition's estimate of the cost of the first four symphonies they have published as 50,000 crowns and agree that Edition should keep one account (for) all of them, that is, *without* keeping a separate account for each symphony.

This is what was agreed between myself and Direktor Hertzka.

Please see that these points are stated precisely and clearly, so that the agreement can be signed.

What is all this about the taxes?

I am becoming more and more flabbergasted!

Do I have to make further declarations of income? Please explain.—

Very best wishes,

Yours,

Gustav

12*

427. *To Siegfried Lipiner*

Toblach, 7 July 1910[1]

Dearest Siegfried,

I cursed and swore when I got that pile of telegrams (imagine just signing a letter of acknowledgment for each)—but when I came on yours, I was really so happy that I gladly put up with all the rest. Since it was dated from the Reichsrat, I take it that you are back in your old routine, and I simply don't dare to ask whether you are again in anything resembling a human condition, whether at least those horrible after-effects of the radium treatment have disappeared by now.—*Where* are you *going* this summer, *and when*? Please let me have a postcard, just a word.—As every year, I have fled here to be alone for the summer, and particularly on this day.—It is always difficult at first trying to come to terms with oneself. Experience, I'm afraid, doesn't seem to help at all, for it is almost as though one had to introduce oneself to oneself all over again.—But probably this applies only to people who lead the sort of life I have always led, burning themselves up at such a pace.

My rehearsals in Munich and Leipzig were pretty satisfactory. *I* am only now beginning to believe the performance on 12 September will actually come off. It would be marvellous if you could come. I'm sure you would enjoy it. I think you would recognize part of your own mind. The hymn, especially, might have come out of your own soul.

The journalistic cloudburst in 'W.[2] and Court Opera' strikes me as having descended out of the blue (which it has every right to do), being apparently based merely on chit-chat between W. and some reporter. The offer to Muck, in particular, strikes me as a put-up job. I'm certain nothing will come of it before the autumn, anyway, and by then I shall doubtless be consulted again.

Love and blessings to both of you from

Yours ever,

Gustav

428. *To Anna Moll*

Undated. Toblach, July 1910

My dear Mamatschili,

(Good heavens, isn't it hard to find a pet name for you!)

What a shock I had today when I got Almschi's letter!—Afterwards, when a second, somewhat calmer one, and especially your sweet letter, came, I felt a

[1] Mahler's fiftieth birthday (o.e.).
[2] Weingartner (K.M.).

little easier, and am now assuming I can stay on here for these last few days without worrying. But I am terribly sad about the recurrence of this tormenting ailment.—I live here, as you know from my letters to Alma, much occupied with you all in my thoughts.

How lucky we are to have you!

And I don't say that out of egoism, for {if}, instead of so sweetly helping us, you were yourself in need of help, it would be a joy to both of us to give back to you all that we ceaselessly receive from you—and I should ever and again say: How lucky we are to have you.

But now everything possible must be done to get Alma well and strong again! I had completely forgotten about my birthday and only your letters reminded me of it so suddenly that I couldn't help smiling at the thought of how unimportant that day seems to me and yet how lovingly you all remember it. Thank you a thousand times for your sweet words, and always remain what you are to me, friend and mother (as dictated by a peculiar whim of fate).

Your old
Gustav

429. *To Anna Moll*†

Undated. Tobelbad, [July] 1910
Postcard

Dearest Mama,

Just a word to let you know I found Almschi much fresher and fitter and am firmly convinced her cure here is doing her a great deal of good. Please make her stay here for as long as you can (for she seems to have dubious intentions as to the length of her stay). Please don't forget to have a similar bed-table made for me and sent to Toblach when it is finished. Lots of love to both of you,

Yours,
Gustav

430. *To Georg Göhler* (Leipzig)†

Undated. [Toblach] July 1910

Dear Dr. Göhler,

Summer is a bad time to try and get a letter out of me. This applies even to you, in whose debt I am doubly, indeed trebly.—There are just a few lines I must write in reply to your letter. I am afraid it is far from certain that I shall be able to get away for a rehearsal on 3 September. The fact is, this is probably the only night in Vienna when I can count on having most, if not all, of the choir there. And this is too *important* to me, I think really essential, so I must simply rely on my proven confidence in you and your valiant throng and leave further rehearsal in your hands.

Your article really warmed the cockles of my heart—I don't think anyone ever *meam rem egit* so exhaustively and so utterly without verbiage.

Thanking you for such a thing would amount to reducing those magnificent words to the level of a newspaper article.

I am greatly looking forward to our meeting in Munich.

Forgive my brevity today—putting it down to my holiday-time-letter-writing indolence, which you will probably be able to interpret correctly.

Yours most sincerely,
Gustav Mahler

431. *To Emil Freund*

Undated. Alt-Schluderbach, 15 July 1910

Dear Emil,

I had to make two corrections, or rather, additions, to the draft contract that was sent to me. They are:

1. *to make agree with the now finally established score.*

(This clause refers not only to the emendations I am now making, but also to all those that have been made in the plates since the first impression),

2. (after 'within six months'), *those made in the final version of the Fourth Symphony as established after performance under my direction.*—This is self-evident.[1]

If I am not mistaken, the sales clause is made irrelevant by the omission of the penalty for non-fulfilment of contract.—If so, I find the contract quite acceptable.—If not, please let me know.—I posted the letter to Flinsch[2] without making any alterations.—I do not think Charlton played a hand; it is the quite naïve, brutal egoism of these people, who simply do not consider their opponent's point of view at all.—No, *vederemo*, the answer.

In greatest haste, with many thanks,

Yours,
Gustav Mahler

[1] The revisions in question were only published in 1964. Mahler conducted his Fourth Symphony for the last time on 20 January 1911 in New York (K.M.).

[2] Secretary to the committee for the organization of Mahler concerts in New York. The letter in question was drafted by Emil Freund (o.e.).

432. *To Emil Gutmann†*

Undated. Vienna, [July] *1910*

Dear Gutmann,

I am simply dumbfounded! Here I have been saying over and over again that I can't manage without a third day of rehearsals! You come here to remove the obstacle—Schalk and I talk ourselves hoarse, explaining to everyone why it is necessary.—You arrange everything, we discuss the *absolutely essential* rehearsal timetable. You send me the final list from Munich. Now you reveal to me that the Singverein is 'ecstatic', that a third rehearsal day is therefore no longer necessary, and that instead of that rehearsal day all that is at my disposal is ecstasy. You are also thinking of fitting in a fourth rehearsal (the three agreed on will take, all in all, about 15 hours—that is why I insisted on a one-hour break at each rehearsal). Indeed, you are even thinking of arranging for yet another rehearsal on the day of the performance. So you are actually expecting a choral society's ecstasy to raise the dead. Because after two such days these people would be dead.—Now *once and for all*, please! Either *every item* in our agreement is kept to—i.e. the full *three days* are at my disposal, without any restriction (incidentally, that is the *minimum* necessary)—or you may take this as my final withdrawal.—Please let us have no further argument about it either now or in the future.

With all good wishes,

Yours very truly,
Mahler

433. *To Emil Gutmann†*

Undated. Munich, [September] *1910*
Grand Hotel Continental

Dear Herr Gutmann,

With the best will in the world I find it impossible to accept the Konzertverein's solo violinist for this unusually difficult task, and I definitely must ask you to suggest another solution. I was really in agonies during today's rehearsals, and I fear that very important passages in my work will be simply incomprehensible. The best way out would be to return to my first suggestion, bring *Rosé* from Vienna for this concert.

With very best wishes,

Yours sincerely,
Mahler

434.   *To Karl Moll†*

Undated. Munich, [5 September] *1910*
Grand Hotel Continental

My dear Karl,

Do forgive these everlasting pesterings and please, when you come to Munich (either via Toblach or direct), bring my gigantic American trunk, with all its contents, just as it is. It is very important—it will do a great deal for domestic peace and quiet and all sorts of things. Above all I need it as a wardrobe, for in the tiny room that Almschi and I live in there is hardly enough space for her things. I was quite miserable to hear that dear little Mama has now fallen a victim too. If only I had you all here again! I myself had to stay in bed yesterday, sweating out a flare-up of my tonsillitis, in a real panic lest it might again go on for days. But I'm glad to say the drastic treatment did some good, so today I was able to hold my first rehearsal[1] as planned. Please give me a day's (if possible two days') notice of your arrival. Fondest greetings,

Yours,
Gustav

The diadem was received with great delight.

I trust the winter coat has already been sent off. It's terribly cold here! You must all come in your winter clothes!

435.   *To Alfred Roller†*[2]

Undated. Munich, [9] *September 1910*
Hotel Continental

Dear Roller,

Am just going to the station to meet my wife—she is arriving about 10 o'clock. Please call at the hotel for us at half-past nine tomorrow morning so that we can go to the rehearsal together.

Yours ever,
Mahler

---

[1] First full rehearsal for the première of the Eighth Symphony (o.e.).
[2] Mahler's last letter to Roller (o.e.).

436. *To Julius v. Weis-Ostborn* (Graz)

Undated. Vienna, 12 October 1910

My dear Ostborn,

My heartfelt thanks for your beautiful and profound words, in response to which I send cordial greetings, on the very point of leaving for America. You have said most beautifully what can be said about art and the artist, and the creative artist could wish for nothing better than always to meet with such response. Alas, I am convinced that these two sides rarely come together. The sense of being so thoroughly understood by you is a great joy to me, and your words will be a precious vade mecum on my way across the great water.

Most cordial greetings both from my {wife} and from

Yours very sincerely,
Gustav Mahler

437. *To Georg Göhler†*

Undated. [October 1910]

My dear Dr. Göhler,

Just a short note, with best wishes, before my departure for America. Preparations have kept me going so hard during the last few weeks that I could not find time to answer your sweet letter. Your score,[1] which I have so far been able only to glance through, definitely interests me. I can only repeat what I have already told you about your songs: I find them genuinely musical. I shall take it to America with me, hoping to have a chance to study it more closely there.—I definitely must get to know your Second when I return. For today do forgive my brevity. I write in very great haste. Once again my warmest thanks for your affection and friendship. My wife also sends her regards.

Yours most sincerely,
Gustav Mahler

My address in America, is: Hotel Savoy, New York.

---

[1] Mahler wanted to know something of Göhler's music and had therefore asked to see the score of his First Symphony (o.e.).

438.   *To Karl Moll*†

Undated. New York, [November] *1910*
⟨Hotel Savoy⟩

My dear Karl,

We received your precious news today. We had both been eagerly awaiting the outcome, and there is a fair and true aim for all our hopes and desires.[1] Almschi will be writing at length about everything. This year I have literally not an hour really to myself, but I am very well and full of energy despite—or indeed, perhaps, because of—all this work.

I should like now, before you finish the plans for the house, to urge you to be sure to include a bathroom ⟨with a W.C.⟩ each (no matter how small) for Almschi and for me for I can hardly find any 'residence' comfortable—or, indeed, really hygienic—without such a convenience. We both really need this, and I beg you to spare no pains on this point.

As for ⟨Gregor's⟩ splendid plans, I have so far received no communication of any kind. But I am by no means inclined to link my destiny for the immediate future in any way with the personality of a man of whom I have never heard anything that was not highly unfavourable.

I do not feel under the least obligation to M[ontenuovo], since I have always emphasized that I can only make a decision when I have a clear view of the situation from the artistic standpoint. We were overjoyed to hear that you were now fully reconciled to dear little Mama's coming to stay with us here for a while. God bless you for it, dear Karl. ⟨Perhaps we can arrange it so that Mama goes to fetch Almschi, who wants to go off about the 1st of March 'in order to supervision [*sic!*] "affaires etrangers" over there', so that the entire female contingent will be turning up over there a month earlier.⟩

Affectionate greetings to you both, my dear ones, from

Your

Gustav

Alma is now for the first time really doing something sensible about her health, and I am *very* satisfied with her progress. She is also in very good spirits and full of hope.[2]

---

[1] Mahler had bought a plot of land in the Semmering and wanted to build a house (o.e.).
[2] In G.E. the postscript is wrongly attached to letter 373 (K.M.).

439. *To Emil Freund*

Undated. New York, 21 November 1910

Dear Emil,

Thank you very much indeed for your news.—I forgot to tell you I should like to have the land registered in both our names (Alma and Gustav Mahler). Perhaps you thought of it yourself—if so, I am very glad. If not, what could be done to put it straight now? You will have been able to read between the lines of the newspaper hoax about my return to the Court Opera. In fact, it had never even occurred to me to work with a person I do not even know and one who, from all accounts, seems thoroughly unlikable.[1]

For heaven's sake hang on to W.[2]

He will not be offered another contract like the one he has in Vienna. Positions with a salary of 12,000 gulden are few and far between. Even I did not receive more in my early years as a director. Thank you again, and all good wishes to you.

I am pretty well at the moment, with a frantic amount of work, which I am coping with very well. Alma and Gucki are, I'm afraid, not in the best of health.

Yours,
Gustav Mahler

Please tell *Hertzka* to send the final amendments when sending the printed score of my Eighth. I should also like to know whether *Mengelberg* has given his firm agreement for the Frankfurt performance.[3]

440. *To Karl Moll*†

Undated. New York [Autumn 1910?]

My dear Karl,

Here I come again with 'business', which is the highest level to which I can ascend in America; this admittedly only where letters are concerned.

What goes on vibrating deep within me is love for home, and home, as you well know, is at the Hohe Warte.—But now to business! Before leaving I gave the score of my Fifth Symphony to my copyist, Herr *Forstig*, of St. Andrä-Wördern an der Stadtbahn (that is his full address), with instructions to enter into the Vienna Konzertverein's parts the numerous corrections I had made,

---

[1] Probably a reference to Hans Gregor, Weingartner's successor as director of the Vienna Opera from March 1911 (K.M.).
[2] Bruno Walter, whose contract with the Vienna Opera was soon to expire. He did not wish to extend it, but was offered new and very favourable terms which he finally accepted (K.M.).
[3] Mengelberg did not perform the Eighth in Frankfurt until February 1912 (K.M.).

and to deliver the corrected material to the Konservatorium, into the hands of Direktor Hammerschlag, while my score was to be delivered to *you* so that you could send it on to me here.—I can make little sense of what Mama has told me. Has Forstig given you the score? Or did he make a muddle and deliver it to the Konservatorium? In the latter case please recover the score (my copy) from Forstig (or, as the case may be, Hammerschlag), but don't send it to me here now, keep it, if you will be so good, in your strongbox until my return.

Fondest greetings to you and dear little Mama,

Yours,
Gustav

441. *To Emil Gutmann†*

Undated. New York [Autumn 1910?]

Dear Gutmann,

I beg to have from 1 June until 1 October always strictly regarded as the 'close season'. Barring extraordinary circumstances I should like to have peace and quiet for physical recuperation and for creative work during these months.—I should prefer not to have my Ninth performed for the present. It is as good as certain that I shall return next season. If the Konzertverein had approached me *in a suitable manner*, I should certainly have conducted a benefit concert.

I *have* got something done: revised my Fifth. I should like to have this semi-novelty performed some time or other (Munich, say, would do, or anywhere else for that matter).

With best wishes,

Yours sincerely,
Mahler

1911

442. *To Anna Moll†*

Undated. New York [February 1911]
Hotel Savoy

My dear little Mama,

For some time your letters have made no mention of your coming, which we are *all* looking forward to so much. I have the feeling that Almscherl is to blame for this, with her temperamental outpourings. Or doesn't Karl want to let you go? Please do write about this instantly. It would be really too absurd if a misunderstanding and some kind of pique should have arisen between us. We have our posh cabins on the finest ship in the German merchant navy, the *George Washington*, for 20 March, and you will be sure to arrange your journey in such a way that the three of us can return together, won't you? That will be wonderful. When are you coming?

This time I can give you the best of news about Almscherl. She is really blossoming—is keeping to a splendid diet, and has *entirely* given up alcohol, looking younger every day. She is hard at work and has written a few delightful new songs that mark great progress. This, of course, also contributes to her well-being.

Her published songs are causing a furore here and will soon be sung by two different singers.[1] Guckerl is also full of life. Now we need only you (as we have to manage without Karl). Almscherl will have written all there is to tell about me. Including that I shall probably be returning here for another year. How much I hope we shall be able to talk it all over together. All I want in writing today is to get you to let us know when you are coming, for I cannot get rid of the feeling, dear little Mama, that there is something on your mind that you are keeping to yourself. Almschi is such a one for upsetting her nearest and dearest. Perhaps she hurt your feelings somehow. But surely I don't have to tell you how well she means?

So please cable just to let us know when you are coming. Thank God I can now sense the first breaths of spring. (I mean, I too have kept very fit this year, but I am tremendously looking forward to being back.)

Lots of hugs to you and to Karl and Maria
from
your faithful
Gustav

443. *To Georg Göhler* (Leipzig)†

New York, 8 February 1911
Hotel Savoy

My dear Göhler,

I have just this minute received your letter and am delighted by the entrancing analysis of my Fourth. I hasten to reply at once, to tell you how touched I

[1] On 2 March 1911 the soprano Frances Alda (1883–1952), who was married to Gatti-Casazza, gave a recital in New York including some of Alma Mahler's songs, which were published in January 1911 (K.M.).

am at being so well understood. In particular, I find your approach to this work quite new and extraordinarily convincing. You actually say what had never before occurred to me whenever *I* had to say something about it. It now seems child's play, so obvious! One thing seems to me to be missing: did you overlook the thematic relationships that are so extremely important both in themselves and in relation to the idea of the whole work? Or was it just that you felt you must spare the general public technical explanations? In either case I do beg you to look for just this in my work. Each of the first three movements is thematically most closely and most significantly related to the last.

I too have often thought of you, dearly wishing I could contribute towards extricating you from the oppressive narrowness of your present life and liberating you, helping you to find a position suited to yourself and your abilities. I shall keep my eyes and ears open. But these things do not happen overnight. Believe me, I myself know where the shoe pinches. What I don't yet know is what shoe fits you.

There is no question of it, we must get to know each other much better. Perhaps this approaching summer we shall be able to meet without having to rush and scramble.

Very best wishes, dear Göhler, from

Your sincere and grateful friend,
Gustav Mahler

I have finished my Fifth—it had to be almost completely re-orchestrated.

I simply can't understand why I still had to make such mistakes, like the merest beginner.

(It is clear that all the experience I had gained in writing the first four symphonies completely let me down in this one—for a completely new style demanded a new technique.)

Fig 8. Admission card to Mahler's funeral, 22 May 1911

IX

SUPPLEMENT

13 Letters to Gustav Mahler from his
parents and sisters

In my Introduction I refer briefly to the other side of Mahler's correspondence, i.e. the letters addressed to him, most of which seem unfortunately to have been destroyed during the Second World War. The discovery of a handful of letters from Mahler's parents and sisters is therefore of such vital importance and interest that I think it justifiable to include them in this volume as a separate supplement to Mahler's own letters.

Through these letters we are allowed to glance into the somewhat depressing circumstances which continually prevailed at Mahler's home, and we get a clear picture of the relations between the young conductor and his immediate family. Moreover, the letters give us an idea of the intensity of the correspondence and consequently of the number of letters lost.

Of the thirteen letters collected here, the first two, both from his mother, date from the autumn of 1882. At that time Mahler had, only seven weeks earlier and after a prolonged holiday in Iglau, returned to Vienna, and he was then waiting for a new offer as Kapellmeister from Gustav Lewy, his agent; in the meantime he scraped a day-to-day living giving piano lessons. (Both letters should be read in conjunction with letter 15 in the main section.)

The remaining letters all date from spring and summer 1886 and were addressed to Prague, where Mahler was about to conclude his one year contract with the German Theatre. After a few days' rest in Iglau he went to Leipzig where, on 25 July, he took up his new appointment at the Stadttheater under the directorship of Max Staegemanan. (These letters are scattered over the period marked by letters 40 and 46 in the main section.)

Mahler's family in Iglau in 1886 consisted of Marie, his mother (age 49), Bernhard, his father (59), the two brothers Alois (19) and Otto (13), and the sisters Justine (17) and Emma (10). Leopoldine (23) had recently married Ludwig Quittner and taken up residence in Vienna.

All footnotes are by the present editor.

K.M.

1. *From Mahler's Mother*

Iglau, 14 November 1882

Dear Gustav,

We are *all* in good health. You must have already got my letter today. I only ask you not to laugh at my anxieties and *take my advice*. Dear Father is quite well. Set your mind at rest. Nothing new has happened here. Good-bye and best wishes

From your ever-loving Mother,
Marie

2. *From Mahler's Mother*

Iglau, 15 December 1882

Dear Gustav,

We have received your welcome letter, and I am now replying to tell you that our opinion would be that you would do better to come home by the excursion train rather than staying in Vienna, since this year the Christmas holidays last for four days and you will not be able to give lessons, and will have to live off ready cash, and this will certainly cost you more than the journey to Iglau. You need not bring any luggage of course. If need be I will help you out with laundry, though if you have any torn socks or shirts you can bring them with you in the coach in your travelling bag and the journey will cost you next to nothing, then you can stay at home for a few days and we will be able to discuss everything fully. The children and the two of us are looking forward to seeing you, so this will be the best idea as it is too tiring for me to travel in winter. Will you write now to let us know if you are coming? and when? so that I can warm your room. I shall also be able to argue out with you those things I can't argue out in letters. Why these endless changes of lodgings? I don't believe there can be a single person apart from you who changes his lodgings every fortnight. Are you going to end up changing your lodgings every time you change your linen? And won't you finally find yourself without any linen or clothes? I know you: you will forget something at each place—and will go on moving until you have nothing left. Am I not right? However I shall leave the rest until I can talk to you. That is enough for today. One more thing, though: if you come home bring with you a bottle of *French brandy*.

Good-bye and warmest regards from us all,

Your ever-loving Mother,
Marie

Otto and little Emma were very pleased with your letters. Emma writes to you several times a day. In fact she devotes all her time exclusively to you when she is home from school. We should be very pleased if you would also stay with Uncle Hermann[1] before you come home, also I have given G. Frank[2] your earlier address and if you have settled into new lodgings again he will naturally not be able to find you. Consequently you must look him up. We have written to him at the Academy of Fine Arts.

3. *From Mahler's Mother*

[Letterhead]: *B. MAHLER OF IGLAU*
Manufacturer of liqueurs, rum, rosolio, punch, essences and vinegar
Iglau, 3 March 1886

My dear Gustav,

At your father's behest I am asking you to go to Uncle Weiner[3] as soon as you receive this letter and to offer him condolences on the sudden death of your Aunt. Upon a misfortune such as this all quarrels and enmities cease. Please also convey our deepest sympathy to your Uncle. We are all in good health here. We read the letter from Neumann, the director, in *Bohemia*.[4] Did he write it to you or did he simply send it to the paper? Write to us in detail about it all soon.

Dear Gustav, I beg you *once again*, go straight away.

Good-bye and warmest regards from your ever-loving

Mother,

Marie

Dr. Freund visits us often and I am extremely glad about this. The talk is mostly about Gustav of course. He is perhaps the best of your friends, besides us.

---

[1] Probably Hermann Mahler (b. 1832), a brother of Mahler's father. La Grange presumes (p. 702) Hermann 'died before 1868', but this must be wrong.
[2] Gustav Frank, Mahler's cousin, mentioned several times in Alma Mahler's *Memories and Letters*.
[3] Not identified. He was probably married to one of Bernhard Mahler's sisters.
[4] Angelo Neumann, the director of the German Theatre in Prague and Mahler's superior, had published a flattering letter about Mahler in *Bohemia*, a leading paper in Prague, after he and Mahler had had a more or less public argument concerning a performance of Gounod's *Faust*.

4. *From Mahler's Father*

Karlsbad, 6 May 1886

Dear Gustav,

I will be brief, because I have a great deal of correspondence here.

Although from the third day of my being here there has been no trace of sugar, yet up till today I have had severe *inflammation of the liver* and the cure has been much hindered by the bad weather.

The way I have lived since my arrival is that apart from when I go out to eat at midday I do not leave my room at all and at night I am already in bed by about half past seven. Hence it is quite impossible to meet with anyone, for it will not occur to anyone to come to me in my room. Hence there is nothing else to be done but that I possess myself in patience and take comfort in the thought that there are others here who are even worse off.

With warmest regards,

Your
Father
B. Mahler

5. *From Justine*

Iglau, 9 May 1886

Dearest Gustav,

I have been intending to write to you for a long time, but with the best will in the world it has not been possible, as ever since your departure we have been constantly involved at home with redecorating. Have you written to dear Father yet? He wrote to us that his condition is highly satisfactory, though he has had much to endure with the bad weather. You don't write to us at all these days. Have you a lot to do? There are certainly no new operas in prospect, so at least you can recuperate now. I am already eagerly looking forward to July when you will be at home again. Your visit will compensate me for many privations I have had to impose on myself. Since dear Father has not been at home I have only twice been out for walks, as dear Mother has been prevented from going with me by her painful feet and having too much to do in the house.

Yesterday we had a letter from dear Leopoldine. She loudly bemoans the fact that in spite of a number of letters she has written to you you have still never replied. If you wanted to you could congratulate her on her birthday on the 18th of this month, as she has never failed to do on yours, and you can have no idea how delighted she would be. I will close now and send you my best regards.

Your ever-loving
Sister [Justine]

6. *From Mahler's Mother*

Iglau, 31 May 1886

Dear Gustav,

Only today am I able to send you a few lines. Dear Father has been at home since Tuesday and he is feeling really well, God be praised. Only he now has to take things very easy and above all avoid vexations and agitations, though this is not at all easy when you are in business. However we are well pleased about him and the doctor holds out the best hopes for him.

Apart from that there is nothing of interest to report. How are things with you, dear Gustav, and will you be coming home in July? I am writing now with great reluctance and so will close with warmest regards and kisses to you from us all—

Your ever-loving Mother
Marie

7. *From Justine*

[Letterhead]: *B. MAHLER OF IGLAU*
Manufacturer of liqueurs, rum, rosolio, punch, essences and vinegar

Iglau, 4 June 1886

Dear Gustav,

I was very pleased to have your letter, and have acted in the way that you advised. I am taking care, to the best of my ability, to get back on good terms with Father. Often I succeed for a short while, then once more in his judgement I make mistakes and all the good is undone again. Dear Mother's health was much better when Father was away from Iglau. I think that her journey to Dr. Pribram in Prague is gradually being forgotten about. You could bring it back to mind in a letter so that we will know what Mother is to do. At present she is drinking Marienbad water but it does not seem to be suiting her. We ought now to set about this matter with a will. And now I am going to tell you about my own personal concerns. The marriage brokers and all sorts of old women are now beginning to come to the house, and it upsets me a great deal to think that my future is to be decided by such people. I feel within myself that it would cost me a great effort of self-control to marry such a man, and yet that will be my fate, for ideals are never attained and what people most wish for never comes to fruition, so that I can take no comfort at all in my future.[1] Don't be angry that I am telling you everything. If you had not permitted it I certainly should not have done so. Already it makes it easier for me that I have shared it with you and am convinced that you will not laugh at me but will sympathize with my feelings.

Good-bye, and kind regards and kisses from

Your ever-loving Sister [Justine]

8. *From Leopoldine*

Vienna, 8 June 1886

Dear Gustav,

I delayed answering your letter because we had little Anna photographed and I wanted to send you a copy; the picture is ready today, so I am doing this. Here there is nothing but good news to report. We are all in excellent health, little Anna is coming on splendidly, and is a very good and lovable child. Ludwig is very well in with his boss and as for me, I now feel really happy and contented. In your last letter you ask what sort of prospects we have for the immediate future. I must candidly admit that I don't properly understand this question. Do you mean perhaps that Ludwig might wish to change his job? I can only assure you that nothing is further from his mind than to change his job. As I've already said, he is very well thought of by his boss, who only recently has given proof of his good will and satisfaction by presenting him with 100 florins for a season ticket on the tramway. And Ludwig himself is as delighted and enthusiastic about his boss as rarely any man is about another. Now, as regards my visit home, I don't as yet know anything definite. Ludwig is going to Hungary and Transylvania in the middle of August and will be away for 3–4 weeks, and I may possibly use this time for a summer holiday. Ludwig never goes to Prague on his trips since he only travels through Hungary, Transylvania and Moravia.

It only remains for me to give you my warmest thanks for your birthday greetings. With best regards,

Your Sister Leopoldine

Have you heard that Minna Frank[2] is married?

My address: L. Qu. Meidling bei Wien, Hufelandgasse 10, 2nd floor.

---

[1] Justine married Arnold Rosé in 1902 at the age of thirty-two.
[2] Not identified. She was possibly a sister of Gustav Frank.

9. *From Mahler's Mother*

[Letterhead]: *B. MAHLER OF IGLAU*

> *Manufacturer of liqueurs, rum, rosolio, punch, essences and vinegar*
>
> Iglau, 10 June 1886

Dear Gustav,

I can't yet tell you the exact date of my arrival, but I hope to come in a fortnight. By that time we think that dear Father will be able to travel. At present he needs as much rest as possible. He is not even supposed to walk about in his room until the swellings on his feet go down. Really I am not sure at present whether it might not be better for us to go to Vienna to see Bamberger. Father does not really know whether he will get good medical treatment, so I do not know what plans to make. I daren't make the journey on my own. Anyway say what you think would be for the best, and whether you are still to conduct anything in Prague? I should like to see you conduct some time— is that not a very modest wish?

It will be quite impossible for me to come to Leipzig. But try *in any case* to come home at least for a few days. We *all* look forward to seeing you.

Warmest regards and kisses from us *all*.

> Your ever-loving Mother
>
> Marie

The letter[1] from Leipzig *will follow immediately.*

10. *From Mahler's Mother*

> Iglau, 16 June 1886

My dear Gustav,

Evidently it must have been written in the stars that I was not to see you conduct in Prague—for though I should very much have liked to see it, it is absolutely out of the question. I cannot risk the journey having only last Friday had another violent attack of asthma. Now I again need as much rest as possible for a long time and cannot expose myself to the journey to Prague. I am *very* glad that you, my dear son, will be coming home for a while, and I hope we shall have some happy days with you here. Dear Father too is very much looking forward to seeing you. Your being here will do him good. He badly needs the distraction, as his feet are still swollen. Despite this, however, he is in general *better*. As for your room, you know what our house is like. We will do all we

---

[1] Possibly from Max Staegemann in answer to Mahler's letter to him of 3 June (see letter 41 in the main section).

can to try to make you comfortable here. Will you, whatever happens, let me know exactly when you are coming?

Bring home *all* your old things and clothes—perhaps I can use some of them (for the children). Meanwhile dear Father joins me in sending you warmest regards and kisses—

Your ever-loving Mother,
Marie

11. *From Justine*

Iglau, 16 June 1886

Dear Gustav,

We received your letter today and I am very glad that you will be coming home for some time. As usual, dear Mother's journey has evaporated into thin air. She has again had a violent attack and on that account cannot venture anything. Perhaps later on she will go to Vienna with dear Father to see Prof. Bamberger. Dear Father will certainly go in order to consult about his health. Already he is doing quite well. We made tests again today and we were all able to see the improvement. But he is still frequently very peevish. Have you yet had little Anna's picture? Don't you think she looks strikingly like our Mother. Poldi will be bringing her here in August for a while as Ludwig is going on a trip to Transylvania. This week Babi Tausig was here from Vienna and told us a lot of nice things about Poldi. She feels very happy and things are now going very well for her. On Sunday Tini Kraus and Fanni Kellner have weddings. Yesterday Doctor Adler Gottlieb from Vienna visited us. He sends you his regards. My health is now very good. Doctor Schwarz prescribed some pills for me, and they have worked remarkably effectively. Everyone is amazed at how well I have been looking for the last three weeks. Dear Father has just told me that he is not going to see the Professor in Vienna, but then as you will be coming home so soon you will be able to arrange it so that you can take dear Mother to Prague or Vienna. She must consult a Professor, since she does not dare to go for walks and that is really her best medicine.

Good-bye and regards from

Your ever-loving Sister Justine

12. *From Justine*

Iglau, 5 July 1886

Dear Gustav,
  Warmest good wishes on your birthday. We hoped that you would be able to spend it with us but Fate has ordained otherwise and robbed us of this great pleasure. I believe it had to be like that: because I was foolishly looking forward to seeing you, and when I look forward very much to anything it does not happen. Dear Mother baked you a birthday cake and I embroidered a bookmark for you, but we will not send them off since the delay will make them no longer appropriate. Yesterday dear Father went to Vienna to see Professor Bamberger and Doctor Schwarz went with him. Dear Mother has been in quite good health for a few days. Dear Father has bought a one-horse wagon and we have ridden out twice. That does her a lot of good as she cannot walk because the country is mountainous all around us and she is not supposed to climb hills. It is, however, a shame that already Alois is going away with the wagon tomorrow. Let us know exactly when you are coming; dear Mother will take advantage of it to come and meet you—otherwise she would not take a wagon.
  Otto is now playing the Beethoven Sonata which you played at the concert with Camilla Ott.[1] He is making good progress. Emma too is starting to learn the piano this week. As for the music I could not find, dear Father had it shut away in boxes with other books.
  Good-bye until soon, then,

Your ever-loving Sister
Justine

Dear Gustav,
  Accept my warmest wishes too on your birthday. I am much looking forward to seeing you. Warmest greetings from your

ever-loving Mother
Marie

[1] A reference to Mahler's last concert in Iglau on 11 August 1883 when he accompanied Milla von Ott in Beethoven's *Kreutzer* Sonata. See letter 226.

13. *From Justine*

Iglau, 14 July [1886]

Dear Brother,

I am sending you our latest greetings from Iglau. We have received your card and propose, in case you cannot come on Friday, to go to meet the train on Saturday, as Friday and Saturday would be too expensive. On Friday too Alois comes home from his trip. I will put off telling you everything until we meet. Our parents have both been in better health, thank God. We are all very much looking forward to seeing you, and it is only a pity that you will be at home for such a short time. Dear Mother already weeps to think that you are going to Leipzig. She always held on to the idea that while you were staying in Prague she would go to see you. However, that is not possible, as she cannot risk any journeys. Schwarz did not allow her to go with dear Father to see the Professor in Vienna, and she cannot bear the cure he has prescribed for her. For her, peace of mind has been the main requirement throughout her illness. The Doctor has examined her and can find nothing organically wrong, it is all a matter of nerves. Dear Father is completely reconciled with Ludwig and Poldi. She is very happy, but they are both upset that you have not answered all their letters, not even when they sent you the picture of little Anna. He is now earning on average 180 florins a month and they can live very well on that. Poldi even puts something on one side every time, which he does not know about. It is not yet certain that she will come in the summer, as he is apparently not going on the trip and therefore she would rather stay with him in Vienna.

Good-bye for today then and warmest regards

from Justine

Until we meet!

NOTES

In the original German edition (hereafter G.E.) the last twenty pages consist of notes to the letters addressed to Friedrich Löhr who precedes his notes with the following introduction:

The editor of this volume [Alma Mahler] has asked me to be responsible for editing the letters addressed by Mahler to myself. The reader will readily sympathize with me: something extremely personal is here given to the world for the sake of making more widely known the innermost nature of a great man. This is something about which I have already written (in *Musikblätter des Anbruch*, April 1920). There I spoke of the purity, like clear water, simplicity and directness of his essential nature, and of his warmth of feeling. That manifests itself, in an incomparably lovable way, in these letters, which, for all their richness of ideas, are made known not for the ideas they express but for their living warmth, for the way they reveal the writer's concern both for weighty matters and with the insistent affairs of day-to-day life.

Many things are touched on in these letters that cannot be recorded in full. Only a complete biography could supply all that the sympathetically interested reader will wish to know. But to prevent the lacunae being too obvious, and in order to give these precious fragments some additional framework, however modest, I have made these notes somewhat fuller than the various relevant passages might be thought to require; and if their tone should seem to err on the personal side, that is because of the subject and because the man whom Mahler is here addressing, the man who experiences all this through him, must himself become the writer—what has counted in my eyes has never been myself, let the reader be assured of that.

A considerable number of letters have been lost. Putting all the undated letters into chronological order has been difficult, requiring much scrupulous consultation of memory and at times what scholars call *divinatio*. I believe I may say I have done my best.

Summer 1923   Friedrich Löhr

Besides Löhr's comments the following pages include notes by the former editor, various other recipients of letters and by the editor of this volume. The numbers correspond to those of the letters. In order to avoid confusion, the notes are preceded by the initials or the full names of the contributors except in the case of the present editor where they appear at the end.

K.M.

I: Vienna, Bad Hall, Laibach and Olmütz (1877–1883)

1877

1 Undated in G.E. Mahler took his *Matura* (school-leaving certificate) in September 1877 in Iglau not having, as he so nicely puts it, come late, but having failed at his first try in July; he thus had to sit the examination again two months later. This time he passed, though hardly with the best marks (K.M.).

1879

2 During the summer of 1879 Mahler was engaged as a piano teacher to a farmer's children in the Puszta-Batta (in Hungary, near Budapest) (K.M.).

3 The village of Seelau (Želiv) is situated about twenty-eight miles north-east of Iglau, near Humpoletz (Humpolec). Mahler spent part of his holidays there in 1879. In the autumn he returned to Vienna where he went into lodgings with Hugo Wolf, amongst others, at 23 Opernring. Later he moved to the so-called Cottageviertel at Währing (then a Viennese suburb) where he rented a small villa which, however, he handed over to Hugo Wolf in the middle of December, when he himself went home to Iglau for Christmas. See letter 6 (K.M.).

4 Not in G.E.

5 Not in G.E. Mahler's short and unhappy love affair with Fräulein Josephine Poisl, daughter of the postmaster in Iglau, is reflected in these letters to Anton Krisper. Mahler's strong feelings for the young lady are expressed in several poems to her, some of which he started setting to music. However, the affair ended abruptly during the spring of 1880 when Mahler had only completed three of the five songs planned: 'Im Lenz' (dated 19 February 1880), 'Winterlied' (27 February) and 'Maitanz im Grünen'

(5 March). The latter, the only one Mahler had published (by Schott in Mainz, 1892), is identical with 'Hans und Grethe' from Vol. I of the 14 early 'Lieder und Gesänge' (K.M.).

6   Not in G.E.

1880

7   Not in G.E.
8   Not in G.E.

Forgotten Love

How desolate my heart! How empty the world! / How great my longing! / O, how the distances endlessly / stretch from valley to valley! / My sweet love! For the last time? / Ah, this torment indeed must burn / in my heart for ever!

How in her glance there once shone radiance true and clear! / I made an end of wandering in spite of Winter's pranks! / And when the springtime passed away, / My love did deck her tresses fair with wreaths of myrtle!

My walking-stick! Come out once more from your corner today! / Long hast thou slept! Prepare thyself! I shall awaken you! / My song of love I long have sung / And yet the earth is broad enough—so come, my faithful staff!

How lovely the smile of hill and dale in their flowery billows! The spring-time made its slow advance with sweetest sounds! / And flowers are blooming everywhere / And everywhere are little crosses—these have told no lies!

9   Not in G.E.
10   (a) Not in G.E.

(b) Bad Hall, twenty-two miles south of Linz, was then a small village of only about 800 inhabitants. As a well-known spa it had its own theatre; it seated about 190 people and was open only for the season, which ran from June to September. Mahler was engaged for the whole season in 1880 (K.M.).

(c) *Rübezahl* was one of Mahler's many opera projects at this time; only part of the libretto has survived. We know from Alma Mahler that Hugo Wolf also had the idea of composing an opera on the same popular subject and that this led to differences between them. Wolf immediately abandoned the project, but Mahler continued working on his libretto for the next four or five years. In 1896 he even suggested that Max Marschalk compose music to it. See letter 164 (K.M.).

11 (a) *E. Freund:* From 1878 until 1883 Mahler used to spend part of his holidays with me at my parents' house in Seelau (about three hours' drive by cart from his native Iglau).

Sensitive as he was to the joys of country life, and thankful for them, he was also ready, in those days, to sit down at the piano and play for us. He was full of spirit and humour, and he rarely failed to carry away his youthful audience, which, in 1878, included a girl, a relative of mine, who found his personality especially inspiring.

The attraction was mutual. Yet such was the moral dignity of the eighteen-year-old-girl's character that he resisted the temptation of indulging in light-hearted flirtation with her. He treated her with warm-hearted friendliness, but in the kindest way warned her against being swept away by passion, lest some day it should bring great trouble upon her. They parted as true friends.

Alas, what he had foreseen did come about. She was scarcely twenty when great trouble came, causing her to take her life. It was my sorrowful task to tell Mahler (near the end of October 1880) what had happened. His letter is in reply to the announcement of her death.

(b) All Souls' Day, a Catholic holiday in memory of the dead, is celebrated on 2 November. Mahler is no doubt referring to the young girl mentioned by Freund in the above note when he writes that the looming All Souls' Day 'is the first I have ever known'. It is interesting to note that Mahler already was 'thinking' as a Catholic even though he was not to become a convert until February 1897 (K.M.).

1881

12 G.E. has a question-mark against the date, but as 18 August 1881 was a Thursday it is obviously correct (K.M.).

13 In G.E. dated (1882), but Mahler was only conductor at Laibach from September 1881 until April 1882 (K.M.).

1882

14 Not in G.E. This letter was written just after the conclusion of the season in Laibach (K.M.).

1883

15 (a) Not in G.E. Original undated, but the reference to the performance at the Iglau Theatre plus Mahler's New Year greetings suggest the beginning

of January 1883. On 10 January Mahler went to Olmütz in order to take over as first conductor at the Royal Municipal Theatre (K.M.).

(b) The young singer who is the butt of Mahler's criticism, Fräulein Hassmann (read: Husmann) seems to have had second thoughts about her ability as a singer, for two years later she had evidently become an actress, though still with the Iglau Theatre (K.M.).

16 (a) Mahler, summoned through his agent Gustav Lewy, arrived in Olmütz on 10 January where he was launched headlong into conducting, until the end of the season (18 March). Owing to a disagreement between Emmanuel Raoul, the director, and Emil Kaiser, the first Kapellmeister, the latter had suddenly resigned his post and left Olmütz. It is perhaps worth mentioning that two years later Raoul and Kaiser joined up again in the small town of Reichenberg (K.M.).

(b) Olmütz then had a population of about 20,000, and the theatre could hold a thousand. The orchestra normally consisted of twenty-four musicians, and a chorus of twenty-eight singers, while the theatre had seventeen soloists at its disposal. Mahler made his début on 15 January with *Les Huguenots* and conducted eight different works during the following eight weeks, including *Carmen*, *Rigoletto* and *Un Ballo in Maschera* (K.M.).

17 (a) During Mahler's stay in Olmütz Richard Wagner suddenly died in Venice on 13 February. No letter from Mahler mentions this sad event, but the baritone, Jacques Manheit who was engaged at the theatre in Olmütz has left a moving account of Mahler's reaction: 'One day I met Mahler in a coffee house completely absorbed in his own thoughts. As I sympathetically asked him why he was sad, he answered, that he had had bad news from home, his father was ill. The following morning, on my way to the theatre, I saw a very confused man running through the street, crying and groaning loudly. Only with difficulty did I discover it was Mahler. I remembered, of course, his sadness concerning his father the previous night, and asked him gently, "For Heaven's sake, has something happened to your father?"—"Disaster, disaster, a catastrophe," Mahler now cried loudly, "the greatest disaster has happened, *Der Meister* is dead!" This was 14 February. It was impossible to deal with Mahler in the weeks following. He only came to rehearsals and to the performances at the theatre, otherwise making himself scarce' (K.M.).

(b) *F. Löhr*: Mahler was at that time—though not for long—a vegetarian. In the preceding period, in Vienna, he had been an habitué of the vegetarian restaurant in the Wallnerstrasse [Café Ramharter]. Through me Mahler got to know my old school-friend Joseph Reiff, with whom he remained in close touch for years. Reiff was an opera singer, theatrical director and then a teacher of singing in Vienna.

II: Kassel (1883–1885)

1883

18 (a) *F.L.:* On 25 June 1883 my elder brother died in his twenty-seventh year. Mahler had had to leave for Kassel a few days earlier, when my brother was already gravely, critically, ill. Mahler and he were very unlike in character, outlook and attitude to life, but nevertheless deeply devoted to each other. I still recall how on the Monday of that week, on the Friday of which my brother died, Mahler and I sat together for the last time, in profound sorrow, in the Café Imperial [in Vienna].

(b) The date of this letter cannot be correct. According to Löhr his brother died on Friday 25 June 1883, but 25 June 1883 was a *Wednesday*! Löhr also states that Mahler had had to leave *for* Kassel a few days earlier, but Mahler departed *from* Kassel on 31 May and did not return until 21 August. The intervening two and a half months he spent partly in Iglau, partly in Vienna and at the Bayreuth festival (see next letter). Löhr has apparently confused the facts concerning his brother's death, or else, perhaps, the original editor mistranscribed his original note to the letter (K.M.).

19 (a) Between 8–30 July Hermann Levi conducted eleven performances of *Parsifal* in Bayreuth. Mahler mentions that he is leaving Iglau in three weeks, on 10 August, from which it can be concluded that the present letter was written on Sunday, 22 July. However, he postponed his departure for another ten days and finally arrived in Kassel on 21 August (K.M.).

(b) *F.L.:* A short time previously Heinrich and Gustl [Augusta] Krzyzanowski had got married, setting out on a tour through Germany before settling down in Starnberg [Bavaria], where Mahler visited them several times during the summer vacations.

20 (a) During his three seasons in Kassel Mahler changed his address three times: from 22 August 1883 to 1 September he rented a room from the gentleman-tailor Adolf Frank at 17 Karlstrasse (Mahler writes 'Mittlere . . .' but only an 'Obere' and an 'Untere Karlstrasse' existed and still exist). For two months (September and October 1883) he stayed with a Fräulein Liese (22 Frankfurter Strasse), and then rented a room from Frau Lauckhard at 13 Wolfsschlucht until he left Kassel at the end of June 1885 (K.M.).

(b) *F.L.:* regarding *Peer Gynt*: The Kassel love affair [i.e. with Johanna Richter, see note 28] had begun to take its exuberant course; the young, tempestuous spirit was unable to escape from its spell during the whole period there. Why Mahler multiplies the Crooked Giant in quoting from Ibsen's *Peer Gynt* (2nd act, towards the end) is hard to understand. Nobody will be surprised to learn that *Peer Gynt* was one of Mahler's favourite works.

(c) Rudolf Krzyzanowski, who was a year older than Mahler and who died four weeks after him, was with Mahler at the Vienna Conservatory, where he studied the violin and the piano from 1872–6; then changed to organ and composition, and graduated in 1878 (K.M.).

21 (a) *F.L.* regarding 'Mountain spirits': Presumably I had asked about his fairy-tale opera *Rübezahl*, on which he had been working with tremendous enthusiasm and delightful inspiration before he went to Kassel.

(b) *F.L.:* Basler, subsequently (if memory serves me right) a provincial civil servant, a tall man, muscular and athletic in build, and in manner very much 'the strong man': he was welcomed as a member of our circle in Vienna and was popular among Viennese Wagnerians. His letter to Mahler was prompted by the attempts he made over a considerable time to turn his powerful bass voice to account as a professional singer.

(c) *F.L.* ('last walk'): No matter when we were together, we always spent a tremendous amount of time going on walks, which we enjoyed enormously. At that period our favourite territory was the countryside stretching from the Leopoldsberg and the Kahlenberg out to Hermannskogel, the wooded hills and the meadows about the Josefswarte on the Parapluiberg, above Perchtoldsdorf, where I used to spend the summers, with my little family, for a number of years from 1882 onward. Although we did not talk much on those walks, they meant a great deal to us: orgiastic abandonment to nature, meditative absorption in the charms of old-world Austrian villages and the historical memories they evoked, and not least the sympathy of two hearts in accord. The first walk out to Heiligenstadt, which Mahler speaks of here and which must surely have taken us along Beethoven's paths to Heiligenstadt and Nussdorf, was almost certainly in 1882, after Mahler's return from Laibach, that being the time when I first really became great friends with him. The 'last' walk to Perchtoldsdorf will have been in the early summer of 1883, before my brother's illness.

1884

23 From Mahler's remark about Löhr's Christmas Day we may presume that the latter too was involved in an unhappy love affair (K.M.).

24 The incidental music to Scheffel's poem *Der Trompeter von Säkkingen* (1854), which Mahler composed in June 1884 must be considered lost for ever, most probably during the Second World War. From contemporary

newspapers and other sources it appears that seven scenes from the poem were selected and arranged by Wilhelm Bennecke for a single stage performance in Kassel on 23 June 1884. The performance was announced as follows: 'Der Trompeter von Säkkingen. Sieben lebende Bilder mit verbindenden Dichtungen nach Victor Scheffel von Wilhelm Bennecke. Musik Mahler'. The selected passages were narrated by an actor (Herr Thies) while members of the cast performed a kind of pantomime illustrating the contents of the poem. In letter 29 Mahler speaks about performances of the work in Mannheim, Wiesbaden and Karlsruhe. My researches show, however, that only the performance in Karlsruhe materialized, on 5 June 1885. The stage designer Herr Ewald from Kassel was in charge of the staging, and a local actor Herr Aloys Prasch was narrator (K.M.).

26   *F.L.:* Mahler arrived at our house in Perchtoldsdorf on 1 July and stayed until after his birthday, 7 July. This visit of Mahler's to us and my visit to him, shortly afterwards, in Iglau, constitute the peak of a period, lasting about two years, during which our friendship was at a pitch of intensity that could not be sustained, since our careers took us in different directions; yet it did lay the foundations of an affection that was to last to the end.

Two things occupied the foreground in those days in Perchtoldsdorf: our walks and music, many hours of music. The windows of my room on the first floor of the Eder-Haus on the market place were kept closed, despite the summer heat, and yet there were always people standing outside, listening. How few people there are today who know what it meant then to hear Mahler at the piano! True, he said himself that five or six years earlier he had been a more able pianist. I have never before or since heard such de-materialization of the human, the technical, process. Mahler rose inexpressibly above what his hands did. He could never have given an account of how he achieved what he did; every thought of technical difficulty was utterly cancelled out; all was disembodied, purely contemplative, passionately and spiritually concentrated on all that, without conscious physical contact, passed from the keys into his being. In a way all his own, comprehending it with the energy and accomplishment of genius, bringing out every nuance, every shade of expression, he caused the music to ring out with all the force with which it had gushed forth from the soul of its creator. In Beethoven's Sonata Op. 111 (No. 32), for instance, the storm at the beginning broke out in a terrible maestoso, shatteringly intense, with a wild ferocity such as I have never heard again; and similarly the finale faded out, pure, utterly luminous, in loveliest beauty, softly and softlier still, from closest touch with this earth out into eternity.

Yet what can words convey of how his playing affected one? I am simply

awed by the exalted happiness that was granted to me—thinking back now to
what Mahler gave me, the sole listener, in those years: all Beethoven's sonatas,
Bach's *Wohltemperiertes Klavier* and many another work of that most beloved master, and yet more, such as, one unforgettable afternoon in the long
house next to the Karlskirche [Vienna], where Mahler was lodging at the
time, the whole of Beethoven's *Missa Solemnis* played right through without
a break. Not long after this Mahler lost interest in playing the piano, and
particularly works written for the piano, since he had become accustomed to
mastering the orchestra in that same way. But anyone who in those early
days heard him at the piano, in the truest sense of the word reproducing the
music, understood him, and what he could do, and his early destiny as a
conductor. Just as he himself reproduced music, being himself the sole
instrument of his will, so it was to be, and had to be, with the orchestra. In
what he did alone everything material was suspended; with an orchestra the
material manifested itself with all its potentialities of resistance. There too
his obsessive energy took over, and increasingly his achievement was to
bestow happiness on many thousands of listeners.

27   *F.L.:* So far as I can recall, he played less during this week that I spent
with him in his parents' house in Iglau. The main thing for me—something
for which I cannot be too thankful—was getting to know the place where he
grew up, the old parts of the town itself and the glorious countryside surrounding Iglau. There in the height of summer we would go for walks lasting
half the day, wandering among flowery meadows, by abundant streams and
pools, through the great woods, and to villages where the peasantry was in
part Slav. And on Sunday afternoon there was an expedition to where
authentic Bohemian musicians set lads and lasses dancing in the open air.
Ah, there was dancing, there was rhythm, causing heart and senses to vibrate
as though intoxicated. There was the zest of life, and sorrow too, just as there
was a profound gravity, all of it veiled by reserve, on the faces of the girls,
their heads bowed towards their partners' breast, their plump, almost naked
limbs exposed by the high whirling of their many-layered bright petti-
coats, in an almost solemn, ritual circling. The archaically earthy charms of
nature and of nature's children, which Mahler came to know in his youth,
prepared the ground for his creative work and never ceased to vitalize his
art.

28   Mahler was evidently an extremely discreet man, even when writing to his
closest friends. If it were not for F. Löhr we should probably never have
known the name of the woman who caused the young Mahler so much heart-
break and anguish during his last two years in Kassel, her identity being
revealed for the first time in Mahler's correspondence not by himself but by

his most intimate friend. Mahler had undoubtedly unburdened his heart to Löhr during the holidays.

Johanna Emma Richter's importance for us lies only in her role as a catalyst for Mahler's innermost feelings and as the inspiration for his song cycle, 'Lieder eines fahrenden Gesellen'. However, apart from some superficial details, collected from various contemporary sources, we do not know much about her and it is difficult if not impossible to create a picture of the person behind the dry and trivial facts. Not even a photograph of her has survived.

Johanna Richter was only about seventeen years old when she made her début in October 1879 at the Stadttheater in Danzig (Gdansk), her native town. After two seasons there she was engaged by the Stadttheater in Königsberg for one season. This was followed by seasons in Mainz and Bremen. In spring 1883 she made a successful guest appearance in Kassel which resulted in a contract from the beginning of the following season, i.e. with Mahler.

Unlike Mahler she lived at the same address (13 Kölnische Strasse) during her four seasons in Kassel, in the same house, incidentally, as Kapellmeister Wilhelm Treiber, a man with whom Mahler was never on good terms. One can easily imagine how much more Mahler suffered when paying the visits to Johanna Richter he describes in his letters to Löhr, from sensing that his enemy was aware, as he presumably was, of his love and despair.

During the 1886–8 seasons Johanna Richter was a member of the German Theatre in Rotterdam, and from there she went to Cologne (1888–91) and Chemnitz (1891–2). This was the end of her career abroad; she went back to Königsberg (until 1895) and finally returned to Danzig for good in 1896, spending a further six seasons at the theatre there. She retired from the stage gradually, now and then making guest appearances. After 1906 it is recorded that she made her living giving singing lessons and recitals.

After World War I Danzig was declared an independent city-state under the protection of the League of Nations but the Second World War put an end to this arrangement in 1939 and Danzig was held again by Germany for some years. The last time we hear of Johanna Richter was in 1943 when she was in her early 80s. Did she survive the war or did she die during the chaotic circumstances at the end of the war?

Her so-to-speak vagrant existence suggests that she never married (she kept her maiden name all these years), and her life as an artist was probably as unimaginative and dreary as that of thousands of other unknown singers before and after her. She was a dramatic soprano who specialized in coloratura parts. Judging from contemporary reviews she was merely an average singer

—which her career seems to confirm. But her looks were often remarked upon. One cannot help wondering if she read these letters to Löhr or was ever herself acquainted with the 'Lieder eines fahrenden Gesellen' (K.M.).

1885

29 The question of whether Mahler conceived the four songs of 'Lieder eines fahrenden Gesellen' as having an orchestral or piano accompaniment has not yet been answered convincingly, and probably never will be unless an earlier manuscript than those known today should turn up unexpectedly.

It is surprising how rarely these songs, now Mahler's most popular, were performed during his lifetime. The music appeared in 1897, printed by Josef Weinberger in Vienna (score and vocal score), but only about eighteen performances are recorded between the first, in 1896, and May 1911—many of these incomplete; in particular the third song was often omitted (K.M.).

30 (a) Not in G.E.

(b) Mahler did not actually sign the contract with the Leipzig Stadttheater (Max Staegemann) until March; and it ran only from July 1886. For the intervening season he was able to secure an appointment at the German Theatre in Prague (K.M.).

31 Bringing the Kassel music festival to life caused Mahler the greatest difficulty. Jealousy and anti-Semitism went hand in hand, with the result that the opera orchestra refused to participate (see letter 33) and the Intendent, von Gilsa of the Court Theatre, would not allow the festival to take place in the theatre. Thus Mahler was forced to find a new orchestra and another concert hall. The former was scraped together from musicians from an infantry regiment and from various Hofkapellen in nearby towns. The 'concert hall' was erected on a military ground in Kassel, and the chorus was made up of the Kassel Music Society Chorus plus choirs from Marburg, Münden and Nordhausen. On 29 June Mahler conducted the first concert which contained Mendelssohn's *St. Paul*. The soloists were the then-famous Rosa Papier-Paumgartner (who later played an important part in Mahler's being appointed to Vienna), Paul Bulss and Heinrich Gudehus—also well-known singers. Paul Bulss gave the first performance of some of Mahler's songs from *Des Knaben Wunderhorn* in Hamburg and Wiesbaden in 1893 (K.M.).

33 *F.L.* comments regarding 'Starnberg': This may refer to the preceding letter [no. 29] of greetings for the New Year; it would have been sent to Starnberg, where I was then staying with Heinrich Krzyzanowski. But several later passages in this letter (of April 1885) show that he must have written in

the first quarter of that year at least *one* letter in which he told me of the music festival for which preparations were already being made and of his being about to enter on a trial period as conductor in Leipzig and it must since have been lost.

35 *F.L.: Deutsche Worte*, a monthly Viennese journal founded in 1881 and edited by Engelbert Pernerstorfer. During those years, the paper published a number of articles written by me under the pseudonym Hanns Maria, and later one or two more under my own name.

36 (a) *F.L.:* Joseph Seemüller, the Germanic philologist, at that time a schoolmaster in Vienna, also lecturing at the University, subsequently professor at the Universities of Innsbruck and Vienna. He was a friend of my brother's from their student days, and he became a dear friend of mine. He met Mahler in our circle, and although I do not think he was in the habit of meeting Mahler alone, he saw a good deal of him together with us. Being a real lover of music, he delighted in Mahler's playing; he also played duets with him, immensely stimulated by having such a partner. A remarkable, indeed astonishing, change took place in Seemüller: just as his buttoned-up attitude to life gave way to something more youthfully relaxed, so too his well-trained, pedantically correct, staid mode of playing the piano was imbued with a lively, flowing quality, an urgently emotional rubato, a liberated intensity of expressive emotion. When Mahler later returned to Vienna, as director of the Court Opera, their acquaintance was not resumed. [Seemüller was born in 1855 and died in 1920. In 1885 he published *Leitfaden zum Unterricht in der deutschen Grammatik am Obergymnasium nach dem neuen Lehrplane* (K.M.).]

(b) *F.L.:* Dr. Seraphim Bondi, a Viennese lawyer, was an active and leading figure in the German Schools Association and collaborated with Theodor Gomperz in the association that founded and supported the Viennese Girls' High School. It was through Seemüller, with whom he had become close friends in early days when both went to school at the Schottengymnasium, that he was introduced into our circle. He was dearly loved by us all until his tragic end in Lake Constance.

38 *F.L.:* Mahler returned home from Kassel via Prague, doubtless in order to make the acquaintance of the director Angelo Neumann. Since the Prague Opera opened on 1 August, he can only have spent a short time in Iglau. I no longer recall anything about the trial period as conductor in Leipzig.

III: Prague and Leipzig (1885–1888)

1885

39   *F.L.:* This letter as well as the following postcard (no. 40) was first published in *Musikblätter des Anbruch* (Vienna, April 1920, cf. my Notes there). Immediately after this I spent several weeks in Prague with Mahler.

1886

43   The G.E. has a question-mark against the date, but the fact that Mahler conducted Gluck's *Iphigenie* on 1 July confirms it. *Fidelio* was performed on 9 July (K.M.).

44   (a) The Hotel Blauer Stern was a well-known hotel in Prague in which Mahler frequently stayed later (K.M.).

(b) On 13 June Staegemann had written to Mahler asking him if he knew Ponchielli's *La Gioconda*, and on the 26th he wrote again and asked Mahler to listen to a young singer, probably Fräulein Hudl. Apparently nothing came of her audition; at any rate she was not engaged at the Leipzig Theatre. It is questionable, incidentally, whether Mahler had correctly understood the young lady's name, as she does not appear in the contemporary German opera annals, nor in the records at Olmütz (K.M.). Mr. Paul Banks (Oxford) adds 'there is a record of a Frl. *Huld* at Olmütz in 1884–5 (see the *Almanach der Genossenschaft Deutscher Bühnen-Angehöriger*, 1885, p. 214). So perhaps the original transcriber of the letter misread Mahler's handwriting.'

(c) Mahler did not perform any works by Smetana, Glinka or Dvořák in Leipzig, but later in Hamburg he conducted four of Smetana's operas (K.M.).

46   (a) In G.E. dated 'August 1886'.

(b) *F.L.* comments on the 'two enclosures': The reference is to Martin Krause's review, in the *Leipziger Tageblatt*, of the performance of *Tannhäuser* on 16 August 1886. What could not fail to be distressing to Mahler was the blatantly personal prejudice evident in this notice. While acknowledging the performance to be very good, even in detail, and deserving all the applause it received, and patting Mahler on the back in the usual manner, granting that he was an unusually gifted artist, the critic denigrated the whole style of his conducting, finding an excess of 'attack', evidently also unusually fast tempi, for instance in the 'Entry of the Guests', and quoting a number of passages from Wagner's writing against Mahler. On 12 August, in the same newspaper, Gustav Schlemüller described the performance of *Rienzi* under Mahler's baton as a complete success, both in box-office and in artistic terms, and praised Mahler's immense dedication, his sureness of touch, his inspired *élan*. That performance was likewise praised in similar terms by Bernhard Vogel in another Leipzig newspaper. Yet the *Leipziger Zeitung* of 21 August published a typically exasperated, conservative notice, signed S——r, on the performance of *Der Freischütz*. I should have liked to give the reader Mahler's brilliant marginalia to that review, but it would necessitate publishing the notice as well, and it does not deserve the honour of being reprinted. The examples I have given are merely a few from among the many, now inconsistent, now downright attacks, which Mahler had to put up with until he was finally in a position to ignore them.

(c) Betty Frank was for many years a regular member of the German Landestheater in Prague. During Mahler's previous season in Prague he had paid special attention to her, probably resulting in a love affair. She was born in 1864 in Breslau where she also made her début. In 1893 she went to Zurich and the following year to Berlin. Soon afterwards she returned, however, to Prague and became a member of the Landestheater once more. According to the German opera annals she was still active as an opera singer and as a singing teacher in 1913. In 1893 she married a Herr Rückert, director of an insurance company in Prague. Betty Frank was the first to perform compositions by Mahler in public: she sang three of his 'Jugendlieder' (of which only 'Hans und Grethe' has been identified) in Prague with Mahler at the piano on 18 April 1886 (K.M.).

47 Max Staegemann's two daughters, Helena and Erna, to whom Mahler refers, later became noted singers. Helena in particular, then only eight years old, became a highly esteemed soprano who at about the turn of the century made herself conspicuous giving recitals all over Germany; these occasionally included Lieder by Mahler (e.g. in October 1905 in Leipzig with Hans Pfitzner at the piano!). In 1910 she married the composer Dr. Botho Sigwart (Count Eulenburg the younger). She died in 1923 (K.M.)

49 *F.L.*: Hans Emmanuel Sax, secretary to the Vienna Chamber of Commerce, lecturer at Vienna University, subsequently Professor of Economics at the Agricultural College in Vienna, and author of *Die Hausindustrie in Thüringen* (Thüringian Domestic Economy), three vols., Jena, 1882–8. A member of our most intimate circle, soon after this time he fell prey to an incurable lung disease; he moved to Merano, where he spent his last years intensely happily married to a noble woman. He bore his sufferings with heroic humour and died, aged 38, on 29 June 1896, at Dreikirchen near Waidbruck.

50 Arthur Nikisch left the Vienna Conservatory two years before Mahler, five years his junior, entered. After having played the violin in the Court Orchestra in Vienna for three years, he went to Leipzig in 1878 to become conductor of the Stadttheater. In July 1889 he was appointed conductor of the Boston Symphony Orchestra, but returned to Europe in 1893 where he was Mahler's successor in Budapest; two years later he was elected conductor of the Leipzig Gewandhaus Orchestra which remained his central interest until his death. It is not known what opinion Nikisch had of Mahler the conductor and if we can judge his opinion of Mahler the composer from the number of performances he gave of his works, it was not very high. To be sure he was the first to perform the second movement of the Third Symphony in 1896, and he even repeated it in Leipzig some months later. In 1905 he conducted the 'Kindertotenlieder' in Berlin as well as in Hamburg, and the Fifth Symphony in Berlin. But after a performance of the Second Symphony in 1906 at a Gewandhaus Concert he did not conduct any of Mahler's works again until after the composer's death. It should however be noted that in 1915 he gave the first performance of *Das Lied von der Erde* in Berlin (K.M.).

1887

56 (a) In G.E. dated 'Leipzig 1887'. As Nikisch announced publicly that he had declined the offer from Budapest in January, the letter can be dated to the same month (K.M.).
(b) *F.L.:* Heinrich Braun was at that time married to Spiegler's sister Josephine, his first wife. Mahler did not keep up with him for long.
59 Mahler conducted *Siegfried* on 13 May, and the following day Nikisch conducted *Götterdämmerung*. The letter was probably written at the end of April as Nikisch returned from Italy at the beginning of May (K.M.).

1888

60 (a) *F.L.:* In the period that elapsed between the foregoing letter [no. 59] and this one we spent a great deal of time together. Writing to me from Iglau, where he was on summer vacation, on 17 July, Mahler announced his arrival as follows:

Dear Fritz, I shall be appearing on the scene on either Wednesday or Thursday. Love to the whole family.
Gustav

(b) Mahler was at that time preparing the first performance of Weber's *Die drei Pintos* which he had 'completed'; he was probably also working on his First Symphony which occupied his life and his mind for the next two months (K.M.).

62 Mahler had been working on his 'performing version' of Weber's skeleton opera *Die drei Pintos* since the previous summer and finished it in October 1887. The première was scheduled for December 1887 but was postponed and finally took place on 20 January 1888. It is a comic opera in three acts consisting, in Mahler's arrangement, of twenty-one scenes, with an *entr'acte* preceding the second act. Weber had only sketched and composed seven pieces when he died, but the music remained in the possession of his family who invited various composers to complete the sketches, all in vain. When Mahler's turn came he was at first sceptical but soon became very enthusiastic. On his own initiative he selected other compositions by Weber and arranged and orchestrated them and the original sketches. The *entr'acte* was composed on themes from the opera. He also had a hand in the libretto which Karl v. Weber, the composer's grandson, had prepared.

The première, awaited with suspense all over Germany and Austria, was a great triumph for Mahler who, of course, conducted it. About fifteen repeat performances were given during that season and it was also produced at four other German opera-houses (Hamburg, Dresden, Munich and Kassel). The, following season it was on the playbill of theatres in Vienna, Coburg, Breslau, Bremen and Prague, and later in Weimar, Berlin (the guest appearance of the Prague ensemble), Brünn and Strassbourg, but interest was fading. However, in the first decade of the new century *Pintos* was revived suddenly in Frankfurt, Hanover, Riga, Leipzig, Dresden and Essen. The music was published in February 1888 and appeared in many different editions and arrangements.

For English readers it might be of interest to learn that the *entr'acte* was the first composition by Mahler (–Weber) to be heard in England, Sir Georg Henschel including it in the programme for his sixth London Symphony Concert on 22 January 1889. As early as 6 June 1888 Anton Seidl introduced the same piece to the Americans at a concert in Brighton Beach, repeating it shortly afterwards (K.M.).

64 (a) *F.L.:* A few of Mahler's letters to me from Leipzig may have been lost. But had there been only these three [nos. 60, 63 and 64], with their unique flow of language, I should still understand everything. In Mahler's life this was a time of tremendous spiritual ferment, the most sublime moments of which he wrapped in holy silence. The work then nearing completion, of which he here writes, is his First Symphony, the beginnings of which date back to the year 1884, when he was in Kassel.

The first of these 1888 letters [no. 60] is the only one that Mahler wrote to me in red ink.

(b) *F.L.* comments on 'your work': I do not know what he meant: there was at that time no 'work' of mine. Possibly he was referring to a collection of verse, essays and translations that I had sent him.

65 Not in G.E. (Written in red ink.)

68 (a) In G.E. dated 'Iglau, Summer 1888'. However, Mahler's negotiations with the Budapest Opera, mentioned below by Löhr, only started in September (K.M.).

(b) *F.L.* on 'business': When his Leipzig appointment came to an end Mahler, who was always pessimistic about such things, imagined he would be without employment, and was tormented with anxiety about his family. All at once, however, the negotiations with Budapest—to which he here refers —began, leading to a swift conclusion. At the beginning of October Mahler took up his duties as director of the Budapest Opera.

(c) *F.L.* on 'in town': At this period I was once more spending the summer holidays in Perchtoldsdorf.

(d) *F.L.:* Mahler's brother Otto was then in his sixteenth year. He had already shown early signs of unusual musical talent. He came to Vienna at this time, first of all staying with his sister Leopoldine, to study music and to take private lessons to make up for the deficiencies in his general education.

IV: Budapest (1888–1891)

1888

69 In G.E. dated 'September 1888': Mahler arrived in Budapest at the end of September, and on taking up his appointment on 10 October he gave this speech to the orchestra and the opera's singers (K.M.).

1889

71 (a) *F.L.:* There are no letters dating from the first months of the year 1889. On 17 April 1889 I went to Budapest, where I spent Easter, from Maundy Thursday until the evening of Easter Monday, with Mahler. We spent much time together in the open air, in the city, in the country around Ofen, on the island of St. Margeret; and then at home he would go to the piano and play me parts of what was to become his Second Symphony. All that was on at the

opera then was *The Barber of Seville* and *Les Dragons de Villars* [by Maillart], under his baton. I have very pleasant memories of the following people, with whom he was then constantly in touch: Herr Ödön von Mihalo-vich [1842–1929]; that excellent serious musician, Professor Hans Kössler, of the Budapest Conservatory, whom I was later to meet again with Mahler in Salzburg and Berchtesgaden; the singer Bianca Bianchi; the actor, Eduard Ujház; and Herr Doktor Ebner and his family. The following may bear witness to the thoroughness and sense of direction with which Mahler, in a foreign country, prepared the ground for what he had in mind: on Holy Saturday he gave an authentically Magyar dinner, in truly princely style, for a small gathering of artists and their families, an occasion at which everyone enjoyed themselves vastly, and which also bore the hoped-for fruits for Mahler's serious plans. Since there was nothing else for me to do during those wonderful days, which passed all too swiftly, I spent time in the museum, where old Pulszky and his staff showed me much kindness, in the Eszterházy Gallery, and visiting Aquincum and some acquaintances of my own.

(b) *F.L.*: From the summer of this year I find only two brief messages from Mahler, as follows:

(1) *Undated Munich. Arrival postmark: Vienna, 16 June 1889*

Dear Fritz,

Enclosed 40 marks for Otto. Have had very satisfactory time here. Writing about it soon. . . .

Mahler's stay in Munich [see also letter 72], preceded by one in Vienna, is confirmed by a letter of mine, 31 May 1889, to my sister Louise, then study-ing painting in Munich. The further news here promised was doubtless given in his letter from Salzburg, the sole evidence for which is now an empty envelope with the clear arrival postmark 'Perchtoldsdorf, 20 July 1889'.— For personal reasons I have omitted one final sentence from the above letter.

(2) Telegram from Prague, 17 August 1889, confirming that Mahler visited Vienna yet again that summer:

Arriving tomorrow Sunday evening eight o'clock Franz-Josef Station. If possible meet me. Mahler.

72 (a) In G.E. dated 'Munich? Summer 1888', and *Löhr* added the following note to this: After deep and scrupulous thought I have decided that this is where this letter belongs, which means it was written in Munich, where Mahler was operated on for the first time for an intestinal trouble that he also suffered from in later years. [However, it was during June and July 1889

that Mahler was in Munich for a haemorrhoid operation. See also Löhr's note to the preceding letter (K.M.).]

(b) *Löhr* had added a further comment, which no longer belongs here since it confirms that the notes thought to have been enclosed in this letter were written in summer 1888. It runs: 'This stay of Mahler's in Vienna is also documented by two pencilled notes, scribbled on scraps of paper sent to me, unsealed, by messenger, the address establishing the date as 1888. They read as follows:

Dear Fritz, This evening shall be with the Spiegler family by the band, Rotunda Park. Please do join us there! Half-past eight or a quarter to nine. Yours, Gustav.

Dear Fritz, do please *instantly* take a cab at my expense, *instantly* coming to Kaubeck's café Zur Schäferin in the *Prater* [at the Aquarium]. With Dr. Bondi awaiting you there till half-past ten! Gustav.

On those occasions, as also after other such meetings with other people, the two of us stayed on alone together at the café, talking over the experiences of previous months or years, as the case might be, cramming a great deal into a few hours.'

73 *F.L.:* Otto had left the house of his sister Leopoldine, who died about this time [on 27 September 1889], and taken a room overlooking the courtyard in the house where we lived in the Breitegasse. We had made ourselves entirely responsible for looking after him.

74 *F.L.:* This was at the time when Mahler's mother was dying after a long illness. His sister Justine was on the verge of collapse from the strain and grief of nursing her and the question was whether she should be allowed to be there to witness her mother's death. So Mahler, who was in the midst of feverish activity in Budapest, hastened to Iglau to see how his mother was, provided a nurse, and took his sister with him for a few days' recuperation in Vienna, where he also had her seen by a doctor. Having obtained medical advice and reassurance, he felt he could let her return to Iglau. Their mother then rallied for a short time. She departed this life on 11 October 1889, a woman richly endowed with the virtues of her sex, one whose tenderness and gentleness, kindliness and warm receptiveness, are an abiding memory of any of those who knew her.

75 In G.E. dated 'Budapest, Autumn 1889'.

76 *F.L.:* After the death of Mahler's mother the Iglau household was dissolved, his father having died on 18 February 1889. Mahler's brother Otto and fourteen-year-old sister Emma spent the next year in lodgings in the

house where we lived. His sister Justine joined him in Budapest, where he had taken lodgings at no. 3 Theresienring.

78 *F.L.:* This must be where this letter belongs. It appears, therefore, that my trip to Budapest must have been postponed for a fortnight.

79 *F.L.:* '. . . after just hearing, with deep emotion, the symphony—I rejoice that I shall be hearing it again tomorrow' I wrote to my wife. This was the First Symphony, for the première of which I travelled to Budapest. I arrived early on Tuesday, 19 November in order to hear the final rehearsal that morning. I assume that Otto came with me, but I have no real recollection. It need scarcely be said that the experience of this performance dominated my visit, all the more so since Mahler himself heard the work for the first time when he rehearsed it. That was the main thing, and a source of continuing encouragement. He also had to work out what the work's reception meant for him. Mahler's own circle in Budapest was deeply moved. A large section of the audience, having, as usual, no taste for formal innovations, was painfully disconcerted by the dynamic force of tragic expression that rages in this work. A fashionable lady sitting near me was so startled by the attacca leading into the last movement that she dropped all the things she was holding. The next day's newspapers carried the reviews that were to be expected: while the *Pester Lloyd* had a warmly appreciative notice by A[ugust] B[eer], the *Neuer Pester Journal* published a damning critique, its repellent arrogance and total misunderstanding merely serving to condemn the taste of that scribbler V[iktor] von Herzfeld. That was the beginning of a long period of suffering for Mahler in his creative life—a period of lonely, often anguished, unfailingly constant superiority to whatever the day might bring.

81 *F.L.:* It was doubtless on his return from Iglau that Mahler joined us in Vienna just as the candles were being lighted on the Christmas tree.

1890

82 *F.L.:* From a friend's postcard of February 1890 I gather that by this time the time of my departure for Budapest was already fixed. Sax's poem, mentioned on that card, was dedicated to Albert Spiegler. Sax was at that time gravely ill, had given up his profession, and was living in retirement at Lainz (a Viennese suburb). Mahler's composition remained a good intention.

84 *F.L.:* We carried out the delightful plan for the summer that is mentioned in the letter of February [no. 82]. Yet Mahler must have been in Vienna as early as March and have discussed it all with me. From a receipt, which I still have, I see that on 1 April we rented a villa in Hinterbrühl (near Vienna) for the summer holiday that Mahler and I and my family were to spend to-

gether. This villa, the property of Frau Lehnhardt, no. 12 Weissenbach-
strasse, with its large garden, assured Mahler of the tranquillity and seclusion
that he needed. First, however, he spent several weeks travelling in Italy with
his sister Justine.

86 *F.L.:* This concerns preparations for a visit to Franzensbad (Bohemia),
where Justine was to take the cure during June and July.

88 *F.L.:* Anyone expecting Mahler to give impressions of his Italian journey
will be disappointed. Apart from the shortness of the period, which was not
conducive to the writing of long letters, the fact is that Mahler lacked what is
so important when travelling in Italy—namely enthusiasm for the incomparable treasures of visual art to be found there. He understood only one artistic
language, that of music, and it possessed him to the exclusion of all else. In
Florence therefore, just as subsequently in Paris in 1900, he did not even
visit the most famous galleries. It was not that he was incapable of receiving
impressions from works of painting and sculpture; if he was confronted with
greatness—as on a later occasion when I showed him photographs of the
Ludovisi Throne, with its reliefs, among them the birth of Aphrodite—he
was profoundly delighted and fascinated. But left to himself, when he visited
new places, he sought out only the never-failing charms of nature, such as the
flowery countryside around Florence and Fiesole or near Paris.

90 *F.L.:* The two and a half months at Hinterbrühl were over for Mahler,
who returned to Budapest in the middle of August, while the rest of us
remained, with my wife keeping house, until the middle of September.
Fortunately the time, so filled with experiences and activity, was long enough
to be of great benefit to Mahler. He could enjoy singular natural beauty,
domestic comfort and, at any moment when he required it, complete personal
freedom; our life there was arranged with him above all in mind. Whenever
he needed, and he often needed it passionately, he could fulfil himself in talk
and discussion.

For the rest he had a delightful room, with an exquisite view, to which he
could withdraw for solitude. There was also a good deal going on, much
coming and going, many visitors to the house, and the peculiar circumstances
of one's own domestic affairs. Until well into July I was kept in town by my
teaching duties, usually spending only Sunday out at Hinterbrühl. For the
sake of his studies Otto remained behind with me. During this period Mahler
often came into town, and once made a brief trip for professional reasons to
Budapest; and occasionally he spent a night with acquaintances at Kalten-
leutgeben nearby.

Later in July, when I was freed from my duties, spending the greater part
of each day alone with Mahler, I did not hesitate to fulfil obligations to another

friend: I spent a week at Aussee with Sax after we heard that his condition, both physical and mental, was deteriorating most gravely. Officials of the Budapest Opera came to report to Mahler. Furthermore, he was already planning ahead for the coming season, reading through possible scores, among them—with growing amazement—one newly arrived: Mascagni's *Cavalleria rusticana*, which he quickly decided to produce. [The world première was in Rome on 17 May 1890; the first performance in Budapest on 26 December 1890 (K.M.).]

His own new period of great creativity had not yet come. What seethed in him, all heat and force, was the variety of that summer life to which he abandoned himself with tumultuous impulse, and he could be cheerfully talkative, unless some sudden reflectiveness caused his surroundings to fade or, if we were alone, he was overwhelmed by agitation at the memory of some agonizing delight he had experienced to the depths of his soul.

91 *F.L.:* Two matters are discussed that had long been the subject of our most earnest consideration. Soon after the date of this letter I set out, for purposes of study, on a journey to the south, accompanied, until March 1891, by my wife and child. I arrived home soon after the middle of September 1891. This meant that at the time when Mahler's letter was written our household in Vienna was temporarily dissolved, so that for this period there was no one to look after his brother and sister. We discussed many possible alternative arrangements. Mahler, who expended himself so devotedly and self-sacrificingly in his care for his brothers and sisters, decided to set up an independent household for Justine in Vienna, where Otto and Emma would also be cared for. A suitable apartment was quickly found in a house already familiar—no. 4 Breitegasse.

I was to have obtained a reduction in the railway fare to Italy, but nothing came of it.—A letter that arrived just before I left is no longer extant.

92 Mahler had had an offer which he had declined from the director of the Hamburg Stadttheater three years earlier. The present correspondence was to lead finally to Mahler's appointment as first conductor in Hamburg (K.M.).

93 Pollini eventually accepted Mahler's demand for an annual salary of 12,000 marks net, from which payments to the pension fund were to be deducted annually. Otto Klemperer writes in his reminiscences that Mahler's salary was raised to 18,000 marks by Pollini after Mahler's first night at the Hamburg theatre, but this is wrong. However Mahler did also receive approximately 1,000 marks at his annual benefit performances and this should be added to his regular income.

Compared with ordinary musicians Mahler was not exactly badly paid: thus the leader of the Berlin Philharmonic Orchestra was paid 3,000 marks gross a year, and the harpist of the Leipzig Stadttheater 2,680 marks a year (including services in the Gewandhaus Orchestra); the oboist of the Royal Chapel in Dresden received between 1,680 and 2,400 marks whereas his colleague the bassoonist only got 1,000 marks. The situation was not, of course, better in Hamburg and the musicians were therefore forced to supplement their income by other means. It ought to be added that Mahler tried many times, not always unsuccessfully, to have the incomes of his musicians increased (K.M.).

1891

95 (a) Brahms who usually declared that he preferred to read the score of *Don Giovanni* rather than listen to a bad performance became so enthusiastic over Mahler's interpretation that he embraced him and exclaimed that he had never in his whole life heard it so well done (K.M.).

(b) *F.L.:* Georg Haussmann, a native of Stuttgart, who was steward of Herr von Dormitzer's estates in Moravia, was on a visit to Stuttgart when, in the prime of his life, he suffered a fatal stroke. Mahler had come to know both him and his wife during their many visits to Vienna, and he delighted in the company of this true-blue German, a man of wide culture.

(c) *F.L.:* My sister Bertha arrived in Rome soon afterwards, accompanied by a woman friend. Just before leaving Vienna she had received from Mahler the following letter:

Undated. Budapest, January 1891

Dear Bertha,

One way or another—for your sake I am delighted that you are coming to Italy. Here is the answer to your question *re* Ancona–Rome–Budapest.[1] So Vienna via Budapest to Venice is nonsense. From Vienna via Budapest and Ancona to Rome is a *small* detour, which is, besides, all the more worth it because it comes cheaper by half, and also because there one can see the celebrated conductor Mahler, who can pipe such lovely mournfulness and who has such a jolly welcome for foreign visitors and who then goes off to Rome along with them. The last, admittedly, looks far from promising.

Please give Ernestine my affectionate greetings—she gets far better marks than you. I mean to buy her a pretty gingerbread heart with 'A souvenir' on it.

Today I wrote to Fritz!

And this very day, too, a volume of Nietzsche goes into the post for you.

[1] In the margin: diagram of the rail-route Vienna–Ancona–Rome (F.L.).

You will then, I hope, cease to pelt me with mean filth. I am glad you are not a reviewer of opera.—I am writing this letter for your autograph collection.

So if you travel via Budapest, see that you let me know nicely in time for me to meet you at the station.

My very best wishes to all.

Write again *instantly*! Do what I say, mind!

Thy well-disposed

Gustav Mahler

(d) *F.L.*: The well-known events that led to Mahler's resignation from his Budapest appointment in March were already in progress. Mahler foresaw the rest and was already negotiating elsewhere, including with Dresden. In the event of his leaving Budapest he was at the time playing with the idea of following me to Rome. It did not come about. Mahler left Budapest on 23 March, together with Justine, who had helped him with his preparations for leaving. After spending two days in Vienna, as I gather from a postcard of 24 March 1891 from my sister Ernestine, he went to Hamburg, where he took up his new appointment on 1 April. [Mahler's first appearance in Hamburg was on 29 March when he conducted *Tannhäuser* (K.M.).]

96   This unfinished letter is probably a draft that was never completed. Only the last of Mahler's demands was accepted: on his departure from Budapest he received 25,000 florins which was then equivalent to about 12,500 marks (K.M.).

V: Hamburg (1891–1897)

1891

97   In G.E. dated 'Autumn 1891'. However, according to Löhr's note to letter 91, Löhr returned to Vienna in the middle of September 1891, thus establishing the date of this letter. Furthermore Mahler mentions that they won't see each other again for nine months, i.e., until June 1892 when the summer holiday starts (K.M.).

98   (a) In G.E. dated 'Autumn 1891' but the reference to Krzyzanowski's opera plans in this as well as the next letter (no. 99) strongly suggests that the present letter was written in November (K.M.).

(b) Considering what we know today about Mahler's output in 1891—and I think that knowledge tallies with the facts—it seems a bit exaggerated when

Mahler talks about the 'many fairy-tales, songs and symphonies in [his] drawer'—at least as regards the symphonies and the fairy-tales. In a letter, dated October 1891, to the music publishing firm B. Schott's Söhne in Mainz, Mahler offers the publisher the following compositions: one symphony (no. 1), a symphonic poem (first movement of his Second Symphony, then named 'Todtenfeier'), 'Ein Märchen' for chorus, soloists and chorus ('Das klagende Lied') and about twenty songs ('Lieder eines fahrenden Gesellen' and the fourteen songs which were later published by Schott as 'Lieder und Gesänge'). I believe that was all he had finished at that time. However, it has been rumoured since 1938 that Mahler left four complete and hitherto unknown early symphonies. These rumours were generated by an article by Paul Stefan in *Musical America* (April 1938) in which he claims that Willem Mengelberg and Max v. Schillings during a visit to Dresden not long before had examined and played on the piano four such symphonies from the manuscripts in the possession of Baroness Marion von Weber. As Schillings had died in July 1933 and Baroness von Weber two years earlier, this event would have taken place before 1931. But when? In my view the whole story was misunderstood by Stefan. In June and July 1907 Mengelberg and Schillings met each other at a festival in Dresden and during this festival they became acquainted with an old friend of Mahler's who for a meeting brought with her a parcel of his manuscripts. Mengelberg and Schillings played the music on the piano, and it turned out to be the discarded 'Blumine' movement of the First Symphony and the original first part of 'Das klagende Lied' known as 'Waldmärchen'. On the last page of the 'Blumine' movement Mahler had written: 'An M. zum Geburtstage'. 'M' almost certainly signifies Marion von Weber with whom Mahler had an affair in Leipzig. In a letter to his wife Mengelberg describes the whole incident. This letter is kept in the Mengelberg Stichting in Amsterdam and is reproduced in Miss B. Heemskerk's book on Mengelberg, published in Holland in 1971 (K.M.).

99 (a) In G.E. dated 'December 1891'.

(b) *F.L.*: Returning to Vienna, I devoted myself once more to supervising Otto and his studies. I was not less anxiously concerned than Mahler over the difficulty of acting as guardian to Otto: constitutionally timid, very reserved, over-sensitive, he had little capacity to get on in life on his own and had proved himself unfitted for any kind of systematic study. He was to take the examination mentioned here in order to qualify for the privilege of doing only one year's 'voluntary' military service. Our fatal mistake lay in deeming this necessary, for it turned out, too late, that he was physically unfit for military service.

(c) As a rule the Stadttheater in Hamburg was closed on Thanksgiving Day (Busstag), but in 1891 Pollini decided to take the opportunity to promote his theatre in the large neighbouring towns. On 27 November he divided his troop into five groups, of which one went to Bremen and performed *Lohengrin*, another to Kiel with Gluck's *Orpheus*, and a third one to Lüneburg, though only to give a recital. Lortzing's *Zar und Zimmermann* was performed together with the ballet *Wiener Walzer* by the fourth force in Flensburg. The fifth group, consisting of an orchestra of eighty-six players plus two solo singers, under Mahler's command, went to Lübeck and played amongst other works Haydn's 'Clock' Symphony (no. 101), Wagner's *Tannhäuser* overture and the prelude to *Die Meistersinger* (K.M.).

100 (a) In G.E. dated '1894', but the references to Mahler's journey to Norway in August 1891 and to Otto's examination suggest the autumn of that year (K.M.).

(b) Dr. Spitz was a lawyer in Iglau who was engaged for some time at the theatre there. Presumably he was involved with the inheritance from Mahler's parents (K.M.).

(c) At the beginning of August 1891 Mahler went on a short journey to Scandinavia. He arrived in Copenhagen on 7 August and left again the following day for Sweden. According to La Grange he visited Hälsingborg, Gothenburg, Oslo (then Christiania), crossed the Skagerak to Frederikshavn in Jutland and returned to Hamburg via Helgoland. The whole trip only lasted about two weeks (K.M.).

(d) Like Gustav, Otto studied music at the Vienna Conservatory and had just begun his fourth year in September 1891. He did not, however, work very hard and was often absent from lessons. He finally left the Conservatory without a diploma in the spring of 1892. Otto also composed but none of his compositions survived him, and they were probably never performed in public. Some writers on Gustav Mahler have mistakenly attributed to Otto some of his elder brother's compositions, referring to a certain passage in Bruno Walter's study of Mahler. The passage in question, however, says nothing about Otto Mahler's compositions but only mentions the several circumstances which at the time (i.e. 1895) were discouraging Gustav Mahler: amongst other things, the suicide of Otto and the sad fate of his own compositions which were never performed (K.M.).

1892

101 (a) In G.E. dated 'Hamburg, 1892', but in the spring of 1892 Mahler rented a two-room flat in 10 Bundesstrasse, and as it seems that Otto was still studying I surmise that the present letter must have been written some time during the spring, probably in early May. The 'enclosed' is probably Mahler's contract with Sir Augustus Harris concerning his guest appearance in London in June and July the same year. As a lawyer Emil Freund used to help Mahler in cases like this (see also Note 102c) (K.M.).

(b) It is interesting to note Mahler's use of a word like 'molecules', a fact no doubt connected with his friendship at that time with the young physicist Arnold Berliner. The latter's doctoral thesis, published in Breslau, 1886, was entitled *Zur Molecularrefraction organischer Flüssigkeiten* (K.M.).

102 (a) The present letter must have been written before 8 June because *Siegfried* was only performed twice on a Wednesday, on 8 June and 6 July and only on the former occasion was the part of Brünnhilde sung by Rosa Sucher; at the second performance it was sung by Katherina Klafsky. However, this does not imply that the letter cannot have been *posted* on 9 June (K.M.).

(b) *o.e.* [probably from Berliner]: Mahler was at that time a guest-conductor [at Covent Garden and] at the Drury Lane Theatre [see below]. The moment this had been arranged, Mahler set about learning English. He kept a vocabulary-notebook in which he entered words and phrases he would need in the theatre. It was Arnold Berliner's task on their daily walks together to hear him and to get him to form whole sentences. Mahler took every opportunity of practising: hence the correspondence in English.

(c) On 2 April 1892 Mahler signed a contract in Hamburg with Sir Augustus Harris as conductor of the latter's German Opera Season in London for that summer. As soon as the annual Wagner Festival in Hamburg was finished on 25 May Mahler went to Cuxhaven where he boarded a steamer bound for Southampton. He travelled with an opera company consisting of about twenty-four soloists, an orchestra of eighty and a chorus of fifty-five. In addition there were two conductors, one stage designer and an attendant— in all about a hundred and sixty people. Six operas were planned for Covent Garden between 8 June and 13 July, including Wagner's *Nibelungen*, *Tristan* and Beethoven's *Fidelio*. However, from the first night the season proved so successful that the operas were not only repeated several times but two more works were included in the repertoire: *Tannhäuser* and Nessler's *Der Trompeter von Säkkingen*. As Mahler was not contractually obliged to conduct the latter work (he never conducted it in Hamburg), his colleague Leo Feld, who was familiar with it, took the baton. The tour was extended for ten days because of the extra performances. Twenty performances were given in all, most of the extra ones at Drury Lane. *Siegfried* and *Tristan* were each put on four times, the others twice. It should be mentioned too that the opera company also gave two afternoon concerts at St. James's Palace (K.M.).

103 In G.E. undated. As *Tristan* was only performed once on a Wednesday (*Mittwoch*), 15 June, and since this was the only time Rosa Sucher sang the part of Isolde, this letter must have been written between 9 and 14 June. In view of Mahler's enthusiasm it was probably written immediately after the first performance on 8 June of *Siegfried*, i.e. on 9 June (K.M.).

104 In G.E. dated '29 June', but in view of Mahler's reference to a forthcoming performance of *Rheingold* on a Wednesday, which could only have been 22 June, the present letter must have been written immediately after the first repeat performance of *Tristan* on 18 June—I would suggest 19 June (K.M.).

105 (a) In G.E. dated '15 June'. However, two remarks in the letter indicate that 14 July is a more probable date: the first performance of *Götterdämmerung* took place on 13 July, and 23 June was a Thursday, whilst 23 July fell on a Saturday (K.M.).

(b) *o.e.:* regarding 'Beethoven': Mahler here refers to Wagner's essay on Beethoven (1870), which he had given Berliner before leaving for London. Mahler often said that apart from Wagner in 'Beethoven' the only writer who had said anything of value about the nature of music was Schopenhauer in *The World as Will and Imagination* (1819). Berliner recalled him once having said that the relevant passage in Schopenhauer's work was the profoundest thing he had ever read about the nature of music.

106 During his six weeks in London Mahler was able to follow the rapid spread of the cholera epidemic from south-east Europe and Russia in both English and German papers. The first case in Hamburg was noted on 16 August (after Mahler's return to Germany) and soon the whole city was at the disease's mercy. More than nine thousand people died in the following months. One of the consequences for Mahler was that the opening of the theatre was postponed to 15 September. Mahler, however, was so panic-stricken that he could not make up his mind whether to return or not, but he eventually arrived in Hamburg at the beginning of October. Soon after he was invited to contribute to a special publication to be sold for the benefit of the destitutes in Hamburg and Altona and on 9 November Mahler wrote the following little poem:

> So reiche Kunst! So grosse Namen?!
> So heller Sterne Schein?!
> Ein farbig Bild in gold'nem Rahmen!
> Da soll ich mit hinein?

> Ich wag's! Gleicht manchmal dem Demanten
> Nicht auch ein Tropfen Thau?
> Zuletzt!—Mit einem Musikanten
> Nimmt man's nicht so genau!

The volume appeared at the end of 1892 entitled: *Deutsche Kunst zu Hamburgs Gunst. Deutsches Künstler- und Schriftsteller-Album herausgegeben zum Besten der Notleidenden in Hamburg und Altona* (K.M.).

107 It has been impossible to identify Kapellmeister Frank, but it has been established that he was never engaged at the Hamburg Theatre. It might have been a certain Karl Frank, Kapellmeister at Nuremberg (K.M.).

108 (a) In G.E. dated 'August', but Mahler's remark about the opening of the theatre on the 16th (read: 15th, i.e. of September) indicates that it must already have been September (K.M.).

(b) *F.L.:* Hamburg was at this time stricken by a serious cholera epidemic. Mahler had reached Berlin, on his way to Hamburg, when he turned back for Berchtesgaden. He spent a week in Munich.

(c) *F.L.:* After many difficulties we did manage to see each other. I was spending the summer holidays, with my wife and child, in St. Gilgen, where I was also teaching a vacation course at the Brunnwinkel settlement, so that I could not entirely dispose of my time. Hence the exchange of letters and telegrams with Mahler, who was likewise not free to do just as he liked. Two of these communications are interpolated here. The first begins with a reference to the fact that my sister Ernestine had been on a visit to Mahler just before coming to join us:

> *Undated. Berchtesgaden, August 1892*
> (A curtain blown about on my table by the
> wind has wrought devastation below it.)

Dear Fritz,
   On any day, at any hour, I am prepared to meet you in the way that Ernestine is going to discuss with you.
   It goes without saying that we must spend all our free time together.
   Let me have all details in good time—I shall be wherever you agree with Ernestine, who is best informed on all the circumstances, that I should be Ever.

Your Gustav

One of the telegrams turned out quaintly comical, and after it had duly disconcerted me we had a good laugh over it. What happened was this:

during the holiday Mahler wanted to coach some songs with a woman singer in Salzburg, and he left instructions in Berchtesgaden that, if a telegram should meanwhile arrive for him concerning this arrangement, it should be forwarded to him by means of a telegram to me. One dispatched from Salzburg indeed arrived from Mahler's old acquaintance, [Max] Steinitzer, and Justine forwarded it with her own additions. The wording that then confronted me was:

Saturday away faring student wanted Steinitzer following by special messenger. Justine.

What was meant was: 'Saturday. Wayfaring Student wanted. Steinitzer. Following by special messenger. Justine.'—meaning that Mahler was also to bring his 'Lieder eines fahrenden Gesellen'.

When the arrangement was finally made, Mahler came for me and we went to Salzburg together, where we spent the night. We returned to Berchtesgaden in the company of the above-mentioned musician from Budapest [i.e. Prof. Hans Kössler, see note 71a], to enjoy a few days of precious communion together before parting again—for another year.

111 (a) In G.E. dated 'September 1895?' to which *Löhr* adds: Addressed to Gross-Lobming in Steiermark (Styria), where we spent our summer holidays in the years 1894–6. These dates strike me as odd in relation to the concert season, but there is no other place where this letter seems to belong.

(b) One understands Löhr's doubts, since Bülow died on 12 February 1894, and had not conducted a concert in Hamburg since the 1892–3 season during which he had twice postponed concerts owing to illness. On a third occasion the same season he let Mahler take over the concert, which took place on 12 December 1892. The programme consisted of Beethoven's Fifth, Wagner's *Siegfried Idyll* and works by Mendelssohn and Lalo. Mahler is no doubt referring to that concert (K.M.).

1893

112 Not in G.E. First published by Paul Nettl in the *Neue Zürcher Zeitung* on 11 May 1958. Miss Tolney-Witt was the well-known musicologist Gisela Selden-Goth who died in 1975. She was author of several books on music and musicians. When she wrote to Mahler she was in fact only eight or nine years old (K.M.).

114 (a) *F.L.:* Nina was our very dear friend Frau Nina Hoffman-Matscheko, wife of the painter Joseph Hoffmann (1831–1900) and author of the well-known book on Dostoevsky (Berlin, 1899) and [translator and editor of *Zwölf* *geistliche Gespräche* by] Madame [Jeanne-Marie de la Motte-] Guyon (1648–1717) (Jena, 1911). She died on 10 October 1914.

Having met Mahler through us, she was for a time in close and affectionate contact with him, and her devoted efforts on his behalf and on that of his brothers and sisters cannot be too highly praised. Mahler was not always so attuned to her sensitive nature as to appreciate it to the full—and life's vicissitudes caused many misunderstandings—but when he was, they were indeed in harmony with each other. Mahler confided in her, telling her a great deal about himself. She would recall with intense emotion his visit to her in Marienbad one summer in the 1890s.

(b) *F.L.:* This is the last time that Otto Mahler is mentioned in these letters. Scarcely two years later, not yet twenty-two years of age, he put an end to his unhappy young life. True, the shackles of imposed study had fallen from him, but his sick soul, with all its pure, highly pitched inwardness, entirely turned in upon itself, had become ever more estranged from the world. Even the musical talent of which his brother thought so highly failed to find expression. It was on 6 February 1895 that he shot himself, under the roof of their old friend Nina [Hoffmann-Matscheko].

115 (a) The date of this letter is questionable since Mahler's (false) engagement in Boston was published in the paper he mentions on 17 June and Mahler's denial appeared on 19 June (K.M.).

(b) The elections Mahler refers to were those to the German Reichstag on 15 June when—as the *Hamburger Correspondenten* put it—'the three Hamburg constituencies were once again, as in 1891, lost to the socialists' (K.M.).

116 (a) *F.L.:* It was not until Thursday 13 July that I got to Mahler, at Steinbach am Attersee, this time together with my youngest sister, Gretel. On the 26th we left for home, Mahler accompanying me as far as Salzburg where I went on to spend a few days with old friends in Munich.

Mahler and his family lodged in a detached house surrounded by meadows, some quarter of an hour's walk from the village and not far from the lake. It was a spacious house, with two terraces as large as the rooms. There I came upon Mahler in the midst of composing. He regularly spent from early morning until noon shut away in the seclusion of his imaginative world. In the afternoon he would relax or, according to each day's requirement, continue.

It was at this period that Mahler, oppressed by the conditions that life imposed on him, the compulsions of the operatic and concert season, which wrung from him the utmost that his artistic temperament could give, and felt in duty bound to give, sought refuge in his system of working with the utmost concentration in the holidays, combining that with abandoning himself to nature in all its waxing bloom and beauty. This system, to which he henceforth kept, regulated the economy of his creative work and saved it for the world—something that cannot be discussed here at such length as it deserves.

Once turned outward to the world again, he doubtless bore traces of what had prevailed within him in his solitude. Yet he also enjoyed dedicating himself to the joys of the summer holidays, to his family, and to being alone with me for many hours of these two weeks, so that the sense of the old times in Perchtoldsdorf and in Hinterbrühl awakened in our hearts again.

Before me are letters I wrote to my wife at this time, testimony to its living quality. Here are two passages:

Last night, after supper, G. played many of his songs, some of them previously unknown to me, and the music touched my heart with strong and deep emotion—oh, you know it is the moods in them which shake one's innermost being to the depths, indescribably moving.

He has again composed some songs, from *Des Knaben Wunderhorn*, of course, for symphony and orchestra [*sic!*] [i.e. for voice and orchestra], and in an amazingly short time scored a whole movement of a symphony. I am to hear it today or tomorrow. I have something like an inkling that this music too is of necessity the self-amusement of a being as peculiar and as great as a man as an artist. One cannot seize it in words, one must simply understand it for oneself.

Surely this resignation on my part is highly characteristic of the situation at that time: how utterly novel and peculiarly audacious Mahler's style inevitably seemed. More than one whole generation has passed since then. (b) In the above passage from a letter to his wife Löhr mentions several newly-written compositions. He was doubtless referring to 'Des Antonius von Padua Fischpredigt', dated 8 July 1893 and 'Rheinlegendchen', dated 9 August 1893. The symphonic movement Mahler scored is the Scherzo from the Second Symphony, dated 'Steinbach Sunday 16 July 93'. He also finished the Andante that summer but only after Löhr had left on 26 July (K.M.).

1894

117 It was not until about 10 May that the announcement that Mahler's First Symphony had been placed on the programme for the festival of the 13th Allgemeiner Deutscher Musikverein (31 May–6 June) was made. The concert took place in Weimar on 3 June with Mahler conducting the symphony for the third time (K.M.).

118   The addressee is unidentified in G.E. The original letter can be seen in the Berlin Staatsbibliothek (Unter den Linden), together with the envelope addressed to Otto Lessmann. Lessmann reviewed the performance of Mahler's symphony in *Allgemeine Deutsche Musik-Zeitung* (22 June 1894), of which he was editor, and his judgement was *very* harsh. His review is valuable as it provides a list of the titles which Mahler gave the movements at the eleventh hour. It appears that the first movement had the following subtitle: 'Erwachen der Natur im Walde am frühesten Morgen' whereas in Hamburg Mahler had called it: 'Erwachen der Natur aus langem Winterschlafe' (K.M.).

119   (a) In G.E. dated 'late 1894 or January 1895', which must however be wrong since the actor Otto Brahm replaced Adolf L'Arronge as director of the Deutschen Theatre in Berlin from July 1894 (K.M.).

(b) *F.L.:* When this letter was first published (*Der Merker*, 1 March 1912, pp. 174 ff.) there was a grave error in the dating, which is herewith corrected [but nevertheless wrongly! (K.M.)]. The letter dates not, as was stated in the introductory note, which is not, incidentally, an accurate rendering of what I wrote, from Mahler's later time in Hamburg. It must have been written at least two years earlier, i.e. before the death of his brother Otto. This is evident from a passage that was then omitted and which is here communicated in full.

For the present the following elucidation must suffice: even in the years before Mahler received his appointment the need for a change had been felt, partly because of Hans Richter's being so busy in Vienna and in England, and partly because of [the director Wilhelm] Jahn's inadequacy. Time and again attention had been drawn to Mahler but in vain owing to the many opponents. The passage in the letter of 29 August 1895 [no. 137], testifying to a conversation with the then Intendant of the Court Theatre, Bezecny—a conversation that probably took place a year earlier—shows that the first steps had been taken.

120   Mahler conducted the Hamburg première of Humperdinck's opera on 25 September 1894. The world première had taken place in Weimar on 23 December the preceding year (K.M.).

121   In the Austrian National Library there is a similar letter addressed to Otto Mahler but dated 30 June (K.M.).

122   (a) Not until the summer of 1893 did Mahler continue the composition of his Second Symphony of which the first movement was composed in 1888. The Andante and the Scherzo were completed in that summer (see note 116b).

14

The funeral of Hans von Bülow in March 1894 gave him the inspiration for the Finale (text) and during the following summer and autumn he finished the symphony. The fourth movement, 'Urlicht', had already been composed (1892?). The basis for the text in the fifth movement is Klopstock's poem 'Die Auferstehung' ('Resurrection') which Mahler adapted and to which he added further stanzas. As is the case with the 'Gesellen-Lieder' he claims paternity of the text, though this is not quite true: he only wrote two-thirds of the texts in both cases. I believe we must take these slight distortions of the truth as a mark of the artist's absorption in and identification with his material (K.M.).

(b) *o.e.*: At Frau Cosima Wagner's request Mahler had rehearsed Birrenkoven in the role of Parsifal [Mahler never conducted this opera (K.M.)]. After the first rehearsal in Bayreuth Frau Cosima Wagner asked Birrenkoven to tell Mahler that no singer had ever come to Bayreuth with this role so thoroughly studied. All that remained to rehearse were passages where costume was essential, e.g. removing the armour in the third act. Birrenkoven was such a great success that Frau Wagner also engaged him to sing Lohengrin the following summer.

123   Is the date of this letter correct? It is strange that Mahler should still have had an account open in Budapest in 1894. On the other hand, the letter seems to have been written from Steinbach, Mahler's summer resort from 1893 onwards (K.M.).

125   *F.L.*: The middle-class, Old-Viennese inn Zum roten Igel, close by St. Stephen's, no longer stands. Even the square where it once stood has fallen prey to architectural changes. This was for a long time Anton Bruckner's regular haunt, and we would sit at a table with him—whether in his last days, when he was seventy, I cannot now say with certainty, though I seem to recall that it was so.

126   The Philharmonic Subscription Concerts in Hamburg were run by the Berlin concert manager Herrmann Wolff who tried unsuccessfully to continue these concerts after Bülow's death. During the 1893–4 season the concerts were conducted by various guest conductors including Felix Mottl, Hermann Levi and Anton Rubinstein .Mahler conducted a memorial concert for Bülow on 26 February 1894, and he was elected conductor for eight concerts the following season, all given in the Hamburg 'Convent Garten' the first on 22 October and the last on 11 March 1895 (Beethoven's Ninth). However, Mahler was not able to draw the hoped-for audiences; Herrmann Wolff therefore dropped these concerts and replaced them with subscription concerts by the Berlin Philharmonic Orchestra (K.M.).

1895

131 (a) In G.E. dated 'Summer 1895', but Mahler's remark concerning the subject of this letter, whom he had last seen in the previous summer 'on my way back to Hamburg', suggests a date between summer 1894 and summer 1895. My preference for the spring of 1895 derives from Mahler's remark in letter 132 about 'the poor fellow', a remark which, I assume, is a reference to the same person. Thus the letter must have been written before 11 May 1895 (K.M.).

(b) *F.L.*: After long and agonizing indecision I believe I do right in resolving not to omit this letter on grounds of its personal nature: such a humane document, throbbing with sympathy, does not deserve to be excluded from Mahler's utterances. My qualms find expression in the suppression of certain passages.

137 The motto for the sixth movement taken from *Des Knaben Wunderhorn* is from the poem 'Erlösung' ('Redemption'), but Mahler has, as usual, made radical changes:

Erlösung

MARIA: Mein Kind, sieh an die Brüste mein,
kein Sünder lass verloren sein

CHRISTUS: Mutter, sieh an die Wunden,
die ich für dein Sünden trag alle Stunden.
Vater, lass dir die Wunden mein
ein Opfer für die Sünde sein.

VATER: Sohn, lieber Sohn mein,
Alles was du begehrst, das soll sein.

Redemption

MARY: Son, behold my breast,
Let no sinner be unredeemed

CHRIST: Mother, behold the wounds
That I have hourly borne for thy sins.
Father, let my wounds
Be a sacrifice to thee for sin.

FATHER: Son, dear son of mine,
All thou desirest shall be so.   (K.M.)

138 (a) In G.E. dated '1894 or 1895'.

(b) Otto Lohse and his wife the soprano Katherina Klafsky (1855–96) could not resist a tempting offer from an American opera company, and they both left Hamburg without warning during the summer of 1895. Frau Klafsky had even received a considerable advance from Pollini. In his anger the latter reported both artists to the Society of German Theatres for breach of contract and they were of course declared guilty and fined. But that did not help Mahler who was left with Karl Pohlig (1858–1928) as his second conductor, and the chorus coaches Bruno Schlesinger (alias Walter; he only changed his name when he left Hamburg) and Walter Henry Rothschild (K.M.).

(c) The reference to 'our little house': Mahler rented the upper part of 86 Bismarckstrasse in the late summer of 1895 (K.M.).

139 Weingartner's *Kain*, referred to in G.E. in footnote no. 3, was not published until 1914, but his book, *Die Lehre von der Wiedergeburt oder das musikalische Drama* (published in September 1895), contains a draft of a mystery play, *Die Erlösung* which is based on the myth of the biblical figure of Cain (K.M.).

141 (a) In G.E. Gernsheim's first name was wrongly given as Julius (K.M.).

(b) In G.E. dated 'October, 1895'. The manuscript bears the date of '12 October' (Saturday), though written in pencil and in another handwriting (K.M.).

145. In G.E. undated.

146 This letter and the following to Anna v. Mildenburg were written in connection with the first complete performance of Mahler's Second Symphony given in Berlin on 13 December 1895 (K.M.).

149 (a) The remark in the last paragraph, here in angle brackets, and the postscript are omitted in G.E. (K.M.).

(b) Max Marschalk was music critic of the *Vossische Zeitung* and he also contributed to several music magazines (K.M.).

(c) The piano reduction (see letter 138) was published in December 1895 by the Leipzig publisher Friedrich Hofmeister who also published the full score two years later. Bruno Walter later made another piano score for four hands which was eventually published by J. Weinberger (K.M.).

151 The theatre was closed for Easter, but the Hamburg Senate had allowed Pollini to arrange choral concerts at the theatre on Good Friday. Mahler often conducted these concerts, and besides the more well-known works like Mozart's *Requiem* and Haydn's *Creation* he included modern works like Bruckner's *Te Deum* (in 1892, 1893 and 1897) and at the concert in 1893 he even conducted Bruckner's D minor Mass, the very first performance of this work in Germany (K.M.).

1896

152 In G.E. dated '1895' but Mildenburg's first appearance as Ortrud in *Lohengrin* establishes a more precise date (K.M.).

154 In G.E. undated. However the letter was most likely written sometime during 1896 (K.M.).

155 In G.E. the date is given as Mahler's, but the manuscript shows it to be a pencil addition in another hand, most probably Marschalk's (K.M.).

156 (a) The end of the letter (in angle brackets) and the postscript are omitted in G.E. (K.M.).

(b) It is evident that Mahler based the text of the first song of his 'Gesellen-Lieder' on a poem from *Des Knaben Wunderhorn*, and he obviously did so unconsciously. In Alma Mahler's *Memories and Letters* (London, 1973), p. 93, she quotes a conversation recorded by Ida Dehmel when Mahler said that the *Knaben Wunderhorn* 'poems were not complete in themselves, but blocks of marble which anyone might make his own'. During the same conversation he also admitted that he had known the poems from his earliest childhood (K.M.).

158 The postscript is omitted in G.E. (K.M.).

159 (a) Not in G.E.

(b) Mozart's *Requiem* was performed on Good Friday, 3 April, and *Fidelio* on 9 April. *Siegfried* was not performed after all. Natalie Bauer-Lechner gives an account in her reminiscences of her visit to Hamburg in April 1896 (K.M.).

160 In G.E. the date is given as Mahler's. It has, however, been added to the manuscript in pencil and in another hand (K.M.).

161 In G.E. undated, but the reference to Mahler's injured hand and the allusion to the Third Symphony's second movement (composed in the summer of 1895 and orchestrated in April 1896) make it possible to date the letter from Natalie Bauer-Lechner's reminiscences (K.M.).

162 (a) In G.E. the date is given as Mahler's. It has, however, been added to the manuscript in pencil and in another hand (K.M.).

(b) Everything in angle brackets was omitted in G.E. (K.M.).

(c) The Hamburg Stadttheater always closed the season with a cycle of Wagner's operas. Mahler was overburdened with work throughout the 1895–6 season, and he conducted on twenty occasions in April 1896 and twenty-one in May, whereas Bruno Walter appeared only seven and Pohlig nine times (in May). Thirty-eight works were performed in the two theatres (Hamburg and Altona) which Pollini ran for that month (K.M.).

163 (a) In G.E. the date is given as Mahler's. It has, however, been added to the manuscript in pencil in another hand. I do not see any reason to dispute the given date (K.M.).

(b) Marschalk's opera *Lobetanz*, like Ludwig Thuille's better-known opera, is based on a text by O. J. Bierbaum. Mahler later accepted Thuille's work for performance in Vienna; see letter 266 (K.M.).

164 (a) The date in G.E. is not Mahler's. The manuscript bears no date, but there is no reason to dispute that given (K.M.).

(b) In an unpublished letter to Marschalk preceding the present one Mahler writes of his *Rübezahl* libretto:

> Herewith I am sending you a *folk-tale*. In the absence of a better one it may perhaps be possible for you to extract a musical impression from this child which is longing to be put to music. . . . All manner of unforeseen circumstances have prevented me from writing the music and it has almost completely passed from my mind. On getting to know your *Lobetanz* music I was involuntarily reminded of it, and I now place it at your disposal in case you can find something of interest in it.

165 Anna v. Mildenburg spent her holidays with her parents in Malborghet, a small village on the little river Fella south-west of the Wörtersee (K.M.).

170 Walter visited Mahler in Steinbach that summer and gives an illuminating description of his stay in his study of Mahler (K.M.).

176 In G.E. dated '1896'.

177 In G.E. dated '1896?'. Mahler's reference to his Third Symphony suggests the summer of 1896 as a likely date for this letter (K.M.).

179 (a) In G.E. dated 'Hamburg, 1896'.

(b) It is obvious from Mahler's remark about Rudolf Krzyzanowski in this letter that his old friend disappointed him, and their collaboration in Hamburg did not improve matters. To make it worse, it seems that Pollini played the two off against each other, for example giving Krzyzanowski those operas which Mahler was contractually engaged to conduct (K.M.).

(c) *F.L.*: The reference is doubtless to my article on Ibsen's *Catalina*, in Pernerstorfer's monthly, *Deutsche Worte* (XVI, 1896).

(d) *F.L.*: Mahler's stay in Vienna the following summer [read: last summer (1896)], and the time we spent together, is confirmed by two postcards, as follows:

(1)   *Undated. Postmark: Vienna, 5 June 1896*

Dear Fritz,
    Here I am, and madly busy! I have reserved Sunday for you. If it is all

right with you, I shall come to lunch with you all about half-past one, and afterwards we'll take a stroll in the country.—When are you free tomorrow (Saturday)? I shall be at Nanna's [Spiegler] in the evening! But during the day?

Ever,

Gustav

Am staying at Natalie's [Bauer-Lechner], Jasomirgottgasse 3.

(2) *Undated. Postmark: Vienna, 9 June 1896*
Pneumatic post

Dear Fritz,

Do you feel like spending a little while with me this evening? Then come to Café Europa at 11, if it is not *inconvenient*.

Ever

Yours,

Gustav

The Café de l'Europe was then on the Stephansplatz [now in the Kärtnerstrasse]. The meeting did take place, and I recall it most tenderly. Mahler arrived in the best of spirits and stayed there with me until late into the summer's night.

180 (a) In G.E. dated 'approx. October 1896'. (b) After only two seasons at the Hamburg Theatre Walter went on Mahler's recommendation to Breslau where he was appointed second conductor. At the beginning everything went well, but soon conditions became intolerable for Walter who disclosed his troubles to Mahler. Leopold Weintraub (18??–19??) was first Kapellmeister in Breslau (K.M.).

181 In G.E. dated 'Hamburg, 1896'.

182 In G.E. the date is given as Mahler's ('Hamburg, 27 January 1896'). The manuscript is undated but bears two postmarks: 'Hamburg, 27 September 1896' and the arrival postmark 'Berlin, 28 September 1896' (K.M.).

183 In G.E. dated [Sunday] '2 February 1896' (with the month in Roman numerals), but the context indicates a later date, possibly November 1896. Mahler's remark, 'the day after tomorrow, which is Wednesday' proves that he is writing the letter on a Monday not a Sunday. If we assume that the letter was written in November the facts fit together rather better: 2 November 1896 was a Monday, and nine days later (11 Nov.) Nikisch conducted the première of the Minuet of the Third Symphony in Berlin (K.M.).

184 In G.E. undated.

185 In G.E. dated '18 February 1896' (with the month in Roman numerals), but Mahler's reference to the 'Flower' piece suggests that the letter ought to be re-dated November 1896. See also letter 188 (K.M.).

186 In G.E. dated '1897' but the context suggests an earlier date, possibly the end of 1896 (K.M.).

187 Walter wrote in a letter to his parents (17 January 1897) that Mahler had written advising him to remain in Breslau. The present letter could well be the one in question, making December 1896 its likely date. Things did not improve for Walter in Breslau, and a month later he gave his notice. See also note 203 (K.M.).

188 (a) In G.E. the date is given as Mahler's, but on the manuscript there is only a pencilled date in another hand ('2 December 1896') and it does not correspond with that in G.E. (K.M.).

(b) Weingartner's performance of three movements from Mahler's Third Symphony took place in Berlin on 9 March 1897 (K.M.).

189 (a) In G.E. dated 'December 1896'. The manuscript bears the date '4 December 1896' added in pencil in another hand, possibly Max Marschalk's (K.M.).

(b) In G.E. the name of Richard Strauss is replaced by an 'X'. In the first draft to this note I wrote: 'I have very strong reason to believe that "X" in this letter stands for Richard Strauss' and I added 'we know from Alma Mahler— and from Mahler himself—that he and Strauss put the best face they could on their relationship because they "needed" each other, especially at the start of their careers and Mahler in particular needed Strauss. The antagonism which prevailed between them is clearly described in Alma Mahler's book and the distance is also obvious from the greetings Strauss sent Mahler on the latter's fiftieth birthday. However, that did not exclude a mutual respect for each other's craftsmanship. The lack of understanding and of interest is also, I believe, to be deduced from the few performances they gave of each other's works. In Mahler's lifetime Strauss only performed the former's First and Fourth symphonies plus some songs. In a memorial concert in 1911 he conducted Mahler's Third Symphony' (K.M.).

(c) The passage in angle brackets was omitted in G.E. (K.M.).

190 In G.E. the date is given as Mahler's, but the manuscript has only a date in pencil probably by Marschalk (K.M.).

191 In G.E. the date is given as Mahler's, but the manuscript only bears Mahler's somewhat cryptic date (omitted in G.E.) in the postscript, presumably meaning: between 8 and 11 December 1896. One notices the question mark against the date which suggests that Mahler is having a lark with Marschalk (K.M.).

192 In G.E. undated.

193 In G.E. undated. The references to *The Water Carrier* and *The Merry Wives* suggest a date in December 1896 (K.M.).

1897

195 In G.E dated 'April 1897' but the reference to the performance of Gernsheim's symphony establishes a more correct date (K.M.).

196 (a) In G.E. dated as though by Mahler, but the manuscript has only a date added in pencil, probably by Marschalk (K.M.).
(b) The remark 'I shall be staying at the Hotel Europa in Sendig' does not make sense. Mahler must have meant the hotel Europäischer Hof in Sidonienstrasse in Dresden (K.M.).

197 In G.E. dated 'January or February 1897'.

198 In G.E. dated '1897'. Mahler handed in his resignation in the middle of January (K.M.).

200 In the first two sentences Mahler is making a pun on the German substantive *Junge* = boy, and the verb *jung* = to be young (K.M.).

201 In G.E. dated 'December 1896' but according to contemporary notices in the Hamburg press Anna v. Mildenburg went to Bayreuth during February 1897. Between 31 January 1897 and 27 March she did not appear in Hamburg (K.M.).

203 In G.E. dated 'approx. Spring 1897'. *Bruno Walter* comments as follows: I had offered my resignation in Breslau as from the end of the season, but had not yet found another job. I wrote to Mahler, explaining that it would be best if I did my year's military service, but that I had not the funds to keep me going. Mahler replied (the letter has unfortunately been lost) that I should do my military service, that he would keep me in funds and that I was to say how much I needed. His entirely spontaneous offer was very touching. How generous he was becomes clear when one knows that his annual income in Hamburg was 13,000 marks (12,000 marks salary and 1,000 marks 'benefit'), so that the 1,200 marks he offered me was more than a month's salary.

204 In G.E. date given as Mahler's, but the manuscript has only a date added in pencil in another hand (K.M.).

205 After the concert in Berlin Mahler went on a month's concert tour to Moscow, Munich and Budapest (K.M.).

206 In G.E. dated 'March 1897' only, but the last rehearsal took place on 8 March and the concert was the following day (K.M.).

207 The music critic of the *Berliner Börsen Courier* was Oscar Eichberg; see letter 129 (K.M.).

14*

210 In G.E. dated 'March 1897'. Written the day after the concert which took place on Monday 15 March (K.M.).

211 In G.E. dated 'Berlin, 19 March 1897', but Mahler refers to his concert in Moscow the previous day. The programme consisted of Beethoven's Fifth, Wagner's *Siegfried Idyll* and the *Rienzi* Overture and Schumann's Piano Concerto, with Victor Staub, who also played several solo piano pieces (K.M.).

212 In G.E. dated 'March 1897' only.

213 *F.L.:* Mahler was then, I believe, travelling from Moscow, where he had been conducting concerts, via Vienna to Hamburg. During this visit the final negotiations between the Vienna Court Theatre authorities and himself began in earnest. The vicissitudes and agitations that they involved are reflected in the next few letters. Once again it seemed at first as if the efforts of those qualified to judge, and those friends of Mahler's who were both intellectually and socially of high standing, would be wrecked by various counter-influences. Finally, however, a surprising decision taken by the Court Chamberlain, Prince Rudolf Liechtenstein, led to Mahler's appointment at the Vienna Opera from 1 May.

214 *F.L.:* Mahler had gone from Vienna to Budapest (he writes on the writing-paper of the Budapest hotel, The Queen of England) in order to conduct a grand special Philharmonic Concert for the benefit of the charitable funds of the Budapest Journalists' Association. The programme consisted of (1) the *Rienzi* Overture, (2) 'Dich, teure Halle' from *Tannhäuser* (Fräulein Sedlmair), (3) Mahler's Third Symphony, 2nd movement, (4) Weber's *Aufforderung zum Tanze* (*Invitation to the Dance*) for orchestra adapted by Felix Weingartner, (5) Leonora's recitative and aria from *Fidelio* (Fräulein Sedlmair) and (6) Beethoven's Fifth Symphony.

216 In G.E. dated '7 April 1897', but according to Karpath's account of Mahler's stay in Vienna (*Begegnung mit dem Genius,* p. 49) as well as the drafts for the G.E. (in my possession) the date should be 4 April. This also tallies with the fact that Mahler returned to Hamburg on 8 April (K.M.).

217 The *Wiener Abendpost* was the official voice of the Austrian government. In the issue of 6 April 1897 the following notice appeared: 'Herr Gustav Mahler has been engaged as Kapellmeister by the Imperial and Royal Court Opera' (K.M.).

221 The first paragraph (in angle brackets) is omitted in G.E. Mahler never performed any of Marschalk's operas (K.M.).

223 (a) In G.E. dated 'approx. Spring 1897', but the reference to Mahler's appointment establishes a more precise date (K.M.).

(b) Walter went to Pressburg (Bratislava) for the 1897–8 season, and from 1898 to 1900 he was first conductor in Riga (K.M.).

225 In G.E. dated '13 April 1897', but Karpath gives 23 April in his memoirs (see note 216) and in his drafts for the original edition of Mahler's letters and this corresponds better with the fact that Mahler's last performance in Hamburg was on 24 April. Although Karpath's account is sometimes confused regarding the dates attributed to the letters included in his memoirs, it is clear that the present letter must have been written during Mahler's last week in Hamburg (K.M.).

226 In G.E. dated 'Hamburg, 25 [?] 1897'.

VI: Vienna (1) (1897–1901)

1897

227 Not in G.E.

228 In G.E. dated 'approx. end of April': Mahler's meeting took place on 2 May, so this letter must be dated either the same day or shortly thereafter (K.M.).

229 (a) In G.E. dated only '1897': Guido Adler was at that time Professor at the German University in Prague. From 1898 he was appointed to the same position in Vienna. Mahler's remark about the 'autumn' convinces me that the letter should be dated spring or early summer 1897 (K.M.).

(b) Adler succeeded in obtaining subsidies for the publication of Mahler's Symphonies 1 and 3, plus the orchestral parts for the Second Symphony, from the Gesellschaft zur Förderung deutscher Wissenschaft, Litteratur und Kunst in Böhmen (Society for the Promotion of German Science, Literature and Art in Bohemia). Mahler signed a contract with the big printing firm Josef Eberle & Co. in Vienna who engraved and printed his works and sold them through the Viennese publisher Josef Weinberger. The various editions and arrangements of these compositions appeared in the course of 1899 and 1900. At the same time Weinberger re-published the score of the Second Symphony including Hermann Behn's arrangement for two pianos. Weinberger also published Mahler's twelve songs from *Des Knaben Wunderhorn* (1900), and 'Das klagende Lied' (1902) (K.M.).

232 In G.E. dated 'June 1897'. The reference to the two Wagner operas establishes the correct date, however, as the only time they were performed in the order Mahler specifies was 5 and 6 June (K.M.).

234 *o.e.* ('Jahn, Richter and Fuchs'): Wilhelm Jahn, Mahler's predecessor as Director of the Vienna Court Opera, and the Court Opera conductors, Hans Richter and Johann Nepomuk Fuchs. Mahler would have liked to be on good terms with Richter, who had acquired a certain dignity from being a pupil of Richard Wagner's, but unfortunately Richter's behaviour and, finally, his departure prevented this.

237 *F.L.:* Forwarded to me from town [Vienna] to Grinzing, where we were spending the summer holidays. The fact that Mahler was tied to Vienna that summer shows what a vast amount of work confronted him on taking up his appointment. [Löhr is wrong as the preceding letters indicate: Mahler was in fact away from Vienna most of June and July, and the Opera opened the new season on 1 August (K.M.).]

239 *o.e.:* It seems that Bruno Walter had asked Mahler if it would not be better for him (Walter) to gain more experience from another year's work in opera, and only then do his year's military service. Shortly afterwards, on Mahler's recommendation he was engaged as first conductor in Pressburg.

240 In G.E. dated 'August 1898', but Schuch's jubilee was in 1897 as he had been Kapellmeister in Dresden since 1872 (K.M.).

241 In G.E. dated 'September 1897', but the postscript, which was omitted in G.E., proves that the letter must have been written before 1 September. The opening of the letter was also omitted in G.E. (K.M.).

242 In G.E. undated, but given note 240 the date is clear (K.M.).

243 In G.E. dated 'about 1898'. I believe, however, that the reference to Mahler's approaching appointment as director of the Court Opera establishes a more definite date (K.M.).

244 (a) In G.E. dated 'Vienna 1897'. It is clear that the letter must be dated after 8 October when Mahler took up his appointment as Director of the Court Opera (K.M.).

(b) The passage in angle brackets is omitted in G.E. (K.M.).

245 The following note by Karpath was among his papers and was intended for the original German edition of the letters:

Between the last letter [it is not clear which letter Karpath means] and this note serious tension arises. I wrote Mahler a very lachrymose letter in which I lamented his disregard. Thereupon I received this note. Even though he met me in the street two hours later, my letter brought not a word of response from him. I must remark that he himself would not have written this if I had not asked for the return of a letter from Eduard Schütt [conductor and pianist active in Vienna, b. 1856, d. 1933 (K.M.)], which was enclosed with the note.

1898

246 (a) Not in G.E.

(b) The two *Wunderhorn* songs referred to are (8) 'Lied des Verfolgten in Turm' and (9) 'Wo die schönen Trumpeten blasen', both sketched and probably also finished during the summer of 1898. Only the sketches for the edition for voice and piano have been found in manuscript, and both are dated July 1898 and dedicated to Nina Spiegler. The numbers are those designated in the printed edition (K.M.).

247 Not in G.E.

248 (a) According to G.E. undated. However the original letter indicates the date clearly in Mahler's hand (K.M.).

(b) *o.e.*: Bruno Walter replied saying he thought it still too soon for him to go to Vienna as conductor; he did not yet feel sufficiently experienced, and he asked Mahler to give him more time to develop. Walter still recalls how heavily Mahler's offer weighed on his youthful mind (he was only 22). Unfortunately, Mahler completely misinterpreted his uncertain, hesitantly negative reply. Having written warmly and joyfully, Mahler was bitterly disappointed that Walter did not leap at the chance with equal warmth and joy. Mahler's resentment, and indeed suspicion, regarding the genuineness of the reasons Walter gave for refusing resulted from his disappointment, combined with the intensity of his feelings about any obstacle to his artistic plans. As the following letter shows, Mahler even put an unfavourable interpretation on Walter's anxious question as to whose successor he would become.

249 In G.E. dated 'Autumn 1898', but according to Walter's *Briefe* (Frankfurt, 1969) November is a more precise date (K.M.).

1899

250 In G.E. dated '3 March 1899'.

251 In G.E. dated 'April, 1899'.

252 (a) In G.E. this letter and no. 253 were dated 'June 1898', but the contents point to 1899 (cf. letter 253 *re* Fuchs's wounded hand) (K.M.).

(b) Lipiner's tragedy *Adam* (3 acts) formed the prologue (Vorspiel) of a trilogy called *Christus*. The other parts were entitled *Maria Magdalena*, *Judas Ischarioth* and *Paulus in Rom*. Only *Adam* was published—posthumously, in Stuttgart, 1913 (K.M.).

254 (a) *F.L.*: What more could one say after such words have said all, with their overwhelmingly sweet affection, their mystical longing for the unfragmented ray of pure light? This is most truly the conclusion of Mahler's *letters* to me, speaking too for many a period in the last decade of his life and our friendship. What follows, dating from about 1900 onwards, are, with a few exceptions arising from particular circumstances, some examples of brief messages with news that I continued to receive: messages sent out of the press of Mahler's unparalleled Vienna work and achievement, from the midst of which he would with difficulty find a chance of our meeting, say to take one of our traditional walks in the Prater or in Heiligenstadt-Nussdorf. Although our relationship remained as constant as ever, its expression could not satisfy us. In any case, the need to put our thoughts into writing, as we had in earlier days when we did not see each other more than once a year, was no longer there. Once the season was over, Mahler took flight—took refuge in his own work, at summer resorts where my material circumstances did not permit me to follow him. Only on one occasion did I visit him at Maiernigg, where I walked through the woods with him up to his hermitage.

(b) From Alma Mahler's *Memories* it is evident that it was Mahler's marriage which prevented Löhr from seeing Mahler as often as before. Alma Mahler particularly disliked Mahler's old friends, and according to her they did not like her either (K.M.).

255 Not in G.E.

1900

259 In G.E. dated 'approx. October 1900'.

260 Not in G.E.

261 Not in G.E.

262 Lipiner's *Hippolytos*, a tragedy in three acts, was sketched and finished in a fortnight. It was posthumously published, in 1913, by Spemann in Stuttgart, in a volume including *Adam* (K.M.).

264 Did Mahler ever consider using Lipiner's *Hippolytos* as the basis for an opera libretto? In 1910 it was rumoured in several Austrian and German newspapers and magazines that Mahler intended to compose an opera called *Theseus*, a subject also based on Greek mythology, in particular the legend of Phaedra. There is no smoke without fire and the rumour can hardly have been utterly unfounded. We know that in the summer of 1910 Mahler was very close to Lipiner and he probably re-read many of his works then (see note 382). I have found many points of resemblance between certain of Lipiner's poems from his *Buch der Freude* (1880) and the dramatic headings Mahler jotted down in the sketches of his Tenth Symphony, e.g. he calls the third movement 'Purgatorio', a title also used for one of the poems (K.M.).

265 In G.E. dated 'end of 1900' but was probably written shortly after Mahler's arrival in Vienna in August or September 1900 (K.M.).

266 In G.E. dated '1900'.

1901

267 (a) in G.E. undated.

(b) *F.L.*: Here is perhaps the place to give some examples of the messages I have (earlier) described (cf. note 254a):

Come to lunch with us at once! Jaunt in afternoon! All Three? If you feel like it! In great haste

Gustav

The utmost I can manage would be a meeting tomorrow (Wednesday) between 2 and 3 o'clock in the Café Imperial.

Yours ever, au revoir,
Gustav

If you are coming to the final rehearsal tomorrow, Tuesday, half past twelve (and Uda etc.), come to the office a few minutes earlier.

Ever yours,
Gustav

Dear Fritz, Sometimes it does strike me as strange, being in *Vienna* and never setting eyes on you. One ought to be able to manage a quarter of an hour for ourselves now and then. There's nothing I *can* contrive except about five o'clock or so in the evening. Well, old friend? When is your Gustav to see you again? Couldn't you come some *evening*?

268 At the world première of 'Das klagende Lied' Mahler called for *two* soprano voices, Elise Elizza and Anna v. Mildenburg. The other soloists were the contralto Edith Walker and the tenor Fritz Schrödter. On 20 January 1902 he gave a repeat performance in Vienna. Mahler once called this composition, not unjustly, his 'child of sorrow', its being one of his most neglected works; aside from these performances he only conducted it once more, in Amsterdam (Macrh 1906, repeated the following day by Mengelberg), and in March 1910 it was performed in Prague and Graz by local conductors. The music was published in 1902 (K.M.).

269 Immediately after the performance of 'Das klagende Lied' Mahler went to Abbazia, spending about a fortnight in a sanatorium there (K.M.).

270 (a) In G.E. dated 'beginning of 1901'. Walter had been engaged to the

singer Elsa Korneck, née Wirtschaft (1871–1945) since Christmas 1898; their marriage establishes the date of the letter.

(b) Like his three earlier symphonies Mahler sold his Fourth to the printing firm Josef Eberle & Co. in Vienna, who, however, leased the publication rights to the Viennese music publishing firm of Ludwig Doblinger. The full score, the piano score and the fourth movement (voice/piano) appeared in January 1902 (K.M.).

271 In G.E. dated 'Spring 1901', but I believe the letter can be placed more exactly as the season at the Vienna Opera usually ended about the middle of June, and as a rule Mahler went to Maiernigg immediately. The date and first sentence of letter 273 suggest Saturday 8 June (K.M.).

272 (a) Not in G.E.

(b) *The original German text:*

Diese Alles, was Du auf der Karte siehst ist die
Ansicht, wie sie hier gewöhnlich ist.
Ich schicke sie, trotz Du sonst nicht meiner Ansicht
bist. Vielleicht bist ihrer sie, wenn Du sie liest!

Da hier noch ein schönes Platzel
so schrieb ich hier ein kleines Satzel
leider nur in Eil' und Hatzel
—von einem Vers ist's nur ein Latzel,
—hoffentlich krieg' ich kein Patzel!

Diese Zeile schrib' ich nur,
weil sie passt in die Architektur!

Ich sitze hier in dem Kaffé
und grüsse Dich, Dein treuer G.
u. auch dabei Natalie!
o je o je! sie fällt in den See
das ist ihr 'Portrait'!

273 (a) *o.e.:* The letters to Max Kalbeck, critic, poet and translator, are for the most part concerned with Kalbeck's new translations of Mozart's libretti. Kalbeck's versions of the libretti for *Figaro* and *Don Giovanni* were used in memorable performances under Mahler's baton. *The Queen of Spades*, *Otello* (Verdi) and later *Tosca* (Puccini) [the latter was not in the repertoire under Mahler (K.M.)] were also translated by Kalbeck. Kalbeck certainly did not unreservedly profess the materialist philosophy against which Mahler polemicizes in this first letter.

(b) Offenbach's *Hoffmanns Erzählungen* was not however abandoned completely and was performed on 11 November. Mahler used the dress-rehearsal as an 'excuse' to arrange a new meeting with Alma Maria Schindler—his future wife—whom he had met for the first time on 7 November (cf. her *Memories and Letters*, London, 1973, pp. 5 and 15) (K.M.).

(c) *The Queen of Spades* was first performed on 9 December 1902 and was repeated about thirty times during the following five years (K.M.).

274 In G.E. dated 'Summer 1901'. Walter had much difficulty releasing himself from his contract with the Royal Opera-House in Berlin and only effected it late in August (K.M.).

275 The projected performance of Mahler's Third Symphony by Richard Strauss did not materialize until November 1911, after Mahler's death. In January 1907 Mahler conducted the symphony in Berlin (K.M.).

277 Not in G.E.

278 (a) In G.E. dated 'probably 1901', with the remark 'just leaving', in which case the letter should be dated August as the new season started on the 18th; according to Bauer-Lechner's *Erinnerungen* Mahler's last day in Maiernigg that summer was 20 August, and this is almost certainly the right date. The same source also tells us that during the summer Mahler composed six of his songs to poems by Friedrich Rückert: 'Ich atmet einen linden Duft', 'Blicke mir nicht in die Lieder', 'Ich bin der Welt abhanden gekommen' and (the first?) three songs of the 'Kindertotenlieder', plus 'Der Tamboursg'sell' and a sketch of his Fifth Symphony, probably the first three movements (K.M.).

(b) Gretchen, mentioned in the postscript, is probably Henriette Mankiewicz's daughter who was studying in Munich at the time (K.M.).

281 In G.E. dated 'November 1901'.

282 In G.E. dated 'December 1901'; Mahler left Vienna on 9 December (K.M.).

VII: Vienna (2) (1902–1907)

1902

283 In G.E. only dated '1902'. Mahler's engagement to Alma was publicly disclosed in a Viennese newspaper on 27 December 1901—to the surprise of everyone, even Mahler's most intimate friends. Bruno Walter described the bridegroom's attitude in a letter to his parents: 'He [Mahler] welcomed me saying, "What do you say, the newspapers have it that I'm engaged! Yes,

actually, I am but, please, do not congratulate me, or rather do it quickly—
right, now we won't talk about it any more" ' (K.M.).

285   In G.E. undated.

286   In G.E. dated 'Summer 1903', but 1902 seems a more suitable date, as
it is recorded that Mahler and Roller met for the first time at the Max
Klinger exhibition arranged by the Vienna *Secession* on 15 April 1902. In
fact, it was Mahler who opened the exhibition, conducting a chorus from
Beethoven's Ninth Symphony which he had arranged for six trombones.
During a subsequent discussion of *Tristan* Mahler became fascinated by
Roller's ideas and shortly after invited him to design a production for the
Court Opera. The première took place the following year, on 21 February
1903. The present letter is no doubt written immediately before Mahler and
Alma went to Krefeld in Germany (K.M.)..

287   In G.E. dated 'Summer 1903', cf. above note (K.M.).

288   (a) In G.E. dated 'Summer 1903', cf. note 286 (K.M.).
(b) Roller's appointment as chief stage designer to the Court Opera took
effect from 1 June 1903 (K.M.).

289   (a) It has proved impossible to identify Herr Kafka who is not mentioned
in the official records of the Court Opera (K.M.).
(b) Professor Johann Ress was a well-known teacher of singing in Vienna
(K.M.).
(c) No further works by J. Reiter were put on at the Opera (K.M.).

291   Not in G.E.

292   In G.E. addressed to the conductor Fritz Steinbach, in Cologne, with a
suggested date of 1902.

The remark in the postscript about the theatre whose acoustics were as yet
untried confirms the year, and as the letter is on Mahler's Maiernigg writing-
paper it was presumably written during the summer vacation. It cannot
therefore have been to Steinbach who was not appointed conductor of the
Cologne Gürzenich Orchestra until March 1903 when he succeeded the then-
famous conductor Franz Wüllner who had died suddenly on 9 September
1902 (in 1902 he was 'only' Kapellmeister of the Meiningen Court Orchestra).

There are two indications that Wüllner was planning a performance of
Mahler's Third Symphony in Cologne, the first in a letter to Guido Adler
from Mahler's sister, Justine Rosé, dated 27 August 1902. She writes from
Edlach (Semmering, Austria): 'Yesterday Gustav stopped here for a day
on his return from Maiernigg to Vienna, bringing with him the completed
Fifth Symphony; as a result he was in high spirits. This winter several
performances of his works are to take place—on 19 November the Third
Symphony in Cologne.' From an article in a Cologne newspaper in con-

nection with Mahler's première of his Fifth Symphony there on 18 October 1904, we learn that a projected performance of his Third Symphony in 1902 had finally been cancelled because of Franz Wüllner's sudden death.

To my mind a closer examination of certain expressions in the letter corroborates my choice of Wüllner as the correct addressee. One should bear in mind that the latter was born in 1832 (thus was seventy in 1902), whereas Steinbach was only five years Mahler's senior, and that Wüllner had behind him a long and extraordinary career which Mahler certainly knew about. Thus it was Wüllner who was in charge of the premières of *Das Rheingold* and *Die Walküre* in Munich. Steinbach, however, did not have and never gained a similar reputation—though he was known as a fine interpreter of Brahms's music—and certainly would never have caused Mahler to use expressions like 'Revered Maestro' (Verehrter Herr und Meister), and 'highly esteemed Herr Doctor' (hochgeehrter Herr Doktor), etc., when addressing himself to him. Steinbach was, moreover, never addressed as Doktor, unlike Wüllner who received this distinction from the University of Munich in 1873; I think it is amply proved in the present collection of letters that Mahler never made excessive use of titles and mere words, and I cannot see why he should have made an exception of Fritz Steinbach. It is my guess that the letter was found in the archives of the Gürzenich Orchestra, without an envelope, and it was assumed that it was written to Steinbach in connection with the 1904 performance of Mahler's Third Symphony. (K.M.).

293 (a) This letter was probably written shortly after the première in Krefeld (K.M.).

(b) Mahler is referring to Nodnagel's book *Jenseits von Wagner und Liszt* (Königsberg, 1902) which includes a short outline of the symphony. When two years later Nodnagel published a separate elaborate study of the symphony Mahler called it—in a letter to his wife—a 'ghastly analysis' (K.M.).

294 In G.E. undated.

1903

295 In G.E. dated 'Autumn 1903'. When Mahler mentions the 'second night of *Tristan*' he is almost certainly referring to the new staging by Roller which had its première on 21 February 1903. The first repeat performance was on 3 March, and the only *Friday* between the two performances was 27 February, indicating a date between 23 and 25 February (K.M.).

296 In G.E. undated.

297 (a) Buths gave a repeat performance of the Second Symphony two years later at the Lower Rhine Music Festival (K.M.).

(b) Mahler could not attend Buths' first performance of the symphony because he was conducting his First Symphony in Lemberg the same evening (K.M.).

299 In G.E. undated. My assumption that this letter has a connection with letter 298 is only guesswork. It might well have been written earlier than no. 298 (K.M.).

300 In G.E. dated 'approximately 1900' but the allusion to Berghof suggests the letter was written during the summer. Furthermore, in a letter dated 15 November 1903 (Austrian National Library) Goldmark writes to a friend that Mahler has refused to perform the revised score of *Merlin* (text by Lipiner) and that he, Goldmark, had therefore offered his opera to Frankfurt/M. (cf. letter 306). The opera was put on there on 14 February 1904 (K.M.).

306 The date of this letter cannot be right as Mahler was in Frankfurt/M. on that day conducting his Third Symphony. According to Alma Mahler he returned, however, to Vienna on the following day (K.M.).

1904

308a,b (a) In G.E. dated 'January 1903'. The 'performance on Saturday' was probably the dress-rehearsal on 16 January, and consequently the letter must have been written between 10 and 14 January (K.M.).

(b) In G.E. these two letters to Kalbeck were numbered as if they were only one, but it is obvious that they are in fact separate, and this is confirmed by the originals in the Austrian National Library in Vienna (K.M.).

309 Specht's monograph appeared in June 1905 (57 pages) and was, incidentally, the second book to have appeared on Mahler. Eight years later, in 1913, Specht published a more extensive volume which remained for many years one of the best books on the composer and his music. It was reprinted several times, and also revised, but owing to the shortage of paper after World War I the music examples and fine illustrations in the first edition were abandoned (K.M.).

310 Mengelberg's difficulties with the Concertgebouw Orchestra nearly led to his resignation as conductor. Regarding Mahler's visit to Amsterdam later that year, cf. letter 316 (K.M.).

313 (a) In G.E. dated 'Summer 1906'. Mahler completed the Sixth Symphony in the summer of 1904. A fair copy of the score (Gesellschaft der Musikfreunde in Vienna) is dated May 1905, and the first performance took place in Essen on 27 May 1906 (K.M.).

(b) *o.e.:* This is Mahler's reply to a letter in which Walter argues against programme-music, criticizing in particular a passage in Wagner's letter about Liszt's symphonic writing. Mahler is replying after completing his Sixth Symphony, that is, in the summer of 1906 [1904], and his letter expresses the gay, almost exuberant mood that always came over him when he had finished a work.

315 Mahler's remark about his Fourth Symphony seems a little unreasonable as this work had had twelve performances since its première in November 1901 (K.M.).

316 For many years it has remained a mystery whether Mahler conducted both performances of the Fourth Symphony in Amsterdam on 23 October 1904 or whether Mengelberg conducted the second one following the interval. The programme (p. 282) establishes Mahler as the conducter in both cases; this is confirmed by a letter written to Alma before the concert, and found among her papers. It reads: 'Well, Almscherl, I am now leaving for the concert in which I shall conduct my Fourth twice in succession.' (K.M.).

1905

318 In G.E. dated 'approx. 1905'. The concert mentioned in the original footnote took place on 29 January 1905 in Vienna and was repeated on 3 February. Besides the 'Kindertotenlieder', four Rückert Songs and seven songs from *Des Knaben Wunderhorn* were performed. Three male singers participated (*not* singing in duets, which is today—to my mind—a bad practice in concert halls and on records) and Mahler conducted the Hofopernorchester. Parts of the same programme were repeated in June that year in Graz (K.M.).

319 Karpath's article quoted the present letter almost verbatim. In his review of the Vienna performance (see above) Karpath had asserted that Mahler's songs from the *Wunderhorn* were the first and only ones which revealed the 'pathetic beauty' of these poems. The editor of the magazine had questioned this, thereby prompting both this letter and some days later a second article by Karpath (K.M.).

320 The music publishing firm Lauterbach & Kuhn (Leipzig) had Mahler's Seventh Symphony scheduled for publication early in 1909, but in the meantime the firm was taken over by Messrs. Bote & Bock in Berlin. This firm published the piano score (prepared by Alfredo Casella) and the full score later in the autumn 1909 (K.M.).

321 In G.E. undated. The allusion to the new production of *Don Giovanni* determines the year in which the letter was written. In addition we know from Alma Mahler's *Memories* (letter 73) that that year the Mahler family went on holiday on 15 June, and from that we can establish the letter's full date (K.M.).

323 In G.E. dated 1904, but the new staging of *Die Walküre* was given its première on 27 February 1906, thus making 1905 a better choice (K.M.).

324 The revised version of *Figaro* by Mahler and Kalbeck was produced in Vienna on 30 March 1906. Kalbeck contributed a new (more literal) German translation and Mahler reinstated the original trial scene in the third act before the sextet. He also composed some new secco recitativos. A vocal score —anonymous—of this version (subtitled: *Bearbeitung der Wiener Hofoper*, and with a short introduction, probably by Mahler and Kalbeck) was published in September 1907 by C. F. Peters in Leipzig. See also letter 370 (K.M.).

325 Mengelberg made his first guest appearance in New York at the beginning of November 1905, with great success. The present letter (in G.E. only dated '1905') was very probably written shortly after his return, in November or December (K.M.).

1906

326 In G.E. dated 'Vienna 1906'.

327 In G.E. dated 'approx. 1906'.

328 In G.E. dated '1906'.

329 In G.E. undated.

330 In G.E. dated 'October 1904'. To my mind the last paragraph suggests the letter should be dated later. Mahler's remark beginning 'Now all at once . . .' could hardly have been written in October 1904 since the Fifth Symphony was performed for the first time that very month, and for the second time the following February—on neither occasion successfully! The letter's continuation 'The Sixth Symphony must just . . .' seems to indicate that this work had just been performed and that the reviews Mahler 'gave up reading after the first one' concern either the première of the Sixth in Essen in May 1906, or possibly the later performance (at which Mahler was present) in Berlin in October 1906 under Oskar Fried's baton. The Berlin critic Leopold Schmidt reviewed both performances. His first comments, appearing on 2 June, were very lukewarm and reserved, but he was, he declared, 'more than willing to change his opinion, should the next performance convince him that he ought to do so'. It didn't! (K.M.).

334 *F.L.:* Understandably enough, Mahler did not trouble himself further about the author of the hymn on which he based the first part of his Eighth Symphony. The poet's identity is not certain, but the ascription to Maurus Hrabanus, which Mahler took from his 'old church book', is wrong. Cf. Blume-Dreves, *Analecta hymnia aevi L.*, 2nd series, Leipzig, 1907, pp. 180 ff., and Dreves, *Hymnologische Studien zu Venantius Fortunatus und Rabanus Maurus*, Munich, 1908, pp. 55 ff.

338 (a) The date of this letter cannot be right as Mahler was in Salzburg between 14 and 21 August to conduct two performances of Mozart's *Figaro*. This is doubtless a misreading of the postmark (the envelope is no longer extant). 28 August would probably be more correct, or perhaps 18 July? (K.M.).

(b) The Cologne horn-player, Max Hesse, had played in the first performance of the Fifth Symphony on 18 October 1904 and had been met with general approval by the critics (K.M.).

339 *o.e.:* Reitler went to Salzburg and discussed all the details of the project with Mahler. The Third Symphony was agreed on, because in his view it was the easiest to understand. Mahler made the stipulation that his symphony was to be the first work in the programme (the concerts of Messrs. Chevillard and Colonne at that time usually included anything from seven to twelve items) and that he should have at least five rehearsals. He intended taking the bells, first trombone and Flügelhorn with him from Vienna. Colonne made petty difficulties, even trying to force a reduction of the orchestra from the size stipulated. That was one reason why he suggested the Fifth or Sixth instead of the Third Symphony.

341 Mahler undertook several revisions of his Fifth Symphony and three editions were published during his lifetime (see also letters 440–1 and 443) (K.M.).

343 At the time Mahler wrote this letter his Sixth Symphony had only been performed once (in Essen), but other performances were scheduled and took place as follows: October 1906 in Berlin; November 1906 in Munich (two performances); January 1907 in Vienna; and in Leipzig and Dresden in March and April 1907. At the latter performance only the two middle movements were given. Mengelberg did not conduct it until 1916 (K.M.).

344 I am very doubtful about the date attributed to this letter, and am most inclined to ascribe it to December 1905 when Mahler performed his Fifth Symphony in Breslau on Wednesday the 20th. In that case Mahler would have arrived in Breslau on the Sunday morning of 17 December, three days before the concert. To my mind it makes no sense for Mahler to give the playing time of his Fifth Symphony when he has come, according to the date in G.E., to conduct his Third (cf. also note 346). The playing time of the Fifth has by the way certainly been wrongly transcribed. The text of the German edition reads: 'Meine Symphonie, die V., dauert knapp 3/4 Stunden.' It should presumably be '5/4 Stunden' i.e. about 75 minutes (K.M.).

345 In G.E. undated.

346 In G.E. dated 'late December 1906', but the letter seems most likely to have been written between Mahler's concerts in Breslau on 24 October 1906 and in Munich on 8 November. At the former the programme consisted of the Third Symphony plus three *Wunderhorn* songs and 'Ich bin der Welt abhanden gekommen' (soloist: Fr. Weidemann), and at the latter Mahler was to conduct his Sixth Symphony, but he was summoned to Vienna at the last minute, and Bernhard Stavenhagen had to substitute for him. Stavenhagen repeated the concert on the 16 November. Dohrn, incidentally, repeated the songs at a concert in Breslau on 23 January 1907 (K.M.).

1907

347 (a) In G.E. dated '12 January 1907'.
   (b) Mahler did not conduct again in Amsterdam until October 1909 (K.M.).
348 In G.E. dated 'Frankfurt 1907'.
350 In G.E. dated '17 July' which I believe, however, is a misreading of the postmark. It had already been officially announced at the beginning of June that Mahler had resigned from the Vienna Opera, and, if the attributed date is correct, it is strange that Mahler does not mention the death of his eldest daughter (K.M.).
352 In G.E. dated 'Vienna, 1908?'. My assumption that Mahler's absence from Vienna in October is linked with his concert in Wiesbaden on 9 October 1907 is more or less guesswork (cf. Alma Mahler, *Memories*, p. 293) (K.M.).
353 In G.E. dated 'Autumn 1907'.
355 In G.E. dated 'Autumn 1907'.
356 In accordance with tradition this letter was ripped off the notice-board and torn to pieces. However, the text was published in numerous newspapers and music magazines during the next few days (K.M.).
357 In G.E. dated 'Spring 1907'.

VIII: The Last Years (1908-1911)

1908

358 Mahler's plans concerning the engagement of Roller at the Metropolitan Opera came to nothing. Nevertheless, Roller left the Vienna Opera in May 1909, to take over the directorship of the School of Art and Craft in Vienna (Kunstgewerbeschule) (K.M.).

359 The manager of the Metropolitan Opera, Heinrich Conried (1848–1909), was forced to retire from his post in the early spring of 1908. In his honour a huge benefit performance was given at the Metropolitan on the evening of 24 March. On this occasion Mahler conducted Beethoven's *Leonora* Overture No. 3 (K.M.).

360 In G.E. dated '1908'.

362 Karl Muck had been in charge of the Boston Symphony Orchestra since 1906 but resigned in 1908 to become conductor of the Berlin Royal Orchestra. Higginson invited Mahler to take over Muck's position in Boston, but he turned it down recommending Mengelberg instead. The latter, however, having just strengthened his position in Amsterdam considerably was not interested either, and the post was then offered to Max Fiedler from Hamburg who finally accepted (K.M.).

363 Conried's successors were the Italian G. Gatti-Casazza (1868–1940), previously director of the Teatro alla Scala in Milan, with the German tenor Johann Andreas Dippel (1866–1932) as joint manager; the latter held the post for only two years (K.M.).

366 In G.E. only dated '1908'. Mahler conducted his last performance of the season at the Metropolitan on 16 April (*Siegfried*). Mahler's first visit to America lasted only sixteen weeks during which he conducted nineteen performances (K.M.).

367 (a) In G.E. dated 'March 1908'.

(b) As mentioned by Alma Mahler in her Foreword (p. 27) certain influential ladies in New York had been considering forming an orchestra, 'The Greater New York Orchestra', and at an informal meeting on 15 April 1908 they secured Mahler's services for the founding of a permanent organization. The report of this meeting, dated 24 April, clearly states that 'the orchestra is not being formed for any conductor'. The Committee's first goal was to arrange four 'Festival Concerts' during the autumn of 1908, and 'it was decided that these concerts should be but the beginning of a permanent orchestra'. The report is signed by 'The Committee for the Four Festival Concerts' which consisted of nine ladies and four gentlemen. The chairman was Mrs. George R. Sheldon, wife of a prominent New York banker.

The progress of events had been as follows. Mahler had been negotiating with Walter Damrosch, conductor of the New York Symphony, since the beginning of March 1908 about three concerts to take place later in the year. Heinrich Conried who already had a contract with Mahler would not, however, give his sanction, because he claimed that the rehearsals for these concerts would keep Mahler from his duties at the Metropolitan. In spite of this, and no doubt also because Conried was being forced to leave the Met, on

22 March Mahler settled terms and details with Damrosch. Only three days later he received an invitation from the 'Ladies' Committee' to conduct a series of concerts, and oddly enough, on the very same day an article appeared in the New York *Sun*, which quoted an anonymous report that a fund had been subscribed for the purpose of having Mahler conduct several symphony concerts the following winter. (It was probably this newspaper Mahler enclosed with his letter to Anna Moll.)

On 24 March Conried retired from the Met, and the Company gave Mahler a free rein, but on condition that he gave up $3,000 of his salary if he conducted the New York Symphony concerts. Mahler was now in a dilemma and he asked for ten days' reflection.

We must assume that during his subsequent negotiations with the 'Ladies' Committee' reimbursement of the $3,000 was agreed since he gave three concerts with the New York Symphony the following autumn, on 29 November, and on 8 and 13 December. At the concert on 8 December his Second Symphony was given its American première.

The 'Ladies' Committee' had however worked on their ideas which finally resulted in the reorganization of the New York Philharmonic Society in early 1909. Owing to Mrs. Mahler's remark in her foreword that 'he [Mahler] had *his* orchestra', it ought to be stressed that Mahler was only engaged as conductor by the Committee, and the Philharmonic was never *his* orchestra in the sense suggested by Alma Mahler (K.M.).

369 In G.E. dated '1909' but the reference to Roller's staging of *Fidelio*, produced in New York in early spring 1908, and of *Figaro* which was to be produced in January 1909, indicate an earlier date. I have suggested June 1908 as it is evident that Mahler is just leaving for Toblach and that the Vienna Opera season is about to close (K.M.).

370 Gablonz (now Jablonec, in Czechoslovakia) situated about 80 miles north-east of Prague, was then a town of about 25,000 inhabitants. Following Mahler's advice Karl Horwitz did not perform *Figaro* (K.M.).

373 In G.E. dated 'Toblach, 1909'.

374 In G.E. dated 'Alt-Schluderbach, 1908 or 1909'.

376 It was Ferdinand Löwe who on 14 February 1910 gave the first Munich performance of Mahler's Fifth Symphony (K.M.).

377 According to Alma Mahler she and Mahler spent a few days in Hamburg ('and did not feel at all well there') at the beginning of May before Mahler's concert in Wiesbaden on 8 May. This concert included a performance of his First Symphony (K.M.).

378 Mahler was on his way to Prague to prepare the première of his Seventh Symphony on 19 September (K.M.).

379 In G.E. dated 'Autumn 1908'.

380 In G.E. dated 'Autumn 1908'. For Lauterbach & Kuhn, cf. letter 320 (K.M.).

1909

381 (a) In G.E. dated 'New York, 1909'.

(b) It was during spring 1909 that Auguste Rodin (1840–1917) made his two busts of Mahler in Paris. The Rodin Museum there has rather strangely labelled one of them 'Mozart' (K.M.).

382 *Bruno Walter* comments: In the last years of his life Mahler was in a unique state of emotional upheaval. He was almost ceaselessly overwhelmed by his feelings. His thoughts and hopes centred at this time with particular intensity on his much-loved and greatly respected friend, Siegfried Lipiner, the author of *Adam* and *Hippolytos*.

Here once again all comment is superfluous. This letter, like the previous ones [nos. 372 and 375], written during Mahler's summer holiday of 1908, is one of the most moving documents of all those agonizing (but also sometimes joyful) emotional crises in which he consumed himself.

383 In G.E. dated 'Spring 1908'. However, it was only in the spring of 1909 that Mahler took charge of the New York Philharmonic Orchestra (K.M.).

384 In G.E. dated 'beginning of 1909'.

385 In G.E. only dated 'Spring 1909'.

388 (a) In G.E. dated 'probably early Summer 1907'. Mahler's last tour of Holland took place in October 1909: he conducted his Seventh Symphony in The Hague on the 2nd, and repeated it twice in Amsterdam, on 3 and 7 October. The projected tour to Frankfurt came to nothing (K.M.).

(b) In early spring 1910 Mengelberg did a tour, conducting the same symphony of which he was very fond, five times: in Amsterdam on 27 February and 10 March; in Frankfurt on 4 March, and in Arnhem and The Hague on 7 and 12 March respectively. At a concert in Haarlem on 8 March he only performed the fourth movement. Alma Mahler later presented the manuscript score of the Seventh Symphony to the Amsterdam Concertgebouw Orchestra (K.M.).

389 In G.E. dated 'Vienna, 1909'.

391 The complex history of Mahler and his publishers finally ended in 1910 when Mahler signed an exclusive contract with the nine-year-old but enterprising Viennese music publishers, Universal Edition. In the meantime nine other publishers had been involved with Mahler's compositions: A.

Bösendorfer's Musikalienhandlung (Vienna, 1880), C. F. Kahnt (Leipzig, 1888, 1905), B. Schott's Söhne (Mainz, 1892), Friedrich Hofmeister (Leipzig, 1895–7), Josef Weinberger (Leipzig–Vienna, 1897–1902), Ludwig Doblinger (Vienna, 1902), C. F. Peters (Leipzig, 1904–7), Bote & Bock (Berlin, 1909), and G. Schirmer (New York, 1910). As early as 1906 Universal Edition had published study scores and piano scores of Mahler's first four symphonies (K.M.).

393 In G.E. dated 'June, 1909'.

396 In G.E. dated 'Toblach, 1910'. My only reason for believing that the present letter should be dated 1909 is Mahler's reference to 'the keys to the flat', by which I presume he refers to his own flat in Auenbruggergasse in Vienna. The Mahlers moved out of this flat in October 1909, and during their last visits to Vienna stayed with the Moll family (K.M.).

397 Mahler refers to the visit he received from Dr. Ernst Decsey (1870–1941) in June 1909 and which the latter described in the June and August issues of *Die Musik*, Berlin, 1911 (K.M.).

399 In G.E. dated 'approximately Autumn 1909'. The last sentence indicates that it must have been written in August (K.M.).

400 (a) In G.E. dated '15 September' but was certainly written in August (K.M.).

(b) Mahler refers to a historical concert which was given in New York on 10 November. The programme consisted of compositions by Handel, Rameau, Grétry, Haydn and finally Bach's Suites Nos. 2 and 3 which Mahler had arranged (see letter 406). Spiering played Bach's E major Violin Concerto (K.M.).

401 In G.E. dated 'Summer 1909', but a surviving letter of Strauss's refers to his visit to Mahler at Toblach which took place at the end of August.

403 *F.L.:* We were never again to spend so long together in affectionate communion. My engagement-book has the entry for that day: '5–8 o'clock w. G'. A year later, on 2 October 1910, I walked with Mahler from the Villa Moll on the Hohe Warte (Vienna) over the Hungerberg to Grinzing, through the cemetery there, past his own future grave [where his daughter Maria was buried], and back to Frau Alma. A week later he called on me briefly to say good-bye before leaving for America. After that I saw him no more in this world.

404 (a) In G.E. dated 'Autumn 1909', but probably written in September (K.M.).

(b) The concert in Nuremberg came to nothing. The local conductor there, Wilhelm Bruch, was a strong Mahler advocate who included Mahler's works in the Philharmonic Concert programmes several times (K.M.).

(c) The 'cyclic concerts' in September 1910 were the occasion of the première of Mahler's Eighth Symphony (K.M.).

405 In G.E. undated, but presumably written after Mahler's departure for America and before the letter he wrote to Emil Herztka (dated 26 November 1909) in which he asks the latter to give Wöss his regards and thanks him for the beautiful arrangement of the symphony (see *Neue Zeitschrift für Musik*, September 1974, where this letter is reproduced). The vocal score of the Eighth Symphony was published by Universal Ed. in April 1910 (K.M.).

407 In G.E. dated 'approx. December 1909'.

1910

411 (a) In G.E. only dated '1910'.
(b) The 'Paris matter' concerned the first Paris performance of Mahler's Second Symphony in April 1910 (K.M.).

412 In G.E. only dated '1910'. The original letter is undated but '27 February 1910' has been added in pencil in another hand, probably Gutmann's or his secretary's, either when the letter was received or when it was answered (K.M.).

413 In G.E. only dated '1910'. The reference to the coming meeting in Paris (for the Second Symphony) suggests a date in March (K.M.).

414 In G.E. undated.

415 Walter not only assisted Mahler in selecting the soloists for the performance of the Eighth but he coached them as well (K.M.).

416 In G.E. dated 'end of March', but the Mahlers arrived in Paris on 12 April (K.M.).

417 (a) Not in G.E. The recipient of this letter is not given, but the contents indicate that it was addressed to the head of C. F. Peters Verlag in Leipzig (Herr Heinrich Hinrichsen), the publisher of Mahler's Fifth Symphony (K.M.).
(b) Mahler was never to perform his Fifth again after his concert tour to Finland and Russia in October and November 1907, when he conducted it in St. Petersburg on 5 November (K.M.).

418 On 21 May 1910 Mahler signed a contract with Universal Edition for his Ninth Symphony and *Das Lied von der Erde* (K.M.).

419 In G.E. dated 'early June' but Mahler only spent the second part of June in Munich, finishing the preliminary rehearsals for his Eighth Symphony on 24 June (K.M.).

420 It seems that Mahler was having a diadem made for Alma (cf. letter 434), a detail which Alma did not remember when she wrote in her *Memories*

(p. 181) that 'Mahler had no notion what gave a girl pleasure' after she had received 'my first piece of jewellery in my life' (from A. Berliner). This happened on the evening of the première of the Eighth, but Mahler gave her the diadem as a birthday present on 31 August (K.M.).

421 (a) Mahler was having trouble with the leader of the Munich Orchestra which was to perform his Eighth, and as a consequence asked his brother-in-law, Arnold Rosé, to replace him. This was, however, strongly opposed by the orchestra, and finally Mahler had to give in (see also letter 433) (K.M.). (b) Owing to the deficit of about $100,000 in the 1909–10 season, the board of the New York Philharmonic engaged Mr. Loudon Charlton as manager of the orchestra. Mahler's salary was approximately $25,000 (or 140,000 in contemporary marks) for the whole season (K.M.).

422 In G.E. dated 'approx. June 1910'. This letter reveals the first signs of the matrimonial crisis that arose between Alma and Gustav Mahler that summer. The whole affair is minutely described and documented by Alma in her *Memories* (pp. 172–9), though only giving her point of view (K.M.).

424 In G.E. dated '1910' only, but the letter is undoubtedly connected with Mahler's rehearsals, concluded on 24 June, in Munich, and, according to a letter to Alma Mahler (no. 158, *Memories and Letters*, London, 1973), Mahler left on Sunday 26 June (K.M.).

429 It appears that Alma Mahler spent three to four weeks in Tobelbad (near Graz) where she took a cure. Mahler visited her two or three times during June and July.

It was in Tobelbad that Alma met the young architect Walter Gropius (1883–1969) with whom she had an affair, and whom she later married (on 18 August 1915) (K.M.).

430 *o.e.:* As Mahler subsequently told Göhler in Munich, what he was referring to was a short piece in the *Dresdner Neueste Nachrichten*, one of a number of articles that Göhler had written in connection with the preparations for the performance of the Eighth Symphony and Mahler's approaching fiftieth birthday. It was as a result of this article that Mahler expressed the wish that Göhler should translate the 'Veni, creator spiritus' into German. [Göhler's translation was printed in the programme for the première (K.M.).]

432 In G.E. dated '1910'. The final rehearsals for the première of the Eighth took place in Munich in the week of 5–11 September. The rehearsal timetable looked as follows:

Monday	5 Sept.	} from 9.30 a.m. orchestral rehearsals
Tuesday	6 „	
Wednesday 7	„	} from 4.00 p.m. rehearsals with choirs

Thursday	8 „	11.00 a.m. orchestra, children's choirs and soloists
Friday	9 „	coaching of children's choirs and soloists
Saturday	10 „	⎰ 10.00 a.m. 1st complete rehearsal of Part I
		⎱ 4.00 p.m. „ „ „ „ „ II
Sunday	11 „	Generalprobe (dress rehearsal) complete symphony
Monday	12 „	7.30 p.m. première
Tuesday	13 „	7.30 p.m. second performance (K.M.)

433 In G.E. dated '1910' only.

434 In G.E. dated 'Autumn 1910'. The original footnote in G.E. claims that Mahler is referring to the 'first full rehearsal', and in view of the following passage in which Mahler asks for one or two days' notice of Karl Moll's arrival in Munich one can only presume that Mahler means the first orchestral rehearsal on 5 September (K.M.).

435 In G.E. dated 'September 1910'. According to Alma's *Memories* (p. 178), she arrived in Munich on 9 September (K.M.).

437 In G.E. undated.

438 In G.E. dated 'Autumn 1910', but I assume that this letter is connected with the following letter, dated 21 November. It is evident from the latter that Alma in fact knew about the plot of land Mahler bought in Semmering, although her *Memories* (p. 186) leaves one with the impression that she only learned about it on Christmas Eve. It seems unlikely to me anyway that Mahler would have gone ahead on his own account without discussing the matter with Alma (K.M.).

440 In G.E. dated '1908 or 1909'. The reference Mahler makes to his revisions of the Fifth Symphony suggests, though, that the present letter belongs to the autumn of 1910, cf. letter 443 to Göhler (K.M.).

441 In G.E. dated '1909?'. See note 440. Furthermore, it should be added that Mahler only completed his Ninth Symphony in the spring of 1910, see letter 415 (K.M.).

1911

442 In G.E. dated 'March 1910'.

443 (a) *Göhler* comments regarding the 'Fourth' Symphony: I had sent Mahler the programme notes of the first Leipzig performance of his Fourth [17 February 1911], which I conducted, together with my explanatory notes, asking him for ruthless criticism of my analysis, since I had never discussed the work with him, nor ever heard it played.

(b) and on the 'Fifth': When Mahler was in Leipzig for the choir rehearsals for his Eighth Symphony, I asked him which of his symphonies he thought I should choose to conduct first in Leipzig. I told him I was very fond of the Fifth, which I had already obtained the rights for and begun organizing for performance in Karlsruhe, only to give it up after one rehearsal because I was not allowed to have the additional string-players required. He told me *the first version of the Fifth was never to be played again*, because it was badly orchestrated. I then had the privilege of conducting not only the first performance in Leipzig of the Fourth, First and Eighth Symphonies, and of *Das Lied von der Erde*, but also the world première of the new version of the Fifth, which, unfortunately, is still neglected.

[Göhler is probably referring to the last revisions of the Fifth Symphony which the composer undertook in 1910 (see letter 417) and which were only published in 1964. The *first* edition was published in September 1904 (study score and piano score, four hands, only), the *second* edition followed in November the same year and the *third* one in spring 1905. One of the most interesting features of the first version is the *repeat* of the first part of the symphony's second movement. This has never been deleted in the piano score for four hands (K.M.).]

ADDENDA

Letter 384, p. 331

The date of this letter was only discovered during the final proof-reading, but it was not possible to transfer the letter to its right chronological place, i.e. *summer 1909* (K.M.).

BIOGRAPHICAL
LIST OF ADDRESSEES

ADLER, Guido (1855–1941), Austrian musicologist, professor of music history and theory at the University of Prague (1885–98) and at the University of Vienna (1898–1927). Like Mahler he spent his early years in Iglau and at the Vienna Conservatory, leaving the latter in 1874, the year before Mahler started there. Thereafter Adler studied law at Vienna University, then returned to music. Adler and Mahler probably met in their youth and they continued to keep in touch. Adler published a study of Mahler in 1916. Their relationship is carefully documented in the study by Edward R. Reilly, *Gustav Mahler und Guido Adler*, Vienna, 1978.

BARTOLOMEY, Franz (1865–19 ?), Austrian clarinettist, member of the Court Opera Orchestra, and of the Vienna Philharmonic Orchestra which he joined in 1894. In 1898 he was appointed professor at the Vienna Conservatory.

BATKA, Richard (1868–1922), Czech musicologist and author of several books on music, including a general history (1908). Batka was music critic on the *Bohemia* in Prague, for a time on the *Prager Neue Musikalische Rundschau*, and on the art magazine *Kunstwart* for which he wrote several articles on Mahler.

BERLINER, Arnold (1862–1942), German physicist. Berliner became acquainted with Mahler during his initial season in Hamburg, and it was he who gave Mahler his first lessons in English. He had graduated from the University in Breslau in 1886 and worked for several years for the Allgemeine Elektrizitäts Gesellschaft, first in Hamburg, later in Berlin. He committed suicide in 1942 when the Nazis came to arrest him.

BIE, Oscar (1864–1938), German writer on music. In 1894 he became editor of the influential Berlin art journal *Neue deutsche Rundschau*, founded in 1890 by Otto Brahm. He was also music critic for the Berlin *Börsen Courier* for a time. Bie wrote several important books on music.

BUTHS, Julius (1851–1920), German pianist and conductor. Born in Wiesbaden and educated by his father, he later studied with Friedrich Gernsheim at the Conservatory in Cologne. He began his career as conductor in Breslau, went on to Elberfeld, and in 1892 was appointed musical director in Düsseldorf, a post he held until 1908. Buths wrote chamber music, a piano concerto and several songs.

Diosy, Béla (18 ?-1930), Hungarian music critic (*Neuer Pester Journal*) and teacher.

Eichberg, Oscar (1845-1898), German music critic, singing teacher and minor composer. Lived in Berlin where he was critic on the *Börsen Courier* and the *Neue Berliner Musikzeitung*.

Epstein, Julius (1832-1926), Austrian pianist and professor at the Vienna Conservatory (1867-1901). He was Mahler's piano teacher and had a special liking for his pupil.

Freund, Emil (1859-1928), Austrian lawyer, a close friend of Mahler, whom he met in 1873. Freund read law at Vienna and afterwards opened his own office in Vienna. He was Mahler's financial adviser and helped him in contractual matters with his publishers.

Gernsheim, Friedrich (1839-1916), German composer, pianist and conductor. In 1890 he became conductor of the famous Sternsche Singverein in Berlin which sang in the first performance of Mahler's Second Symphony, 13 December 1895.

Göhler, (Karl) Georg (1874-1954), German conductor, composer and writer on music. Having completed his doctorate in 1896, Göhler was appointed conductor of the Riedel Chorus Society in Leipzig, and he returned to his post there following a short interval as conductor in Karlsruhe (1907-9). He came into contact with Mahler in 1910 when he was preparing the première of Mahler's Eighth Symphony. Göhler remained a faithful advocate of Mahler's, conducting his music in Hamburg, Berlin, Lübeck, Altenberg and Halle. He resigned all his positions in 1932.

Goldmark, Karl (1830-1915), Austrian composer and teacher. Goldmark's numerous operas were highly popular during his lifetime and were performed all over Germany and Austria. He also composed two symphonies, various overtures and chamber music. Goldmark was a member of the jury in 1881 when Mahler competed for the Beethoven prize with his 'Klagende Lied'.

Gutmann, Emil (18 ?-19 ?), German impresario in Munich, later in Berlin. Gutmann organized the première in 1910 of Mahler's Eighth Symphony and was also responsible for its nickname, 'Symphony of a Thousand'.

Hammerschlag, Paul (1860-1933), Austrian banker, director of the Austrian Credit-Anstalt in Vienna and president of the Austrian Bankers' Society. Hammerschlag was born on 7 July 1860 and studied law at Vienna University. He was a member of the board of directors for the Wiener Konzertverein. Hammerschlag's younger brother, Albert (1863–1935) was a well-known Viennese doctor of medicine.

HESCH, Wilhelm (1860–1908), Czech name: Vilem Hes. Bass singer, made his début in Prague in 1880. In 1893 he joined the Hamburg Stadttheater where he and Mahler first met. From August 1896 to 1908 he was a highly esteemed member of the Vienna Court Opera.

HINRICHSEN, Heinrich (Henri or Henry) (1868–1942), German music publisher, director of the famous C. F. Peters Verlag in Leipzig from 1900 to 1941. In 1904 he purchased Mahler's Fifth Symphony for 10,000 Dutch guilders, and he published it that year. Two years later, however, when he was offered Mahler's first four symphonies together with all Bruckner's for 160,000 marks (by the Viennese printers J. Eberle & Co.), he turned them down. Hinrichsen died in the German concentration camp Theresienstadt in 1942.

HORN, Richard (18 ? –19 ?), Austrian lawyer. His relationship to Mahler is not clear.

HORWITZ, Karl (1884–1925), Austrian composer and conductor, pupil of Schönberg. From 1908 till 1914 he conducted in various smaller opera houses in Austria.

KALBECK, Max (1850–1921), Austrian writer on music and one of the most influential music critics in Vienna. A close friend of Brahms whose biography he published between 1904–15, he collaborated with Mahler on a new (German) edition of Mozart's *Le Nozze di Figaro*.

KARPATH, Ludwig (1866–1936), Austrian music critic. Karpath met Mahler when he attempted to join the Royal Opera in Budapest in 1888 as a bass singer. Within a few days Mahler had both appointed and dismissed him and he then decided to take up music criticism. He worked on the *Neues Wiener Tagblatt* from 1894 to 1923 and also contributed to foreign newspapers and magazines. From 1914 to 1917 he was editor of the leading Viennese art journal, *Der Merker*. In his book *Begegnung mit dem Genius* (Vienna, 1934) Karpath gives a detailed account of his relationship with Mahler, particularly stressing his rôle during the hectic days of April 1897, when Mahler was trying to secure his post in Vienna. Relations soon cooled, however, to Karpath's disappointment. The most precise characterization of Karpath is perhaps given by Bruno Walter in a letter to Hans Pfitzner (25 Sept. 1904): 'Keep Karpath warm—he is stupid but good-natured, and he has a talent for promotion!' Probably an opinion shared by Mahler.

KASTNER, Rudolf (18 ? –19 ?), German musician and writer on music, with the *Berlin Morgenpost* for a time.

KRISPER, Anton (1858–1914), Austrian composer, born in Laibach and for two years a fellow-pupil of Mahler's at the Vienna Conservatory. In 1882 he completed a doctoral thesis on the philosophy of music at the University of Leipzig. According to La Grange an opera of his was staged in Prague (in 1885), but its failure led him to abandon music completely. He died in Graz, suffering from mental illness. ~ *Mahler predicted it.*

KRUG-WALDSEE, Josef (1858–1915) (original name, Josef Wenzel Krug), German conductor and composer, born in the small town of Waldsee in Swabia. He studied music in Stuttgart, and in 1889 became chorus conductor at the Hamburg Stadttheater where he met Mahler. In December 1891 he left Hamburg for Brünn, then went on to be Kapellmeister in Nuremberg and Augsburg. In 1901, he took up a permanent post in Magdeburg as conductor of the municipal symphony orchestra.

KRZYZANOWSKI, Heinrich (1855–192?), like his younger brother, the musician Rudolf Krzyzanowski, was one of Mahler's closest friends in his youth. Born in Eger, he studied German philology at Vienna University and, for a short time, taught in a grammar school. After his marriage to Auguste Tschuppik, he settled in Germany, living there as a writer in Starnberg, Munich and for a while in Berlin. Author of the novel, *Im Bruch* (Spemann, 1885). Many years later he returned to Vienna as a private tutor and lecturer, finally moving to the Tyrol.

LESSMANN, (W. J.) Otto (1844–1918), German music critic, editor and owner of the influential Berlin music journal *Allgemeine Musik-Zeitung*. Besides his activities as critic Lessmann held important posts in Berlin teaching piano and singing. Lessmann remained an opponent of Mahler's music all his life.

LEWY, Gustav (18 ?–1901), Austrian music dealer and impresario. On 12 May 1880, Mahler signed a five-year contract with him, according to which Mahler had to pay Lewy five per cent of his total earnings. It was Lewy who helped Mahler obtain his appointments in Bad Hall, Laibach, Olmütz and Kassel, and who assisted him in spring 1883 in getting his post as chorus conductor at the Carl Theatre in Vienna.

LIPINER, Siegfried (1856–1911), Austrian writer, poet and philosopher. Lipiner and Mahler became friends during Mahler's early years in Vienna, and they remained close until Mahler's marriage. Alma disliked Lipiner ('my avowed enemy', she called him), and according to La Grange's *Mahler*, p. 698, Lipiner did not have a high regard for her either. Lipiner studied at Vienna and Leipzig. He published his first poems, *Der entfesselte Prometheus* (Prometheus Unbound) in 1876; these awakened Wagner's, as well as Nietzsche's, interest in him. Two years later he published two more books (*Über die Elemente der Erneuerung religiöser Ideen in der Gegenwart*, and *Renatus. Epische Dichtung*). His last volume of poems, *Buch der Freude*, appeared in 1880. From then on Lipiner published no further works of his own. However, he began to translate the poetical works of the Polish national poet Adam Mickiewicz (1798–1855), the first volume, *Todtenfeier* (Funeral Rites) appearing in 1887, the next in 1898 (*Herr Thaddäus oder der letzte Eintritt in Lithauen*). In the meantime Lipiner had sketched his *Christus* trilogy (see p. 429) never completed and only posthumously published. Lipiner made his living as librarian for the Austrian Reichsrat. He married twice, his first wife being Nina Matscheko, who later married the painter Joseph Hoffmann, and his second wife being Clementine, the sister of Albert Spiegler. Clementine and Lipiner had a daughter, Walli.

LÖHR, Friedrich (Fritz) (1859–1924), original name, Löwi. Friedrich Löhr studied archaeology in Vienna and Rome. It appears that he taught privately for a time, and was then appointed Secretary of the Austrian Archaeological Society in Vienna—a post he held until his death.

LÖWE, Theodor (1855–1936), Director of the Stadttheater in Breslau, It was Löwe who suggested that Bruno Schlesinger should change his surname when taking up his new appointment there.

MANKIEWICZ, Henriette (1854–1906), Austrian artist, especially known for her embroidery. Mankiewicz was an invalid who according to Natalie Bauer-Lechner bore her sufferings with angelic fortitude. Mahler met her at the beginning of 1900, but their contact probably came to an end when Mahler married.

MARCUS, Adele (1854–1927). Mahler got to know her during his Hamburg years. She was a widow (née Hertz) of high society, and took a great interest in Mahler.

MARSCHALK, Max (1863–1940), German composer, music critic and publisher. In 1895 Marschalk became critic at the Berlin *Vossische Zeitung*, and it was as a result of his favourable review of Mahler's Second Symphony that the latter contacted him. Although Marschalk rejected the direction Mahler took with his Fifth Symphony and was only drawn to his music again with *Das Lied von der Erde* (at least according to Bruno Walter), they remained friends until Mahler's death. Marschalk was a composer on a smaller scale, mostly concentrating on Lieder, and writing the music for several plays, in particular those of his brother-in-law, Gerhardt Hauptmann.

MENGELBERG, Willem (Josef) (1871–1951), Dutch conductor, taught by Franz Wüllner in Cologne. He began his career as conductor in Lucerne, but in 1895 he took on the famous Concertgebouw Orchestra in Amsterdam, remaining there for fifty years. Mengelberg first met Mahler in Krefeld in 1902 at the première of Mahler's Third Symphony; the following year Mahler was invited to conduct the Concertgebouw Orchestra, and this visit was so successful that Mahler repeated it almost every year, the last occasion being October 1909. Mahler found in Mengelberg an unusual friend and admirer to whom—I believe—Mahler's music owes more than any other conductor, not discounting Bruno Walter. No one else has ever performed Mahler's works so often: between 1903 and 1920 Mahler's name is to be found in Mengelberg's programme over 230 times.

MILDENBURG, Anna von (1872–1947), Austrian soprano, studied in Vienna, a pupil of Rosa Papier-Paumgartner. She made her début in Hamburg in September 1895 and Mahler almost immediately fell for her and a passionate love affair soon developed. On leaving Hamburg however Mahler put an end to the relationship. The following year Mildenburg was engaged by the Vienna Opera and remained a member of that company until 1923. In 1909 she married the Austrian poet Hermann Bahr.

MOLL, Anna (18 ?–1938) (née Bergen), Mahler's mother-in-law, born in Hamburg. In 1878 she married the Austrian painter Emil Jacob Schindler (1842–92) and they settled in Vienna. The following year she gave birth to Alma, Mahler's future wife. Five years after Schindler's death Anan Schindler married his pupil, *Karl Moll* (1861–1945). Alma Mahler has left unfavourable accounts of her mother as well as of her stepfather. Mahler, however, as is clear from his letters to both, was very fond of his parents-in-law and retained a filial love towards them all his life.—Karl Moll became a Nazi during his last years and he committed suicide in 1945 when the Russian Army besieged Vienna.

NEISSER, Albert (1855–1916), German dermatologist and professor at the University of Breslau. He was president of the Breslau Music Society and invited Mahler, whose music he was fond of, to conduct in Breslau.

POLLINI, Bernhard (1838–1897) (real name: Baruch Pohl), German impresario, Director of the Hamburg Stadttheater. Pollini began his career as a baritone singer and toured all over Central Europe. In 1874 he leased the Hamburg Stadttheater from the Hamburg Senate and, as Director, turned the Hamburg Opera into one of the best in Germany, and won himself a leading reputation. In 1891 he engaged Mahler for three seasons as his first Kapellmeister, but although he renewed the contract in 1894, relations between the two men were consistently strained and drove Mahler to seek a new post.

REICHENBERGER, Hugo (1873–1938), German conductor, pupil of Ludwig Thuille, Reichenberger was Kapellmeister in various German towns (Breslau, Aachen, Bremen, Stuttgart, Munich and Frankfurt) before his engagement at the Vienna Court Opera in September 1908, where he stayed until 1935.

REITLER, Josef (1883–1948), Austrian conductor, music critic, later Director of the Neues Wiener Konservatorium. He studied music in Berlin, Paris and Vienna. From 1907 he was music critic for the *Neue freie Presse* in Vienna.

ROLLER, Alfred (1864-1935), Austrian painter and stage designer. Mahler and Roller first met in 1902 and during subsequent meetings discussed the latter's plans for a new production of *Tristan*. These were enthusiastically received by Mahler who, the following year, engaged Roller as chief stage designer. Together they were responsible for historic productions of works by Mozart, Wagner, Beethoven and Gluck.

SEIDL, Arthur (1863-1928), German music critic, professor and author of several books on music. He lived in the small town of Dessau where he was musical manager of the Court Theatre and from 1904 he also taught the history of music at Leipzig University. Seidl published several books, mainly on modern composers (Wagner, Richard Strauss and Pfitzner). He was a great admirer of Mahler.

SPECHT, Richard (1870-1932), Austrian music critic and author of books on music. He first studied architecture in Vienna, but owing to an eye disease had to give up and for some years worked in commerce. During this period he began writing poems, plays and essays on various subjects. He studied music privately with Ignaz Brüll, A. Zemlinsky and Franz Schrecker, and met Mahler for the first time in 1895. In 1904 he became music critic on the Vienna paper *Die Zeit*, and in 1909 he founded the famous periodical *Der Merker* (Vienna) of which he was editor-in-chief until 1919. He published his first book on Mahler in 1905, followed by a large biographical study in 1913.

SPIEGLER, Albert (18 ? -1938), Austrian doctor of medicine and research chemist in dietetics, always prepared to sacrifice his scientific career to more philanthropic enterprises. He and his wife (Nanna) were close to prominent members of the Austrian Social Democratic movement. His sister was married to Siegfried Lipiner.

SPIEGLER, Nanna (or Nina) (1855-1937), wife of Albert Spiegler, and, according to Bruno Walter, a woman of extraordinary charm and intelligence, and with a musical understanding that led to a close friendship with Mahler. In order to assist her son's studies she fully mastered Latin and Greek. She suffered increasingly from delicate health.

SPIERING, Theodor (1871-1925), American violinist, conductor, composer, and teacher. In 1909 Mahler appointed him leader of the reorganized New York Philharmonic Orchestra.

STAEGEMANN, Max (1843-1905), German singer, actor and, from 1882, Director of the Leipzig Neue Stadttheater.

STEFANOVIC-VILOVSKA, Camilla von (18 ? -19 ?) (maiden name, Camilla Ott,

Edle von Ottenfeld). Austrian violinist. She studied the violin at the Vienna Conservatory and became well known during the 1880s under the stage-name Milla von Ott. She played with Mahler at a concert in Iglau on 11 August 1883. When she married she gave up her career and taught the violin privately. In 1910 she was appointed vice-president of the Society of Female Music Teachers in Vienna.

STEINER, Josef (1857–1913), Austrian lawyer. I am much indebted to Dr. Felix Steiner (New York) for the following information about his father: 'My father was born on 29 August 1857 in Habern, Bohemia—not far from Iglau—where his father Ignatz Steiner had a store. My grandfather was actually the first to recognize young Mahler's extraordinary musical gifts and introduced him in 1874 to Gustav Schwarz, manager for the Morawan estates, and through the latter's recommendation Mahler was later directed to Vienna where he enrolled in the Conservatory in 1875. My father studied at the Gymnasium (Grammar School) in Iglau which takes eight years. Mahler studied at the same Gymnasium, so if Mahler studied all the eight years, he might well have been together with my father in Iglau from 1872 to 1875. Mahler then continued as a "Privatist", 1875–7, because he took up studies at the Vienna Conservatory, whereas my father finished Gymnasium in 1875 and went to Vienna where he studied at the University from 1875 to 1879.

In the years 1875 and 1876 Mahler and my father spent some of their holidays at Ronow in a country home of my father's aunt. During holidays in 1875 my father wrote the libretto to the opera *Herzog Ernst von Schwaben* and worked with Mahler on the musical score. When they returned to Ronow for a holiday in 1876 and wanted to continue their work, they learned that my father's aunt had thrown away and burned all the papers they had stored in the attic. The two young men were rather upset, but apparently did not resume the work on the opera again—although my mother told me that my father—about 30 years later—played fragments of *Herzog Ernst* to her from memory. My father probably did lose touch with Mahler soon after 1879, since Mahler was resident in Vienna, and both friends were engaged in strenuous uphill-fights. The only work by my father which I have a printed copy of, is a volume of poetry *Aus meinen Sommertagen*, published in Vienna in 1908. Two documents relating to Mahler's friendship with my father are in my possession: an autograph manuscript of "Das klagende Lied", dated 27 February 1879, and a postcard written by Mahler from Iglau (28 April 1879) to my father in Vienna.'

THUILLE, Ludwig (1861–1907), Austrian-German composer, pupil of Pembauer and Rheinberger. From 1883 he taught piano and music theory at the

Conservatory in Munich. Composed operas (*Lobetanz* the most important), chamber music, Lieder and piano works.

TOLNEY-WITT, Gisella (1884–1975), alias Gisela Selden-Goth, wrote a book on Busoni (1923) and published several articles.

WALTER, Bruno (1876–1962) (real name Schlesinger), German-Austrian conductor, born in Berlin. Walter studied in Berlin, and gave his first public concert in 1886. From 1893 to 1894 he was chorus coach at the theatre in Cologne. In 1894 he was engaged at the Hamburg Opera where he remained for the following two seasons. During these Hamburg years he became a close friend of Mahler's, a friendship which was strengthened during the years (1901–7) they worked together at the Vienna Opera. Walter gave the first performances of Mahler's *Das Lied von der Erde* (1911) and Ninth Symphony (1912). In 1936 he published his monograph on Mahler. His auto-biography, *Themes and Variations* (1947), is invaluable for all Mahler enthusiasts.

WEIS-OSTBORN, Julius von (1862–1929), Austrian conductor who spent most of his life in Graz in Austria.

WÜLLNER, Franz (1832–1902), German conductor and composer, began his career as a piano virtuoso. From 1858 conductor in Aachen, and from 1869 at the Court Theatre in Munich. It was during these years that Wüllner was ordered to conduct the first performances of Wagner's *Rheingold* and *Walküre*, much against Wagner's wishes. In 1884 Wüllner was invited to Cologne as Kapellmeister of the Gürzenich Orchestra and director of the Conservatory.

WYDENBRUCK-EZSTERHAZY, Mysa (1859–1926), Austrian Countess married to August, Count Wydenbruck.

ZEMLINSKY, Alexander von (1871–1942), Austrian composer and conductor, born in Vienna where he studied at the Conservatory under Franz Krenn and Robert Fuchs. Conductor at various Viennese theatres, including the Court Opera, between 1900 and 1908. 1911–27 he was engaged by the German Opera in Prague. Although he had a passionate affair with Alma Schindler during the year preceding her engagement to Mahler, he remained a close friend of theirs. Zemlinsky made the piano-score for four hands of Mahler's Sixth Symphony.

ZICHY, Geza von (1849–1924), Hungarian composer and pianist, who at the age of fourteen lost his right arm. Intendant of the Budapest Opera from 1891 to 1894. Zichy composed several operas and songs and one piano concerto.

INDICES

Index of Mahler's Compositions

(The numbers refer to pages, not letters)

General Index of Names and Places

Names of towns and places which have been changed since Mahler's time are indexed as they appear in the text, with the modern equivalent given after an oblique stroke. Similarly, an oblique stroke separates a person's Christian name from his familiar name, e.g. Friedrich/Fritz Löhr. Names of the recipients of letters from Mahler are followed by bold-type numbers referring to the letters addressed to them, except for those letters in the supplement, which are referred to by their page numbers. Asterisked names are unidentifiable and/or date(s) unknown.

Marschner, Heinrich (1795–1861): *Hans Heiling*, 225
Marsyas (Greek legendary figure), 205
Marwege, Friedrich (1841–19?), German violinist, 157, 228
Mascagni, Pietro (1863–1945), 196; *Cavalleria rusticana*, 406
Matscheko, Nina *see* Hoffmann
Maximilianplatz (Munich), 359
Méhul, Joseph Etienne Nicolas (1763–1817): *Joseph in Egypt*, 68
Meidling (Vienna), 380
Meier, Herr*, 127
Meiningen (Germany), 434
Meissl & Schadn, Hotel (Vienna), 327
Melion, Franz (Mahler's teacher), 56
Mendelssohn-Bartholdy, Felix (1809–47), 98, 414; *St. Paul*, 395; Violin Concerto, 399
Mengelberg, Mathilde/Tilly*, wife of Willem M., 273, 277–8, 281, 294, 296, 314
— Willem, 303, 310, 316, 325–6, 338, 341, 343, 347, 362, 388, 27, 352, 369, 409, 438–9, 441, 443, 453–4; *Rembrandt Improvisationen*, 294
Mengelberg Stichting, Willem (Amsterdam), 21, 409
Menzies, Maggie (18?–87), Australian pianist, 98n, 100
Merano (Italy), 398
Merker, Der (Vienna), 417, 455
Messchaert, Johannes (1857–1922), Dutch baritone, 287–88
Metropolitan Opera House (New York), 18, 301n, 309–10, 314–16, 330n, 346, 440–2
Meyerbeer, Giacomo (1791–1864), 68; *Les Huguenots*, 389; *Robert der Teufel*, 74
Michaelergasse (Olmütz), 67
Michaels, Fr[iedrich?], 158
Michalek (-Merlitschek), Margarethe/Rita (1875–19?), Austrian soprano, 261n
Mickiewicz, Adam (1798–1855), Polish poet: *Herr Thäddäus*, 453; *Todtenfeier*, 346n, 453
Mihalovich, Ödön/Edmund (1842–1929), Hungarian composer, 402
Milan, 126–7, 441
Milano, Hotel (Milan), 126–7
Mildenburg von Bellschau, Anna, 145–8, 152, 165–7, 169, 171–5, 201, 206, 208–10,

212, 230, 232–3, 355, 169, 198n, 420–2, 425, 431, 454
— Father of, 186
Misurina, *see* Lago di Misurina
'Mittlere' Karlstrasse (Kassel), 74–5, 390
Mödling (Vienna), 126
Moll, Anna, 282, 366, 367, 381, 395, 413, 422, 428, 429, 442, 278, 323, 333, 340, 358, 366, 368, 370, 442, 454
— Karl: 281, 373, 386–7, 396, 419–20, 423, 434, 438, 440, 318–19, 328, 343, 353, 359, 371, 447, 454
Montenuovo, Alfred Prince (1854–1927), 225n, 368
Moravia, 380, 407
Morawan (Bohemia), 55
Morawetz, Fräulein*, 66
Moscow, 213–16, 425–6
Moser, Kolo/Koloman (1868–1918), Austrian painter and designer, 262
Mossel, Isaac*, (Dutch cellist), 278
Motte-Guyon, Jeanne-Marie Bouveres de la, 415
Mottl, Felix (1856–1911), Austrian conductor, 104, 213, 274, 418
Mozart, Wolfgang Amadeus (1756–91), 68, 289, 316, 455; *Così fan tutte*, 80; *Don Giovanni*, 68, 105, 130, 225, 285–6, 316, 407, 432, 437; *Le nozze de Figaro*, 170, 226, 286, 293, 296, 320, 332, 432, 438–9, 442, 451; *Requiem*, 420–1; *Il Seraglio*, 296; *Die Zauberflöte*, 226, 257
Mozart festival (Salzburg, 1906), 293
Muck, Karl (1859–1940), German conductor, 99, 138n, 185, 195, 202, 313, 362, 441
Munich, 12, 15, 27, 119, 122, 152, 208, 213–14, 216, 219, 246, 247n, 254n, 272–3, 299n, 325, 327–8, 351, 355, 358–360, 362, 364–6, 370, 400, 402–3, 413, 415, 425, 433, 435, 439, 442, 445–7, 450, 454, 457
— Court Opera, 122
— University, 435
Münchener Neueste Nachrichten, 283
Münden (Germany), 89, 395
Musical America, 409
Musik, Die (Berlin), 13n, 444
Musikblätter des Anbruch (Vienna), 11n, 385, 397
Musikverein (Vienna), 277, 329